D1559603

# AIRCREW

# MEMORIES

The Victoria Publishing Company Inc.

309-11 Cooperage Place,

Victoria British Columbia V9A 7J9

THE AIRCREW ASSOCIATION

VANCOUVER ISLAND BRANCH

ACKNOWLEDGES WITH THANKS

THE FINANCIAL ASSISTANCE OF

# THRIFTY FOODS

IN PUBLISHING THIS VOLUME OF MEMOIRS

# AIRCREW
# MEMORIES

The collected World War II
and later memories
of members of the
Aircrew Association,
Vancouver Island Branch
Victoria, B.C.

Sixty-five stories of service with the

Royal Canadian Air Force

and

Royal Air Force

In war and peace

Main entry under title:

    . Aircrew memories: being the collected World War II and later memories of the
Air Crew Association, Vancouver Island Branch, Victoria, B.C.: sixty-five stories of
service with the Royal Canadian Air Force and Royal Air Force in war and peace

Includes bibliographical references.
ISBN 0-9698699-5-9

Canadian Cataloguing In Publication Data

02   Canada. Royal Canadian Air Force–Biography

02   Great Britain. Royal Air Force–Biography.

02   Flight crews–Canada–Biography.

02   World War, 1939-1945–Aerial operations

02   World War, 1939-1945–Personal narratives, Canadian

02   Title

D811.A2A52 1999    940.54'8171   C98-900714-6

First published 1999
02 01 00   3 2 1

Printed in Canada

# INTRODUCTION

With the passage of half a century, it is to be expected that a very large compilation of official histories, scholarly works, studies, technical analyses, etcetera would now document the momentous events of World War II. Indeed, one may wonder what remains to be explored so many years later.

In fact the least explored, and perhaps potentially richest source of greater insight into many dimensions of that conflict, may devolve from thoughtful personal accounts by those who fought the war. A degree of intimacy and insight into the nature of the operations involved emanates from these contributions, a degree not present in any of the many other works available. Moreover, as one reads these fascinating accounts, important qualities of balance and perspective that only time can yield become evident. The Aircrew Association of Vancouver Island is to be congratulated for undertaking the compilation of such works, this being its second publication of the kind. Also to be congratulated are the individual authors. The publication is both particularly timely and suggested by a concentration of distinguished WWII airmen who have retired in the region.

General Thériault BA CMM CD

Chief of Defence Staff 1983-1986

# About the RCAF and RAF

We spoke in slang. We wrote and spoke in abbreviations. To lose these would be to lose some of the vitality of those days. We provide below a guide to terms used in all the stories. Before each section we clarify the specialized terms that have been used therein.

**Ranks**
Except during the very early days of WWII, when a few aircrew were Leading Aircraftsmen (LAC), when aircrew were awarded their wings or brevet they were either promoted to sergeant or commissioned.

Sgt    Sergeant.
F/Sgt   Flight Sergeant
W/O    Warrant Officer
P/O    Pilot Officer
F/O    Flying Officer
F/L    Flight Lieutenant
S/L    Squadron Leader
W/C    Wing Commander
G/C    Group Captain

**Decorations**
DSO    Distinguished Service Order
DFC    Distinguished Flying Cross. A second award (DFC*) would be worn as a bar to the Cross
DFM    Distinguished Flying Medal

**Cu-Nim**: Cumulo-nimbus, also known as cb's. An anvil-headed thundercloud that could contain dangerous upcurrents capable of throwing around even a heavy bomber.

**IFF**: Transmitter-receiver carried by Allied aircraft. When interrogated by a ground signal, it would respond to identify the aircraft as friendly. German aircraft carried a similar device.

**Mayday**: International voice distress signal. From the French "m'aidez"?

**Caterpillar**: Silkworm lapel badge given to aircrew who baled out.

**Goldfish**: Winged badge given to aircrew who "ditched".

**Roger**: Radio code meaning "message received and understood".

**Very Pistol**: Wide-mouthed hand gun used to fire coloured signal flares.

**Flak**: Ack-Ack, AA, Anti-aircraft fire.

## PREFACE

Looking at them today, all some may see is a bunch of weather-beaten old timers who have raised their families, paid their taxes, tend their gardens and live in our communities. But Oh no, they're way more than that! Sure, now they may not be all that remarkable to look at – but what they did as teenagers borders on the incredible. A nineteen-year old engaged in fighter combat; piloting a four-engined bomber over Berlin; spending seventeen hours in a Catalina hunting U-Boats; or a sixteen-year old manning a tail-gun.

And this is their story – when the searchlights were blinding, the stench of cordite stifling, and the skipper struggling to fly the aircraft straight so his bomb-aimer could do his stuff.

These are our flying veterans. These are their stories. This is their oral history. Telling it the way it was. Telling what they went through.

We owe all of them a lot - an awful lot.

Read it!

Garde B. Gardom, Q.C.
Lieutenant-Governor of British Columbia

# MAPS

# CONTENTS

# PHOTOGRAPHS

# BRYON SIMS

*Bryon enlisted in the RAF in 1942 at the age of nineteen. He received his pilot wings in Canada in March 1944 and returned to the UK, where he was selected as a flying instructor. He says, "I cannot claim instructing was anything but a tedious job, not likely to stir the pulse of any reader. However, I can write about a different aspect of war, one etched in my memory. It concerns a young lad of eleven and a navvy (a labourer) of fifty or so, a veteran of World War I. Here is that story*

## The Navvy

To the boy in his early teens, England between the wars was a paradise. To the boy, the world of flying between the wars was the ultimate adventure. Farnborough, or South Farnborough as it was correctly known in flying circles, was full of new wonders and old friends. It held him bewitched. Not for him the stressful years of the discovery of girls with which many boys filled their teens. He found his first love, the aeroplane, in the days when Jim and Amy Mollison made the first flight to the USA, in thirty-nine hours. They were the years of men like Cobham, Kingsford Smith, Waghorn, Clouston and Adam, of the truly glamorous girls, Amy Johnson, Amelia Earhart, and the Duchess of Bedford.

He lived their world, devoured newspapers and magazines for news of their wonderful machines, and learned sadness as death so

11

regularly took its toll of those he never knew, yet knew so well. Farnborough was his temple. From the age of ten he plagued his parents for permission to cycle there on holidays and weekends. But it was not until he was thirteen that his parents allowed him to go. From that day he started to live.

From his home in Farnham to Farnborough was six miles; the first three being all uphill to the village of Heath End, where Caesar had camped on nearby Laffans Plain, camped in the open, free from the attacks of Celtic tribes. Today this area is called Aldershot, a place loved or hated by many of the Canadians who camped there in two wars. The journey took him an hour, but anticipation made light of the steep hills. Upon his return the downhill runs would be filled with memories of the treasures he had seen.

Of all his heroes, one was special: Flying Officer Adam. He'd seen Adam once, near the Queen's Hotel in Farnborough, and had even spoken to him, which took a lot of nerve. That had been a few weeks after Adam had broken the world altitude record. He'd reached over 53,000 feet. In his shy way the boy had approached Adam and asked,

"Was it very scary, sir?"

"It was super."

Adam smiled. The boy never forgot Adam, but the next time he saw his hero he couldn't recognize him.

In those days flying was in its early years and airfields were not large; take-off and landing runs were quite short. The airfield at Farnborough was fairly small and bounded by roads that were not thoroughfares for traffic but were open to the public. Thus the boy could take a viewing spot just outside the wire fence and still have a clear distant view of the hangars and buildings of the RAF Heyfords, Whitleys, Battles, Furies and Harts. All and more he saw and learned to love.

Some he saw and did not know. The prototypes of the Spitfire, the Hurricane and even the forerunner of the Lancaster. When he saw a prototype, he looked for more information; he searched "Flight", "The Aeroplane" and any other magazines he could get hold of.

These planes were not weapons of war. They were beautiful, sleek things with which his heroes broke the barriers of speed and distance. War was a remote thing that ages ago had scarred his father; but war was gone and England was mighty enough and wealthy enough to preserve this boy's dreams.

12

BUT WAR DID COME. It came early and suddenly on a quiet English summer afternoon. It came as harsh and as brutal and as terrifying as hell itself. It left the boy much closer to a child, yet in many ways closer to a man and certainly closer to reality.

It was the latter part of May. School exams were over and the boy looked forward to a summer of Farnborough afternoons. On this afternoon, a Wednesday, the weatherman had smiled. Flying would be good.

As Farnborough had no runways then, aircraft could take off pretty close to the wind. Today the wind was from the north-west and the boy took his place on the north side just outside the low, four-strand, wire fence at a spot where he knew he would not be directly under the plane taking off, but slightly to one side. It was an excellent position as most aircraft would be no more than 200 feet away as they passed his position.

He settled down on the warm scrub ground of Laffans Plain. This was the life. There was no one around to disturb him. In fact, the only person near was a labourer, a navvy, working about two hundred feet away, just inside the perimeter.

The navvy was clearing the land drains that drain the excess water from the low-lying part of the field. He was a nondescript man, typical of so many ex-soldiers of the 1914-1918 war and, like so many, laboured for 44 hours a week for a meagre two pounds a week. He wore a grey peaked cap and a heavy gingery-brown moustache, and his face had that rugged look of old leather. He wore a shirt with no collar made of flannel with a blue stripe running vertically. Around his neck he had a red choker that sopped up the perspiration rolling off his face as he worked. His jacket was of a heavy greyish material and had obviously seen more summers than had the boy. His trousers were brown corduroy. Tucked into the string around his left leg was a little chip of wood that he used to scrape mud adhering to his shovel. His boots were neither black nor brown, just the colour of age. Across his back lay a sack, the kind navvies used as rain cover.

Periodically he would stop, straighten up slowly, lift off his cap and wipe away the sweat with the sleeve of his jacket. He took no notice of the boy and even less of the aircraft that passed so close over his head.

The boy watched.

A Hawker Hart taxied away from the far-distant buildings over to the south side and turned into the wind. It started to move and the sound of its engine did not reach the boy for a couple of seconds. Halfway across the field it lifted its tail and roared directly towards the boy. As it passed over him the man in the gunner's seat looked over and waved down to him; the boy waved back; his afternoon was made.

Slowly, very slowly, almost like a dowager duchess, a Whitley detached itself from the aircraft near it at the hangars and taxied across the grass to the same position from which the Hart had just taken off. It turned its nose into wind and paused. This was a surprise for the boy. The Whitley was the biggest heavy bomber the Royal Air Force had at this period between the wars. It was twin-engined, had a wing span of almost sixty feet, and was one of the first heavy bombers to have enclosed gunner positions in the front and rear of the fuselage. The boy had never seen one up close or even seen one fly; but he had read about it in "Flight".

Far across the airfield the boy heard the roar as each engine was run to full power to test the magnetos before take-off. A peculiar thing happened as the port engine was being run up. At full power it coughed slightly and a large sheet of flame ran down from the exhaust and quickly disappeared.

The pilot was evidently satisfied and throttled back. The sound of engines gave way to silence. Then, very shortly afterwards, the aircraft started to move and in a few short seconds the roar of those big engines again reached its way across the airfield. The Whitley came towards the boy slowly, for it was a heavy beast. When it was about halfway across the airfield, the boy could see the 25 degrees of flap the pilot had lowered to shorten his take-off run. A few seconds later the wheels lifted off the grass and almost immediately started to retract.

The monster came over the airfield toward the boy, gradually increasing its height as it came. It swept across the airfield fence at maybe a hundred feet in the air. The boy watched, fascinated.

Then it happened. A large cold hand of fear gripped the boy and he watched in horror the most ghastly tragedy he was ever to see. One engine coughed and faltered and slowly the starboard wing began to drop. Many years later the boy learned there was only one thing to do in the circumstances, and that was for the pilot to throttle back the other engine and dump the machine straight ahead. But this the pilot didn't do. He must have tried to maintain his height on one engine, and he paid the final penalty for his misjudgement.

Slowly the Whitley dropped her wing, rolled over on her back, and nosed upside down into the sandy scrub of Laffans Plain.

Suddenly, within 200 feet of the boy, the aircraft broke into many pieces, partly from the impact and partly from the massive explosion. The heat lifted the down from the boy's face and he felt the crinkle of his eyebrows singed by the initial flash.

He seemed surrounded by fire. He was terrified. He ran. He ran as fast as his feet would carry him from this scene of horror.

Seemingly from the far distance—a voice.

"Where are you going?"

The boy stopped and dumbly looked at the navvy. The navvy beckoned.

"Come with me."

The navvy clutched at the boy's sleeve and dragged him towards the crash.

"How many inside?"

"Five I think."

"I'll try to get them." The navvy took the sack from his back and gave it to the boy. "You stay here and put them out. Use this." The instructions were terse, the boy was just a boy, and the crash was a mass of burning wreckage.

The navvy disappeared into a group of maybe half a dozen individual small fires. The boy watched in fascination and fear. Soon, through the smoke he saw the navvy coming out. He ran quickly to help drag the first body to a safe distance, maybe twenty feet from the nearest fire, but his hands were bare and his efforts useless. The navvy disappeared again.

The boy was overcome with the smell of burning human flesh. He looked down at the man—or what had been a man. Whatever it was it had a parachute with the pack slightly open. Pure white silk blossomed out and made a clean sterile bed to honour the human mess that lay at the boy's feet. He pulled off the body's flying glove, and with the sack he started to beat the smouldering flames that had more or less devoured the flying suit. He threw sand onto the more stubborn flames; this body was at least "out". It was just smoking. He covered it over with the folds of the parachute.

He glanced at the face, at what once had been a face and was now a black mask horribly contrasted against the white. He turned his head aside and stumbled away. He retched and threw up.

"Boy!"

That distant voice again. Body number two was on its way out. He ran to the navvy, who dragged the second 'whatever it was' over towards the first. Once again the navvy disappeared and once again the boy started the job of 'putting it out'. The left leg of the flying suit was still burning badly and would not be doused. The boy reached down and ripped the material away. As he did so he was aghast, for the remnant of flying suit came away with flesh attached. Black molten flesh.

"Hurry."

He had no time to vomit again. The voice was calling. Blindly he ran over to help with the third man.

"You take him; there is another one."

The navvy disappeared back into the inferno. The youngster could not lift the man under the armpits or drag him to safety from the fire that was now beginning to spread through the scrub. He doused the flames on the flying suit and pulled off a pair of flying boots that were not burnt. The socks came off with the flying boots and for the first time the boy saw pink unharmed flesh. He felt encouraged.

"Boy!"

The navvy was dragging the fourth man. The young boy ran to help. This one was completely "out". There was no flame, just a few wisps of smoke from the smouldering flying helmet. The boy took it off.

"I can't find the fifth one."

"There might not be five." The boy had thought there were five, but he wasn't certain.

"Come", said the navvy tersely and the two of them dodged their way between the fires to look. To this day the boy cannot remember if there was another body.

"Get back! Out!"

The boy ran back to the four waiting bodies. He stood and watched for the fifth man. Suddenly there was a blinding sheet of flame as a fuel tank exploded. The boy was terror stricken. The navvy had been killed as well? He was all alone!

But he wasn't alone. Through the filthy, black, swirling smoke came the navvy, slowly, almost as if he were too tired to walk. As he straightened up, two large tears ran down from his eyes and worked a trail through the black smoke stains across his cheeks. He looked at the bodies and looked at the boy.

"I wonder if any of them is alive."

16

"I don't think so. None of them have moved."

"Poor buggers", said the navvy, stooping to pulled the parachute folds from underneath one of the bodies and drape it across the face, or what had once been a face, and then standing back helpless–for neither he nor the boy knew what to do next.

Far away the bell of the fire truck from the airfield hangar clanged as it charged across the airfield grass. Not even stopping for the fencing wire, it came right through the fence and drew up some thirty feet from the bodies.

The navvy and the boy withdrew to let the specialists commence their grisly work. They did stay and watch to see if any of them were alive. Presently an RAF staff car came over and four officers alighted. The navvy and the boy once again withdrew from the scene. All four were pilots, their white wings standing out upon their blue grey uniforms.

One of the officers would have been F/Lt Clouston. The boy recognised him as one of his heroes whose photograph he had seen many times in the newspaper in recent years. Clouston walked to the bodies. Without bending down he put his shoe under the folds of the parachute and lifted them from the *one-time* face. He looked, then shrugged and turned away. He stood looking away for quite a time, saying nothing.

The boy hated him. Why could he not have bent down and lifted the parachute folds with his hand? Was he afraid? The boy who stood with a blackened glove in his right hand felt as if he had been insulted by one of his heroes. For many days he could not forgive Clouston; but he did as he grew older.

The ambulance arrived anon and the boy withdrew further from the scene. Eventually the fire was put out and the bodies loaded into the ambulance. The navvy returned to his job of digging the land drains. Before he left he looked at the boy.

"You all right?"

The boy assured him he was and the navvy went back to his digging, hitting his cap against his cords. The boy wandered away, picked up his bicycle and moved along the fence so that he was some four hundred feet from the demolished Whitley. He recommenced his watching, but this wasn't as good a position as his other spot. Yet it was the best he could do.

He recommenced his watch for other aircraft, but none came. For some reason or other there was an anti-climax about 'watching airplanes' and after a while he climbed on his bicycle and started his journey home.

Apart from vomiting at the sight of the first body he felt no ill effects from the experience. He cycled out onto the main Farnborough road and turned west. As he cycled he wondered whether he and the navvy should have interfered. Both the navvy and he were typical products of a working-class English upbringing. They backed away from any form of officialdom, particularly anyone in uniform. It was for this reason that he and the navvy had backed away when the fire-truck turned up, and again when the staff car arrived with the air force officers. It was for the same reason that the navvy had gone back to his trench digging and the boy had withdrawn to a safe distance to continue his watching.

He wondered if he would get into trouble for still having the flying glove he had used to douse the flames. It now rested in his saddlebag.

He wondered whether he and the navvy should have kept away until the fire-truck and ambulance arrived and let them do what was necessary.

His feeling of insecurity about the whole situation started to weigh on him and added to the onset of a reaction that started very shortly after he passed the Queen's Hotel and started the long straight run towards Heath End. After about a mile he found his legs starting to tremble on the pedals of his bicycle and soon he was shaking and unable to ride. He got off, went over to the sidewalk, and sat on the grass. His shaking continued and in one terrible wrench he threw up again. He lay upon the grass, trembling.

"Well, what's going on here?"

The boy looked up and again was afraid. There looking down at him standing by his bicycle was a policeman, a member of the Aldershot Constabulary on his daily bicycle beat.

The boy was unable to speak and even if he could, he would have been afraid to tell the constable the truth of what he had done. He kept quiet and continued his shaking. The policeman was very kind. He was concerned to see a young boy in such a state, perhaps assuming he was having an epileptic attack of some sort. Anyway, in the typical manner of the English bobby, he stood beside the boy and calmed and encouraged him. Eventually the shaking ceased.

"Do you feel okay to get back on your bike now?"

"I think so, sir."

"I'll cycle with you to Heath End; that's the end of my beat."

They set off together riding side by side.

When they reached the top of the hill by the pub in Heath End the policeman asked, "Well, it is all downhill from here, will you be all right?" The boy nodded and went on his way.

When he arrived home at 6:30 looking as white as a ghost, his mother took him to task for having been so late and missing "Tea". The boy made the excuse that he had wanted to watch a special aircraft and had been delayed in waiting for it.

"If you are not going to be home in time for Tea we will stop you from going to Farnborough again", said his mother. And his father nodded in agreement.

They need not have worried. He did not return to Farnborough for many years. He often wondered why he didn't go back. He still worshipped airplanes. He still searched the magazines for information and still knew everything it was possible to know about all the developments in aviation. But he never went back to Farnborough. He didn't analyse why.

Another factor the boy never analysed was the fact that he had transferred his hero worship without even knowing it. To him the navvy was a greater hero than any man he had ever met or was ever to meet in the rest of his life. A quiet unsung world-class hero. To this day the boy does not know whether the navvy received any recognition. Approximately one month after the crash the boy wondered if he could write to the officer commanding Royal Air Force Station South Farnborough and inquire in his naive way whether 'anything had been done for the navvy who looked after the men in the crash'. He did not write in case he got into trouble too.

\* \* \* \* \*

*I understand that in the issue of the "Farnborough News" shortly after the crash there was a small paragraph stating that F/Lt Adam had died upon the steps of Farnborough Hospital after a crash involving his crew. It was terse, and typical of the Air Force releases in relation to accidents. So, Adam, his hero had gone too!*

*The young boy is an old man now; during his working years in publishing and at his Aircrew Association meetings he met many heroes.*

*But I guess not all heroes flew. The navvy taught me that.*

# FIGHTER OPERATIONS

The words Spitfire and Hurricane invariably connote the Battle of Britain and 1940. On Sunday 15 September, the date originally planned for Germany's invasion of Britain, the Luftwaffe sent hundreds and thousands of bombers to bomb London, and Britain, into submission. They were escorted by Me109s. Our Hurricanes and Spitfires were outnumbered five to one but they won the day. The cost on that day was 26 pilots killed; those who survived claimed 185 German aircraft destroyed, a tally understandably overestimated in the heat and lightning thrust of fierce combat; but whatever the count it was undeniably Fighter Command's greatest day.

Our stories cover accounts from the Battle of France to D-Day and beyond. Not only Spitfires and Hurricanes, but also Tempests, Mustangs, Mosquitos, Beaufighters and even Mohawks and other obsolescent aircraft in the Far East–all fought the good fight. They fought over Britain, France, NW Europe, Malta, Italy, Singapore, North Africa, Burma, Siam, and Malaya. They fought over oceans and mountains; deserts and jungles.

Typically armed with various combinations of .303 Browning machine guns and 20-mm cannon in each wing, the RCAF and RAF and their Allies secured and maintained air supremacy. They escorted bombers, para-drops, troop ships, destroyers and gliders; they attacked artillery placements, trains, tanks, warships, U-boats, V-bomb sites, and the V-bombs themselves. Sometimes the fighter would carry small bombs, torpedoes, or rockets.

Always on the offensive, fighter pilots provided protection and support for their brothers in bombers, in coastal operations, in every branch of the service, in every activity. Their stories are fascinating.

Ken Pask

# CONTRIBUTORS
## Fighter Operations

| | |
|---|---|
| **Rhubarb:** | An operation in which pilots seek out targets of opportunity–such as road and rail traffic or enemy airfields. |
| **Jumped:** | Probably most Allied fighter pilots who were shot down by an enemy fighter did not see the fighter in time to take evasive action. Pilots talked of being "jumped" by an enemy when that enemy attacked unseen. |
| **Readiness:** | Aircraft and pilots ready to take-off |
| **Scramble:** | GO NOW |
| **Bogey:** | Unidentified aircraft. May or may not be an enemy. |
| **Friendly:** | One of ours |
| **Bandit:** | One of theirs |
| **Dead stick:** | Without power. |

# T.P.M. COOPER-SLIPPER

*Mike was born on 11 January 1921 and educated in England. He was commissioned in the RAF in 1938 and he flew as a fighter pilot in England, France, Singapore, and the Middle East.*

*He served as a test pilot both in the Middle East and in England. He held the rank of squadron leader and was awarded the DFC.*

*In 1947 Mike moved to Canada to become a test pilot with A. V Roe. He was Chief Test Pilot for Orenda Engines, moved on to sales and worked for five years with De Havilland. He then spent a further five years in marketing with Field Aviation.*

*He worked for the Government of Ontario before retiring to British Columbia in 1986. He is married to Rita. They have one son, Chris, who is Vice-President and General Manager Sales, Field Aviation.*

## The Battle of France, May 1940
### A Week to Remember

May 21. My squadron, No. 605, was at Wick in the very north of Scotland, where it had been since late in 1939. I had joined the squadron from 11 Group Pool (the first of the OTUs) in January, with about ten hours on Spitfires and fifty on Hurricanes.

We lived in Wick, in a hotel run by two old sisters who were not completely up to date on the somewhat irregular behaviour of the modern fighter pilot. The biggest problem was getting booze, as Wick was a dry town; however, the squadron Magister brought some in from a pub in Lybster (I think) and the Navy gave us a barrel of rum.

At about noon we were told we would be moving south that same day and to get our small kit ready to take with us; our main baggage would have to follow by rail with the ground crews. A Flight got off first and B Flight left soon afterwards. We stopped twice to refuel on the way to Hawkinge, near Folkestone, in Kent. I remember the countryside looked greener and more like summer the further south we got. Hawkinge was very busy; we parked our aircraft with some strange ground crew, had a meal, and went to bed.

**May 22**

We were called at about 0400 hours and took off at first light. We were very keen to have a go at the Germans, having spent a rather uncomfortable winter chasing them around the north of Scotland, in terrible weather, from a somewhat primitive airfield, with very little success.

The squadron carried out a patrol into France, behind Calais and Boulogne, without seeing any other aircraft. It was the last time we had that pleasure during our stay at Hawkinge.

We took off again at about 1000 hours. Two flights got separated over France. A Flight was jumped by 109s and lost a couple of pilots. B Flight got itself split into two sections in cloud. My section, in which I was number three, came across two Hel11s at about 5000 feet; they were some five hundred feet below us. The section leader saw them but did not attack. Number 2 and I took one each and set them on fire. I was excited and went alongside, whereupon the front gunner gave me a burst, including two through the canopy. I then dropped back and shot a couple of crewmembers getting out of the top of their canopy. The Heinkel went down in a spin and crashed in a field.

On getting back to Hawkinge, I got an enormous strip torn off for leaving my Section Leader. I was never credited with destroying that 111.

**May 23**

Early morning patrol, this time escorting a Blenheim squadron on a mission to bomb a squadron of German tanks that had spent the night in a small wooded area. There was intense light flak, and the bomber boys, at about 2500 feet, lost some of the Blenheims; even the ones that got home were all hit by something. We were at about 3500 feet, and as soon as the remaining Blenheims were clear, we continued our patrol to the Arras area, where we had a brush with some Me110s.

After landing at Hawkinge, we went to see Basil Embry's Blenheim; someone took a photograph of two people standing in a hole in his starboard wing where it had been hit by flak.

Patrolled towards Ostend, tangled with some 109s; I think we lost one pilot. We were short of fuel and just made it back to base. I remember that the Goodwin Sands looked like land to begin with; then I realized we still had quite a way to go. My thumb was sore from pressing the fuel gauge.

Patrolled Dunkirk area. I was jumped by 109s and badly shot up but my armour plate, installed the night before, saved my life. My compass and several other instruments were shot up. I was down to sea level in fairly bad visibility and had quite a job deciding which way was home. I was quite wrong at first and wandered in over Calais where lots of black flak soon set me on the right course—German flak was black and ours was white. When I landed there were fifty-five bullet holes in my aircraft and the core of an armour-piercing round had ended up in my map case.

**May 24**

I cannot recall anything about this day. It was probably the day we saw a tanker burning in the Channel, its upper works glowing white-hot.

**May 25**

Another early morning Blenheim escort patrol. We all hated these bomber-escort flights; the Blenheims took terrible casualties from light flak, and we were much too low to deal effectively with any enemy fighters. Luckily they did not interfere too much with these raids. Someone got a Henschel Hs126 or a Lysander; they both look much the same!

Patrol to cover a supply drop to the Rifle Brigade in the Citadel at Calais. It was quite a sight to see the Lysanders, Swordfish, Blenheims and one or two other types crossing the Channel at zero feet. They pulled up to drop their loads to our people, but most of the supplies went to the Germans. We climbed to attack some Ju87s that were dive-bombing ships in the Channel. I fired a long burst into one of them and think he went down; I then went after another, but my ammo ran out almost immediately.

**May 26**

Patrolled over Dunkirk and saw several Ju88s below. We attacked. I gave one a long burst and followed him through the smoke just in time to see him roll onto his back and crash into the sea. There were Blenheims in the area. Had I shot down one of our own aircraft? But another pilot confirmed my kill as an 88. All was well.

**May 27**

Early morning Blenheim escort patrol. Again the bomber boys took a terrible beating. We fought some 109s on the way home; my Hurricane was becoming rather tired and tattered, as I seemed to get shot on every patrol.

Early in the afternoon we got mixed up with a lot of 109s to the south of Dunkirk; we lost the Squadron Leader and one or two other pilots. I was getting very tired and jumpy; I had been lucky but knew it was only a matter of time before my turn came. I was much relieved by the news that we were to go north in the near future.

**May 28**

The squadron was withdrawn. We had lost half our pilots either dead or missing; our aircraft were all shot up and in bad shape. I had about seventy-five bullet holes through my Hurricane.

There was quite a collection of shot-up aircraft that had made it back to Hawkinge. Apart from all the aircraft that operated from there and had had various adventures, several others dropped in with sundry complaints. I remember a Lysander with the whole rear fuselage a mass of congealed blood. When they lifted the occupant of the rear cockpit, his whole lower part was smashed to pieces by a flak shell that had hit him.

A Hurricane came in with all the fabric on the fuselage streaming back over the tail of the aircraft.

My rigger always took my forage cap when he helped to strap me into my aircraft, and when we returned he was always the first one there—to hand me my cap back. He said it was for good luck. His pilot couldn't be killed so long as he had his cap!

The batmen were full of news when they woke us in the morning. One prize bit of news was that the Germans had landed during the night and were fighting down in Folkestone at that moment.

The Air Transport Auxiliary brought us three Hurricanes, all brand spanking new, and did a formation landing right through the far side of the aerodrome.

We all went to a hotel in Folkestone for a squadron dinner one night. A senior flight lieutenant said that he would take over as Commanding Officer so long as he didn't have to fly. He was posted next day.

We were to fly to Drem, near Edinburgh, to reform the squadron and were instructed to stop at Shawbury for the night. Shawbury was one of the flying-training schools, and we were to impress the students with the bullet holes in our aircraft.

On the way I did a low pass across my home, misjudged the height of the trees and collected some branches in my radiator. The students were certainly impressed with the bullet holes and I was carried to bed, shot down at last, by Alsops Best Bitter.

The next day four of us went further north. The clouds were down on the Scottish hills and so we landed somewhere to spend the night–at least three of us did; a sergeant pilot went off into the clouds and was never seen again. We were back in the land where people killed themselves in flying accidents.

Looking back, it was all rather unreal. People in the rest of the United Kingdom carried on much as they had throughout that beautiful summer of 1940.

Yet in that little area of the South Coast and a small piece of France and Belgium, a desperate battle was going on; thousands were being killed, ships were being sunk, aircraft were being shot down, and France was dying.

My own thoughts of the week I had been fighting were too mixed up to make much sense. I had grown up certainly, I had flown every patrol the Squadron had carried out, I had killed, I had seen a lot of dead people, and I was cold and untouched by it. I could put down a gallon of good old English beer at one sitting.

I was nineteen years old, and I was a Fighter Pilot.

Ed. And what a fighter! In the Battle of Britain. (which followed the Battle of France) Mike claimed two more Me109s, three Dornier 17s, and a share in other victories before he rammed another Do17. He was thrown from his aircraft and landed safely in the Thames estuary. He was awarded the DFC in November 1940.

# PERRY BAUCHMAN

*Perry was born in Windsor, Nova Scotia, in 1920. He joined the RCAF in August 1941 and was awarded his pilot wings in October 1942. Perry served in North Africa and Britain. He returned to Canada in 1944 and was demobbed in September 1945. Post-war, Perry gained a law degree at Dalhousie University in 1949.*

## A Year to Remember

The year 1944 was undoubtedly the most outstanding one of my life. I was flying Spitfire Mark IXb's with 165 Squadron, near Taunton in Somerset. The Spitfire was indeed a spirited steed and I was on cloud nine. Very soon after I arrived at the squadron, it moved to Colerne, near Bath. This was a permanent RAF station with peacetime-style buildings and what was, to me, a luxurious Sergeants' Mess. It was here that I met Rosemary, the beautiful WAAF sergeant who later became my wife.

Some time thereafter she and I were on leave in the pretty little village of Didmarton in the beautiful Cotswolds, at Rosemary's home, our wedding date fixed a month away. Into this blissful interlude came the voice of stark reality in the morning news over the BBC–all travel to the south of England was banned, effective immediately.

I then realised why our squadron had been transferred from Colerne to Predannack, on the Lizard peninsula in Cornwall, and I knew I had to get back to Predannack pronto. We were all aware of the build-up of materiel, vehicles, tanks, guns and aircraft across the southern countryside, in woods, under trees, and in any area that offered concealment from aerial reconnaissance. The travel ban could only mean one thing–the long awaited invasion. D-Day was upon us and I had a role to play in this history in the making. Kissing my sweetheart good-bye, I took off in my old jalopy to drive the 200-odd miles to my squadron's base.

At that time aircrew were allowed a few gallons of gasoline for personal use in lieu of travel warrants. This was a great privilege; few people had petrol for personal use. I had been a little profligate with my allowance and I was doubtful I had enough to get back to Cornwall. So in every town on the way back I purchased all the lighter fuel that I could get. Like everything else it was in short supply, but it made effective–if expensive–emergency fuel. It was just as well I did this; it fuelled my faithful old heap the last ten miles.

At first light next morning our squadron was briefed to fly top cover over the Normandy beachhead. By the time we arrived the first troops had landed and penetrated a few miles into France in the face of very heavy resistance. In our sector the Luftwaffe was noteworthy for its scarcity. The spectacle on the beaches was awe-inspiring. The coast was hidden in billowing black smoke; warships of all sizes from battleships to destroyers sat off the coast pounding it with everything from the giant guns of the battleships to salvo after salvo of rockets from the cruisers. The rockets trailed continuous streams of fire as they disappeared into the smoke to pulverise the German defence constructions of Fortress Europe.

It was hard to believe that anything could survive such a pounding, but survive Jerry did, to put up a punishing defence. Our troops were still going ashore in landing craft and we noticed some of them suffering hits.

The quantity of shipping was unbelievable, stretching from the Normandy coast across the Channel and around the tip of Cornwall in an unbroken line, disappearing into the distance towards the Irish Sea. It was as though one could walk across the Channel on this bridge of ships. This, more than anything else, brought home the fantastic scope of the operation, the virtually impossible degree of planning and logistics that had gone into Operation Overlord.

Allied aircraft formed a continuous stream that flowed across the Channel into France and back out again. For immediate identification every aircraft had broad white stripes painted across both the upper and lower surfaces of each wing. When we encountered little opposition from the Luftwaffe, we became overconfident. This proved to be a fatal error for two of my comrades who were bounced by Fw190s while we were gaping at the bombing pattern on the ground instead of being alert to provide proper cross-cover.

These were our only losses that day although we were flying from dawn to dusk, returning to base only long enough to refuel and re-arm, and then back to the fray. From then on we were continuously engaged in rhubarbs, ground level attacks on enemy installations, troop movements, road and rail transport, and so on. The Spitfire's main fuel tank only held 85 gallons of fuel. On these sorties, each aircraft was fitted with a 90-gallon drop tank that was used on the trip out. The drop tank was jettisoned as soon as it was empty, or immediately if one was attacked. It was a source of concern to us that we might proceed out on ninety gallons and then try to get home on eighty-five gallons.

One day the inevitable happened. We were engaged on a four-man sweep over France in the area beyond Cherbourg. The flight leader's call sign was Drumroll. He was Red One and his number two was Red Two. My section leader was Green One and I was Green Two. We flew at sea level to escape detection by German radar but as we approached Cherbourg the flight leader, for some odd reason, climbed up to about three hundred feet. Jerry anti-aircraft batteries opened fire with everything but the kitchen sink. The flight commander and his number two were boxed in by anti-aircraft fire. My number one called me.

"The hell with this game, Green Two, follow me up the river."

We continued up the river valley, flying at sea and ground level so that Jerry couldn't depress his anti-aircraft guns enough to bear on us, and we were pretty well out of range of small-arms fire. We cruised up the valley under a canopy of exploding red balls. Red Section had by now passed the coast defences, returned to ground level, and joined us. The flight commander called.

"Good show, Green One. Actually I just wanted to see if there was any shipping in the harbour. Glad you stayed down."

They must have had a host of guardian angels surrounding them to come through that maelstrom unscathed. A few miles further inland we spotted a locomotive just on the horizon. As we got nearer we saw this was a freight train, and judging by the three flak cars interspersed through the line of freight cars it was transporting strategic material.

We opened fire and immediately the locomotive was enveloped in steam and stopped. It was going to be out of action for quite a while. Several of the freight cars burst into flame and the flak cars, although taken by surprise by our low-level approach, opened a discouraging concentration of anti-aircraft fire. We made another pass at the end of the train we had missed previously and then beat a judicious retreat. While we were cruising over the fields behind the Lombardy poplars bordering the highway, a farmer standing in the doorway of his house was excitedly jumping up and down and madly waving his hat at us by way of greeting.

Shortly thereafter we spotted a military motor convoy of about a dozen trucks on the highway. We climbed to about three hundred feet and dropped our slipper tanks while we circled into position to attack. I noticed that one of our slipper tanks landed in the road and exploded. We proceeded to strafe the vehicles from end to end. Red Two made a steep dive and either waited too long to pull up from strafing or was hit by small arms fire. He flew into the end of the convoy, taking about four vehicles out in a great explosion and ball of fire. What actually happened we were never sure, but the devastation was spectacular. We carried out a final sweep of the convoy leaving it in a shambles and our dead comrade behind us.

We set out on a return course, much to my relief, since my slipper tank had run out of fuel not long before I dropped it. I hoped I would get back on my eighty-five gallons. We pulled up to five thousand feet over the Channel. About half-way across, Green One called the flight commander:

"Red One, this is Green One, I've got problems, my engine is running very rough."

"Roger, Green One. You may have picked up some flak or small arms fire; reduce rpm and throttle back. We'll stay with you."

A few minutes later my number one called again:

"Red One, my engine has quit, I'm baling out."

"Roger, Green One. Good luck. We'll call Mayday and give you top cover."

Jimmie dived over the side, his 'chute opened, and his aircraft made a parabola as it fell into the channel, where it left a very prominent oil slick. The flight leader called me.

"Green Two, I'll go down to see if he's OK. You stay up here, give us top cover, and call Mayday."

"Wilco, Green One. Mayday, Mayday, Mayday. This is

Drumroll Green Two calling Mayday, over."

"Drumroll Green Two, this is Rescue. Transmit for fix."

"Rescue, this is Green Two. Green One had to bale out and Red One went down to check on him while I give top cover. Green One's aircraft has left a large and very visible oil slick. Green One entered the water about one mile west of the oil slick. Over."

"Roger, Green Two, thank you. We got a good fix on you and rescue is on the way."

"Oh, good show, Rescue. Thank you. Green Two out."

The flight leader's voice came over the RT.

"Green Two, this is Red One, I copied you and Rescue. I couldn't find Jimmie. His aircraft tail or rudder may have hit him when he baled out or he may have been pulled under by his 'chute. He didn't get into his dinghy. We'd better go home."

"Roger, Red One. I hope I have enough fuel to make it. I've reduced rpm to twenty two hundred."

"Good show, Green Two. Keep me posted. Out."

We continued on course at angels five, with my fingers crossed. Just as we approached the coast my engine started to cough and splutter and finally gave up the struggle. I called the flight leader.

"Red One, my engine has quit. I can see Bolt Head 'drome and with a bit of luck I might be able to glide that far."

"Roger, Green Two. Good luck. Call me when you get down."

"Wilco, Red One. Out. Bolt Head control, this is Drumroll Green Two approaching base and requesting permission to come straight in dead-stick."

"Roger, Green Two. We have been copying. Come straight in on the runway in front of you and good luck."

"Wilco, thank you. Green Two out."

It looked like I would be able to stretch my glide to the runway, but with no engine I would have no air pressure to operate the flaps, nor hydraulic pressure to operate the undercarriage mechanism. I felt this should be quite a spectacular landing. Thanks to an updraft at the approach to the coast I made the runway comfortably but the wheels-up, flapless landing didn't do much for my aircraft. I certainly wasn't going to fly it off again.

"Drumroll Red One, this is Green Two. I made it down all right, but I'm afraid my aircraft is unserviceable. Over."

"Roger, Green Two. Congratulations, very glad you're OK. We'll send the Tiger Moth to pick you up."

"Thank you, Red One. Green Two Out."

I made my way up to the control tower to thank them for their assistance. They told me that Air Sea Rescue would like to see me. They told me they had discovered the oil slick but could find no trace of the pilot and wanted to know just where he had entered the water in relation to it. I explained that he had touched down about one mile west of the oil slick. They told me they'd been tracking us and had actually followed the parachute on its way down but just wanted to double check with me as to the correct location. It was obvious they had responded promptly and accurately, but we never did learn what had happened to Jimmie. There was gloom and consternation back at the squadron when the flight commander was the only aircraft of four to return from our flight.

A few hours later the Tiger Moth arrived to trundle me back to base. And soon after that I had a week's leave to get married.

About this time we began to hear rumours of unmanned flying bombs, a sort of aerial torpedo sporting a 2000-lb warhead and a tail of flame and snorting like an ill-tuned motorbike. With their usual penchant for understatement, the British nicknamed them 'Doodlebugs'. (*When the fire goes out, take cover, it's about to dive in*) We heard that a great many lunatic fighter pilots were actually engaged in shooting them down. Imagine shooting at a one- ton bomb; not bloody likely!

Two days later the squadron was transferred to do just that, and we found ourselves flying in to Detling, near Maidstone, Kent. We had a little trouble catching up with these things at first, particularly if the controller brought us in at the same level on a nearly reciprocal vector that required a turn of 90° or more onto the target. Once they learned to bring us in a little above, we had no trouble overtaking them.

One day I was flying Number Two to an Australian pal, "Happy" Armstrong, when we were vectored in on a Doodlebug over Dungeness. We let it get well inland and away from built-up areas when Happy fired at it from dead astern at about a hundred yards. Big mistake! The Doodlebug exploded and Happy disappeared into a huge ball of flame and black smoke. Good-bye Happy! I thought, but a few seconds later he emerged going straight up and jet-black all over as though his aircraft had been spray painted, and with the fabric of the elevators and rudder afire. In a few seconds the fabric was burned off hence no more fire. Happy levelled out but flew on somewhat erratically, slipping and skidding, climbing and diving. I called him.

"Happy, are you all right?" No answer. I was getting a little worried. I called again,

"Drumhead Green One, are you OK? Answer please." Still no response. All this time I'd been at full boost trying to catch up with him. As I drew alongside, there was Happy with his canopy and cockpit door open, leaning out industriously cleaning off his windscreen with his scarf. When he finally sat back I called again and this time he replied.

"Yeah, I'm OK, but there seems to be something wrong with the controls; they don't respond."

I told him the fabric had been burned off his rudder and elevators and that he had better bring her in fast on his landing approach in order to maintain control.

"Yeah, OK Jack, I'll do that." He did that all right, making a wheel landing at about 150 mph, taking up the whole length of the runway in braking to a stop without putting the aircraft up on its nose.

After flying through the one-ton bomb blast, his plane had no damage other than to the control surfaces–and the black-paint job. The next day reporters and photographers arrived from London and a couple of days later Happy and his aircraft made the front page of the Daily Mirror. Happy said he would rather have been inside with Jane (the scantily clad heroine of a Daily Mirror cartoon strip).

Eventually our squadron was transferred to Lympne in Kent, a wartime aerodrome with a grass landing area bordered by trees that made it necessary to slip off height after clearing the trees on the approach in order to get into the landing area without running into the trees at the other side of the field. The grass turned muddy, and runways of steel mesh were laid down. One day after destroying a Doodlebug, I returned to base to refuel and crashed on landing. To this day I have no recollection of what happened. The last thing I remember is passing through some white cumulus cloud on the way back to the aerodrome. The physician informed me the memory loss was caused by concussion and that I might not recall it later. On landing, my undercarriage had caught in the steel matting at the start of the runway and I had cartwheeled. I was medically grounded and so ended my flying career. A black day.

Bolt Head aerodrome, where Perry made his dead-stick landing, is on the coast of Devon. See map on page s 242/243.

# J. C. HUGHES

*Jack was born in Dauphin, Manitoba, in 1919. He enlisted in the RCAF in 1941 and was accepted for pilot training. He was awarded his wings in September of that year and left for Britain. He joined 402 Squadron to fly Hurricanes and later Spitfire Vs over France. By October 1942, Jack had moved to Malta (249 Squadron) where he stayed until July 1943. In March 1944, he was posted to 401 (RCAF) Squadron flying Spitfire IXs and covered the D-Day operations. Jack finished his tour in Holland and was demobbed in 1945.*

## The Dunking

On 15 July 1942, 402 Squadron was stationed just south of London at Redhill. This was the secondary airfield of the Kenley wing. We were sharing it with 602 Squadron led by W/Cdr Paddy Finucane, and a Polish Squadron. At that time Paddy had more victories than any other living pilot in the RAF.

The weather was bad. A low-pressure system off the west coast. We had ten-tenths cloud, rain, and a ceiling less than 1000 feet. Lousy weather, but ideal for rhubarbs. 602 Squadron and the Poles would fly into France on the deck and go a-hunting. In this weather, the enemy would take advantage of the cover to keep the railways, canals, and roads busy. There would be lots of targets! If things got too hot, we could just pop up into the cloud and fly instruments for a while.

We had been assigned to handle defence. We were standing by for take-off in squadron strength to repel any enemy attack. The Germans knew all about rhubarb. They knew we just loved to drop in for tea and blow up a few locomotives on the way.

At about 1100 hours Paddy and his crew taxied out on to the runway and were off into the mist. We were now at fifteen minutes readiness instead of immediate readiness. I wandered out to my aircraft to gather my gear and chew the fat with the ground crew. We were discussing available entertainment in London for leave when it happened. Two red flares. "Scramble!"

We leapt into action. In no time I was strapped in, helmeted, with engine running. The CO came barrelling along the taxi strip, and I pulled in right behind him as his No. 2 We swung on to the runway and were off. The boss reported "airborne" and air control replied, "Buster 180 deck" (Maximum speed due south below cloud). We crossed the coast and dropped down to the Channel. Our controller came on the blower and advised us that some of our friends were down in the water and the rescue boats under attack by Me109s. We were to see what we could do about it.

We were about seven miles off Le Touquet. I could only see the CO, but the rest were on their way. As we approached the French coast we could see a big break in the overcast several miles across. The Germans must have been waiting there for our Spitfires coming out of France low on ammo and fuel. I could see several boats burning and Me109s diving in pairs to attack them. There must have been about twenty of them. The CO attacked the nearest pair and they broke off the attack. The 109s then joined up to assess the new threat. They had been sent out to destroy the boats and had done a pretty good job. They must be low on ammo by now.

Our CO gave the order to circle the boats to port and form a defensive circle. The enemy formed another circle outside ours, circling to starboard. It was obvious they were not very interested in the boats now and we were the targets. I didn't like it one bit. We had given the enemy the initiative and were now purely defensive.

Then another enemy squadron, Fw190s, got into the act. These boys were not short of anything. The Me109s reformed and were preparing to leave when a pair of them broke off and made a pass at the boats. I decided to have a go. I was in position and dove to intercept the 109s. I picked a spot on the lead 109's line of flight and fired a short burst of cannon. I made a couple of hits and he broke off.

I was ready to finish the job, but first took a glance back and I was looking down the barrels of a Fw190's cannon less than 100 yards away. I slammed everything into the corner to make a break, but I was too late. I saw the rounds coming out of his guns like a volley of red-hot tennis balls.

The Spitfire Vb had a landing light in the leading edge of the port wing, and the quadrant to aim it was located about six inches above the throttle. The first round from the 190 hit the quadrant; it smashed a hole in the port side of the fuselage that I could stick my leg through, and another hole on the starboard side where the whole kit and caboodle exited. My hand on the throttle picked up a splinter of steel and was slammed across my body. I glanced down; blood was coming in spurts through a slit in my glove. The next round exploded on the corner of the instrument panel. The flying instruments were smashed. There was broken glass everywhere. I was looking at a regular fireworks display of sparks in the black hole where the panel had been. My left leg felt as if a baseball bat had hit it and there was a strong smell of cordite. Another round hit somewhere in the engine; glycol coolant was being sucked into the cylinders and blown out the exhaust as white smoke. Time was running out. I called the boss.

"Red Two, hit and baling out."

"I see you. Try to get away from the coast; we'll cover you."

It was good to hear my leader's voice. I shed the canopy, throttled back and set the prop in coarse pitch to get the most of what was left of the engine. I was too low to jump and tried to pick up some height. I was down to about 180 mph. I looked back to starboard and saw an aircraft coming up; it was very comforting. Then I checked to port and there was another aircraft coming up and fast; it had a big yellow spinner. It was an Fw190. I stuffed the nose down and hauled the Spit around to meet it. He pulled straight up into the clouds. He had done his job. They had me boxed in, and he had drawn me into attack so his buddy could close and blast me from behind. I slammed the Spit to starboard to meet the attack.

At my speed, I could turn around on a nickel. I am sure the Fw pilot didn't realise how slow I was going. He was barrelling along trying to bring his guns to bear on me, and overshot. I had turned inside him. He was committed to the attack, and it was too late to break off. He couldn't turn sharply enough to bring his guns to bear on me and would pay for his error. I turned to meet him and opened fire as he approached. He must have passed less than 100 yards from my guns. My windshield was oiled up but I saw several flashes as the cannon shells found their mark. The Fw vanished into the cloud.

The whole operation had started in a large break in the overcast. I was back to overcast and less than 1000-ft. ceiling. The Spitfire has a firewall between cockpit and fuel tank. However, the controls passed through it, and it only had a delaying effect. I saw the fire sucked through the floor by the draft from the open cockpit, and soon it was everywhere. I was well covered: gauntlets, boots, heavy glass goggles, and a slow-burning wool scarf.

I had to move fast. It is suicide to jump from an aircraft at low altitude and hit the water at over 100 mph. I decided to reduce my ground speed by pulling up in a loop so that when I had negative g I could pull the pin and pop out like a cork from a bottle. We had a saying, "When in trouble, do something, even if it is wrong".

I had run through this in my mind a hundred times. Full fine pitch, full throttle, it may blow up, but what the hell! Back on the stick and up we went. I had a routine: right hand pulls oxygen fitting, down to radio and pull the plug, down to seat lever and drop the seat, pull the pin on seat harness, stand on the seat, and kick the stick forward.

It's amazing how little things come to mind. The RAF provided radio plugs and cords in one size only, with about seven feet of cord. I guess this was so the bomber boys could go to the 'can' and still hear the music. For single-seat fighters, two feet would have been adequate. We solved the problem by folding the wire back on itself, wrapping the rest around the folds, and pulling the plug through the end loop. We called it a "hangman's knot"–how appropriate!

I followed the fixed routine until it came to standing on the seat; I couldn't get up. I glanced down and saw the hangman's knot was jammed between the lever and seat, and the cord was holding me back. Time had run out and the aircraft was stalling. I crouched down, got my feet on the seat, hands on the edge of the cockpit and heaved with every bit of strength I could muster. The oxygen mask ripped off my face and the earphones popped out of their rubber cups. I was clear of the aircraft and hanging flat on my back looking at it. I prayed it wouldn't fall back on me; it fell off on its port wing.

Then I made another mistake. I hooked my left thumb in the D ring, straightened my arm, and pulled the ripcord. I felt the 'chute being pulled from its bag. It should be flowing up my back and opening over my head. But it wasn't–it was all going down below.

When I left the aircraft, it was doing about 150 mph straight up and so was I. If I'd had my wits about me I'd have waited until I started to fall before pulling the cord. There was a downward pull on the shoulder straps and I did a back flip. I was hanging head down looking at the mess of 'chute and shrouds. I prayed I would not dive into the 'chute. I fell beside it and eventually was pulled head up. The 'chute was OK. I worried about my bleeding left hand and made a couple of wraps of the ripcord around my wrist.

Then I hit the water. The instructions were to release the harness before entering water, but I was too busy with the ripcord. I went a long way down but found the release buckle, and pressed it with my right hand. Three straps fell away but not the one on my left leg. I reached for it and there was a sudden jerk as the parachute started to drag me. I wore pull-on flying boots. I kicked off my left boot. I was free. I pulled the $CO_2$ bottle lever to inflate my Mae West. I popped out of the water and enjoyed a deep breath.

A strong wind was blowing and big swells from the west were about 7 feet high and 150 feet apart. There was a strong cross wind from the south building up quite a chop and about every third wave was breaking. There was fine rain, mist, and a low ceiling. I must have been about seven or eight miles off shore and well into enemy territory. I hadn't given a Mayday and couldn't expect to be picked up. I thought that was just as well. The enemy monitors all such calls and would have sent out a boat or an Me109 to eliminate me. I had just seen how they dealt with enemy pilots in the water.

My dinghy was in a seat pack on top of the parachute, at the end of a lanyard clipped to my Mae West. I hauled it in and set it up. I pulled myself aboard and found the anchor drogue had set itself. I pulled in the seat pack and opened up the first aid pocket. It was empty. I then opened the escape pocket and it too was empty. I would miss the rain bag. My parachute was floating on the water and I decided to pull it into the dinghy. I rolled it up as best I could. If I heard a Merlin engine, I would let the 'chute blow open to be seen. If it were something else, I would stuff it under the dinghy. I remembered when I had been first hit and thought of the message I had received that I would be covered. Perhaps my side was out of ammo and couldn't drive off the 190s. They may have followed and reported my position. Then there was the 190 I'd hit. I thought there was a good chance I had put him down. He might be near me right now. There could be a boat out searching for him.

I decided to leave the anchor out and stay put until dark. Then if the wind settled down a bit, I would hoist anchor, put on the harness, open the 'chute, and sail home in style. The wind was close to south, and I should be able to move along pretty good. I was about sixty miles from England and at least would be nearer friendly waters where the 'chute could be seen. I figured there was nothing more to be done. I was tired. I had secured everything to the dinghy. I lay back to take a nap and passed out. When I came to, it was dusk, hazy and drizzling. Then I heard it again and that must have been what woke me. Bunga–bunga–bunga! I raised myself up and when the dinghy got to the top of next swell, looked back to where the sound came from. In the mist and on my left about a hundred yards off was the prow of a boat. It was just sitting there.

There was another boat off to the right. The boat to starboard started "bunga–bunga" again and slowly turned and moved at right angles to me. I tried to stand up (it isn't easy in a dinghy), waved my arms, and shouted as loud as I could. They couldn't just leave me here. When he was exactly up wind of me, he stopped, and I realised he was breaking the seas for me. The port boat began its bunga–bunga, turned its prow toward me, and crept forward.

I recognized the boats. They were the same as the B.C. Fraser River fishing boats: wood construction, overlap planking, pilothouse forward, rigging, drum and lines astern. Overall length about forty feet.

One boat pulled alongside the dinghy, reversed the engine, and held its position. A face appeared over the side and looked down at me. It looked up and studied the water all around. The face gave an order and netting was flung out. Two athletic youths leapt over the side and scrambled down the netting into the water. They each caught hold of a shoulder strap of my Mae West and flew back up the netting dragging me with them. They pulled me over the rail and flopped me face first on the deck. While one pinned me down, the other began running his hands all over me. I figured he was checking my wounds so I tried to tell him. Then they flipped me over on my back and the same procedure down my front. When they had finished, they reported to the skipper.

"He's clean. Not even a pocket knife."

The skipper ordered them to take me below and went back to fishing with a boat hook for my equipment. I realised I was on a minesweeper. Wooden boats were used to avoid triggering magnetic mines. There were two groups in the crew: the army looked after the sweeping gear and Bofors gun, and the navy sailed the boat. I asked the navy how they found me. They said it was quite simple. They saw the fireball and took a bearing on it. The other skipper did the same. They marked the chart where the two bearings crossed. They had been assigned a task and had a lot of sweeping to do before taking on anything else. When they finished their task, the skipper had decided to take a look. The two boats went to the mark and sailed down wind. They spotted the dinghy long before they expected. I told them I was dragging a sea anchor, and they said that would do it. They were pleased it wasn't their error. They said they had not known whether it was one of ours or the enemy's, so they were ordered to take cover. They didn't know how many crew to expect, or if they would be carrying guns or grenades, so they followed prescribed procedures.

Down in the hull the soldiers stood guard over me and in a few minutes a doctor (or medical orderly) arrived. He opened his bag, brought out a big pair of shears, and cut off all my clothes. Then he brought out a bottle of alcohol and swabs of cotton wool and cleaned up my wounds. The bleeding had stopped. He dressed the wounds.

The skipper came down and saw me standing there in the nude shivering so hard I was stuttering. He picked up a blanket from the bunk and wrapped it around me. He told one of the boys to get some coveralls and asked if I would like a bowl of hot soup. Remembering that I was dealing with the navy, I asked for a tot of rum. The skipper said he would see what he could do and left me to go above deck. Soon a sailor came down with a water glass in one hand and a bottle of rum in the other. He handed me the glass, pulled the cork and started pouring.

"Say when."

I lost my voice. When the glass was about half full, he stopped pouring and left. I took a big swig and the rum burned all the way down. Straight uncut navy rum! I wasn't cold any more. I took another shot and my body felt alive again. I knew I couldn't stand up, but what was there to stand for? Sitting on the edge of the bunk I drained the glass and just sat there with the glass in my hand and a silly grin on my face. An army boy came in:

"We haven't any rum but would a little brandy do?" I held out the glass and he poured a good-sized shot. I started sipping it and that is the last I remember.

I awoke with a start; something was wrong. The engine had stopped. A thump on the hull had woken me up. The blue light was still on in the hull but the boat was empty. I knew it; they had abandoned ship and left me to go down with it. I dragged myself to the ladder and pulled myself up into the wheelhouse. The compass shed a blue light, and in a few minutes I could see that we were tied to a float at the base of a big dock about thirty feet high. I was at Dover. A gangplank led from the boat to the float. I was not too stable on my feet, and all I wanted to do was to get on shore. I went down the gangplank and on to the float. Then I discovered there were a lot of boats, and many of them were further out. I could hear the crews calling to each other, and then I heard men running toward me on the float. I stepped behind a piling and let them run past. Then I took stock: I didn't know where I was, I had no shoes, and the only clothes I had were the coveralls. I had no money, no identification (other than dog tags), and there was a lot of activity on the float under some blue lights toward the shore. I wish I had stayed on board and waited for the crew but it was too late to go back now—I'd never find mine. The boats all looked the same and I didn't know the name of the boat or its identification number, nor did I know the name of anyone on board, and to top it all, I had had too much to drink.

I was feeling woozy and the main thing was to get on to solid land. I decided to fake it. I would march right down the centre of the float swinging my arms, keep looking straight ahead, and look like I was on an important mission. I marched out into the blue light and saw there were about a dozen stretchers spread out along the float. On the side was a sergeant major type with a clipboard and a loud high-pitched voice. I marched right past him.

"That man. Halt!"

I was the only one moving so I stopped. He pointed at a stretcher and ordered me to pick up one end of it. That did it; I couldn't pick up anything with my left hand.

I turned to face him and shouted. "No."

Then I heard a familiar voice: "There he is, the ungrateful beggar; after all we done for him. We go to get a stretcher and he skoffs off."

They grabbed me and plunked me down on their stretcher. They paraded with me to the sergeant major type with the clipboard. He glared at me and started his routine:

"Name, rank and number?"

My friends gave him their sheet. "Name and address of next of kin?" I mumbled that I didn't have any. He hesitated and then went on. "Have you ever had measles, mumps, meningitis, malaria, (or a dozen other ailments)?"

"Yeah."

One of my stretcher-bearers spoke out, "He won't tell you anything. He's drunk!" I should have made an effort to cooperate, but I didn't like the way I was being shouted at. I was exhausted, I had lost a lot of blood, and I was in quite a bit of pain. I just closed my eyes and passed out. The last thing I remember was the voice of that sergeant major:

"He'll bloody well stay on this dock until he does answer."

I came to as an unidentified casualty on a stretcher in an ambulance and spent six weeks in an English hospital

Paddy Finucane and a lot of others were missing and never turned up. The CO thought it was Bill Dewar who had called for help and escorted him back to England, where Bill crash landed. Bill lost an eye in the operation. The CO said the last he saw of me I was chasing a 109 into France, and as I didn't turn up for a couple of days (being unidentified), he reported me as "missing, presumed killed in action". RCAF Headquarters immediately cut pay and allowances, and my name appeared on a casualty list.

The CO was quite satisfied; we had succeeded in protecting the boats. We lost two Spitfires, but destroyed an Me109 and an Fw190, and we had third party confirmation of this. The score was even.

I returned to the squadron, flew a Spit again on 5 September and volunteered for a posting to the sunny Mediterranean to recuperate. I was posted to Takali, Malta.

I never heard of Paddy Finucane again. It was as if he had never existed. That is the philosophy of fighter pilots: "The war is over for the dead, but the living must return to the sky to fight again. It will only end when there are none left." The German Me109 pilots began fighting in the Spanish Civil war, and the few survivors were still at it at the end of our war.

# DAN NOONAN

*Dan was born in Kingston, Ontario, in 1921. He completed first year at Queen's University before volunteering for RCAF aircrew duties in September 1940. Dan was awarded his wings in 1941, and after a year or so as an instructor, he was posted to 416 Squadron.*

*Dan returned to Queen's and, subsequently, to Trinity College, Toronto, obtaining BA and BD degrees. Dan was an Anglican priest in Manitoba until 1979, then served his church in Victoria until retirement in 1986. Dan is one of the select few ministers of the church who have been awarded the DFC.*

## War: a Necessary Evil

It was 1 November 1940 when I arrived at 6 EFTS, Prince Albert; I had passed all the tests and was going to be a pilot. The first snow fell that day. It stayed all winter. I was awarded my wings in the spring of 1941 and sent to Brandon as an instructor. I did my stint of instructing and finally got the call I was waiting for. I took a month's leave; then it was off to the QEII, and Bournemouth, England. In Halifax I contacted Padre Grant Sparling, our former rector at St. Peter's, Brockville, and had a meal with him at a restaurant. He gave me a prayer card, which I kept in my wallet from then on.

At Bournemouth, ex-instructors were allowed to choose which Command they preferred, and several of us chose Fighter Command. I joined forces with Dave Prentice, who had instructed at Dauphin; we were together right through our ops time.

## MAY '43

I was a Spitfire pilot. I arrived at 416 Squadron at Kenley, near Croydon, and asked to see the CO, S/Ldr Foss Boulton; he had been my flight commander at Brandon. They said he was out on the line, so I went and spoke to him as he climbed into his aircraft. He said, "Can't talk to you now, see you when we get back." On that trip he was shot down over France and taken prisoner.

My first op. We escorted forty-two Beaufighters to attack a German convoy off The Hague: two Beau's lost, hit by flak, no bandits sighted.

## SEPTEMBER '43

We flew cover to a mass of ships in the Channel, a rehearsal for D-Day. On most of our do's so far, no Huns appeared, but on August 22 we had run into a bunch over Beaumont-le-Roger; only the CO of 402 Squadron got one. Usually they would come in high, dive on us, then dive away fast. On one escort job, as we all turned around over the target area and formed up again, right in our midst was a single aircraft; it was an Fw190. As soon as we realised what it was, it dove away.

## OCTOBER '43

One of our tasks was to go in pairs on low-level sorties, shooting up trains and road transport. These sorties were called "rhubarbs". On one of these I was No. 2 to Art Sager. He was hit by flak and his radio quit and we returned early. When bad weather cancelled flying, we did rhubarbs on local pubs.

## NOVEMBER '43

We were escorting Marauders again, and again we ran into a bunch of 109s. My flight leader, Art Sager, chased one and fired, but ran out of ammo, so I moved in and finished it. His wingman, Bill Jacobs, was shot down. After I fired I turned and climbed–and was by myself. As I climbed away from the coast I met a 109 slightly above and coming at me on the starboard side. We both started circling, and I heard myself say, "He's trying to kill me!" In a couple of turns, the good ol' Spit was on his tail. I fired and saw his canopy fly off. I looked down and saw him crash in an urban area

*In 1987 I received a letter from a young man in Zandvoort who was writing a history of wartime events in that town and had obtained names and addresses of members of the squadron. In my reply I mentioned that I would be in Holland in 1988 with my son, Michael, and son-in-law, Terry. He wrote back to arrange to meet us at the* train station at Zandvoort. He had also written to Art Sager now living in Aix-en-Provence. So we met with Rob, and an older friend of his, a ten-year old when the battle occurred in 1943, who had watched it with binoculars from the roof of his house. They took us on a tour of the street where the 109 had crashed; then we had lunch in a restaurant by the beach. It was fascinating to share wartime memories and to hear how the Dutch endured the German Occupation.

On landing at Coltishall, near Norwich, a CBC crew greeted us, and the Wingco, Chad, was given the mike and asked to interview some of us for broadcast. But first he gave us our instructions. We should say it was great but that we'd have done better if we'd had better aircraft. (We had been hoping to get the new Spit IXs to replace our mark Vs.) We all gave this spiel, and later we heard the CBC scrapped the whole thing.

JANUARY '44

We were heading for Digby and landed at Blyton to refuel. The guy coming in behind me, "Black" Campbell, landed faster and too close, and with his tail down. His plane charged into mine with his prop chewing my right wing and his left wing sliding up over my cockpit. That gave me a hefty bump on the head. They took me off to the Doc with a bleeding pate. It turned out to be nothing more than a scalp wound, but I had to go the rest of the way by train.

Another time at a south-coast stop, we all went to a pub and I left my fur-lined flying jacket–squadron crest and "Dan" painted on the back–on a hall rack. After dinner, it was gone. A month or so later a friend saw it in a pub in the west of England, grabbed it, and returned it to me. Now our son Mike has it, in Amsterdam.

FEBRUARY '44

We finally got the Spit IXs. On 4 February, I was made Flight Commander, B Flight and we moved to Kenley again. While we were there, "Buzz" Beurling was posted to one of our squadrons. He was a real loner, seldom being seen in the Mess, but he had great eyesight. On patrol one day he kept reporting "Huns above, at 11 o'clock", but nobody else could spot them for a while.

Dave Greenberg was shot down in France and picked up by the French underground. They got him to the coast and onto a fishing boat that brought him across the Channel. He was back on the squadron in about ten days.

At 8000 ft over France, a Spitfire attacks an Me109.
The engine explodes and the 109 begins to break up
Filmed by the Spitfire's camera gun.

In April we moved to Tangmere with Chad our Wingco. We began dive-bombing missions, going after V1 launching sites and railroad bridges. On our sixth go there was ten-tenths cloud; instead of dropping our 500-lb bombs in the Channel, we were ordered to return with them. Those things hung under the belly of the Spit, so with tail down on the runway the bomb was only inches off the ground. That day the whole dozen of us made perfect landings. It was the one and only time they made us land with bombs on. Throughout May we were busy doing two or three runs a day, escorting bombers and dive-bombing.

**5 JUNE '44**

We patrolled the Channel and saw a "bridge of ships," the invasion fleet, Operation Overlord. The night before, we'd had a visit from Ike Eisenhower, giving us a pep talk.

**D-DAY 6 JUNE**

I flew three patrols of two hours each. In my logbook I wrote, "St. Catherine's Point to Swanage. What a Bridge of Ships! Grand view of naval bombardment and beach landings." On one patrol, I saw gliders landing near Bayeux and watched as one ran smack into a barn, with its tail flipping over. On the second patrol we cruised off the Cherbourg peninsula and saw shore batteries shelling a US cruiser. After two near misses, a shell hit about midships and the lifeboats began to leave; it sank in about ten minutes.

**7-9 JUNE '44**

Lost one of our boys, hit by flak; he bailed out, but his 'chute didn't open. Another lad went the same way on the 8th. On the 9th, some of our boys were hit by flak from our own navy. The weather was bad.

**12 JUNE '44**

Chad collided in mid-air with Frank Clark of 421 Squadron. It was in low cloud. Both Chad and Frank were killed. In my logbook, I wrote: "Black day for our Wing. Wingco Chad and Frank Clark in head-on crash..." We were devastated, but had no time to grieve.

*In 1994 I received a letter from England, signed "Andy Cockshott", the son of our Chad, Lloyd Chadburn. He said he was writing to all ex-416 types. His mother was a WAAF in the plotting room at Hornchurch, Dover. Chad was sent back to Canada on leave in February/March of '44, and when he returned in May he was kept busy and never met up with her again. Andy's mother kept him for ten months before placing him for adoption. She kept in touch with him,* and told him about his father after being reunited with him in 1991. Andy came over to Oshawa in 1995 for a Chadburn Squadron Air Cadet memorial "do".

### 14 JUNE '44

Made our first landing on French soil, at Crépon. On the 16th we moved over to the landing strip there (B2). The next day, one of our guys brought a drop-tank (hung below the Spit fuselage) full of beer, to our base at B2. The tank had been scoured out first with steam but, tough luck; it still tasted of petrol.

Another day, a light plane landed at B2, a Fieseler Storch in RAF colours, flown by Air Marshal Cunningham, with Winston Churchill aboard. Winnie climbed out smoking his cigar, climbed up on a truck, gave a short pep talk, and left.

### 28 JUNE '44

Ran into six Fw190s east of Caen. I shot down the first one, then my No. 3 got another. Our boys got two more later that day. We kept busy patrolling the front lines daily. On the 29th our CO, Freddy Green, was hit by flak and crash-landed, injuring his back. The next day we had S/Ldr Jack McElroy as our CO. After his first or second go leading our squadron, McElroy was mad; he had fired at a 190 and missed. He was sure his guns must have been out of alignment and ordered them to be checked. Result: all in order.

### 12 JULY '44

We were escorting Mitchells to Chartres. "Black" Campbell ran out of gas and bailed out. We heard the story later when back in London. He said he had landed in the front lines among German soldiers, was captured, and put in a farmhouse under guard for the night, until he and another prisoner could be sent to the rear. They snuck into the kitchen at night, got a hacksaw, and cut a way out, then joined the French underground.

When the US army broke through, the Yanks were startled to see a very typical native in a black beret, waving at them and shouting, "Hyah, Buddies!"

### 14 JULY '44

I was leading my flight on patrol and met three 109s. I shot down one, then finished off another after Bud Fraser fired and ran out of ammo.

That same day, Dick Forbes-Roberts shot down a 109 right over our airstrip. The pilot bailed out into the midst of our camp. He was a Hungarian, just 17 years old.

## 18 JULY '44

I was about to land but decided to dump the dust and gravel out of the cockpit; the runways were wire mesh and the dust swirled around on take-off and landing. So I turned the plane over with the hood open. Fine; but on rolling back, the engine quit and I was too low to reach B2. There was another landing strip right below, so I came in there sans engine, and downwind, surprising the guys on the ground, who were watching the other direction and didn't hear me come in. I had a visit there with an old friend from Brandon, then refuelled and returned to B2.

On another do we saw what looked like an armoured car on an open road. Two of us dove down and as we got near, flak guns opened up from both sides. We poured on the coal and climbed away unscathed. On another patrol (*we were told to shoot at anything on the ground behind the front lines*) I dove down on a car that looked like an old coupé with a rumble seat. As I was about to shoot, a man got out and started running, flailing his arms. It looked like he was a civilian so I didn't shoot. Could have been a doctor on his rounds. Another time, I saw what looked like a wagon with a big load of hay. I shot, and the thing blazed up in a ball of fire, probably army fuel tanks.

## 27 JULY '44

We were patrolling near Alençon and saw a plane starting to take off below us. I dove down and then got behind him (it was an Fw190) then realized that by picking up speed in the dive I could overshoot him, so I hauled back on the throttle just in time. I actually lost sight of him under the Spit's nose for a second or two, but then dropped back behind him and was about to fire when he flipped over to starboard and crashed. Obviously his 190 had a higher stalling speed than my Spit; lucky for me. That was credited to me as another destroyed, making four, plus two shared, for a total of five.

On 6 October while instructing at 52 OTU, near Lincoln, I was notified that I had been awarded the DFC. On the 14th I was made a Flight Commander. We had pilots from the UK, Australia, New Zealand, Norway, France, and the US.

During this time I was sent on a course at the RAF College, Cranwell. What I remember most was the study of LMF, the RAF's punishment for what it called "lack of moral fibre". I'm sure they were having doubts about it. Many examples given were shameful: such as a pilot returning with half his crew dead, wounded himself, and the plane in shreds, and being told to fly the next day and refusing; then being declared LMF, and stripped of wings, rank, and sent off to oblivion. The RCAF didn't follow suit for long, but sent people for rest and treatment instead, as in WW1 for shell shock.

*See article on LMF.*

On February 9th I was granted home leave, and left for the Repatriation Depot at Warrington, near Liverpool. I suddenly felt a surge of relief. I had survived.

I had to return to Britain after my leave, but the European war was at an end. I got back to Canada around the end of July '45. Spent most of August fishing on Lake Ontario with a friend, an army vet. Then in September, back to Queen's, in first year Science (later I switched to Arts, and went into the ministry). Later that month, I received my DFC at Government House in Toronto, presented by Governor General Alexander.

*I am sometimes asked how I feel about being part of a shooting war. I don't believe many of my contemporaries felt it was a great noble cause, like the slogans that were common in the First World War. But I felt at the time that Hitler, the evil monster, must be stopped, so war was the only way–a necessary evil. I never remember any feeling of hate of the German people; there was no propaganda about "the wicked Huns", as in WW1.*

*And I certainly didn't feel like a hero. I was just thankful to have survived knowing that much better men than I had not, and that I had so often been fortunate to have been in the right place at the right time and to have had great comrades backing me up.*

*I wasn't very devout, but I prayed every night for God's help and many times gave thanks for a narrow escape and safe return. My wartime experience made me want to do something worthwhile with the rest of my life, although I wasn't sure what that would be. Since responding to God's call to the ministry, and being blessed by finding Franny, the love of my life, I am ever grateful for all my blessings, and I thank God always. Often I have wondered about those on the other side whom I had to kill in the war against fascism, what those young men might have done with their lives; and I've said a prayer often for their families.*

*I thank God, too, for our wonderful family: our son Michael and daughter Sarah, and their spouses Joanne and Terry; and our three beautiful grandsons, Dan and Alex Noonan and Adrian Chowanec. I pray they will never be involved in a war, but will live their lives to the full, in the service of God and a better world.*

# KEN PASK

*Ken was born in Alfreton, Derbyshire, in 1922. He joined the RAF in December 1940, was awarded his pilot wings in January 1942, and was posted to Kirkbride for test pilot training. In August 1943 he was posted to India, joined 155 (F) Squadron in Burma, South East Asia Command. In May 1945 he moved to 226 Group, Delhi, and on to Risalpur and Karachi on test pilot duties until returning to Britain in June 1946. After the war, Ken returned to university and graduated in 1947. He joined Pfizer Canada Inc. and retired in 1987 as Regional Manager, Western Canada*

## The Forgotten War

It was 1941. The Japanese were swarming over South East Asia, an unstoppable yellow tide. The Burma Corps of British, Indian, and Gurkha troops fought with courage and honour—more VCs were awarded in Burma than in Normandy and Italy combined—but they suffered humiliating defeats throughout that year and 1942 before turning the tide. The ferocity of the conflict was often inhuman; the obscene treatment given the POWs by the Japanese is a matter of shameful record.

The Japanese had been at war since 1937; when Singapore fell they moved into Burma. Veterans of the Burma Campaign refer to it as "The Forgotten War". Certainly it was a different war for the RAF. There were no major centres with weapon-producing factories to be bombed, no navy to seek out and destroy. It was a soldier's war, and the RAF flew in support of the Burma Corps, providing airborne artillery on the front lines, destroying supplies and supply lines behind the lines, and protecting supply para-drops to our own army.

With the Allies concentrating on the "Germany First" policy, resources to contain the Japanese in Burma had a low priority. The RAF was equipped with obsolescent aircraft, the Hurricane Mk I, Mohawk, Vengeance, and the like. Except at high altitude, even the Hurricane could not match the *Zero* and *Oscar* fighters. We were simply outclassed.

In 1943 squadrons of Spitfire Vs and VIIIs, Hurricane IIc's, P47 Thunderbolts, Beaufighters and other aircraft arrived and pilots were trained in army support roles. With these aircraft we regained air superiority and by the end of the year seized air supremacy.

The Japanese plan for 1944 was to cut all supplies to the Allied armies in the Imphal-Kohima area and push them back into Bengal. They were faced by a determined, reinforced and re-supplied 14th Army, and a refreshed and equally determined 224 Group, RAF. Our role was to give total air support to the 14th in whatever form was needed.

On 1 August 1944 our squadron moved to Palel on the Tamu-Imphal road. We stayed in that area for the next four months giving the best support we could. Endless days of heavy fighting cost our army dearly as it began the slow, arduous road back into Burma. We moved with them. We were under canvas, a somewhat euphemistic way of describing life in little more than a pup tent shared with another pilot, with one very large tent housing the kitchen and mess. Toilets were slit trenches bordered with bamboo poles stuck in the ground for support while crouched. Water was often rationed to one mug-full for cleaning teeth and shaving. The rest went to the kitchen. Bathing and laundry were luxuries enjoyed when we were camped near a river. Mosquitoes, always dangerous pests, flew in cloud formations during the monsoon, which dropped 200 inches of rain that year.

One morning I was on readiness alert when somebody called my name. I got up, and the next thing I knew I was in the British Military Hospital in Imphal, under canvas and on a stretcher. A particularly malicious mosquito had given me dengue fever. Two days later I developed amoebic dysentery. It was eight weeks before I returned to my squadron.

On my first day back I took off for a refresher flight. As I lifted off, the control tower called to say I had blown my left tyre. Since there was nothing I could do about it I continued my flight, but when I joined the circuit the controller reminded me of the problem. Should I belly-land? What if the tyre were OK and I wrecked a Spitfire needlessly? Should I try for a normal landing? But what if the tyre really was flat? Chances were excellent I would cartwheel and end my flying days somewhat dramatically. I was still undecided as I began to turn in to land. Finally I thought *What the heck?* and put my wheels down. I managed to make a fairly decent landing on the grass, keeping the left wheel off the ground until the speed dropped and I could no longer control it. As the wheel touched, the Spit began to ground loop, then slowly the nose went down and the prop hit the ground. I thought, *If I flip over and catch fire, I've had it.* Then I remembered that with the ignition switch off, the chances of fire were reduced. Off went the switch. The tail went up and I was high off the ground; I slid down the wing and ran for my life. There was no fire, and damage was minimal. The CO congratulated me on my flying skills; I was happy to receive that in person rather than inscribed on my tombstone.

Generally speaking our squadron had twelve Spits on readiness to answer calls for army support, six beside the strip with pilots ready to run at the sound of the siren, and six more at the dispersal. Sometimes the place was jumping with activity; at others it was a hot and boring wait. A unique factor of single-engine fighters was the absence of a pilot-relief tube. A sudden urge brought on by the cold at high altitude could be quite devastating. Consequently relief on the spot by those on readiness was common. On one occasion, as the CO was tending to his need, a newly arrived young airman walked by and threw up a natty salute. Only momentarily at a loss, the CO waved back.—with his hands full.

The only year-round road in Burma ran from Lashio on the China border through Mandalay to Rangoon. So when the Japanese moved large groups, usually accompanied by tanks and trucks, it was likely to be by this road or the railway alongside. Lesser roads, trails really, such as the Mandalay–Assam road, were few in number and mostly impassable to vehicles (including tanks) during the monsoon. Only small groups of soldiers–ours and theirs–could use these jungle-covered trails.

Our job was to maintain air supremacy, to harass and destroy Japanese forces and equipment, and to support our ground forces in every possible way. Our armament was two 20-mm cannons plus six .303 machine guns in the wings. On long-distance sorties we carried 90-gallon overload tanks which could be dropped when empty, and a couple of 250-lb bombs, well suited to dealing with artillery placements.

We maintained dawn to dusk patrols, usually in sections of two, leader and #2, with ground controllers helping us to seek out "targets of opportunity" along the road, rails, and trails. Sometimes the terrain allowed us to fly to the target at treetop height particularly if that target was on elevated ground. More often, we needed to pull up to 100 feet or so and then shove the nose down to fire into the target. This was the norm when attacking troops hidden in the trees. It got a bit dicey at the top of the pull up, exposed and vulnerable to their guns.

Trucks and other vehicles on the move were better targets. We could come down the trail very low, presenting a slim and difficult target for their guns. Conversely, they presented a beautiful target dead ahead.

Engaging heavily armed forces is significantly different from engaging enemy aircraft, although either activity can disqualify you from obtaining life insurance. There would be an element of surprise about our first run, but after that they were ready and waiting for the next attack. Such was the case on 24 February on a patrol south of Mandalay, where a terrific battle was raging. I was flying with W/O Murphy as my #2.

BALE OUT

Murph and I were flying on what would in Europe have been called a rhubarb: Search out the enemy and attack. We spotted a Japanese column of about fifty men and two trucks moving south along a trail. We went straight in, firing all guns, and caught them by surprise. On our second run they were ready for us but we hit the trucks and got away unscathed. Rather foolishly perhaps, we went in again. This time I was hit, probably by a Japanese version of a pom-pom light ack-ack gun.

Smoke poured from my engine. Murph slipped underneath to my starboard side and called me on the R/T:

"Heavy glycol leak.

As he slipped back underneath to my starboard side, flame licked its way from the engine compartment into the cockpit. A Spit has a firewall between engine and pilot to stop this kind of thing happening. At the very least, the firewall is supposed to delay the flames but these were hungry and intent on spreading throughout the cockpit.

If I remember correctly, the regulations decreed we should be covered from head to foot in flying gear and wearing gauntlets. But like all of us flying in Burma, we wore lightweight khaki slacks and shirts. The flames were about to have a field day and there was nothing I could do to stop them. My forward vision was disappearing in oil and smoke.

There isn't a lot of time to think in a situation like that. *OmiGod, I'm in deep doodoo* was about my limit. Up to now I'd looked upon the Spit as my home and now it was time I left. I was six feet tall, about the maximum height allowed for a Spitfire pilot. Climbing out wasn't going to be so easy

I unbuckled the harness, opened the canopy, trimmed the nose fully forward (down) and let the stick fly forward. I catapulted out. I was on my way.

Murph told me later he was above me at 500 feet and guessed I was at about 450 feet when I jumped; that's about half the recommended height. It was going to be a hard landing.

I don't remember much about the drop down into the jungle. I recall seeing an opening between the trees to the right but had no time to worry or plan any action. With a great stroke of luck the blazing Spit hit the ground two hundred yards away and I landed in a grass clearing

I was near a small village; the inhabitants gathered on the outskirts, and. we eyed each other warily. Were they friend or foe?

The Burmese leader, Aung San, had formed a Burmese Independence Army (BIA) to fight alongside the Japanese. During the retreat to Imphal in 1942, Allied troops were frequent victims of treachery from both (Burmese) military and civilians. As the Allies slowly got the upper hand, Aung San decided it would be expedient to desert the Japanese and join up with the Burma Corps–but there were many stories of treachery on the part of villagers.

A man walked towards me waving and calling "Hello! Are you all right?" Now the last thing you expect to hear when you have baled out in Burma is a Burmese villager speaking impeccable English. He

Source: National Defence publication "Official History of the Royal Canadian Air Force, Volume III-The Crucible of War"

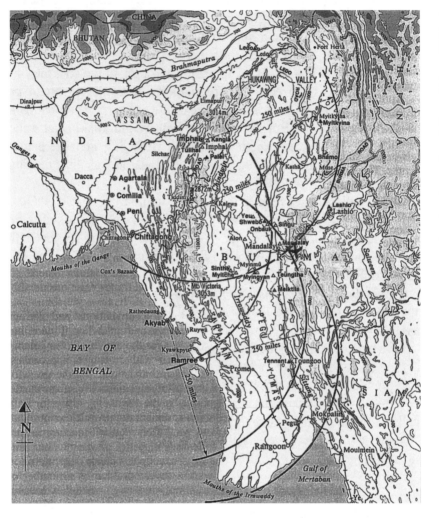

Peter Lake served at Chittagong and in Calcutta
Bob O'Brien served at Kangla and later moved to Akyab and then Ramree Island
The position where Ken Pask baled out over the jungle is marked: ✈

approached and held out his hand for a handshake. I cautiously obliged and asked if any Japanese were nearby. He told me a large group with two trucks had passed by a few hours earlier, heading south-west. Presumably they were the group Murph and I had pranged. If they got hold of me, they were might not be sympathetic.

The man pointed north and added that there were Gurkha soldiers *"over there"*. North it would be. By this time I felt that I could trust him–actually, I didn't have a whole lot of choice. We were surrounded by curious villagers talking excitedly and pointing to the parachute I was dragging. It seemed pointless to attempt to bury it, as they would only dig it up. So I gave it to them.

It turned out my new friend had attended grammar school in Britain, which explained his fluency. He had been in Burma at the outbreak of war, attempting to teach better agricultural practices to the farmers, and been trapped by the Japanese invasion. I didn't stop to chat. Hoping to find the Gurkhas I headed off up the trail.

I was barely out of sight of the village when a jeep appeared. The Gurkhas had seen me come down and come to find me. Now, if you are in Burma in the middle of a war, and somewhat lost, you could not find better friends than Gurkha soldiers. Great guys. I knew that all was well, and that I would be OK. They drove me to their base, where about two hours later my CO and the "Spy" (Intelligence Officer) arrived by jeep and took me back to my squadron. It was great to be home.

In January 1945, the Japanese army, including two squadrons of JAAF, had established a major command centre at Meiktila, roughly halfway between Mandalay and Rangoon. They were losing the battle for Mandalay, and the 14th Army was planning to advance on Meiktila once that great battle was over. The RAF was ordered to "soften up" this enemy command centre. On the afternoon of 15 January, Wing Commander Phil Lee arrived from Schwebo (Wing HQ) and announced that three squadrons (ours and two from nearby strips) would mount continuing rhubarbs on the Japanese positions. He would lead the first flight of four on a dawn raid the following morning. I was to fly as his #2. Our CO, with Jock Dalrymple as his #2, would complete the flight. We carried 90-gallon overload tanks to take us far south of our normal range; we were not expected. We came over the Meiktila airfield perimeter at treetop height in loose line abreast and far too low, too fast, and too suddenly for their perimeter light ack-ack guns to get into action. The hangar doors–wide open–lay straight ahead with about fifteen aircraft parked in front. I bagged a Zero and got off a three-second burst–all my guns–into "my" hangar.

Wingco Lee called for a 270° sweep left into loose line astern, and we came in again along the dispersal in front of the hangars. The perimeter guns fired at us on the way in, but once we were over the field we were so low they couldn't fire at us without also firing on their own personnel and planes.

Between us we destroyed three more kites and a lorry. Another 270°, to the right this time, and we had one more crack at them. We were fired at from gun carriers beside the hangars, but no one was hit. A miracle. Guns empty, we headed for home and claimed seven destroyed plus one lorry plus unknown damage inside the hangars.

The pre-monsoon heat tended to make us somewhat socially unacceptable; so when the opportunity arose, on squadron stand-down, to drive to the river Mu with soap and towel, we set off with great enthusiasm. What a delight! We bathed, washed our clothes, and swam naked in the warm water. After about an hour, we were joined by a truckload of soldiers bent on similar pleasures. They told us they intended to do some fishing and would we care to join them? We regretted that we had no fishing gear, but that we would welcome any excess catch they might have. They grinned and lined up along the bank then threw what looked like large stones into the deep water. As it turned out, these were not stones. If you have ever been standing naked and waist-deep when a series of grenades explodes in the water nearby, you will appreciate our momentary panic. Vision of a monastic life flashed before us, evidently reflected on our faces, as the soldiers hooted with laughter. The only damage was psychological, and that healed as we gathered what we could of the several dozen stunned fish floating belly up on the river.

On 5 May 1945, three days before V-E Day, I left the squadron. We were glad it was over for those in the European Theatre, but it was not over for us. I was posted to Drigh Road, Karachi, on test pilot duties, where we received brand new Spitfire IXs, XVIIIs, and XXIs. As the only test pilot checked out on Spitfires, I was lucky enough to fly all of them. The Japanese surrender (15 August) was a great time for celebration in the mess. All three test pilots were sick with flu the next day–so many bugs in that tropical climate.

# HARRY PILKINGTON

*Harry was born in Darwen, Lancashire, in September 1922. He enlisted in the RAF in March 1942 and was accepted for aircrew training. He was awarded his Navigator brevet in August 1943 and completed two tours of operations–83 trips. He was awarded the DFC in November 1944. Harry was demobbed in August 1946 and emigrated to Canada. Post-war he joined Bell Canada and retired 35 years later as V.P. Marketing.*

## Ambition Fulfilled-and Then Some

In the second week of ITW, we were marching along the Paignton promenade when we were startled by an aircraft flying very low over the sea at what appeared to be a tremendous speed. It was a de Havilland Mosquito, otherwise known as "The Wooden Wonder". It was the only WWII aircraft on either side of the Atlantic that was made of wood. Ever since hearing about this wonderful aircraft it became my ambition to fly in a Mossie.

The first operational mission flown by the Wooden Wonder was carried out on 19 September 1941 and Mossies saw action till the end of the war. No fewer than twenty-seven versions were built for service during the war years, making it probably the most versatile aircraft ever to enter service in any air force. It was originally conceived as a bomber, but its versatility saw it serving as a long range photo-reconnaissance plane, minelayer, pathfinder, high speed military transport, long-range day and night fighter and last, but not least, as a fighter-bomber. Over 1400 were built in Canada, mainly of Sitka Spruce from British Columbia, about 400 in Australia; and the remainder in England. It is interesting to compare the relative effectiveness, per pound, of aircraft produced for several leading British and American bombers. This task was carried out by the production staff of the de Havilland Aircraft Company in Toronto. They used a 'merit' figure obtained by multiplying the weight of bombs carried by the striking range, and factoring in the tare weight per crewman. The resultant ratio read: Mosquito 80, Lancaster 68, Halifax 62, Liberator 26, and Flying Fortress 24. About this wonderful craft Hermann Goering is quoted as saying:

> *I turn green and yellow with envy when I see a Mosquito. The British knock together a beautiful wooden aircraft that every piano factory over there is building.*

After ITW, I was classified as Wireless/Navigator and my real training began. Three months of radio training at Cranwell, Lincolnshire, then to Mount Hope, Ontario, for eight months of intensive navigation instruction. Among the things we were told was that the four top students would be commissioned and given the opportunity to volunteer for operational duty on a Mosquito squadron. What better incentive could I have to work night and day to fulfil my ambition? I did work hard and came top of my class.

Then, with my navigator's wing safely attached to my new officer's uniform, I arrived at my next posting, Greenwood, Nova Scotia. There I was crewed up with Flight Lieutenant Ken Winder, an experienced pilot with some 3000 hours of flying to his credit, and I had the first of many flights in a Mosquito.

After two months at Greenwood we were posted back to England where we had a further six weeks of familiarization on the Mosquito. I was then introduced to the latest navigation aid–the wonderful Gee-box. This was an electronic device for pinpointing one's position. It was useful as far as the French coast but not so good after that. What it did very well was to get us to the Continent, from whence it was dead reckoning and map reading to the target.

At long last, on 11 March 1944, Ken and I were posted to 21 Squadron in Second Tactical Air force, at Hunsdon. For me it was the culmination of almost two years' intensive training and a dream come true. We were assigned a Mosquito Mk VI fighter-bomber with the call signal D-Dog, an aircraft in which we flew over sixty trips, by which time we felt as though we were an integral part of the machine.

The Mark VI was powered by two Rolls Royce Merlin engines rated at 1460 horsepower and armed with four 20-mm cannon and four Browning .303 machine guns all mounted in the nose. It could carry two 500-lb bombs in the belly and one underneath each wing. One version of the Mossie was actually equipped to carry a 4000-lb bomb. Top speed was about 350 mph and it had a range of about 1500 miles. An interesting innovation was the installation of a tank of nitrous oxide. Pulling a lever injected this gas into the carburettor of each engine and for a short period of time accelerated the aircraft by some 30 to 40 mph, ideal for getting away from the German jet aircraft that were beginning to appear in late 1944.

On one of our infrequent 48-hour leaves I was home visiting my uncle Sam when the idea came to me that I might personalize D-Dog. My uncle was the Town Clerk and he gave me a decal of the town coat of arms which, on our return to base, was duly installed on my side of the aircraft. Needless to say my pilot wasn't to be outdone and before long he had the Wigan coat-of-arms on his side of the aircraft. Shortly thereafter our Wing Commander asked us to fly to an airfield in Lancashire and deliver a parcel for him. We landed and taxied in and were amazed to be greeted by a small army guard-of-honour led by an army major. He had been in the control tower as we came in, had seen the coat of arms and assumed royalty had arrived for an unscheduled visit. Hence the royal welcome—for the one and only time in our careers.

After about 60 trips D-Dog went to a maintenance centre for a complete overhaul and one of life's many coincidences occurred. The officer in charge of the unit was from my home town and recognized the coat-of-arms; he had it removed and sent to the mayor. A few questions around City Hall brought forth the full story. The coat-of-arms is now framed and hangs on the wall of my memorabilia room.

Ken and I did 83 trips, mostly night intruder and anti-movement patrols attacking virtually anything we could see: moving trains, troop convoys, etc. Some trips were daylight low-level trips to specific targets such as a barrack block at Nijmegen, or a radar station at Cherbourg. These were very demanding and dangerous jobs requiring both skilful low-level (50 ft) flying and accurate navigation.

Apart from the obvious hazards of flying over enemy territory, two other problems had to be coped with on such trips, most of which took us over Holland. The country was criss-crossed with an electrical network of high-tension wires that were not easy to see when flying low-level. The safe way was to fly over them, but my friend Bertie Willer hit one and came home with several yards of wire wrapped around his wing. The wire was between the engine and the fuselage, the only part of the leading edge of the wing that is metal, being the housing for the engine air intake. Had it been outboard of the engine it could have cut right through the wing with obvious dire consequences for the crew.

The other hazard consisted of flocks of birds that had a habit of becoming airborne as you approached. A bird or two in the air intake could cause the engine to overheat and you would face the job of getting home on one engine. On one trip a large bird hit our windshield and almost completely covered it with blood and feathers. Ken had only about three square inches clear enough to see through, but his skill got us home and we landed safely. Any one of our many sorties, including the one that earned us the DFC, would make a good yarn. I have, however, chosen the three that are still most vividly etched in my mind.

We attacked the barrack block at Nijmegen on Sunday morning 17 September 1944, the day of the ill-fated para-drop at Arnhem. It was intended as a diversionary raid. Six of us took off at 10 am. We were in the Number Two position immediately behind our leader, Squadron Leader George Muffay. The trip across Holland was uneventful. However, about five minutes from the target our leader radioed that he had been hit and we were to take the lead. Our course took us south and east of the target. About ten miles east of the target we changed course 180 degrees and attacked from the east. Our bombs were equipped with a 15-second delay, so the five aircraft had to drop their bombs and be out of the way in less than 15 seconds.

All went well until tail-end Charlie made his bombing run. He misjudged the height of the building and scraped the bottom of his aircraft on the parapet on top of the building. In the process he lost an engine but was still airworthy (the Mossie could fly at a steady 200 mph on one engine). Ken throttled back to 200 mph and accompanied him back to base. The trip was amazing; every few minutes some piece of the aircraft would drop off. The last but not least item was a 20-mm cannon. However, both aircraft landed safely and we were all none the worse for wear except for having slightly tattered nerves.

Probably the biggest scare we had didn't come from German opposition—it came from a malfunction of the bomb-release gear in the belly of the aircraft. We made a bombing run over a marshalling yard and the bomb-release failed. We closed the bomb-bay doors and headed for home. The last thing we did after taxiing in was to open the bomb-bay doors and cut the engines. To our immense surprise the ground crew who greeted us ran off like scared rabbits. The reason was obvious when we got out of the aircraft. On the ground were the two bombs that had failed to drop on our bombing run. Fortunately for everyone the bombs weren't fused or I wouldn't be relating this tale.

Our leader of the squadron was the highly respected W/Cdr Ivor Dale DFC, otherwise known as Daddy Dale. Daddy was a pre-war RAF officer, about 40 years old (almost antique to us young pups) who had already done two tours of operations. He was really too old for operational flying, but every once in a while he would take off for another crack at Jerry. One of the training exercises we did occasionally was designed to see how fast we could bale out of the Mossie. We would be strapped into the aircraft, the sergeant would blow the whistle, and we had to jettison the door and jump out on to an air mattress. The sergeant timed us with a stopwatch. Daddy took his turn at the drill and being somewhat overweight, he got stuck in the door. As the sergeant pried him loose, we had a hard time to refrain from laughing; but the last thing we wished to do was to hurt Daddy's feelings.

This incident proved to be tragically prophetic. On 2 February 1945, we were programmed for an anti-movement patrol over the Ruhr. When one of the squadron's aircraft developed engine trouble, Daddy took over for the grounded aircraft. Ken and I took off about two hours after Daddy's departure, heading for Hengelo, Osnabrück and Münster.

Our course took us over the North Sea to Texel in the Friesian Islands and from there south over the Zuider Zee, then east into northern Germany. We were briefed to fly at about 50 feet crossing the North Sea in order to avoid Jerry radar. While doing so we picked out a faint distress signal, "Mayday, Mayday!" I said, "My God, Ken, it's old Daddy!"

Winder reacted quickly. He took us up to 7000 feet to improve radio transmission, and we got in touch with Daddy. He told us he had lost an engine and was losing height rapidly. He had been trying to contact Dover. While we were attempting to relay his message to Dover we heard his last transmission:

"I'm going in, chaps, goodbye."

B Flight ready to roll. Mosquitos fully armed and ready for take-off

For the second and last time Daddy had been unable to bail out of his aircraft. We carried on and successfully attacked a convoy in the Osnabrück area before returning to base. At our debriefing session, to the dismay and genuine sorrow of everyone present, we reported the sad news about Daddy.

The story of Daddy Dale was not to end yet. A Mosquito Aircrew Association was formed several years ago. The quarterly magazine runs a column designed to help members get in touch with old friends. In one issue was a request from a chap in Holland for information about W/Cdr Ivor Dale and his navigator F/Lt Hacket who were buried in a war cemetery near this man's home. I wrote to him with the information in this story and asked him what had aroused his curiosity about my old leader and his navigator. He replied that he made a hobby of trying to find out as much as he could about airmen buried in the local cemetery.

After completing my second tour of ops I married a marvellous and beautiful Canadian girl whose first husband had been killed flying a Beaufighter on ops. She had a baby daughter and was the sister of my pilot's wife. After the war we took up residence in Canada and had two children of our own. We have enjoyed a wonderful life together.

As a closing note to my tale, I watched a TV program about the Gulf War and the American Stealth Bomber, so-called because it did not reflect radar signals well and was thus almost invisible to enemy radar. The show opened with a picture of a Mosquito, which the commentator claimed was the original Stealth Bomber because wood is a poor reflector. Since some of our most dangerous sorties were flying over water at low level to avoid the enemy radar, had we been indulging in a great deal of unnecessarily dangerous flying?

The position where W/Cdr "Daddy" Dale
went in is shown on the map on pages 254/255. Ed.

# ALEC UYDENS

*Alec was born in Shanghai in 1922 and joined the British army in December 1941. He transferred to the RAF in June 1942, receiving his pilot wings in August 1943. He was posted to 349 (Spitfire) Squadron in July 1944 and received the Belgian Croix de Guerre in 1945. Alec was demobbed in 1946 and emigrated to Canada to join Avro Aircraft as a flight test engineer on the CF-100 and Avro Arrow. In 1959 he joined Transport Canada as Regional Aeronautical Engineer in Vancouver, retiring in 1985 as Regional Director.*

## Strike Home, Strike Hard
### 349 Squadron Motto

I had just begun as an engineering student at Loughborough College in Leicestershire when the war began on 3 September 1939, about month short of my 17th birthday. I was a Belgian national, although I had never lived in Belgium and did not speak French or Flemish.

In December 1941 I joined the Belgian army in England, which consisted of a battalion of two companies of infantry based at Great Malvern. As I had been studying aeronautical engineering, I applied to switch to the RAF. In June of 1942 along with a group of twenty-five other young Belgians, I traded in my army gear for RAF blue at the Aircrew Receiving Centre.

Our flying training began at 31 EFTS, DeWinton, near Calgary, on Tiger Moths and after two months we were sent to 34 SFTS Medicine Hat where we trained on Harvard aircraft, receiving our wings in August 1943.

We shipped back to England on the QE II and went on to 5 AFU, Ternhill, to fly Master II aircraft from the rear seat to get us accustomed to the long nose of the fighter aircraft we were hoping to fly.

In April 1944 we were posted to 53 Operational Training Unit at Kirton-in-Lindsey, Lincolnshire, a fighter OTU for Spitfire pilots. The OTU was equipped with Spitfire Mk I and Mk II aircraft; on my course were pilots from France, Belgium, Norway, Canada, South Africa and Britain. The competition among the various pilots to out-do each other in dogfights was very keen. After some fifty hours of Spitfire flying, we were ready to take on anybody.

Early in June 1944 I was posted to 84 Group Support Unit at Lasham. We supplied aircraft and pilots to the squadrons of 84 Group, which formed part of the 2nd Tactical Air Force.

In July I was posted to 349 Squadron. This squadron was one of two Belgian Spitfire squadrons (the other being 350 Squadron) that were sponsored by the Belgian Government-in-Exile. The squadron formed part of 135 Wing. We lived under canvas at Aston Down but moved shortly after to Funtington, a wartime field about eight miles from Chichester. The wing commander was Ray Harries DSO DFC, and our squadron leader was Count du Monceau de Bergendal DFC, a tall and distinguished looking man whom Harries called "Duke".

My operational career began immediately with convoy patrols to the Normandy beachheads. We were warned to stay well clear of our own navy ships, as they would fire at any plane, friend or foe, that came too close. We also began landing on the beachhead landing strips to refuel and re-arm as our operations took us further into France. From Funtingdon we did a lot of bomber escorts and fighter sweeps but saw few enemy aircraft.

On 18 July we escorted a thousand heavy bombers to Caen. We flew top cover, which meant we were over the bombers in the target area and well clear of the flak. At least two bombers were hit and the crews baled out. The town was pulverized in a couple of hours and the army was able to take it.

Two weeks after this raid the wing moved to Carpiquet, outside Caen. We were issued with khaki battledress to avoid being mistaken for Germans in our blue battle dress and we carried .38 revolvers for self-defence on the ground. Our Spitfires were now fitted with bomb racks to carry a 500-lb bomb under the belly and our role changed to close army support.

No. 84 Group supported the Canadian army as it fought its way up the north coast of France and into Belgium, Holland and Germany. Every day we were out dive-bombing or skip-bombing or shooting up trains and anything else that moved in enemy territory. We caught the Germans at the Falaise gap, strafing the choked roads and creating chaos. Our dive bombing efforts were more of a miss than a hit affair. As the squadron approached its target at 10,000 feet we would slip into an echelon starboard formation and when the target passed by the trailing edge of the port wing, the aircraft would wing over into a steep dive, the pilot keeping the target in sight just over the nose of the Spitfire. At about 7000 feet the pilot would sweep the nose of his aircraft past the target, count to three and then with his thumb press the bomb release button which was set in the throttle twist grip in his left hand. By this time the aircraft would be diving at 350 to 400 miles per hour and in pulling out at 3000 feet the G forces were enough to cause partial blackout.

Skip-bombing was low-level bombing and very accurate though it could be deadly for the pilot. The aircraft would be put in to a shallow dive from about 500 feet while the pilot concentrated his aim on the target using his gyro gun sight. At one hundred feet he would release his bomb and it would travel more or less in a straight line to the target. This type of bombing began to cost us pilots both from flak and the aircraft flying into the target or other obstructions.

The wing kept moving its base as the front moved east. From Carpiquet we went to a place called Eu, between Dieppe and Abbeville, and then to Maldegem in Belgium. We had been living in tents since before leaving England but as it got colder and wetter in November we were billeted in houses in Maldegem. During the last two weeks in October we were attacking targets in the Breskens pocket, where the Germans were holding out to prevent our forces from clearing the entrance to the river Scheldt. For the attack on Walcheren Island we supplied top cover and could see HMS Warspite shelling the German positions as the Canadians landed at Westkapelle.

By 1 November 1944 the army had moved into Holland and we were attacking trains and shipping on the canals. On 8 November four of us were doing a rail interdiction or low-level bombing in the Leerdam area. Our 500-lb. bombs were fitted with 11-second delays that allowed the aircraft to clear the blast area as it skimmed over the target. I was lead aircraft of my pair. I saw the first Spitfire drop its bomb and the second aircraft follow a little way behind. I followed this one down aiming for the same part of the rail line embankment.

As I flew over the line I felt an explosion under my aircraft and knew that I had flown into the blast of the second bomb. I pulled up into a climbing turn. I could see glycol streaming from the radiator under my starboard wing. I headed back for base and hoped at least to make our side of the front line. The radiator temperature began rising immediately; as I reached about three thousand feet, the engine seized up. I was six miles south east of Bergen-op-Zoom and in the vicinity of the bomb line, which was the line ahead of the front line behind which we were not to attack. As I put the nose down to keep up a speed of 90 knots I began to lose height rapidly. At about 500 feet I had settled into a glide and had the aircraft trimmed, the canopy jettisoned and my harness very tightly secured. I have no recollection of what happened after that.

My number two had accompanied me, and as he told me some months later, he saw my aircraft do a fairly decent belly landing before turning over on its back. As he circled over me he saw a Canadian tank making its way to my position, but at this point he had to leave as he was running short of fuel. I came to some time later in an ambulance. It was quite dark and I threw up a lot of blood. Before losing consciousness again, I heard a disembodied voice:

"This one's in a bad way."

When I came to I was being carried by two German soldiers into a hospital. The hospital was an advanced Canadian army hospital in Antwerp, and the Germans were POWs helping out. I lay there for eight days, well looked after and listening to the explosions of the V-1 flying bombs with which the Germans were now attacking Antwerp. I was then taken to a large hall filled with stretcher cases and we were flown back to England in a Dakota aircraft. I was taken to the RAF hospital at Wroughton where I spent a month. The medics couldn't find anything seriously wrong with me other than a sore back, and I spent another three or four weeks at the RAF convalescent hospital at Cleveleys, near Blackpool.

There were three types of inmates there I was told: mental, medical and surgical. Since the locals never knew which category we belonged to, they put us all in the first and kept well clear.

In January 1945, I was cleared fit to fly again and after a week at 84 GSU rejoined my squadron, which was now based at GilsRijn, between Breda and Tilburg in Holland.

We spent the time ranging over Holland and into Germany attacking enemy transports. The trains travelled only at night now and we had to attack them in the rail yards in the towns. But in the yards batteries of Ack-Ack guns protected them and we could be sure of a warm reception. There was very little future in that game.

Towards the end of February the squadron moved back to England and we finished up at Predannack in Cornwall. We were to re-equip with Hawker Tempest aircraft and for a month flew Typhoons while we waited for delivery of the Tempests. We lived like lords in the Pollurian Hotel, which the RAF had taken over. The hotel is still there.

For some reason the Tempest aircraft never materialized and we were sent back to Holland by motor transport and on into Germany to a field called Varelbusch.

The devastation of some of the German towns we passed was appalling. The Spitfire aircraft we received were tired Mk XVIs from a Norwegian squadron. We were operating over Germany attacking the enemy in his own country. We lost three pilots in as many days towards the end of April.

On 3 May I flew two sorties attacking transports on the roads. These were my last operational flights. We ceased operations the next day as rumours of the end of the war came through. I was due for a week's leave in England and heard about the cease-fire on 8 May while waiting for a Dakota transport.

Later in May the wing moved to the German field at Wunstorf, near the city of Oldenburg. Here we could relax at last. We kept in flying practice and on 10 June took part in a victory flypast over Frankfurt with 2500 aircraft, mainly to impress the Russians.

In this same year I was awarded the Belgian Croix de Guerre.

The squadron took part in the Victory Parade in London on 8 June 1946. We were camped in Hyde Park for three days for the occasion.

We were also invited to a garden party at Hampton Court Palace with about three thousand other guests and were presented to the King and Queen.

I left the Air Force in August 1946 and towards the end of the month went back to Loughborough College to continue my interrupted engineering studies.

# CONTRIBUTORS
# BOMBER OPERATIONS

# BOMBER OPERATIONS

Bomber aircrews were formed at OTU (Operational Training Unit) and/or at HCU (Heavy Conversion Unit). These courses came after a long period of training undertaken in Canada, the USA or Southern Africa. Sir Arthur Harris, Chief of Bomber Command, reckoned that the education of each bomber crewmember was the most expensive in the world at £10,000 per man.

The formation of a crew was left to the airmen themselves without intervention by RAF authorities. At first blush the procedure seemed haphazard but in the long run it worked well. Usually a pilot would take the initiative as leader and look for a navigator on whom he thought he could rely. The two of them would then seek a bomb-aimer, wireless operator, and gunners. Then the group would meet to obtain a sense of comfortable compatibility. A flight engineer might be recruited later at HCU.

At OTU a crew received five months of intensive training on two-engine aircraft from instructors who had completed an operational tour. This encompassed technical instruction in classrooms and eighty hours of in-flight training. The most valuable feature of this training, apart from the technical experience and confidence it instilled, was the welding together of a crew that would survive or succumb as a team. Occasionally OTU crews would fly an "op" to make up the required numbers on a raid

At HCU the crew learned to fly four-engine aircraft such as the Lancaster, Halifax, and Stirling. They flew as a team, and when considered ready for a baptism by fire they were posted to an operational squadron.

A "tour" was 30 operational sorties, almost always at night and usually accompanied by up to 800 planes until 1943 and later, when numbers increased to 1,000 or more. Beginning in September 1942 pathfinders (PFF) would precede them to mark the target with a pyrotechnic display. They directed the traffic, if you will. They were followed by the Master Bomber who made sure markers were correctly placed before giving the command to commence bombing. The Master Bomber also monitored bombing accuracy.

*Bill Weighton*

# BOMBER COMMAND

**Master Searchlights**. Radar-controlled lights that first marked the bomber and were then joined by the other lights in an attempt to "cone" the bomber.

**Box Barrage**. All Ack-Ack guns firing simultaneously at the same area of the sky and with fuses set for the same height.

**Window**: Strips of metal foil cut (usually) to a quarter of the wavelength of the enemy radars to be jammed. Bundles of foil strips were pushed out through a flare chute and dispersed over the sky. The RAF first used Window (over Hamburg) on 24/25 July 1943 and totally confused the radar-controlled Ack-Ack. (One pilot described the scene as "Master searchlights and all others waving aimlessly about the sky".) Germany had also developed a version of Window they called "Duppel" but they never used it.

**GEE**: a navigation device working ~20 mc/s. Three stations in England transmitted radio pulses. The navigator operating the Gee set could refer to a chart that plotted the time differences between receipt of pulses and thus determine his position. Germany soon found the equipment in downed bombers and produced a jammer that made Gee pretty useless over enemy territory.

**H2S**: a radar designed to paint a picture of the ground beneath the aircraft even through heavy cloud. It worked well in identifying lakes, rivers, and built-up areas. Germany found the equipment in a downed bomber and designed equipment to detect the H2S signals. Until the Allies realized this, Germany tracked bombers as they were forming up for a raid and could mobilize its air defences.

**Cookie**: a 4000-lb bomb designed to explode before penetrating the ground.

**Hi-capacity bomb**: an 8000-lb bomb similarly designed

**Darky**: short-range radio working on the Bomber Command R/T Guard–6440 kc/s–used by aircrew if they were lost over the UK.

**Nickel:** Leaflet dropping

# BILL STILES

*Bill was born in London, England, in December 1924 and joined the RAF in 1943. He received his pilot wings just as WWII ended and transferred to the permanent force intending to make flying his career. However, "the best laid schemes of mice and men gang aft agley". Bill took his discharge in 1948 and emigrated to Canada. He worked in the federal government, attaining the post of Chief of Information Dissemination Division, Library of Parliament, Ottawa.*

## The Net of an Evil Time

It was the summer of 1944. We were lost sheep, "on detachment aircrew trainees in waiting" sent to RAF airfields to broaden our experience. With a ringside seat, we were witness to much that was off-limits to others. One evening is burned indelibly into my memory. Our detachment was at RAF Spilsby, ten miles west of Skegness, in Lincolnshire. It was evening and the countryside was succumbing to the delightful August twilight. Overhead a massive force of bombers was assembling into formations for another raid on the German mainland. The air reverberated with the thunder of hundreds of engines. Looking up you could detect some of the force finding their way to their appointed positions. They would disappear from view but not from earshot.

A small group of us had decided to go along and watch the Lancasters take off. At the end of the runway, three officers were standing side by side: the Commanding Officer, the adjutant, and the Queen Bee. Queen Bee was the popular although far from official term for the senior WAAF officer on the station.

As each bomber lined itself up for take-off, then rolled down the runway with engines roaring, these three would come to attention and salute the departing airmen. The turrets of the air gunners were palely visible, and the young occupants looked back at us, giving a thumbs-up salute while simulating cheerfulness.

What else could they do? They were caught up within the time when, "as the fishes that are taken in an evil net, and as the birds that are caught in the snare, so are the sons of men snared in an evil time". This was the evil time, as written of by the scribe in the Book of Ecclesiastes. An evil time indeed had descended on the world. All of us were caught up in that net; the cherished values of normal times were stood on their heads. For nearly five years we had been subjected to this perverted philosophy.

Yet for all that, it was necessary. We stood there behind the three officers, awe-struck, identifying ourselves entirely with the crews beginning their perilous journey into the dark. Behind us, incongruously, the ground-crew and other off-duty personnel were playing cricket.

As the bombers pulled round to align themselves, the players were obliged to desist for a few minutes. There was some evidence of vexation and impatience as the game was held up. The precious light was slowly ebbing. Other nations salute with pomp and ceremony their fighting men going off into battle. The English play cricket. Undoubtedly, the aircrew themselves would have endorsed wholeheartedly the notion of a quick game of cricket at such a time.

Each Lancaster would move ponderously forward, the four engines thrashing the air at full throttle, striving furiously to lift the craft and its heavy load of bombs off the ground. The display of aerial might was terrifying to behold. As the last bomber took off one of our party, an East-Ender, summed up our feelings.

"Bleeding 'eroes."

What were my feelings, then, as I stood watching the bombers taking death to unknown souls in similar fashion? Not revenge, I like to think. St Augustine put it best in a passage found in his <u>City of God</u>:

*Even wars, then, are waged with peace as their object, even when they are waged by those who are concerned to exercise their warlike prowess, either in command or in the actual fighting. Hence it is an established fact that peace is the desired end of war. For every man is in quest of peace even in waging war, whereas none is in quest of war when making peace. In fact, even when men wish a state of peace to be disturbed, they do so not because they hate peace, but because they desire the present peace to be exchanged for one on their terms. Thus their desire is not that there should not be peace but that the peace must meet their terms.*

Those terms on which we sought peace had been dictated by circumstances. We had seen the future in the enslavement of most of Europe; deceit, brutality, treachery, the slaughter of innocents. We knew full well what we were up against and how we had to reply in kind. To reach the peace we all desired there were difficult and dangerous measures to be undertaken. Contentious, perhaps, but we had to trust the judgement of those in command if we sought peace. Irony, indeed, for those brave souls taking off into the dark, but we understood perfectly their motivation. Not an easy sentiment to convey across the generations.

Mingling with the aircrews was easy; in fact it was part of our seasoning. They were incredibly cheerful. Their precarious existence had to be countered by a jollity that was there for good reason. Fear must never be allowed to intrude and it seemed that the next mission could be faced only if the façade of merriment were sustained. Occasionally we heard of some airman cracking, but he disappeared immediately from view.

On one occasion, a crew was witnessed dancing for joy on learning the mission had been scrubbed. One impression was paramount: Everything relating to the aeroplanes was new, the Lancasters, the parachute harnesses, the flying suits, the boots, even in many cases the crews themselves seemed to have just arrived. An exception comes to mind. We became friendly with a crew whose stand was near the bomb dump where our mediocre efforts were required. This was a crew all from Lancashire, NCOs only. One air gunner appeared to be about seventeen. The others pulled his leg about a recent incident, one saying, "'e almost got himself shot oop t'arse, t'other night!" This was followed by a gale of laughter, the obligatory clowning where extreme peril had been encountered.

One morning after a mission we went to the stand and found it empty. On looking at that empty space I felt a sickening within me. What had happened to them? Did they go down in some screaming, precipitate fall with all ablaze around them, controls locked? Had the diminutive air gunner been "shot oop t'arse" at last, all clowning ended? Or did they have time to bale out, floating down in the darkness to imprisonment, or death at the hands of civilians? Or an uncertain existence on the run with the Resistance forces? We never found out. A flight sergeant strode by briskly, a clipboard under one arm, unperturbed.

Communiqués concerning losses were, we knew, doctored to understate the actual numbers lost. One summer morning we were awakened to the news that our station had lost eleven planes. Blyton, the nearest other station, had fared similarly, and gradually a picture of disaster built up as the grapevine leaked reports from other stations in the Group.

Revisionist historians theorize with the benefit of hindsight and tell us how we ought to have behaved during that evil time. Doubtless our enemies desired peace also, but on their terms, and they would have employed any measures to achieve it. What kind of enslavement would that have meant for those defeated? The worst of it is that the distortion of reality created by revisionists is to be disseminated to schools. The realities of our World War will thus be perverted to besmirch the memory of those fine men we watched take off into the darkness.

Our chastened group on that airfield saw things differently. Later we, too, were to gain our wings, just as an age of hard-won peace was dawning upon the world. But we remembered, and we remember, always deep within us, those of our number caught up in the net of the evil time.

# ARTHUR FORGEARD

*Arthur joined the RAF as an apprentice in 1927 and had a fascinating career both in the Air Force and the Fleet Air Arm. He trained as an Air Observer and as a pilot. He flew to Finland in that curious expeditionary force to help Finland defend itself against the Soviet Union and he took part in the earliest bombing raids of the war. Presented here are just a few of his multifarious experiences.*

## No. 2 Group and Beyond

For some time I had been applying, without success, for flying training. In June 1936, Group Captain Robb, who had been my Wing Commander Flying on HMS Eagle, helped me get a posting to RAF Leconfield for an Air Observer's course. We flew in Handley Page biplane bombers. I graduated as a corporal air observer and applied for sergeant-pilot's course. I was selected and posted to RAF Wittering Flying Training School. We were trained on Tiger Moths and Avro Tutors. I soon went solo on both types. On passing out in early 1938, I was posted to RAF Bicester to 101 Squadron to fly Blenheims. A sister squadron, No. 90, had Mk I Blenheims, gradually being replaced by the Mk III. On the outbreak of war both squadrons moved to West Raynham, Norfolk, one of the many new bases on the east coast.

### TO FINLAND

Just before Christmas 1939 there was a call for volunteers from all aircrew types for a special mission: my crew and I volunteered. We had to wear civilian clothes and remove our identity tags, and were given civilian passports; mine described me as an engineer and a member of the Bristol Flying Club. We reported to RAF Bicester on 21 February.

Twelve Mk I Blenheims were there, complete with Finnish swastikas on wings and rudders, similar to the German ones. We all objected, as we had to fly them up the east coast to Dyce, Aberdeen. The authorities whitewashed the swastikas but as we left Bicester rain removed the whitewash.

After a night stop we took off for Stavanger in four flights of three aircraft, with very strict orders as to priority for landing. I was number two in the third flight, which consisted of 101 Squadron members. Immediately after take-off we encountered snow and cloud, requiring very tight formation flying until twenty miles from Stavanger when we got clear sunny weather. We had drifted slightly south of the airfield, but No. 1 and No. 2 flights were much farther south in the Skagerrak. We did our usual squadron beat-up and landing, which earned us a good dressing down from the Officer Commanding, since we were supposed to be part time fliers.

Next day in brilliant sunshine we took off for the Swedish Air Force base at Vasterras for a night stop and refuelling. Facilities were excellent; they used their heating systems to hand over to us fully heated aircraft for our next stage. Air temperature was -40°C.

All flight leaders had Finnish Air Force pilots with them to fly the next stage to a frozen lake near Juva, Finland, where the ice was eight feet thick, with the runways rolled by huge logs towed by teams of horses. The aircraft were placed at dispersal sites under the trees. We stayed as Finnish Air Force guests in nearby villages for two days and then proceeded to Helsinki by military bus. After being entertained by the Finnish government for two days, we were taken again by night coach to Turku airfield, all thirty-six aircrew. We boarded a Ju52, with two seats on either side of the cabin, to fly to Stockholm; since there was no luggage compartment our equipment was piled in the middle. The windows had blackout curtains drawn. Eventually the sole pilot, about four feet six inches tall, scrambled over our belongings, entered the cockpit, switched off all our lights, started his engines, and with the minimum of run up started a very fast zigzag run to get off as swiftly as he could. Bombs were bursting on the airfield.

We landed at Stockholm and the CO warned us the place was a hotbed of spies and we should be guarded in what we said and did.

Photograph courtesy of George "Lefty" Whitman

Marshalling yard under attack.
Train tracks at 3 o'clock and the thousand-pounder going down at 12 o'clock

At a stall on the main street where I bought a paper, the woman running it said in perfect English:

"Go and buy yourself a hat and tell all your English friends to do the same. You stick out like sore thumbs."

We stayed in Stockholm for sixteen days. Five of us were flown out at night in a Lockheed Hudson with a very mixed load of passengers to Dyce, near Aberdeen, Scotland.

*In 1944 when I was based in Freetown, West Africa, a letter came from Air Ministry saying I owed them 240 kronor for an overdrawn imprest account. I ignored it.*

*After the end of the war, I was awarded the Finnish War Medal and was told at the presentation that I was the only non-Finnish subject living in Canada to receive it*

EARLY BOMBING RAIDS

My first flight over German territory was to attack the oil-refinery on the south-eastern shore of the Kiel Canal. In those days we were given the target, but we chose the approach and method of attack. We decided to go from Cromer to a position north-east of Heligoland, then south-east to the mouth of the Elbe, past the Kiel Canal, then north-west again and attack the target on our homeward course. We had excellent cloud cover, with tops near 6500 feet and base about 1200 feet, allowing us to test for wind-drift readings at sea level, which was a great help for navigation. We commenced our attack with a steep dive from 5000 feet, broke cloud a 1200 feet, and released the bombs. Hang up! By this time we had alarmed the defences and continuous evasive action was necessary; we attacked again and dropped the bombs in the target area. Because of the evasive action the gyrocompass had toppled, making our course uncertain. We settled on a course for home. Our landing was routine, but we soon had a large audience round our starboard wing where an ack-ack shell had gone through the fifteen-inch gap between the inboard and outboard tanks without exploding. How lucky can you be? At debriefing a strip was torn off me for risking crew and aircraft on a second attack, but the station sergeant photographer came in to show a direct hit on the second run and the target in flames. We were then congratulated on a good attack.

We did a few more night raids, mainly in the Ruhr area, but nothing spectacular happened. On 13 August 1940, however, No. 82 Squadron based at Watton lost eleven out of twelve aircraft. Apparently one aircraft had a microphone left on and was giving details of the target and approach tactics. The German fighters were waiting off shore and shot them all down. My crew joined 82 Squadron on 14 August after an urgent call for replacements. We started right away to carry out night raids on the German barges assembled for the invasion of Britain, which were heavily protected by ack-ack and small arms fire. It was a matter of quickly in and out. We preferred a very low jinking attack from south to north to assist in selecting targets to attack and at the same time to assess the numbers.

We made a single aircraft attack on a Cologne railway station at 9 am, when German army reinforcements were due to arrive on their way to join the invasion forces. Again this was a case of choose your own route. We decided on a very low altitude route over southern Holland towards Koblenz, and turning northward toward Siegen, about fifteen miles north of Koblenz. We then turned westerly for Cologne and scraped around the Cathedral dead on nine o'clock. We received a very hot reception from the railway station, which we hit, but it was too hot to stick around. Our route out was to pass well north of Paris, still at very low level, and turn north to cross the coast between Dieppe and Fécamp.

Our luck changed. Flying north, we went straight in line with a runway with six Heinkel IIIs lined up on each side of the runway firing at us. The only thing to do was to keep low, almost scraping the runway, hoping that they would hit one another with their fire. It was a very hot forty seconds. We made the coast still at low level until halfway across, when we climbed to 1200 feet and made a Mayday call to Thorney Island. They replied with a course to steer and we landed safely, just about out of fuel and with a few holes, but none in dangerous places.

Because of a shortage of trained crews, the flight routine was pretty intense: Take off at 0300 to attack the invasion barges; back to base at 0600. Rest period to 1400, then an attack on coastal shipping, with a return to base at 1800. A further night sortie against road and railway bridges from 2100 until midnight. This would be followed by a rest period until 1400 the next day. After two weeks of this the crew had a forty-eight hour rest period in which we always tried to get away.

One day I was at our dispersal helping the air gunner recalibrate our radio, when the air raid siren sounded, and out of the clouds a Heinkel 111 came, firing at our aircraft. We just had time to adopt the prone position, when he missed, and went on towards the hangars and dropped a large bomb that hit the gantry of a hangar door. Luckily it proved to be a dud. The German was shot down, and the very frightened pilot was brought to Watton for interrogation. He had been told that we killed prisoners.

We engaged in low-level formation flying to bomb Brest and Lannion in daylight, the former in the hope of catching U-boats entering or exiting the docks. On these raids we wore our tin hats to give a certain amount of protection against ground fire.

Navigation aids for returning to base were primitive, consisting of visually coded light beacons whose position and code were changed every night, and the short-range system called "Darky". One night we could not raise Darky, and I was cautiously letting down to see if we could find a hole. At 1200 feet I decided to climb up again and have another attempt at Darky; at 6000 feet the starboard engine cut out and we went into an inverted spin at night in cloud. I told the crew to stand by to bail out and went through the remedial procedure. I got the engine restarted and we broke cloud at 1200 feet right over West Raynham beacon. I said my prayers on the way down. I thought we had bought it. The next day we found that the cause was small pieces of flexible lining of the petrol pipe getting into the carburettor. All aircraft were grounded until the trouble was rectified.

On a daylight single aircraft raid on Bremen, the cloud was solid down to the ground, so we abandoned the attack and continued on course for the sea. Our secondary target was shipping. Suddenly through a gap in the cloud, I saw the inland port of Oldenburg with a coastal vessel unloading at the docks. We made a diving attack through cloud to drop both our 250-pounders between the dockside and the vessel. The attack was perfect and we had photos to prove it.

On one occasion, I was flying second dickie on the way back from Osnabrück. The first pilot was highly experienced but had night blindness that made it difficult for him to judge height and distance when landing at night. We had no luck with Darky and decided to use the ZZ procedure. The W/AG tuned into the appropriate station, gave our code, and was given courses to steer to reach base. Everything was perfect, flare path straight ahead, when I suddenly realized we were too low and directly ahead was a house with two chimneys. My immediate reaction was to pull the captain's arm back, causing him to lift the nose. We actually climbed up the roof of the house and hit the chimneys, but carried straight on to the flare path and landed. I expected the undercarriage to collapse but it functioned correctly.

Before leaving 82 Squadron I had applied for a Specialist Navigation course which would entitle me to a large N behind my name. My ultimate desire was to return to Bomber Command on operations in a Pathfinder capacity, a new idea being developed at that time. I took the course in Canada, got my "Spec N" qualification, and returned to UK where I was soon sent on my way: Casablanca, Freetown, and Takoradi.

### TAKORADI, GOLD COAST

To eliminate the problems of flying across the Med, with its lack of staging airfields and the risk of enemy attack, the Allies established the Takoradi-Cairo reinforcement route. Aircraft were shipped from the UK to the Gold Coast, assembled there, tested, and then flown in loose formation, in company with Bostons as escort, along the reinforcement route to the Middle East. The route was over 3000 miles long and made use of staging posts in Nigeria, Chad (which had declared for the Allies), and the Sudan. My duties were mostly concerned with navigation. The route is shown on the map inside the back cover.

### FREETOWN, SIERRA LEONE

In March 1943 I was transferred to AHQ, West Africa at Freetown as the Command Navigation Officer, where I planned anti-submarine patrols. Our territory extended from the vicinity of the Canary Isles in the north to Luanda (Angola) in the south–from 29°N to 9°S. Aircraft types and crew nationalities were mixed:

| | |
|---|---|
| At Lagos, | Sunderlands by Australian crews |
| | Catalinas by New Zealand crews |
| | Wellingtons by South African crews |
| At Freetown, | Sunderlands by British crews |
| At Bathurst, | Liberators by mixed Commonwealth crews |
| At Dakar, | Sunderlands by Free French crews |

There always appeared to be at least five submarines operating on the coast, in addition to long distance ones returning from the Indian Ocean. Their usual routine was to refuel at or near the Canary Islands, whether going north or going south. Our task was to keep them submerged by attacking them both day and night. Our success was largely due to our knowledge of their positions and tactics, and being able to move our aircraft up and down the coast.

# DAVID R. ADAMSON

*David was born and educated in Alberta and joined the RCAF in March 1941. He received his pilot wings in June 1942 and served with 180 Squadron, 2nd Tactical Air Force, in Britain and Europe. David was commissioned in February 1944. When the war ended, he chose to make his career in the RCAF, and some 30 years later became the Deputy Commander of the North American Air Defence Command, with the rank of Lieutenant General. David retired in 1978, and spent the next 12 years in sales and marketing with de Havilland Canada, Boeing Aircraft, and Air BC. He retired in 1990.*

## 180 Squadron, 2nd Tactical Air Force

I joined 180 Squadron on B-25 Mitchell aircraft in December 1942 a few months after the squadron had been formed. Other 2nd TAF squadrons were 98, our sister squadron, 88 and 107 on A-20 Bostons, and later 226 and 320 also on B-25s.

The Commander of 2nd TAF was the redoubtable Air Vice Marshal Sir Basil Embry who was shot down twice in the early days of the war. The first time he escaped by killing his guard after being captured, and evaded capture the second time. He was fearless and fixated on destroying the enemy wherever he could be found, and he imparted a sense of invincibility to everybody under his command.

By a quirk of circumstance I'd ended up flying the very aircraft on which I had set my sights before I was awarded my wings. It never hurts to dream they say. Well, dream I did about that airplane from the day I read about it in an aviation magazine at Claresholm, Alberta, while we were finishing up our service flying training leading up to getting our wings in June of 1942. The article was all about General Jimmy Doolittle and the raid on Tokyo in April of 1942 by a force of United States Army Air Force B-25s launched from a carrier. There and then I said, "That's the airplane for me." Little did I realize then the twists and turns of fate that would lead to that wish coming true.

On graduation I failed to be among the ten per cent or so chosen for commissions, my less than impressive academic marks and young age, nineteen, leaving little doubt that I needed some seasoning before being allowed in the officers' mess. However, what I did have going for me was that my name began with the letter A, a dubious benefit when fatigue, latrine, and kitchen duties were being handed out. However, on balance, I learned it was an asset when it came to clothing and pay parades. Mind you, I was always the first broke, but in the end it resulted in my B-25 wish coming true. Neither was I considered to be of the quality required to be an instructor, an unwelcome fate anyway for those itching to get overseas and find out what war was all about. Accordingly, along with fifty or so other young sergeant pilots it was off to Halifax and the high altitude indoctrination course while awaiting a ship to get us to England. After ten days or so our turn came, and we were marched off to the Cameronia, a middling-sized passenger liner that we were told would travel by convoy; now fate and the letter A intervened.

Assigned to cabins in alphabetical order, we were tucking away our worldly belongings, all in one blue kit bag, when over the Tannoy came "Now hear this" or its equivalent. "The following sergeant pilots are to disembark immediately and assemble on the pier at the foot of gangway B: Abbot, Ackerman, Adamson, Allan, Anderson, and so on for a total of twelve. On assembling on the pier we were advised that we were going to a Royal Air Force OTU at Pennfield Ridge, New Brunswick, to complete our operational training on the Vega Ventura, a medium bomber. Well, it wasn't a B-25, but it was close, and it looked as if we were headed for duties with the Tactical Air Force rather than heavy bombers or coastal or fighters. Completing that course in eight weeks, we were back in Halifax going through the same routine, waiting for a ship. By this time, of course, we were veterans compared with those just graduating and found ourselves in a group of flight sergeants and warrant officers who, having completed a tour of instructional or staff duties, were getting their chance to see where the real war was going on. Another parade to the ship. We found we had been assigned to Queen Elizabeth and would be making the crossing on our own, relying on speed to evade the waiting U-boat wolf packs. So in late November 1942 we sailed out of Halifax harbour one calm evening with, it has been reported, some 17,000-19,000 other United States and Canadian service personnel on board.

One night I was assigned to a stint of duty on the open deck, checking that no lights were showing. It was dark, windy, and cold as the ship ploughed her way through the North Atlantic swells. My station was somewhere near the bridge. I could hear the bell signals that were being received and dispatched from there. Suddenly the signal for full speed ahead was given, or so I conjectured because the ship gave a tremendous lurch and turned sharply starboard. Some minutes later, after I had pondered my fate and my chances in the North Atlantic, she turned back to port and resumed what I supposed was the original course. The officer of the watch advised us, as we were being relieved by the next watch, that a contact had been made and the ship had taken avoidance action.

*That night was recalled for me fifty years later in a 1992 TV documentary about the Battle of the Atlantic and the role of the U-boats. Toward the end of that program a former German Navy captain was interviewed. He described in some detail the tactics that were employed. He had apparently sunk many merchant ships but emphasized that the ambition of every U-boat Captain was to get one of the Queens. When asked if he had ever had the opportunity he said that in late November 1942, he had fired two non-homing torpedoes at Queen Elizabeth but that she was too fast and had detected the submarine and taken evasive action. Could it have been?*

On the fourth morning we sailed into Greenock and boarded the train for Bournemouth. There we set about waiting for our assignment to an operational squadron, and since there were Venturas operating in 2nd TAF we surmized that was where we would end up. What we did not know was that the RAF had introduced the B-25 Mitchell into 2nd TAF and while we were waiting in Bournemouth the aircraft was assigned to its first mission, a low-level raid on an airfield near Amsterdam. In the event the mission was a shambles. Of twelve aircraft, four went down over the target and two ditched on the way out. Those lost included the Commanding Officer of 180 Squadron and other experienced crews who had been reassigned from other 2nd TAF Squadrons.

We were later to learn that a mistake was made in using the Mustang as close escort on the raid, which was into an area that was heavily defended by Me109s, with the result the gunners were hard pressed to tell one from the other. A further complication arose with the upper turrets when the guns jammed as soon as corkscrewing evasive action was initiated. Thus, they were defenceless against the hordes of fighters that intercepted them before they ever reached the target. Finally, it became evident that, good as the B-25 was, it was no A-20 Boston or Mosquito when it came to low-level raids. It was slower, less manoeuvrable and thus more vulnerable to light flak although it could carry a larger bomb load and had more range than the A-20.

The upshot of that first B-25 raid was an agonizing reappraisal of the tactics employed and the need for some technical changes in the ammunition feeding trays to the upper turret. That would take time and in the meantime there was a need for replacement crews. Four crews, including mine, were chosen in alphabetical order, from our OTU course and were posted to 180 and 98 B-25 squadrons at RAF Station Foulsham, near Norwich.

Foulsham was a new base, and there was mud everywhere. The second day there each crew was interviewed by the Station Commander, who explained the unfortunate first raid the two squadrons had undertaken the week before we arrived. He ended the interview by asking me how much flying time I had.

"285 hours, Sir."

"I say, that is a lot of flying time. When I went to France in the first war I only had 35 hours."

That admission, although no doubt well intentioned, did little to calm the apprehension that was being instilled in us by our new hut-mates who had survived the first B-25 raid and were not reluctant to describe the experience on the slightest provocation. Chief among those were F/Sgt Joe Atkinson and Sgt Knobby Clarke who were the wireless air gunner and air gunner in the crew of S/Ldr Hanafy, the A Flight Commander and acting CO of 180 squadron pending the arrival of a new Wing Commander.

Hanafy was one of those typical RAF officers with a balding pate and a huge flowing moustache, which he had much difficulty crowding into his oxygen mask. He had a highly Oxford-accented manner of speaking and his speech was characterized by many "h'mms", "I say chaps", "Oh! Good show", all the while stuffing his pipe and using many matches to get it going. He was a great operational type and on interviewing the new pilots made the point that "If you have come here looking for gongs you have probably come to the wrong place. On the 2$^{nd}$ TAF record thus far three of every five crews may expect to finish a tour of thirty trips". My thought at the time was: *That's rather impressive; it's certainly too bad for the two crews concerned but we'll be around for the full tour.*

Hanafy was also an avid practical joker who attracted reprisals in kind. One particularly effective prank was played on him more than once by the squadron gunnery leader. This prankster had discovered that the powder charge from one Very cartridge placed in the small stove in Hanafy's office was precisely the charge needed to bring the stove pipes down, to say nothing of spraying soot on everything and everyone in the office. Since Hanafy's first actions on getting to his office were to get a cup of tea, light the small stove, and stuff his pipe, in that order, we were more than once treated to the show of a loud bang followed by a black-faced Squadron Leader roaring around looking for that "buggah" Swannick.

After three months of concentrated training under the new commander, Wing Commander "Digger" Magill, and some technical improvements to the aircraft, the B-25s were again declared ready. That was in early 1943 and operations began in earnest. The roles assigned were "circus and ramrod" operations.

Circus operations were flown against airfields and were designed to encourage enemy fighters–mainly 109s and 190s and sometimes Me210s–to engage. The tactic employed was for the B-25s to cross the Channel in a loose formation at sea level to limit early radar detection and then climb at the last moment to cross the coast at ten thousand feet to avoid the light flak. We were always heavily escorted by Spitfires of 11 Group, some sweeping at tree top level, some flying close escort, and others out of sight above twenty-thousand.

A ramrod operation was aimed at a specific target, e.g., marshalling yards, harbours, industrial factories, blockade-runners in harbour and later, in 1943, the V1 and V2 sites.

Generally speaking, the ramrod operations were the more difficult and, I believe, presented the greater risk. By mid-1943 we were operating in formations of twenty-four B-25s in four boxes of six and were often joined over the target by similar numbers of A-20s.

At 10,000 feet it was reckoned that if you flew straight and level for more than fifteen seconds, the predicted heavy flak had an odds-on chance of hitting you. The enemy also employed what was called a box-barrage technique, which meant that the opening volley came with all guns firing simultaneously at the same point with fuses set for the same altitude.

As 1943 wore on, momentum was building and the squadrons had settled into what seemed to be a steady routine of operations; sometimes the crews would complete two trips in one day, especially in the summer when there was extended daylight. Much attention was being given to interrupting railway lines of communication, and it was on one such trip that S/Ldr Hanafy and crew were lost in perhaps as spectacular a fashion as any one could imagine. The raid was on the marshalling yards at Amiens, and Hanafy was leading the twelve-plane formation. Amiens was always heavily defended by several batteries of heavy flak since it was one of the principal terminal yards that supplied support to the Channel ports.

On the run-up to the target, the flak was finding the range. Just as the bomb doors opened Hanafy's aircraft disappeared in a blinding flash. Momentarily there was nothing there but two Wright Cyclone engines boring through the air with the propellers still turning, and then all the aircraft in the formation were showered by metal of all shapes and sizes. The starboard windscreen was gone from number four, and a complete electrical failure ensued. With wind pouring through the aircraft and no communication from the pilot, the wireless air gunner baled out, only to look up as he was floating earthward to see the airplane recover and turn for home. He was a POW for the next two years. Gone, however, were Hanafy and Clarke, and gone with Clarke was my favourite turtle neck sweater I had just received from home and never worn. The gunners were always cold and the pilots were always hot. Gone, too, was perhaps the greatest unsung war hero of my acquaintance: Joe Atkinson. He had been on continuous operations for more than three years and, to say the least, was more than a little "flak happy" but so believed in Hanafy that he could never say no.

The tempo was not interrupted. A new squadron leader arrived and operations went on as if Hanafy and crew had never been there. Some days later, during an attack on a V2 site in the St. Omer area, we encountered an air battle as large as any I witnessed during my tour. We were later told there were more than fifty squadrons of

Spitfires engaged and yet the Fw190s were still getting through to the formation. Over the VHF you could hear W/Cdr Johnny Johnson, who was leading the operation, calling for fighter reserves.

"Send reserves; we are being heavily engaged."

The sky was filled with contrails high above, and enemy fighters flew head-on straight through the formation with all guns blazing. They were so close you could see the pilots in their cockpits. They scored no kills and departed. But suddenly, the smoke seemed to clear and just as we were breathing a little easier the heavy flak opened up. Curly Motherall, a hard rock miner from Red Lake, had been leading the second box. The first volley disabled his controls and set his aircraft on fire. My gunner said: "There goes Motherall. I can see three 'chutes".

My tour came to an end in March 1944 and I returned to Canada thinking I would be back on operations in six months. By the fall of 1944 the war was obviously in its final months and the powers-that-be disclaimed any knowledge of my request to return to operations. Thus, my close relationship with the RAF ended. I had been very lucky and privileged throughout my tour in 2$^{nd}$ TAF with 180 Squadron. Regrettable as the war was, it was an experience that I would not have missed for the world. I will always retain a tremendous admiration for, and fond memories of, the RAF and especially those squadron mates who were denied, in the bloom of their youth, my good luck and fortune.

---

Curly Motherall survived and got back to his squadron to tell the tale. This is what happened, as related to the Medium Bomber Association and as remembered by Dave Adamson.

*On August 30$^{th}$, 1943, we were shot down while bombing a V2 site near Watten, France. The ack-ack marker shot broke in the bomb bay killing Vic Scuse, my W/AG, and cutting the flying control cables.*

*The B-25 started to climb, so I rolled the trim wheel ahead and it just spun. The plane did a power stall, pulled out, and started to climb.*

*As the starboard engine and bomb bay were on fire and the flames were licking up into the cockpit, I decided it was time to get out and walk. Di (Ephremius) Lewis, air gunner, Bill Dumsday, navigator, and I all baled out. Di had thirteen slugs through him from machine-gun fire from the ground. They only hit me twice.*

*Bill weighed about 160 lb; I was 235 lb, and as a 24-foot 'chute* was made for 180 lb, I passed Bill so fast he must have thought he was going back up. He landed between a red barn and a slough. I landed in a ploughed field near a main road. I buried my 'chute in a dirt furrow and lay still. The Germans were in the field within two minutes but searched the willows in the ditch around the field with their backs to me and moved into the next field when they were finished. I crawled to the willows thinking they might be as lazy as I was and wouldn't search the same place twice.

When it was dark I made my way to a nearby farmhouse, appropriated a bicycle, and took off up the road. After I had gone about four miles I saw car lights approaching a bend, so I rode into the ditch and through the hedge. I walked to a farmhouse and after looking under the blackout curtains and seeing a farmer, his wife, and two daughters, I knocked at the door. The farmer opened it.

"Anglais?"

I replied, "Canadian".

"Oh, Canadian!" and he embraced me and kissed me on both cheeks. They invited me in and gave me supper. They could speak no English and I no French. One daughter washed my leg off, and I dug the bullet out with a penknife.

They sent for a schoolteacher who could speak English, and when I told them where Bill had landed they went and got him. We spent that night and the next day in a ditch in the willows on the farm as the Germans were searching every building in the area. Our new-found friends took our photos that afternoon and wined and dined us. We slept in the hay that night. The next day the mayor of Armentières arrived with identity cards for us, and we were given civilian clothes. We rode bicycles about eight kilometres to a railway station where we boarded a train with the mayor.

We changed trains several times and at one stop we were sitting on a bench pretending to read a French newspaper while a Gestapo officer walked by us a couple of times, looking us over. Just then a German troop train pulled in on the track behind the bench. I wasn't too comfortable with so many German soldiers so close to us. We had to go past six Gestapo as we were handing in our tickets. I was sure glad I didn't look like any of the pilots on recruiting posters. We walked straight ahead and came out of the city on a main road, over a bridge guarded by Germans, old men and fourteen year old boys, through Pont-de-Nieppe and la Crèche. When it got dark we rested in a ditch.

I decided to check out the house we had just passed, and left Bill on guard. The same ritual was gone through again: "Anglais?" "No, Canadian" and the kisses. After deciding that we were okay, I called Bill in. It was the home of John Somerville Dirrech, his wife and six-year-old son. John was in the French Resistance and took us to a house a few miles away that he rented out. We stayed there a few days and then were moved to Pont-de-Nieppe, where we stayed with an old lady, Madame Pankhart, who was a herbalist. She only spoke French. After about a week, John took us back to his home, and I worked with him smuggling on the French-Belgian border until I learned to speak some French and the habits of the people.

One night we had gone out to take an arms drop. I had to signal the pilot to the new drop site as the Germans were on to the old one. After stowing away the guns, ammo, and explosives, we started home on our bikes. It was after curfew. John, Bill, and I were stopped by three Gestapo and questioned. John gave the signal we used when we were in trouble in our smuggling operations; so we both started shooting at the same time. I got two and John got the other one. We sent Bill and the other man to get a shovel while John and I dragged the bodies through the ditch and into the field where we planted them. John contacted a British spy in Lille, and the next morning Bill and I took a bus to Lille where we stayed with Captain Michelle and his paramour. He was the bravest man I ever met.

We stayed with them for a couple of days. He took us on a train to another town where we caught a train for Arras. When we got off the first train and were walking up the platform, he spotted a Gestapo officer (who was looking for him). He pulled out his .22 revolver with a silencer and shot him between the eyes. We walked by the corpse and got on the train for Arras, where we had been told to walk to a certain bridge and stop at a house at the foot of the bridge. We stayed overnight there and were taken out in the country to a farm where we spent another night.

An eighty year old lady, who was a Corsican and who had nursed Edith Cavell, acted as guide to Paris but didn't let on we knew her. On arriving at the Gare du Nord, we were told to go to a certain cathedral where we would be contacted. Simone and another lady contacted us there and took us on the Métro to go to her place. The train was packed, and after a while Simone told us a Gestapo officer was after us, working his way through the crowd. As the train slowed to a stop, she pushed the button to open the back door. We jumped out *of the train and into a duct that led to a sewer. I wasn't as afraid of the bullets bouncing off the walls as I was of the rats, bigger than any cat I ever saw. Simone led us up one sewer and down many others and then told me to climb an iron ladder and push off a manhole cover. We were in her courtyard. She hid us out for over a week and put us on a train for Prepping where a Spanish guide was to take us over the mountains to Spain.*

*On the way, I put Bill and Frank (a GI I had picked up in Paris) on another route to meet up again before our destination. I was changing trains at Lyons and hadn't eaten since Paris and had no food coupons. I decided to enter the café and have a beer. The only customer was a Gestapo officer sitting at the bar so I went up and sat beside him. In poorer French than mine he asked if he could buy me a beer. I accepted and bought him one later. Neither one tasted very good but that may have been my nerves.*

*We made our contact in Perpignan with the Spanish guide who had been paid to take us over the mountains into Spain. Twenty-six of us started out. The other twenty-three were European. We were crossing a vineyard after midnight when machine guns opened up. Bill, Frank and I dropped among the vines while the others tried to run. They were all shot. When the Germans moved up to finish off the wounded, we crawled back to the road, borrowed their jeep, and took off. We upset the jeep in a 20-foot ditch and started walking through the mountains. Every ridge had a German patrol on it. After five cold, wet days, we arrived in Spain, where we were picked up by a border patrol and incarcerated in a local prison.*

*The next morning we were taken to the city jail in Figueras, where police interrogated us. The Red Cross brought us our first meal in over five days. I didn't understand the trial as it was in Spanish, but that night we were marched to the outskirts and put in a dungeon. I managed to bribe our way into the custody of the American Air Attaché. We were moved to Gerona, Barcelona, Zaragossa, Madrid, and then by train to La Linea, from where we walked over the border to Gibraltar and tied one on. The next day we flew to England. It was an interesting Cook's tour.*

# FRED ASHBAUGH

*Fred was born in Busby, Alberta, in 1919 and enlisted in the RCAF in early 1940. He was awarded his pilot wings in April 1941, was posted to 149 (Stirling) Squadron in Britain, and completed a tour of operations in September 1942. Fred then spent fourteen months instructing at 15 OTU before being posted to the Middle East for a second tour. Subsequently he served with 168 Transport in Ottawa, flying the Atlantic route to Biggin Hill before being demobilized in early 1946.*

## A Tribute to Pancho

Well, there they were, my crew. I'd come a long way in a short time to reach this point. A twenty-one year old on the second course through Cap-de-la-Madeleine, Quebec, in 1940. The first course through Flying Training School on Harvards at Summerside, PEI. Along with buddies Bate, Brown, and Bishop (not to forget unilingual Vzina, "Vez", who was later to die a hero's death), we got our wings. Then overseas. The first bunch in Bournemouth. No small bottles of Canadian beer there. Had to buy quarts, and sat around on lawns celebrating Dominion Day till we were hauled off.

Off to Lossiemouth, Scotland, for OTU, 15 August 1941. Into the drink in the North Sea, a hundred and twenty miles off Wick. A "shaky do". After throwing out the navigator, I got hung up on my parachute harness, and started down with the Wimpey. Calmed down enough to reach around and unclip the damned thing. Popped to the surface and swam over to the dinghy and the rest of the crew. A convoy passed us by; it dared not stop. Sent back HMS Gleaner four hours later to pick up a sorry bunch. One with his eye out. One with his scalp hanging over his face, which we'd slapped back into place. Too many in the dinghy; I hung on outside. That North Sea was damned cold, but the rum aboard Gleaner was only too damned welcome.

Now to Whitton, 15 Sqn, and conversion to Stirlings. Posted to 149 Squadron, Mildenhall, Suffolk. Found myself and an Aussie pilot, Muir, having to toss a coin to see who would go to 7 Squadron and a chance to go on ops right away. Muir won. He was posted on Friday. Killed on Saturday. His first op. Next to Brest with Charles (Lofty) Lofthouse, the darling of the WAAF. A handsome bugger. Did five more ops with S/Ldr Watt, the only truly fearless man I ever met. Here I was in the 149 Conversion Unit flight hut, being introduced by Squadron Leader Speare to my first, my own, crew:

Sgt Art Potts, second dickie; Sgt Doug Phillips, navigator
Sgt Gregory, wireless op; Sgt Lawson, front gunner & wireless op
Sgt Sam Curtis, engineer; Sgt Davies, rear gunner
and, ah yes, Sgt "Pancho" MacGillivray, mid-upper gunner.

Nice looking bunch. All Brits except "Pancho". He was a BLAV, *a British Latin American Volunteer*. Small, scruffy, nondescript, face like an impish gnome. The skipper was not impressed. Pancho had run away from home in Uruguay and stowed away in a ship bound for Britain. The powers-that-be didn't know what to do with him. He said he was eighteen, so they let him enrol in the RAF Gunnery School. He had a bad time with English, spoke a mixture of Spanish and broken English. To my astonishment he was hitting the drogue at least twice as many times as the front or rear gunner. His new skipper was now impressed.

It was now time to pack up and move to Lakenheath, a satellite of Mildenhall, for some serious business. The endless trips together. Coming into the mess in the mornings to find many empty places. The pub piss-ups, when we took the ground crew to the pub twice a month, on payday. Their money was no good there.

On a mine-laying trip over the Baltic at five hundred feet we spotted German E-boats. My gunners had a good go at them, and I banked to let Pancho at 'em. Did a helluva job.

We did the thousand-bomber raids to Cologne and Essen. One hairy night, when I was manoeuvring the very manoeuvrable Stirling to avoid flak, some shrapnel clipped the hold-downs on the Elsan. The contents ended up on Doug's desk and on him. "Too much ribald laughter." he stormed. "You've had your last damn course from me."

Our little WAAF MT driver met us with "Rough trip, eh, chaps?" as stinking Doug exited the kite. This same little MT driver was now dating Pancho, and warned us every trip, "You look after him, you hear!"

Our aircraft G–George, N6080, was now fitted with Gee. On June 16 1942, Bomber Command in its wisdom sent us off to bomb the Krupp works in Essen. It was supposed to be covered in ten-tenths cloud.

The Met man goofed. No clouds. There was the Krupp works right below. We let them have it. Got caught in the searchlights. We were well pounded. Fifteen minutes later I got down between two layers of cloud. More hell broke loose. We were being attacked by an Me110. Davies's rear turret was shot to pieces. Torn off. Somehow he crawled back inside and hit the bunk. (He broke down after this trip and was taken off ops.) Sammy Curtis almost fell through a huge hole in the fuselage, going to see what had happened to Davies. The Me110 came up underneath. Then got above us, where Pancho and I could see him. I turned underneath him. Pancho let fly until pieces fell off. I then broke off engagement by diving into cloud. A confirmed kill.

Next thing I heard over the intercom was a wild war-whoop, a stream of Spanish—then, "This is a helluva way to celebrate my seventeenth birthday!" What a shock. He must have been sixteen when he started ops. We all sang Happy Birthday, Pancho. Headed home.

Old kite whistling like a teakettle, full of holes from flak and Me110 shells. Landed wheels up. The Stirling had a bad name, but she sure was sturdy. She had a thousand holes in the fuselage from main spar to tail, and still she got us home. Never to be used again. Before we had left that night, Gregory the wireless op couldn't find his air cushion. He folded a blanket to sit on, grumbling the while. When we landed he found a piece of shrapnel had penetrated the folded blanket up to the last layer. Said it felt like someone had kicked him hard in the arse. Told us later that he had a black eye where the sun don't shine. Lady Luck was with us again.

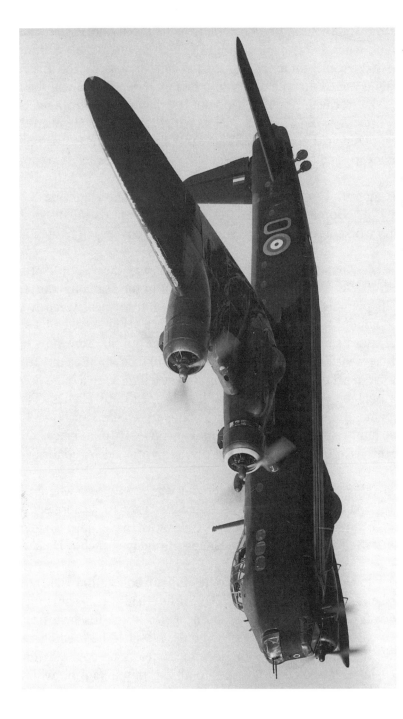

The Short Stirling entered service in August 1940 but did not begin operating until February 1941. Its maximum altitude was only about 12000 ft, making it vulnerable to light and heavy Ack-Ack. They suffered heavy losses and were gradually withdrawn from the main force. In 1944 Stirlings were flown by 138 Squadron on special duties

Photograph courtesy of George "Lefty" Whitman

No. 149 Sqn was one of the first to be completely fitted with battledress for aircrew. King George VI had had a direct hand in authorizing battledress for aircrew and wished to inspect us. He and Queen Elizabeth and the two princesses slowly traversed our line. Noting my CANADA patch, the King stopped. He recalled with pleasure their trip to Grouse Mountain. His warmth and sincerity touched me deeply. He wanted to know who "the little fellow with the BLAV shoulder patches" was. I explained where Pancho was from, why he was with us, and said that the lad's English was not good. The King and Queen went back to Pancho. From the corner of my eye I could see a protracted and animated conversation taking place. Pancho's chest was out like a pouter pigeon's. He didn't come down for a week. I had always rubbed my CANADA patches for fun among the Brits. He now rubbed his BLAVs.

So ended my first tour: 32 ops, 559 hours and 5 minutes total, all service flying. Said goodbye to my great crew, and we all dispersed to instruct. Exactly one year to the day I "wangled" a second tour, this time to the Middle East. Met my second crew at Moreton-in-Marsh:

P/O Dennis Wilburn, Navigator; Sgt Gordon Martin, W/Op; F/Sgt Hacker, RAAF, Bomb-Aimer; Sgt Cross, Aussie in RAF, Rear Gunner.

We flew our Wimpey to Rabat, then Cairo, and were posted to 104 Sqn, 205 Group, Foggia, Italy. I am now "The Old Man" at 24.

We are in support of the Americans at Anzio, doing two trips a night, dropping bombs with "screamers." Two hours over the enemy with scattered bombing. Get back home for tea and a wad, then back out again. One of our trips to Niksic, Yugoslavia, a hundred miles south of Sarajevo, with three Wimpeys, was the only daytime raid made by Wimpeys in this area. The Partisans had a German unit penned up and needed our help.

On a night trip to Steyr, only two aircraft found the target, an airframe factory. The Met was completely off the beam. Thanks once again to a terrific navigator, Dennis Wilburn, we were spot-on, got a great picture. Did two bomb runs with two sticks on a small target.

Shooting the breeze in our mess tent about enemy fighters, I happened to mention that on my first tour my mid-upper gunner Pancho had scored a kill. "Oh him!" I was told. "He was here." Seemed he wasn't well liked. Scruffy, out of place, a braggart about his prowess. "They bought it, damaged by flak, crashed into the mountains in northern Italy." Little Pancho. Dead at eighteen, on the 29th op of his second tour. Buried somewhere up in those mountains.

# REG PRICE

*Born in Lloydminster, Saskatchewan, Reg enlisted in the RCAF in June 1941, completed pilot training, and joined 625 Squadron in October '43. During his tour of Ops, Reg was awarded the DFC. He left the squadron in May '44 and returned to Canada in 1945.*

*Reg went back to the UK in 1947 and re-enlisted with the RAF, subsequently transferring to the RCAF to serve until 1964. He acquired a civilian pilot's licence and flew within Canada until he retired in 1984.*

## From 82 to 125

I had been interested in aircraft from an early age, when I built model aircraft as a hobby. One day in 1937 when visiting an uncle at a farm just outside Aylmer, Ontario, I heard a strange noise. Looking up, I saw a huge silver aircraft flying over–a DC3. The sight and sound confirmed for me that come what may I was destined to be a pilot. My goal was realized although not immediately.

I joined the RCAF hoping to be trained as a pilot. First came square bashing at Valcartier, north of Quebec City, followed by ITS at Victoriaville and guard duty at St Hubert. At long last I arrived at 20 EFTS, Oshawa Flying Club. At last I had a chance actually to get into an aircraft, a Tiger Moth. I knew I had made the correct decision.

After EFTS I went to 16 SFTS at Hagersville, Ontario, to fly Ansons, where after graduation I was awarded pilot wings. The first phase was over. I was a pilot. Now the hard part began.

In December 1942 I went to England on the Queen Mary, along with about 20,000 others, mostly Americans. In the UK I was sent back to flying school, first to 16 EFTS, for a short refresher course on Tiger Moths, with open cockpits and tail skids, no brakes and on a grass airfield, then to 2O AFU at Croughton. After graduating from there, I was sent to 81 OTU at Tilstock, Shropshire, on Whitley Vs. There I met Jim Harris, who became my W/Op, and Frank Sutton who became my rear gunner.

Our first taste of what was to come was on the night of 17 July 1943 on a "nickel", a leaflet-dropping raid, in north-west France. On our return we must have disturbed someone on the ground, as suddenly all sorts of exciting things began to happen, with us the target of searchlights and explosions. Since the Whitley was already going as fast as we could persuade it to go, someone thought that firing the colours of the day might let those on the ground know we were aware of their attention.

Almost immediately all their action stopped and we returned with no further excitement. On examining the aircraft after landing, we found a hole in the starboard tailplane big enough to stand up in. Fortunately, because it was between the leading edge and main spar, no serious structural damage was done. It did provide a hint of things to come.

We then went to 166T Heavy Conversion Unit at Faldingworth in Lincolnshire for training on Halifax V aircraft and then onto Lancasters. Here I met the rest of the crew, a most interesting and diverse group. Starting from the rear, they were:

Sgt Frank Sutton, RAF, rear gunner
Sgt Harry Powter, RAF, mid-upper gunner
Sgt Jim Harris, RAF, W/Op
Sgt Dudley Ball, RAAF, (later Pilot Officer, DFC) navigator
Sgt Les Knowles, RAF, Flight Engineer
Sgt Jack Conley, RAAF (later Pilot Officer, DFC) bomb aimer.

No. 625 Squadron was formed on 1 October 1943, and we arrived a few days later, a new crew with no experience to speak of. Since half the squadron was made up of experienced crews from other units, it was an interesting unit.

We did our first trip to Leipzig on the night of 20 October 1943–over seven hours–followed by thirty more in the winter of 1943/44 to various Bomber Command targets: eight trips to Berlin and others to Kassel, Stettin, Stuttgart, Frankfurt, etc. On 30 March

1944 we went to Nuremberg, the disastrous operation on which so many aircraft were lost. For the most part these operations were routine (a relative term) and although the crew returned on a few occasions with the odd hole in the aircraft, no one was injured.

Throughout the tour the entire crew flew together on every trip except when a couple of the crew were grounded for colds. The last eighteen ops were all done in the same aircraft. We completed thirty-one ops instead of the normal thirty. When the crew had completed twenty-nine, with just one to go, it was decided the next few ops were to be on French railway marshalling yards, which were considered to be less hazardous. As a result it was decreed that it would be necessary to do three of these to count for one operation. After two of these, the policy was again changed and each op was counted as one instead of one-third. Thus the crew finished their tour with one extra.

One other crew, also with a Canadian pilot, Sid Middlemiss, completed their tour at the same time, and we became the first two crews to do a complete tour with 625 Squadron. Of course, other crews completed their tours earlier, having done part of a tour before joining 625.

An event of interest occurred whilst we were based at Kelstern on the Lincolnshire Wold. The Wold consists of a series of fairly level areas 400-500 feet above sea level, separated by deep valleys. The ground slopes gently eastward to the shores of the North Sea. A number of Bomber Command bases were located in these level areas. (See map on page 246)

On this occasion a crew had been briefed for an op to Dusseldorf, normally about a five hour flight, fuelled accordingly, and loaded with a 4000-pound bomb plus the usual assortment of smaller bombs. At about 300 feet after take-off, fortunately to the east, both inner engines failed. Since it was a night op, visibility was not great. The aircraft began to lose height; however, the ground ahead sloped downwards. The crew lightened the aircraft as much as possible and flew around over the sea trying to get as much altitude as possible while using up fuel. Eventually they were able to get close to 4000 feet and released the load. The aircraft received quite a jolt as the big bomb went off. Power was reduced on the good engines and a normal landing was made at base. Total flight time was 1¼ hours.

While at Kelstern I met Elsie, a member of the WAAF, who was driving crew buses and other large vehicles. This was a dangerous occupation while driving on the airfield at night amid taxiing aircraft.

Elsie and I were married in August 1944. Of my crew, two are still alive and well. Jack Conley, bomb-aimer, lives in Kincumber, about ninety kilometres north of Sydney, Australia, and Jim Harris, the wireless op, lives in Lincoln, England. Frank Sutton died after the war, as did Les Knowles the flight engineer. Harry Powter, the mid-upper gunner, was killed whilst he was on leave. The night before he was to return to duty, a flying bomb landed on his girlfriend's house in north London and killed him; he was 19 years old.

Dudley Ball, the navigator, was the best man when Elsie and I were married. Our son is named after him. He was promoted to flight lieutenant after the tour, and joined an RAAF squadron. He was killed in a flying accident while training for a second tour on Mosquitoes.

After my tour I was posted to an OTU on Wellingtons and Hurricanes, training air gunners. I returned to Canada in the summer of 1945, followed a few weeks later by Elsie.

I am convinced that even though luck was involved, it was the ability of my crew of six exceptional people from different parts of the world to work together that made it possible to survive. Not to be forgotten are the ground crews, who worked under very difficult conditions, particularly in the miserable weather of the winter of 1943-44, and always had the aircraft ready to go when required.

One concern I had is that the two Australians, Jack and Dudley, and I were commissioned and awarded the DFC, while the four RAF sergeants received no such recognition although they all flew in the same aircraft on the same operations. Without their valuable contribution it is doubtful we would have survived. They were more deserving than I and braver. I only had to put up with the enemy, while they had that, plus they had to be subjected to the questionable skills of the pilot without being able to do anything about it.

After a year and a half in Canada, still bitten by the flying bug, I applied for a commission in the RAF and was accepted. 1947 found me back in England. I spent two years flying Lancasters, first from St. Eval in Cornwall, and then from Benson near Oxford. After a conversion course at Dishforth, in Yorkshire, I was posted to 511 Squadron at Lyneham, where I flew Hastings from the UK to Singapore for two years, outbound mostly with freight and returning with British troops wounded in the fighting in Korea. A couple of months were spent living in tents at RAF Fayid, in the Canal Zone of Egypt, flying Hastings from there to Dhahran or the Persian Gulf at the time of the Iranian oil crisis.

While I was at Lyneham I met a fellow Canadian, Keith Murphy, who was in the RCAF, on exchange to 511 Squadron as a navigation officer. He eventually persuaded me I should return to Canada, since the RCAF was expanding and with my experience on four-engined aircraft I would probably get a posting to No. 426 Squadron to fly North Stars. I returned to Canada. After the required training I ended up on 426 Squadron at Dorval flying North Stars. I should point out, however, that a flying instructor course at Trenton and four years instructing at Claresholm, Alberta, preceded 426 Squadron.

While on North Stars with 426 Squadron and at 4 OTU I was involved with UN operations flying to such places as Belgian Congo (now Zaire), Saudi Arabia, and Yemen. Other flights took me all across Canada, to the arctic with one trip to the geographic north pole, and also to Ascension Island, Hong Kong, and Saigon. All told I made sixty-five round trips across the Atlantic Ocean.

All good things come to an end, and in the summer of 1964, permanent commission notwithstanding, I found I was one of some five hundred aircrew the Air Force no longer wanted. Determined not to let this little problem deter me from my chosen career, I used the last few weeks of my time in the RCAF to obtain my Airline Transport Pilot licence and Class I Instrument Rating, doing flight tests at Toronto in a North Star with a DOT inspector in the jump seat.

*Postscript*

*The first aircraft I flew was a Tiger Moth, built by de Havilland Aircraft, in April 1942. The last aircraft, some 20,000 hours and 35 different types later, was an HS 125-700, the last aircraft designed by de Havilland in the UK as a separate company. De Havilland was absorbed into the Hawker Siddeley Group and subsequently into the British Aerospace empire. It progressed from the early DH125 IA series to the HS 125 and eventually the BAC 125. My first and last aircraft were both de Havilland, but what a difference between the two!*

# REG LANE

*Reg Lane was born in Victoria, BC, He joined the RCAF in July 1940 and went overseas in 1941. As a pilot, he completed three tours of ops: 65 operational sorties of which 35 were as a Pathfinder. He was Mentioned in Despatches and returned to Canada in June 1946 as Group Captain Lane, DSO, DFC and Bar. He remained with the RCAF and served as Chief of Staff, 1 Air Division and Deputy Commander-in-Chief NORAD. Lt. General Lane was made an Officer of the Legion of Merit (U.S.A.). He retired in 1974 to become a consultant to Systems Development Corp. of Santa Monica. General Lane retired in 1976.*

## Leadership and Determination

Anyone who was a member of a bomber crew in Bomber Command during WW II will have his favourite story to tell. Some are humorous and a joy to relate over and over again while others describe the heroism of other aircrew, many leading to death. I have two such stories to tell, the first about leadership leading to survival, and the second about dedication leading to death.

In October 1941, I joined 35 Sqn in 4 Group at Linton-on-Ouse, Yorkshire. My flight commander was S/Ldr G.L. Cheshire, DSO, DFC. He was an amazing officer who went on to survive the war as a brilliant operational leader with many more awards including the VC. About the same time, another Canadian, P/O D.P. MacIntyre, joined the squadron and after the usual five or six second-pilot operational trips, we were selected to be converted to the Halifax Mk II.

Now we began ops in earnest. Not surprisingly, a number of Bomber Command's operations during the fall of 1941 and early 1942 were directed against German warships, culminating in the raids against the 'Tirpitz' in Norway in the spring of 1942. The War Cabinet was concerned that these warships would create havoc with the convoys in the North Atlantic if they should escape from their ports. The Scharnhorst and the Gneisenau were two such ships berthed in Brest on the French coast. From early November 1941 through to early February 1942, some nineteen attacks were made against these ships in Brest at the cost of 127 aircraft. The Germans decided to move them to a safer port and on 12 February 1942, under the protection of very low cloud and poor visibility, they raced through the English Channel to German ports, arriving practically unscathed although slowed down by mines off the Frisian Islands.

We were one of the squadrons detailed for two daylight attacks on Brest on the 18th and 30th December 1941. These were my fourth and fifth operations and anything but a quiet introduction to bomber operations. We flew in formation from Linton-on-Ouse and attacked from 17,000 feet in the line astern formation. The weather was clear and the anti-aircraft fire intense; every aircraft in the squadron was hit. The Squadron Commander, who went in first, was severely damaged and lost both port engines. He lost height rapidly and finally ditched some sixty miles off the English coast. We watched fascinated as his aircraft approached the water since at this point in the war we had no knowledge of the ability of the Halifax to stay together and to float after a ditching. When the spray settled, we saw the squadron commander emerge from the escape hatch and walk up and down the wing. Our wireless operator was sending out SOS calls and we stayed with the downed aircraft and dinghy until we could see the Air Sea Rescue launches approaching at full speed to the rescue.

The second raid was similar to the first except for more accurate flak and Me109s who attacked as we were leaving the target. One of the six aircraft from my squadron. was shot down and others were heavily damaged before a Polish squadron of Spitfires arrived to drive off the 109s. Our crew went from a state of fear to one of exhilaration and joy as the Spits turned up. I am sure the Polish pilots could hear the shouts of relief.

On 27 March 1942, the Squadron was ordered to an advance base at Kinloss with no indication of the reason for the move other than that we would be on a highly secret operation.

The next day we were briefed that the battleship Tirpitz had left Germany and was tied up in a narrow fjord near Trondheim, Norway. The Royal Navy was concerned that she might exit to the Atlantic to play havoc with the North Atlantic convoys. The Navy wanted Bomber Command to sink the Tirpitz or damage her to the extent that she would have to return to a German port for repairs where she would be within range of the whole of Bomber Command. The attack was to be carried out at mast-head height using special mines to be dropped between the ship and the side of the fjord, a gap of less than fifty feet. A few of the Halifaxes were to carry special incendiary cans with the hope of creating fires on the deck and so reduce the light AA fire from her many guns. Mine was one of the aircraft carrying the incendiaries.

The operations briefing on the afternoon of 30 March was straightforward. The weather was excellent with a full moon and no cloud forecast over the target. Little was known of the defences except that there would probably be lots of light AA guns on Tirpitz and on the surrounding sides of the fjord. The attack was to be carried out at mast-head height to enhance bombing accuracy. No mention was made of any smoke screen or that two months earlier a force of sixteen Halifaxes and Stirlings had attacked without any success. Apparently only two aircraft reached the Norwegian coast (and attacked some small ships); one Stirling had been lost. Secrecy was emphasised in the vain hope of a surprise attack. The 35 Squadron Operations Record Book does not record the take-off or return times or any of the debriefing intelligence.

Our trip out was normal. We made landfall on course, proceeded towards Trondheim and on to the fjord where Tirpitz was moored. The AA was very active but the target was totally hidden by a smoke screen. Obviously there was no surprise factor. We did not drop our incendiaries but pulled up to go over the high hill north of the Tirpitz and jettisoned the load on what looked like a glacier. Visibility was unlimited in the moonlight and snow-covered ground. We headed for base and landed after eight-and-a-half hours flying. The Squadron lost three of the twelve Halifaxes detailed for the attack.

On 4 April the squadron returned to Linton-on-Ouse to be told that at the insistence of the Royal Navy, we were on standby for another attempt to get Tirpitz. The squadron sat twiddling its thumbs, not allowed to go on any operations until the weather improved over the target. On 23 April we returned to Kinloss.

The German warship TIRPITZ, one of the Germany's largest, tied up in a narrow fjord near Trondheim,

The operations briefing was held on the afternoon of 27 April with a much more strained atmosphere than the one a month earlier. The loss of three of twelve aircraft and the effectiveness of the AA defences had a very sobering effect. This time the smoke screen was expected and a timed run was to be made from a small island at the mouth of the fjord. The island would be quite visible in the moonlight. After the briefing, Don MacIntyre and I decided we would fly in formation and whoever was leading at the target would go in first. We both carried mines.

This time the Germans were ready for us with increased defences and searchlights that were probably meant to blind the pilots rather than to assist the light AA defences.

Don started his bombing run just ahead of me, having let down over the water to about 250 feet. The AA fire was intense on the run in, with shells bouncing off the water from the guns placed up higher on the sides of the fjord. The little island was easy to see and a timed run was possible. However, Don was being badly shot up and his aircraft was on fire. He was losing what little height he had.

I received several hits from the light AA but none of the crew were injured and all four engines kept running. We carried out our attack after the timed run, dropping our mines through the smoke screen and hoping they would land between the ship and the side of the fjord.

We did not hang around for an attack assessment but pulled up to get over the high hill north of the Tirpitz, nearly stalling the aircraft before we slid down the other side into the next fjord, where we were greeted by fire from another naval ship. We escaped with no further damage and after almost nine hours flying arrived back at Kinloss. I reported seeing Don MacIntyre on fire and was not surprised when his was one of the two aircraft the squadron lost on the operation.

The following day, 28 April, a repeat attack was laid on. My aircraft was undergoing repair to the main spar after being hit by a 20-mm shell and we missed the operation. Only seven aircraft were serviceable; of these seven, only three reached the target with two returning early and two missing. Of the twelve aircraft the squadron flew to Kinloss for the three attacks on the Tirpitz only six returned to Linton-on-Ouse.

The attacks on Scharnhorst, Gneisenau, and Tirpitz were a tough introduction to bomber operations and a hard way to gain experience, but they provided a basis for three tours of operations.

About six weeks later I was sitting in the ante-room of the Mess when I was certain I was seeing a ghost. Don MacIntyre, whom I had long since given up as dead, walked into the room. His story is quite remarkable.

On the run in to the Tirpitz his aircraft received several direct hits from the light AA causing severe fires. The cockpit soon filled with smoke and he had to release the escape hatch over his head, stand on his seat and fly the Halifax on the ailerons with his head out in the slipstream. He knew the airplane was about to blow up and he had two options: he could try to climb to an altitude where the crew could bail out, or cut what power he still had from the engines and crash-land. The odds for the former were almost nil as the aircraft might blow up or disintegrate before reaching any altitude. He opted for a crash landing in the mountains of Norway knowing full well that the odds were almost as bad as his other option. With that he prepared for a crash landing or more likely a crash into the side of a mountain.

He was trying to fly up a valley at the head of the fjord when he spotted a frozen lake and decided to make a wheels-up landing on the ice. This he did even though the aircraft was still burning badly. The aircraft slid across the lake coming to a stop only a few feet from a rock precipice on the edge of the lake. Up to this point the shrapnel had injured none of the crew and they all exited from the Halifax in a hurry, still expecting the aircraft to explode. Unfortunately, the tail-gunner broke his ankle in his haste to get out of his turret and had to be helped to the shore, where the crew watched the aircraft burn its way through the ice.

*(This aircraft was salvaged a few years ago and is now in the RAF Museum at Hendon.)*

Don realized they could not remain by the lake, as the Germans would already be searching for the crashed aircraft. He told the crew they were "quite close" to Sweden and should therefore try to get across the border before they were picked up and made POWs. They started out using the small map they had, walking through deep snow. He realized they were leaving an easily followed track in the snow, and tried to throw the Germans off by walking along any road they came to that had had traffic. There was a risk in doing so, but they would hide on the edge of the road when they heard any traffic approaching. In addition, they travelled mainly at night and rested during the day. The moon and snow on the ground helped the visibility.

The navigator, a slight RAF officer, was wearing his lined flying boots. His feet soon blistered to the point where he could walk no farther. He asked Don to leave him and for the rest to carry on to Sweden. Don would have none of that and from then on carried his navigator on his back. The crew took turns breaking trail through the snow when they had to leave any road. There were several close calls as the Germans continued an intensive search knowing that the crew were travelling on foot. It was not long before fatigue became the enemy and not the German search parties.

After two nights the crew were exhausted and wanted to give up the attempt to reach the border. Don kept encouraging them to hold on:

"The border is just over the next hill."

The crew finally rebelled and said they would go to the next farm and seek food and shelter to regain their strength before resuming their escape walk. Again Don, who was exhausted himself, had to call on all his powers of persuasion and leadership to convince the crew to continue. He did compromise by agreeing to follow such a plan if the border was not over the next hill. And so after three days and two nights of exhausting conditions with no food, they did reach the border, where, they gave themselves up to the Swedish border guards.

When they were being interrogated by the Swedes they described how the night before they had almost gone to a farm for help. They were told that the farmer was a "quisling" and would have called the Germans immediately. They were thankful Don had persuaded them to carry on. Thus the crew, minus the tail-gunner, became guests of the Swedish Government. Arrangements were made for Don to be flown back to England in a Mosquito. He was transferred to the Middle East where he did a tour on Liberators before being repatriated to the Liberator OTU at Boundary Bay, BC.

Thus we have a remarkable story where sheer will power, superb pilotage under extreme conditions, and magnificent leadership by Don MacIntyre saved not only himself but also his crew. For all this he was never recognized.

The second story occurred much later in the war, when I was CO of 405 (PFF) Squadron, based at Gransden Lodge near Cambridge. During the spring of 1944, Bomber Command carried out many raids on marshalling yards in Belgium and France to disrupt the movement of military equipment, particularly tanks, to the German forces along the coast of France once the invasion had started.

Many such attacks were carried out during this period. Most targets were considered to be a piece of cake as they were lightly defended and did not require a deep penetration into Germany. Such a target was the marshalling yard at Montzen, Belgium, on the night of 27 April 1944 when 120 Halifaxes and 16 Lancasters from 4, 6 and 8 Groups were ordered to attack. I was the Master Bomber and S/Ldr E.M. Blenkinsop DFC, also from 405 Squadron, was the Deputy Master Bomber. Teddy was from Victoria and on his 38th operation. He was an excellent pilot with a first class crew and had the leadership qualities necessary for me to consider him as my replacement as CO when I became tour-expired.

Take-off was just before midnight for a three-hour operation. The defences consisted of a few light AA guns but no searchlights. Flares dropped by other PFF aircraft illuminated the target and I dropped my target markers from 4500 feet. The raid began and I called on the Deputy Master Bomber to back up my markers as they were disappearing in the bombs from the main force. This Teddy did and after some twenty minutes over the target I told him to head for base and that I would stay a little longer to take care of any late arrivals. After twenty-four minutes over the target I also started the return trip. We had not gone very far before I saw the first bomber being attacked by a night fighter and shot down. This was not unusual on a raid, but after seeing seven more go down I realized that the fighters were well and truly in the bomber stream and having great success. With each casualty I dropped down a little lower until I was at a low enough height for the ground to interfere with the German night fighters' intercept radar.

I was wondering how many more bombers would "buy it" when the ninth aircraft was attacked and blew up just ahead of me. I was horrified to see target markers exploding and falling from this aircraft. The colours could only come from the Deputy Master Bomber's aircraft and with the explosion it was difficult to see how anyone could survive. Fifteen bombers, including Teddy Blenkinsop's, were lost on this "piece of cake" operation.

The epilogue to the Blenkinsop story did not come to light until well after the war. One of the incredible and unbelievable incidents that occasionally happened during the war is the follow-up story to the Montzen raid. Teddy's aircraft did blow up but he was thrown clear and, still conscious, pulled the ripcord to his parachute. The rest of his crew went down with the aircraft.

He landed uninjured and, being fluent in French, managed to find the Belgian underground who wanted to put him in the "pipe" to escape back to England. He refused, arguing that he might not make it and that he probably could do more harm to the Germans if he stayed and became an active member of the underground. This he did, assisting them in acts of sabotage. He obtained false papers to pass himself off as a Belgian national.

Information on his activities is very thin, particularly dates. We do know that while living in the town of Meensel-Kiezegem he was picked up along with eighty others by the Gestapo and transported to the St Gilles Prison in Brussels. This is confirmed by another prisoner who lived to report after the war that he had communicated with Teddy by tapping in Morse Code on the steam pipes, not that there was any heat.

He was subsequently transferred to Hamburg to work in the shipyards, still hiding his identity. There is an apocryphal story that he escaped and found his way back to Belgium to again join the underground, only to be caught once more by the Gestapo. What is known is that in November 1944, he became ill with tuberculosis and was transferred to the tuberculosis section of the infamous Belsen prison camp where he is reported to have died at the end of January 1945. While he is reported to have been cremated, there is no proof of this and, hence, no known grave. However, the Belgians have a headstone marker for him in a cemetery in Neuengamme, Belgium.

He was never recognized by his own country for his great unselfish determination and final sacrifice, but in 1948 the Belgians awarded him (posthumously) the Croix de Guerre and Palm. His story can be added to the many others of gallantry that, for whatever reason, did not come to light and hence went unrecognized. We shall remember them!

# GERRY WALLS

*Gerry was born in October 1920 in Saskatchewan. He joined the RCAF in 1941 and graduated with his Navigator brevet in September 1942. Gerry completed his operational training overseas and joined 427 (Halifax) Squadron. He was with the squadron from July to November 1943; then he was posted to 433 Squadron and stayed with them until March 1944. He was awarded the DFC in June 1944 and demobbed in June 1945. He later earned a Commerce degree and worked with the Government of Canada until retiring to Victoria in 1978.*

## Listen to the Navigator

No. 433 Squadron was the first squadron in 6 Group to be equipped with the new Halifax III, and what a big improvement the III was over the Halifax V–considerably faster, more manoeuvrable, and capable of a much higher ceiling. My crew was the senior crew; it was our duty and privilege to perform a number of air tests with the Bristol chief engineer on this new kite. Our last test lasted 7 hours and 20 minutes; it was a 1500-mile endurance test at 20,000 feet, near the end of which the Bristol engineer had us feather engines. We shut down three, in succession, and as we achieved single-engine flight we were descending through 10,000 feet at a rate of 50 feet per minute. The Bristol fellow estimated the aircraft would maintain level flight on one engine, at 5,000 feet altitude. We didn't try it.

At OTU I crewed up with three other Canucks: pilot Gerry Wolton, bomb-aimer Don Wilson, and rear gunner Ray Potentier. Our wireless operator was Dublin-Irishman Stevie Byrne. At 1659 HCU we picked up English engineer Jack Brown and American mid-upper gunner Otis 'Yank' Mohler.

I expect my bomber tour was somewhat less eventful than that of many others. Our crew never had an enemy fighter fire on us, thanks to a very sharp-eyed rear gunner who always spotted the enemy early and quickly and called for evasive action. In fact, the only occasion he fired his guns over Germany was to ward off a Lancaster that was overtaking us from above, on a return trip from Berlin. And as for flak, we were hit only twice during the tour.

However, we did have our exciting moments. On 12 August 1943, we were coming back from a long, boring trip to Milan. To our dismay we encountered strong headwinds, and after a breathless crossing of the Channel with fuel gauges showing empty, we made an emergency landing at Thorney Island. One engine quit on landing; a second, also on the port side, quit just after we turned off the runway! We had to be towed to the dispersal area.

On 27 August we got into a bit of trouble returning from Nuremberg. We were on-target and on time, so I was confident of my navigation. Our route home was to take us between Frankfurt and Mannheim through a gap in the anti-aircraft defences. As we approached the area the pilot decided, over my objections, to alter course 15° to port, to where he thought the gap was. Suddenly the flak opened up. The next few minutes seemed an eternity–the smell of burning cordite stung our nostrils and the aircraft rattled with a sound like hail on a tin roof! We nosed down, dodging and weaving until we were clear. We made our way home without further hindrance and found that the aircraft damage was limited to a few flak holes. From then on my navigation was never questioned.

On the night of 23 September, Mannheim was the target. As was our custom when the bomb-aimer took over control for the bombing run, I had gone up to the cockpit to set the next course on the pilot's compass, and to stand beside the pilot to keep watch out the starboard side. Unfortunately just as we started the bomb run, searchlights suddenly coned us. Gerry–our Gerry that is–slammed the control column forward and we went into a steep dive. As the lights followed us down, he pulled the controls back sharply to the stall point, then dove again and we were free of the beams.

When he first bunted the aircraft over, I hit my head hard on the overhead cockpit Perspex, only to crash down to the flight deck as he followed the nose-over with the positive-g manoeuvre. We managed to complete the bomb run, but I noticed Gerry was having a hard time keeping the kite level. (He later told me he thought we had been hit and had lost part of our starboard wing.) As I reached over to set the new course on his compass, I saw that I had knocked both starboard throttles back when I had fallen to the deck. No wonder Gerry was having trouble keeping us level. I immediately reached to push them back up. As I put my hand on the throttles Gerry happened to glance down and saw me about to touch his engine controls. He hit my hand so hard I thought he had broken it! He raised up towards me as far as his harness would let him, ready for a fight, he said later.

We had completed the bomb run on only two of the four good engines and lost eight thousand feet altitude, but so far we were completely untouched. The excitement was about to change form.

After clearing the target area the bomb-aimer went back to the rest position, to start throwing out Window (strips of foil intended to thwart enemy radar). When he got there he loudly exclaimed on the intercom that the bundles of Window had broken open, obviously during the violent manoeuvring, and that the stuff was all loose in the back of the kite. Of greater concern was that the lanyard for the photoflash had come out of the flare chute, which meant that the photo flash, with the explosive power of a 250-pound bomb, was armed and rolling around loose at the back of the aircraft. We were a very nervous crew until the bomb-aimer and the engineer managed to get it under control and wrestle it out the escape hatch. We felt the concussion as it went off, clear of the aircraft.

Near the end of March 1944, and just off a week's leave, our crew was told that pilot Gerry Wolton and I were to be screened from operations early and allocated to other duties. Experienced pilots and navigators were needed at 22 OTU to train new aircrews.

Unhappily Gerry and I were not able to persuade higher authority to keep our crew intact: our bomb-aimer and our mid-upper gunner were later killed. Our rear gunner spent several months in Belgium as an evader.

After instructing at 22 OTU for a year, I returned to Canada in April 1945, for a month's leave. The war in Europe ended. I returned home and was discharged on 1 June 1945.

# DOUGLAS HUDSON

*Doug was born in rural Manitoba. In 1942 he joined the RCAF and was accepted for aircrew training as a Wireless Air Gunner. Soon after receiving his W/AG brevet, Doug was posted overseas to operational duty with 420 Squadron. After 31 ops he returned to Canada and participated in training in Nova Scotia for service in the Far East. Doug completed his course on VJ Day and was demobbed in September 1945.*

## Landing—with Bombs

We were a crew of Canadians of 420 (Snowy Owl) City of London (Ontario) Squadron on Halifax Mk.III heavy bombers at Thalthorp, Yorkshire, a satellite of Linton, some twelve miles from the historic and beautiful old walled city of York. Our regular aircraft was T-Tare, with which we were all comfortable. The night in question was 30 December 1944.

We had completed nine ops and now had some confidence in ourselves and, more importantly, in each other. The target was Cologne marshalling yards. The hydraulics of Halifax T-Tare had been badly damaged by flak over our target the previous night, and so the aircraft was not serviceable. We were assigned to K-King for this op—the usual run up to the target, searchlights plus flak evasion. The gunners reported fighter sightings, but we were unscathed.

Our bomb load consisted of one 2000-pounder and a number of smaller ordnance. We dropped the smaller stuff over the target, but the 2000-pound high-explosive cookie hung up; it stubbornly refused to fall. The bomb-aimer and engineer worked frantically to effect a release, but to no avail. They continued their efforts until we crossed the German border. At that point, they gave up. It was Air Force policy not to jettison bombs over occupied territory.

With the cookie still hung up, we headed for the jettison area in the North Sea.

We kept trying to get rid of the thing. Then our gunners saw what appeared to be an Me110 stooging the area, presumably on the prowl for aircraft seeking to dump its bombs. We immediately abandoned all jettison efforts and set course for Woodbridge Emergency Field. Woodbridge had a massive runway designed for cripples and other emergency landings.

On the approach the crew took crash positions. The skipper reported an aircraft burning on the runway, but there was ample runway space left for us. The cookie had been fused and selected, and we had no idea what would happen on touch-down.

The landing was smooth and, to our huge relief, we were still intact. As we lost speed the skipper turned off onto the grass and shut down. The crew jumped out and ran, the adrenaline still pumping. The skipper later told of running as hard as he could and the tail gunner passing him as though he were standing still.

We ate and went to bed. The following day we returned to our aircraft. The riggers and bomb disposal crew had removed the cookie and left it lying on the grass beside K-King. It had been our tenth op and our sixth diversion.

Diversions were a common event for us, usually due to fuel shortages, flak damage, and the terrible weather in Yorkshire that winter. We made nine diversions during our tour. On each occasion we had slept in a strange bed–but in England.

Our crew went on to complete a tour. On our 28th trip we were told that due to the state of the war a tour would now be 35 trips. However, at the briefing that was to be our 32nd trip it was announced that any crew with 30 or over trips was screened. It was over.

Our final trip had been to Kiel, where predicted flak, searchlights, and fighter activities had been intense. It resulted in our ninth diversion, this time to Honeybourne.

# JACK SHEEHAN

*Jack was born in Montreal on 11 November 1922. He enlisted in the RCAF in August 1942, was awarded his pilot wings in November 1943, and went to England to complete all phases of operational training. He arrived on 207 Squadron RAF on 15 February 1945 and was screened on 30 May. He was discharged from the Service in September 1945. In 1951, he earned a degree in mechanical engineering from McGill.*

## Violent Evasion

My crew consisted of F/O Norm Hancock, navigator; F/O Rocky Shaffik, bomb-aimer; P/O Ernie Van Slyke, mid-upper gunner; F/Sgt Mac McArthur, rear gunner (all RCAF); together with F/Sgt "Scotty" Scott, flight engineer, and F/Sgt Fred Howard, wireless operator (both RAF). I was the pilot and captain of the crew.

Our training on Short Stirlings was completed at 1654 Heavy Conversion Unit on 17 December 1944. We were happy to receive a posting to 5 Lancaster Finishing School although the weather kept us from beginning the flying part of our course until February 1st.

Our first flight in a Lancaster lasted two hours and forty minutes. It included familiarization, three-engine overshoots, and a few take-offs and landings. The instructor got out at the control tower and sent us up for solo landings. On our first solo we heard a loud noise and felt vibrations as we reached take-off speed. As we climbed, the rear gunner reported large strips of tyre wrapped round his guns.

I informed the tower and was directed us to make a low pass over the them so that they could view the damage. I cycled the undercarriage up and down and discovered that the starboard wheel was jammed near the "up" position. We were directed to make a landing at the emergency aerodrome at Woodbridge. This we did, and made what was presumably a successful landing–we all walked away from it. The remainder of the training was uneventful by comparison.

On 16 February we were posted to 707 Squadron at Spalsby in 5 Group RAF. We began squadron training, and on 19 February I flew as second dickey with an experienced crew to Böhlen, Germany. Then on 7 March we were sent on our first operation as a crew to Harburg, Germany, to attack an oil refinery.

Immediately following our bombing run, and as soon as we were clear of the flak, we resumed a banking search in which I banked the aircraft to allow the mid-upper gunner to see below the aircraft. Almost immediately, while banked to port, the rear gunner gave me the command: "Starboard–Go!" Since it would have been fatal to return to a level position to start the manoeuvre, I went into the down starboard position directly from the port bank. As a result the negative gravity threw everything and everybody in the aircraft to the ceiling.

As soon as the attack by the enemy aircraft was over, I checked the crew: the bomb aimer was OK except that he had been hit on the head with his parachute, which he immediately put on; the flight engineer had struck his head on the ceiling and collapsed to the floor unconscious; the navigator thought he might have been hit since his legs were numb from being jammed under the table; and the mid-upper gunner's head had collided with the turret and smashed his goggles. The rear gunner and the wireless operator were OK. The two gunners and I continued our comments on the intercom throughout the evasive action.

The bomb-aimer examined the flight engineer and the navigator, checking them with a beam of light from a flashlight shining through a pinhole in a piece of cardboard. Sensation was returning to the navigator's legs; he thought he was probably OK. The flight engineer was lying on the floor covered with aluminium strips of 'window' and the navigator's vomit. The conversation for the next few minutes was unprintable. We returned to base with no further excitement. The station commander decided that seven days' leave was in order. Reporters took pictures, and we left to prepare for our holiday.

# JIM BAILLIE

*Jim was born in Saskatchewan in 1916 and spent most of his life in Saskatoon–at least, that part that was not given to the RCAF. He joined the Air Force in the spring of 1941 and was awarded his pilot wings in November. Jim became a flying instructor, and for more than two years taught young recruits the art of flying. In March 1944 he arrived in Britain and began an operational tour in Bomber Command, a tour that ended when Germany surrendered.*

*Jim was demobilized in September 1945 and began a career with the Department of Veterans Affairs in Saskatoon. In 1947, he became the Commanding Officer of 406 Auxiliary Squadron in Saskatoon, a position he held to his retirement from the RCAF in 1952.*

## Yorkshire by Moonlight

By November 1941, I had won my pilot wings and been selected for training as a flying instructor. During the course I had been detailed to do a test flight on a Fleet Finch. It was winter, the field was snow covered, and one landed on the packed down runway. Upon landing, in my wisdom or otherwise, I decided to shorten the landing run a bit and applied the brakes. Unfortunately I hit the bare concrete part of a runway crossing my landing path. As a result I was flat on my back looking at the concrete. The fire brigade and the blood wagon came and rescued me.

The aftermath to this story is now quite laughable although the mishap wasn't funny at the time. It was a Friday afternoon and the OC Flying was W/Cdr Joe Stevenson. He and one of his staff officers were congratulating themselves on having an accident-free week, until they looked out the window and there was Baillie on his back. I paid the price for that escapade, becoming Orderly Officer for ten days for my sins.

There is an amusing postscript to the episode. I brought my wife to the New Year party. Whilst she was dancing with the Station Commander, he asked her if she was having a good time. She replied to the effect that:

"Some so-and-so had made him do Orderly Officer duties for ten days".

The group captain took her words in good grace and did not reveal he was the culprit.

My time at CFS was very interesting and we managed to fly such various types as the Fleet, Harvard, and Cessna, and I even got a chance at some dual on a Lockheed 10. I spent many hours learning the approved "patter" and taking the patter test. You really haven't lived until you have tried to talk a student through a slow roll in a Fleet or Harvard using the old Gosport tube, which never stayed in one place. Moreover landing a Mark I Harvard at night from the back seat–with a huge instructor in the front–on a flare path in the winter can be a challenge to an embryo instructor.

Eventually I graduated from CFS and was posted back to Claresholm, Alberta, flying Cessna Cranes. Life as an instructor at SFTS was quite interesting. Students were not only Canadian, but included personnel of the RAF, RAAF, RNZAF, and quite a few Americans who had come up from the USA to fly.

Once you became an experienced instructor your chances of getting overseas appeared very poor. Representations were made to higher authority and a small quota were posted overseas each month. Our Chief Instructor at Claresholm was S/Ldr Charlie Burgess.

After putting in 1300 hours at the instructional business I eventually arrived overseas. However I must say that my time as an instructor was a great learning experience from a flying point of view and in developing relationships with other people, other nationalities.

I was posted to an AFU at South Cerney in Gloucestershire (Oxfords) and then to an OTU at Long Marston, Warwickshire. After familiarization on Wellingtons, I managed to put together a crew.

They were all Canadians; the youngest (tail gunner) was barely eighteen years old. I was an old man of twenty-seven.

After OTU, we were posted to a heavy conversion unit at Wombleton, Yorkshire, and thence to 426 Squadron. in 6 Group, stationed at Linton-on-Ouse, Yorkshire. To my surprise the CO of 426 was my old Chief Instructor from Claresholm, W/Cdr Burgess, who quickly checked me out on a Halifax VII. My operational career started three days later with a trip to Hagen. Germany at last.

My crew and I were indeed fortunate during our 24 missions to have survived. We had our moments with fighters and flak. There are many tales to tell but a couple should suffice to give an idea of our lives.

MAGDEBURG

A night trip to Magdeburg started off badly. On take-off, the first aircraft off blew a tire and blocked the runway. This caused a runway change and delay of 15 minutes, which made us late on target. Not only did we arrive late, but very much alone. We had just made our run and got out of the target area when we picked up a night fighter. We did our evasion tactics and managed to get into cloud. Sometime after this episode the starboard inner prop ran away. If you, as a pilot, have experienced one of these, they are terrifying to say the least. In a Halifax that prop is with you even in the cockpit and images of its flying off can be unsettling. With the help of my flight engineer we got our airspeed down to 120 knots and with 15 degrees of flap managed to get the RPM down to about 2250. As the starboard inner tachometer had broken, we used the shadow method to synchronize the prop with the starboard outer. Eventually we arrived back at base safe and sound. It had been a long, lonely trip.

CHEMNITZ

Another operation that comes to mind is a trip to Chemnitz. During take-off a line squall fell on bases in 6 Group. Severe icing caused the loss of nine Halifaxes: Three of these were 426 Squadron aircraft. Only one crew member survived. One of our aircraft crashed in York killing some civilians. My crew and I were indeed fortunate as we managed to avoid icing conditions. To avoid oncoming aircraft it was a habit of mine to turn west after take-off. By good luck it took us out of the icing conditions. We were not aware of what was happening, as there was R/T silence. We were diverted to Mildenhall and landed there 8½ hours later. Among those killed over base was my flight commander.

## DUSSELDORF

On Christmas Eve we were detailed for a daylight operation to Dusseldorf and I thought what a dreadful present we were delivering to the German people. All our ops to that time had been done at night. On the way in my bomb-aimer, never having seen daylight flak, said, "What's that funny bunch of stuff at our height straight ahead?" It was barrage flak. We went straight through, picked up a little but no serious damage.

As an aftermath to this trip we were diverted to Great Dunmow, Essex. Eight Halifaxes landed. The CO explained that rations had been saved for months to provide a Christmas banquet for his personnel and that it was out of the question to invite an additional 56 aircrew to the feast. He did his very best by providing lots of beer and ordinary rations. .

## RETURN TO CANADA

We finished our operational tour with the end of the war. At that time I was A Flight Commander, 426 Squadron. One of my new duties was to prepare for return to Canada those of my crews who had volunteered for action in the war in the Pacific.

I got home shortly before the atomic bomb brought an end to that war. I took my discharge in September 1945 and returned to my wife and family in Saskatoon.

*I was fortunate after discharge to obtain a position with the Department of Veterans Affairs in Saskatoon in late 1945 and remained with that department until my retirement in 1974. This service together with my wartime service totalled some 35 years.*

*In early 1947 I was approached by the RCAF to build an Auxiliary Squadron and become its first Commanding Officer.*

*Recruiting began and we finally got 406 Squadron off the ground. Our first aircraft were Harvards, followed by Beech 18s (Expediter) and then eventually B-25s (Mitchells). The role of 406 originally was as a light bomber squadron. in defence of our country.*

*I stepped down as CO in 1952.*

*My activities since that time have included a period as Provincial Chairman of the RCAF Benevolent Fund, and Chairman of the Saskatoon Corps of Commissionaires. When I retired to Victoria, I joined the British Columbia Air Museum. I am a tour guide and enjoying this association.*

# IAN CAMPBELL

*Ian graduated from High School in Quebec and volunteered to join the RCAF. He was hoping to become a pilot, but the Service decreed otherwise. Jim travelled the usual route, Manning Depot (at Lachine) to learn the ways of the RCAF and then off to Elementary Flying Training School.*

## My Life in the RCAF

At EFTS I was introduced to the Tiger Moth. It was a wonderful aeroplane made up of cloth among other things; it carried 19 gallons of gas, had a bit of tin on a spring for air speed indicator, a couple of cockpit instruments, and a half inch rubber tube with two funnels (the Gosport tube) as an intercom system between the fore and aft seats. But it was an aeroplane. And it flew.

On to SFTS. My familiarization flight was simply fantastic; as we taxied out to the runway the instructor asked if it was my first flight in a Harvard. It was and he said, "I'll show you what a Harvard can do". Boy did he ever. I am still not sure what we did and admit to being surprised when we landed safely.

Someone, somewhere, decided I might be better employed in some trade other than pilot and sent me to Rivers to learn navigation. I was issued a watch, an octant rather than a sextant, a Dalton computer that wasn't a computer at all but a mechanical device used to work out drift, ground speed, course and so on, and last but not least a huge green canvass bag or purse in which to carry everything.

At Rivers we learned to identify various stars and planets; in time we learned to take and work out an astro fix that put us somewhere in the correct vicinity. By the end of the course, like a modern major-general, we were "teeming with a lot of news". We flew in Ansons, probably Mk Is; the crew consisted of pilot, wireless operator, student navigator and student-bomb aimer. The navigator or bomb-aimer had the privilege of winding up the undercarriage; I can't remember how this was decided.

On one of our first night flights after flying over Winnipeg and admiring the jewel-like lights we flew north-west over Lake Winnipeg, a big lake something like 250 miles long. Shortly after we left the south shore, the port engine began to surge oddly, and we saw a bright red flash off the port side. Pilot tells student bomb-aimer to have W/AG send a Mayday. Student bomb-aimer returns wide eyed.

"He's gone and the door is open."

At this point pilot can't help laughing. He and W/AG had cooked it up. Pilot plays with engine, fires red Very flare out window, W/AG grabs 'chute, opens door then crawls into luggage area and closes that door. Dumb students panic.

Two other incidents stick in my mind during the course, one weird and the other tragic.

The weird one was on a cross country; we iced up so badly the pilot decided we had to make an emergency landing, we made a wheels-up in a snowy clearing in northern Manitoba. As I remember it we just tightened our seat belts and sat there; the landing was reasonably smooth but extremely noisy and raised all the dust in the aircraft

Shortly afterwards a trapper arrived and offered to show us a trail to a road where we could get a ride to civilization. The pilot decided someone should stay with the aircraft. We drew lots. Guess who won. Or was it lost?

The trapper gave me some supper, and as we sat smoking he told me many stories, each more amazing than the last. When he told me of his ability to point at a moose and having a bolt of lightning from his finger kill it instantly, I became a little concerned. His shaggy beard and strange demeanour reminded me of a wild-eyed Rasputin and I decided I'd better get on with the job of guarding the Anson. I spent the rest of the night and most of the next day huddled there until rescue arrived. Thank God for my flying suit. The other thing that sticks in my mind was the death of two crews, including a classmate.

This was the first indication we had that we were not immortal. I had gone on sick parade with a cold that day and the Medical Officer had grounded me. I had been slated to fly that night, but couldn't go. On return in the circuit, the plane collided with another Anson, and all seven in the two aircraft were killed.

After wings parade, commando training, and spot of leave, we boarded RMS Andes for Liverpool and Bournemouth. At Bournemouth we lived like kings for several weeks. A day or two after we arrived, the sirens sounded while we were on the way to breakfast, as it was a new experience for us we didn't know what to do. We began to run looking for an air raid shelter when we noticed a young mother pushing her baby in a pram quite unconcernedly. In embarrassed confusion we stopped running and never did see any action that day; we watched the contrails of dog fighting but it was too far away to recognize any aircraft.

From Bournemouth we went to AFU at Llangefni and then to OTU for crewing up and training on Wellingtons. Then it was off to HCU to convert on to Halifaxes. We did more circuits and bumps, cross countries, practice bombing and fighter affiliation; it was great fun as one could soar weightless for a moment amongst all the dust when you came up and over and banked into another dive. On completion of our course at heavy conversion unit we joined 415 squadron at East Moor.

East Moor was some eight miles north of York; both squadrons there flew Halifaxes. Our skipper did a second dickey trip and after more fighter-affiliation, practice bombing, cross countries and so on, we were a sprog crew ready for a couple of Nickel raids before being considered operational. One autumn evening we were lying on the grass beside our aircraft ready for a trip to Duisberg and making nervous jokes. I found a four leaf clover, the one and only one I have ever found; then after "Boots" (our rear gunner was named for his size 12 flying boots) had a final pee on the tail wheel, we climbed aboard.

During take-off, while sitting behind the main spar and eating an orange, a perk for every op, I noticed our mid-upper gunner had an odd expression on his face. Since I had been working at my table, and storing my gear, I hadn't bothered to plug into the intercom. Now I realized we had a problem. The aircraft veered sharply to the right; we all braced ourselves as the monster bounced around and finally wound up in the middle of some woods.

Fire broke out before we stopped. The rest of the crew rushed to the rear door to get out. I thought I'd be smart, avoid the rush, and exit from my escape hatch near the nose. I didn't think we had been airborne and assumed the undercarriage hadn't been retracted. Unfortunately the frame was so distorted that I had considerable difficulty in opening the hatch. When I finally got it open, to my horror I found the belly of the plane flush with the ground so there was no escape there. The Perspex nose was intact; obviously we had not hit any trees head on; .I wouldn't be able to get out there. By this time the centre of the Halifax was a mass of flames, and I tried to exit through the pilot's escape hatch, which was still closed. It was so hot up there I could feel the skin on my face blistering. I dropped to the deck and crawled to the rear door through the flames as the ammunition in the mid-upper turret began to explode. As I tumbled out the door a WAAF lorry driver, who was later mentioned in dispatches, was running from the plane, I called and she helped me to her lorry, which was nearby with the engine running. As we were driving away the bombs exploded, nearly throwing the lorry on its side. The explosion left a huge water-filled hole in the woods but caused us no serious damage

The WAAF drove to sick bay, where I was given a shot of morphine before being taken to Fulford Hospital in York. I remember being carried on a stretcher and feeling as if I was floating on a cloud while I hummed away to myself. I felt so-o-o-o good. I have stayed away from drugs ever since as I know I would surely become an addict. My thoughts while in the fire were oddly enough not fear as much as disbelief that this was happening to me; things like that only happen to other people. My only other thought apart from escape was that the damn fire was taking all the oxygen, so I had trouble breathing. While in hospital, after some minor skin grafting, I made an excellent recovery due to a new treatment for burn patients. It was so successful that the well-known plastic surgeon Dr. McIndoe came to have a look at the way I was healing.

By the time I was discharged from hospital some months later, the war was winding down. My crew had been dispersed to other crews and other places; most had finished their tours or gone. As a spare navigator I hung around the station for a while; I did one trip with the CO, and eventually joined our flight commander's crew who had lost their Nav. VE Day came before I finished my tour; the fire may have saved my life.

# RAY FISK

*Ray was born, raised and educated in Prince George, BC. He joined the RCAF early in 1943. Following his graduation as a navigator in Winnipeg later that year, he went overseas to complete operational training and subsequently joined 49 Squadron, RAF Bomber Command to start his operational tour. Ray came home to Canada in 1945 to attend UBC, where he graduated in Civil Engineering. After thirty years with CN Rail in senior engineering positions throughout Canada, Ray retired to run his own consulting business.*

## Too Young For War

The most significant move on my part while I was at No. 3 Manning Depot was to sign up for a picnic on Easter Sunday 1943. At this picnic I offered Mary Young some mustard for her hamburgers. It was the first of a chain of events that included marriage (fifty-one years and counting) three children and four grandchildren.

At ITS, borderline night vision removed any option for pilot training. My "score" was originally 5 (out of 32). I was re-tested and achieved cat's vision of 6, which was evidently good enough to become a navigator. So it was on to Air Observer School, Winnipeg, for five months training in air navigation.

At Air Observer School our first familiarization flight took place on a beautiful day in late summer, the sky dotted with beautiful puffy white cumulus cloud. No one warned us that flying in these pretty clouds included being tossed about like a cork in a whirlpool, resulting in our intrepid navigator being airsick on his very first flight.

However, this proved to be the only instance of such embarrassment and after five months of flying out of Stevenson Field, we all graduated with shiny new wings and set off for embarkation leave and transfer to the British Isles. There we found ourselves attached to the RAF but paid by the RCAF. In due course I was posted to AFU at Bishop's Court, Northern Ireland.

The only thing of any moment that occurred at AFU was the realization that the Station Commander and I held quite different concepts on the accuracy of air navigation. The Wingco, a permanent-force type, had to go to a meeting at a station near Liverpool and believed in giving a member of the current training course an extra opportunity to practise navigation. I thought hitting the airfield perimeter a pretty good effort, but the Wingco's standard of good effort was that you flew over the exact centre of the field exactly on your ETA–not glimpsing it about three miles off the port wingtip at roughly the right time.

The posting to OTU started a very significant chain of events, for it was here that the make-up of crews, on a volunteer basis, took place. It was a sobering thought that you are making choices which will have a large impact on your life expectancy. We wound up with four RCAF and three RAF crew members.

We also left the sturdy Anson behind and started flying Wellingtons. On this aircraft we learned such sobering things as baling out drill, ditching and dinghy drill, oxygen drill, procedure when lost at night, fire drill, petrol and oil system, all the while fervently praying we wouldn't have to do any of them.

At HCU we moved on to Stirlings for training on four-engine aircraft. Here we came into much too close a chance to practise our recently learned baling out drill. We were flying over Wales one night on a cross-country training trip when suddenly all went quiet. You've no idea how silent it can get when four big engines have been droning away and suddenly stop.

"Prepare to abandon aircraft."

It was the Skipper's voice. I clipped on my chest pack. I leaned back toward the wireless op. It was obvious he was busily engaged with something on his wireless, perhaps wasn't on the intercom, and hadn't heard the *Prepare to abandon* order. I have never forgotten the startled expression on Danny's face when the message reached his brain.

"Surely you jest. You're not kidding, are you?"

It was at about this point that the engines started coughing and resumed their task, much to our relief. The flight engineer had forgotten to switch over tanks at appropriate times; it was a very quiet trip home.

From Heavy Conversion Unit (HCU) we were posted to No. 5 Lancaster Finishing School (LFS) for final training on Lancs before our squadron posting. Among other training sessions, we were given practice drills on feathering various combinations of four propellers, including all four at the same time–a nice approach to fuel conservation.

While at 5 LFS, non-pilot aircrew were given hands-on experience to enable them to nurse an aircraft back to English skies with enough altitude for survivors to bale out. Finally we were posted to 49 Squadron, 5 Group RAF., at Fulbeck one week before Christmas 1944. This was at the time of the ten-day period of fog. The Squadron had been diverted elsewhere and the only occupants of the station were the ground people, plus us two or three newly posted aircrews.

After two months on squadron, we were assigned a brand new replacement Lanc with the identity S, full name "EA-S". She was complete with the latest in paddle-blade props, all the bells and whistles, and a very jealous crew (us) when anyone else got to fly her. The Air Ministry thought this aircraft belonged to them; our crew thought it was ours; but everyone knew that the real owners were the ground crew who looked after her and us. We were able to look after her fairly well until the end of hostilities.

On 11 March 1945, we took part in one of the massive daylight raids on the Ruhr. EA-S was one of more than a thousand Lancasters and Halifaxes that dropped some 4500 tons of bombs on Essen. At that time the Allied armies had advanced to within fifteen miles of the city, a rail and communications centre of some importance. On that same day, 1200 USAAF bombers plastered Hamburg, Bremen, and Kiel.

Because of the specialized nature of our targets, a lot of our time was spent in training and practice. Between 14 Jan and 25 April 1945 we completed eleven sorties. Six of these targets were synthetic oil plants, deep in East Germany, Czechoslovakia and Poland, with trip lengths in the order of nine to ten hours. These oil plants, sometimes occupying 100 acres or more, were heavily defended by flak and fighters, and further protected by construction of dummy plants nearby.

On Wednesday 25 April, we were given the fascinating task of striking Berchtesgaden, Hitler's redoubt in the Bavarian mountains, and the barracks situated about five miles away. Two 12,000-lb bombs, fused for deep penetration, hit the redoubt. Photographs taken during the attack confirmed the hit.

Nine of our eleven trips were night ops with each crew being responsible for its own navigation and bombing. In the first week of May, we were feeling joyous and thankful that it was all but over. We flew two *Exodus* flights, each of twenty-four POW, from Juvincourt and Brussels. On 15 May we flew a reconnaissance flight over the Ruhr area, with ground personnel as passengers, to get a first-hand look at the devastation. Not long after VE Day, our crew was disbanded. The bond that had grown among our group in quite a short time was nothing short of amazing.

I had volunteered for service in the Pacific Theatre, and was posted temporarily to 427 Squadron in Leeming. During the last week of June, with pick-up crews, we made several bomb-disposal trips to designated areas in the North Sea. VJ Day occurred while I was on the way home, so that instead of reporting for Pacific service, I reported to the discharge centre at Jericho Beach in Vancouver in September.

Soon after returning to Canada, I paid a visit to Mary Young in Calgary to complete some plans we had started a couple of years earlier. While in Calgary, we learned that a Lancaster bomber was on display at Calgary Airport and could be visited by the public. We joined the line-up and as we reached the "sandwich board" which listed the specifications and characteristics of the Lancaster, I commented quietly on several minor differences between this information and that which I was used to with RAF aircraft. A neighbour in the line-up said, "What does that punk kid know about these things—he's never had a uniform on his back!"

I just smiled.

Sad to relate, Ray Fisk died before this book was published. Ed.

# BOB GOATCHER

*Bob was born, raised, and educated in Winnipeg. In June 1942 he joined the RCAF, graduated as a navigator in August 1943, completed his operational training, and joined 420 Squadron RCAF in Britain at the beginning of 1944. Bob was awarded the DFC during his operational tour, and stayed with his squadron post-operations as the Navigation Training Officer. He came home in August 1945, achieved a degree in Commerce, and ultimately served on the faculty at Red River Community College, Winnipeg. Bob retired in 1988 and lives in Nanaimo, BC.*

## A Navigator's Nightmare

Our crew was stationed at Tholthorpe, Yorkshire, with 420 Squadron, one of fourteen such units in 6 Group (RCAF) Bomber Command. We had been together for four months and had done twenty-one bombing trips to targets in Germany, France, Belgium, and Holland. Many were daylights; some were night raids. We had seen plenty of enemy fighters, flak, and searchlights, and had also had our share of diversions on the return journey because of weather, shortage of fuel due to pierced petrol tanks, or other semi-emergencies.

Our crew had also survived a serious crash in which we lost our flight engineer and which put the rest of us out of action for a month. Our engineer's name ironically was Monument and we had

133

nicknamed him "Tombstone". The aircraft was a complete write-off, having blown up within a few seconds of our having got out and over to a ditch about one hundred feet away. Because we had landed on top of seven cows, our Pilot's nickname was changed from Allan "Tubal" Cain to "Killer" Cain.

The rest of the crew consisted of F/Sgt John "Johnny" King, bomb-aimer; Sgt Jim Danberger (Danny), wireless operator; Sgt Ted Frayne, mid-upper gunner; and Sgt Earl Cruikshank, rear gunner. Earl was the only member who had been with me on a previous crew. We were ready to go on op twenty-two and had just that day acquired a new flight engineer, our third, P/O Erick Herrod.

The briefing was over and we were headed for dispersal to board our Halifax III, A-Able. It was the night of 15/16 September 1944 and we had been assigned to attack the German naval base at Kiel. We took off at 2205 hours just as darkness was about to set in (double daylight-saving time) and climbed eastward after setting course over base. It was a short run to the coast of England and Johnny got me a pinpoint. We were nearly ten miles off track! I gave Killer a new course to steer and wondered how we could be that far out in such a short time. Surely the Met wind forecasts could not be that far out. Earl got me a gunsight bearing on Whitby that put us even more off track. Something was wrong.

I checked the DR compass; it was not operating properly. I checked the repeaters: they were going around in lazy circles and not all reading alike. I tried resetting the master compass twice–but to no avail. Danny tried to reset it but with the same negative result. By this time we were well over the North Sea, position not known exactly.

I quickly estimated where we were, gave Killer a new course to steer on the P4 compass, and asked him to reset his gyro. At this time, Gee was being jammed so badly we couldn't use it and even if it had been okay we were nearly out of range anyway.

It was a partly cloudy night, but some stars were visible. I hauled out the astro compass and set it up as quickly as I could. We were at about 55° north, so I set the correct angle and began looking for Polaris, the North Star. Fortunately there was a good break in the clouds and only one star anywhere near my line of sight. After some adjustments I confirmed the true course we were on. I reckoned we were now headed for the right place on the Danish coast. We would have to recheck our course against the North Star and reset the gyro every ten minutes or so for the rest of the trip.

We were just beginning to settle down and I was contemplating my next move when Killer reported that his Air Speed Indicator was now reading zero. There must have been moisture in the pitot tube and it I had frozen as we climbed. I wondered what would happen next. The API (Air Position Indicator) had not been working because of the duff compass. Killer had said that he could estimate the air speed within about ten knots by the throttle settings. There was little else we could do now unless we returned to base but we quickly discarded that idea. I told the crew that if we could just get a pinpoint on the Danish coast, we would be okay.

We droned on for what seemed like hours. Some of the crew members had become very apprehensive because of our lack of navigation aids and my resulting inability to determine our exact location. You could hear the tension in all their voices over the inter-com. I had lots of time to think and the words of my navigation instructor, F/O McBroom, at Portage AOS (Manitoba) came to mind:

"A navigator is never lost, he is merely sometimes a little less sure of his exact position."

These thoughts fitted me to a tee at that particular moment. With nothing much else to do except re-check the course whenever Polaris decided to show itself I reluctantly opened the case containing the sextant. I couldn't remember when I had last taken a star shot. I lined up Polaris first and took a shot noting the time. I picked out two other stars at different angles and repeated the procedure. I carefully plotted the three position lines making sure to advance the first and second lines to the time of the third.

The result was a large cocked hat (triangle). I carefully bisected the three angles and plotted a position about ten miles from where I thought we were. So much for astro navigation.

Tension mounted as we approached the coast of Denmark. Visibility was not the best and I had alerted Johnny to keep his eyes skinned about ten minutes before we were due to cross as I needed a pinpoint badly. "I see the coast", Johnny yelled excitedly over the inter-com. "We are crossing it now". He couldn't get me a pinpoint but at least I had a roughly north-south position line and was able to calculate a fairly accurate ground speed.

It was now time to watch for the east coast of Denmark. Again no pinpoint but at least a time of crossing. I took the elapsed time and put that distance in nautical miles on my dividers. I then took the dividers and ran them up and down Denmark on my chart. I did it twice to make sure; there was only one place that fit, so I decided that this *had* to be where we crossed.

I dead-reckoned ahead to the last turning point before the target, and gave Killer a new course to steer. I felt confident now. I had also found that we were three minutes early so as soon as we reached the turning point and headed south toward Kiel, I asked Killer for a three-minute dogleg, in order to waste time. We did the standard 60° port, 120° starboard; then back on course. I was now sure we were headed directly for the target.

The weather had cleared considerably and we could see lots of stars. Off to starboard perhaps thirty or forty miles away, we could see fires and searchlights. Someone asked if that could be the target, but I reckoned it must be Flensburg. I remembered that at the briefing we had been told of a spoof or small diversionary raid there.

"No. We still have five minutes to go; the target should be dead ahead."

Our assigned bombing altitude was 21,000 feet, but we were still at 20,000 and unable to climb higher. I had begun to count down ... *three minutes... two minutes ... and ... one minute... If we don't see markers in the next fifteen seconds we'll have to orbit.*

Just then white flares went down in front of us followed almost immediately by a string of red TIs (Target Indicators). Immediately over the radio came the voice of the Master Bomber.

"Bomb on the red TIs."

"Steady. Steady. Steady. Bombs gone."

We'd done it. I was emotionally exhausted and elated at the same time. As soon as our load had gone, the aircraft jumped up to twenty-one thousand feet. We had made our altitude at last.

The mood of the crew had noticeably changed for the better. The flak had started and searchlights came on but somehow it did not seem to bother us now. The most important thing on our minds was that we had got to the target and dropped our bombs and now we were getting out. We followed our flight plan courses through the target area and on to the next leg and finally headed for home.

It had been a navigator's nightmare. We returned to base without further incident, landed and went to de-briefing, or interrogation as we sometimes called it. We told our story.

The CO heard it and said, "*I would have turned back*".

# N.G. "DOC" GORDON

*Born and educated in Halifax, Nova Scotia, Doc Gordon enlisted in the RCAF in April 1939 at twenty years of age. In 1942 he received his pilot wings, and was in Britain by October 1943 where he completed his operational training. Doc reported to 158 Squadron in September 1944, and during his tour of operations he was awarded the DFC. After the war S/Ldr Gordon continued his career with the RCAF at home and overseas until 1965, when he served the Ontario Ministry of Labour until he retired to Victoria in 1977.*

## Memories of a Bomber Pilot

The passage of time has a way of mellowing one's memories so that only the highlights or pleasant recollections remain. Events of twenty years ago often become blended together and it becomes more difficult as the years pass to separate them or to vouch for their accuracy.

Though this be true, I still regard the twenty months spent in England, beginning in October 1943, as the best years of my life.

The trip overseas via Boston, New York, and Greenock was a thrill to a young man of twenty-five who, prior to this, had done very little travelling. The introduction to the English way of life was quite pleasant, even under wartime conditions. Perhaps war added spice to the whole experience.

Upon settling in at Bournemouth, I discovered that my previous aircrew training was destined to influence my future and extend my stay in this beautiful south coast town. Prior to this I had been destined for service with Coastal Command but as I was single-engine trained and because there was no shortage of trained pilots, no operational unit wished to spend the time required to convert a replacement pilot. Thus it was that I found myself one of fourteen pilots reporting to RAF Station Kidlington, near Oxford, where we soon learned that we were to undergo training for service in Bomber Command. Many months were to pass while we struggled to master the art of flying multi-engined aircraft. We still had to experience flight in the Whitley at Kinloss and Hallie II at Rufforth spaced by a short "invigorating" stay at Acaster Malbis to attend a survival course.

It was 20 September 1944. I can recall the journey to Lissett quite vividly, undoubtedly because we were so pleased to be on our way to join an operational squadron; it meant we had at last arrived. As the newest members of 158 Squadron, we soon found we were in the advance guard of replacement aircrews that would, eventually, upset the aircrew balance to the point where the majority of crews on this RAF station were Canadian. During the next two days we were allotted billets and given a familiarization flight in a Hallie III. On 27 September we had our baptism of fire during a raid on Calais.

The attack was carried out without opposition from the enemy, but being novices we created our own thrills. The briefing had directed that the bombing run be executed at nine thousand feet from seaward. Poor reception prevented our hearing the Master-Bomber's instruction "Basement 5" until we had arrived directly over the target above a solid cloud layer. After a few moments of indecision concerning the meaning of this order, we began a descending 180° turn toward the target and emerged from the base of the cloud cover with the fortress at Calais directly ahead. We had just enough time to release our bombs and alter course to avoid the mainstream of bombers approaching from the west. Having stumbled through our first trip, we felt we were ready for ops.

I have always been thankful that RAF operational training was of the highest possible calibre. I rate this as the chief reason for our successful, if not uneventful, tour of operations. Having said that, I recall an incident that occurred early in our tour when we found ourselves sitting on top of a cone of searchlights. I quickly realized I had not been trained for this and that a drastic change in course, speed and altitude was needed. The manoeuvre can best be described as a stall, sliding off into a steep dive. The procedure may have been unorthodox, but it worked. Needless to say, it became standard practice for this crew.

Things were never boring on operations. Even if there was no enemy opposition during a trip, it was essential that everyone be on the alert for enemy fighters or our own bombers, as sometimes the traffic became very heavy, especially at turning points or over the target area. Judging by the number and variety of demoralizing devices introduced into the air battle toward the end of 1944, it was evident the German was an ingenious fellow who could be counted upon to key your interest. Although these devices did not achieve their intended purpose, they were distracting and you could never be sure whether or not they were lethal objects.

Many crews lived through nerve-wracking experiences, suffering injury and misfortune of every kind, but we were more fortunate. Aside from the usual encounters with flak and enemy aircraft, the possibility of collision with one of our own aircraft constituted the greatest danger. It was our good fortune to have received only minor damage from enemy action and we were lucky enough to emerge from two encounters with other aircraft. The first, with an Fw190, occurred on 14 March 1945 as we were leaving Hamburg on a night raid with the two aircraft flying opposing courses. I'll never know why we did not collide or why that fighter pilot didn't fire his guns, especially as we would have been silhouetted against the fires in the target areas. The second incident or near miss involved a Lanc, and it too occurred at night. The identity of this aircraft will never be known, but from its location and direction of flight, I assumed it was a radar-screen aircraft.

Not all aircraft losses resulted from enemy action or adverse weather conditions; human error often played its part. Those who lived through an incident of this nature learned a vivid lesson and could later laugh at their stupidity or carelessness. I believe every crew was guilty of at least one error of this nature during their tour of operations. Ours occurred on 5 March 1945 during our return flight from Chemnitz, a long trip for a Halifax. Our briefing was normal but it did include a warning to stay well away from Frankfurt and Mainz on our return flight because the ack-ack defences in the area had been greatly strengthened.

Having left our target well behind, we continued to follow our flight plan, which included several changes of height and direction. Then, while maintaining five thousand feet, the lowest of our assigned altitudes, our aircraft lurched to port. A cockpit check revealed that the port outer throttle had disconnected. I instructed my flight engineer to feather the port outer and I applied power to the three remaining engines. This action caused ice to break free of the propellers and strike the fuselage. I immediately activated the pilot's de-icing pump to clear the windscreen; however the gremlins were at it again. The plunger came free in my hand and released a stream of de-icing fluid up my arm. My wireless op was presented with this problem and soon the flow of fluid was stopped. While this was going on, the aircraft again veered to port. The cause was evident. The solution: unfeather the port outer and feather the port inner. Simple, except that the propeller would not respond and we were left with a windmilling prop.

This mishap, compounded by the ice we carried, prevented our climbing to an ice-free zone, and therefore our only alternative was to descend below the cloud base.

My navigator and bomb-aimer were busily assessing our situation relative to the rest of the stream when I requested information relating to the height of the terrain along our track. The answer was *three hundred* so I began my descent and levelled off just beneath the cloud at 1200 feet. The ice began to melt and we settled down to our trip back to base.

It was not long before both gunners came on the intercom to announce that they could see trees. I opened my cockpit window and peered into the night, but could see nothing. Almost immediately thereafter, we cleared a ridge and found ourselves directly over Frankfurt and Mainz. It seems their defences were not prepared for our visit; we saw only a few searchlights and no shots were fired. I immediately sought shelter in the clouds and continued to climb to our next assigned height. All the while we were falling farther behind the bomber stream and had become, in effect, a sitting duck. I decided to return to the safety of the clouds, hoping that the icing condition had diminished. We soon found it hadn't, and once more our only recourse was to descend. The elevation of the terrain was checked and this time it was reported to be *three hundred and fifty*.

For a second time we found ourselves flying just beneath the cloud base at approximately 1200 feet. This time the gunners, supported by the flight engineer, became disturbed and reported that they could now see even the hedgerows. From my vantage point the ground was not visible, but directly ahead I could see two lights that resembled unshaded windows in a Frenchman's cottage. This was nothing unusual now that the front had moved far to the east and I remarked sarcastically, "I'll show you just how low we are". Then I turned the aircraft toward the lights. As we approached, the lights suddenly veered to my port side. They were, without doubt, the headlights of a vehicle whose passengers must have thought their time had arrived. This incident brought me to my senses with the realization that I had accepted the reported elevation of the terrain as being measurements in feet rather than in metres. Just how close we had come to parking on a point of high ground we will never know.

This macabre trip was not over yet. Later on, as we approached the French coast, I instructed my wireless op. to send a message to base to advise them we were more than half an hour late. This was a precaution to prevent our own ack-ack batteries from using Halifax Friday the 13th for target practice. Now it was his turn to blunder: instead of sending his message as we crossed the French coast, he was waiting for word that we'd reached the English coast. By this time tempers were becoming a little ragged, which is understandable in the circumstances. Fortunately, this was the only occasion during our tour when we were not all pulling together.

No one had spoken for some time and I was concerned as to where we would make our landfall in the Dover area. Not wishing to invite the wrath of the "office" by questioning their navigation, I tuned in on the emergency or Darky frequency in the hope that I'd obtain my own fix. Instead I was startled to hear operatic music followed by the deep voice of a German announcer. Slight though the incident seems, it was sufficiently disconcerting to cause me to check my compass heading and turn off the receiver in the hope that the crew had not heard it.

About this time we received orders to divert to an RAF station at Blackbushe, not far from London. The area was experiencing heavy rain and, as we approached Blackbushe, visibility was extremely poor, so much so that I had trouble seeing the glide-path indicators. At this stage of the flight, de-icer fluid was the last thing on anyone's mind. Only when we neared the perimeter on our final approach did we realize that the stuff had vaporised and condensed on every window and glass panel in the cockpit. It was then that my bomb-aimer improved my view of the runway with one swipe of his hand. Moments later we touched down. I assure you it was not one of my better landings.

Friday the 13th, Halifax III of 158 Squadron, completed 118 operational flights. It was reconstructed after the war and

Photograph courtesy of Donnie MacFarlane.
Copyright: Jo Jameson, Irthlingborough, Northants

When we got out of the aircraft, we saw that a large piece of Perspex was missing from the radome. We found the broken pieces inside the radome and could only surmise that we had struck a chimney pot whilst we were flying low over the Continent, or perhaps some object on our rather erratic final approach at Blackbushe.

After a cup of tea laced with rum and a cigarette, we got over our show of temper and laughed at our own stupidity, as I have done so many times since.

There is one other experience associated with operations that is quite vivid in my memory, aside from the recollection of seeing one thousand bombers forming up for a raid. This was the exhilaration I experienced whenever I became the target of "predicted flak". Relying on knowledge of the time required for the German gun-layers to react to their radar information and fire six shots, we would begin flying an erratic course, changing direction every thirty seconds in an attempt to avoid serious damage or destruction. The suspense would be broken repeatedly by the appearance of six bursts of flak where you had been a few seconds before; that is if you had any luck at all. This form of Russian roulette would continue until you were out of range of the battery in question and had settled back on course.

I am sure every pilot thought his crew as the best crew that ever graced an English pub. Me, I am convinced that Friday-the-Thirteenth's crew were good types who were extremely proficient in their fields and completely compatible. Our teamwork was 100 per cent both in the air and on the ground. The exception, of course, has to be the sortie to Chemnitz.

Although we were stationed at Lissett for only six months, we met many Yorkshiremen and enjoyed the friendship of the people of Bridlington and surrounding countryside, who warmly included us in their social activities. Life between ops was not unlike that which we had led while undergoing training in various parts of Britain. We were well paid, young and single. We studied and worked hard, but on our time off or during leave periods we sought entertainment and relaxation at dances and in pubs, wherever we were located. That wonderful institution, the English pub, in addition to being the local watering hole, was the social centre of the district. One was always sure of good company there. I believe every Canadian serviceman who served in England reserves a soft spot in his heart for his favourite pub and the friends he made there.

# PETER W. LAKE

*Peter joined the RAF in 1941, aged twenty, and received his Wireless Operator/Air Gunner brevet in September 1942. After completing operational training he was sent to the Middle East in March 1943 to join 203 Squadron flying Baltimores. At the end of that year, the Squadron converted to Wellingtons and moved to India, where Peter completed his tour. Peter returned to the Middle East briefly (Cairo) before returning to the UK to serve with Transport Command. He returned to India with 48 Squadron.*

In September 1940 the RAF was advertising for aircrew. I applied, passed my medical, was sworn into the RAFVR, and was accepted for pilot/navigator training. On 13 January '41 I was on my way to Babbacombe, Devon. This was a great revelation for me, joining in with a crowd of fellows my own age.

At ITW I ploughed the navigator's exams and was remustered to Wireless/Air Gunner training. No leave, straight off to Blackpool to learn Morse code. What a new lifestyle this was. Met guys from all over the world, including the son of an earl – he even had a castle and his own apartment in Blackpool complete with bar. The Winter Gardens, the bars, monster dance floors, a palace, were just other worlds for me and all very exciting.

The place was flooded with girls from mills and factories. Wow!

When I had completed the wireless course, off I went to Felixstowe, a pre-war flying boat station. Very cold on the exposed coastline. Huge 80-foot cranes to lift seaplanes out of the water. The Schneider-Trophy planes were housed here pre-war when not competing. Then off I went to a gunnery course in Pembrey, South Wales, and on 19 September 1942 I graduated as a Wireless Operator/Air Gunner. We were offered a choice of Hampdens or Beauforts; I chose Beauforts. Then off to Turnberry to 5 OTU where I crewed up with a pilot, navigator, and W/AG, all in their late twenties. Then to TTU (Torpedo Training Unit) and finally to Portreath in Cornwall for despatch overseas.

We flew to Gibraltar, a seven hour thirty five minute flight, and landed with fuel for only five minutes. Then on to Cairo where we lost our Beaufort to another crew headed for Malta. My crew travelled five days by truck convoy to Benghazi. There were three airfields there called Berka I, II & III. My squadron, 203, flew Baltimores from Berka III and in our first week or so we were busy converting. We flew our first operational flight on 15 April 1943, a daylight sortie over the Aegean. On the way out we flew at wave-top height; I discovered all our ops would be below 5000 ft and often at virtually zero altitude.

The Baltimore was a noisy aircraft for the gunner, especially the earlier Marks I & II which had no gun turrets. Camp facilities were primitive. Our tent lines were in a direct line off the end of the runway. We had a couple of near misses.

One time, a Blenheim overshot the runway and hit the ground between the tent line, breaking an olive tree then bouncing over the tents and crashing into a parked Baltimore and catching fire. Amazingly, the crew got out relatively untouched.

Another time, a Halifax undershot the runway, and when he was over our tents opened up all four engines in a deafening roar and landed on the grass just at the end of the tent lines. Then a Liberator took off from Berka II across the road and its engines caught fire. He too crash landed at the end of our row of tents and his nose wheel collapsed. It flipped on its back and blew up. We got some crew members out, but not all. Don't ask why we didn't move the tents; I don't know.

Dust storms played havoc with the engines. We had our starboard engine cut on take-off; we just made it to the grass at the end of the runway, ground looped and walked away. Two days later, after maintenance said it was now OK, another crew took it off. The starboard engine again cut, and they pranged just off the field. It caught fire and both W/AGs died from their burns.

We always carried pigeons, and one crew had them to thank for their survival. They had to ditch in the late evening, and our search aircraft could not find them. Next morning, pigeons arrived with a message and their position and they were picked up. We lost some crews who just never came back. Six aircraft were lost on one sortie, and only one crew survived. Except for those times when we did formation bombing all our sorties were solo. Enemy fighters in that area were mostly Ju88s, Arado156s and Me109s.

In October 1943 just after a short leave in Alexandria and although our tour was only two-thirds done, the squadron was posted to Santa Cruz, India. We converted to Wellingtons, and our old crew got broken up. I completed my operational tour having made sixty sorties of average time five hours each.

I was sent back to Cairo to do a wireless instructor's course. I came home by boat for leave and was then posted to 108 OTU Transport Command to fly the DC3. Whilst I was at OTU the war ended. I celebrated VE Day in Loughborough; it was pretty wild. At the end of OTU I was posted back to the Far East: Karachi, Baroda, Calcutta, then on to join 48 (Dakota) Squadron. at Chittagong in the NW corner of Burma. *See map on page 56.*

I was off duty for two weeks getting physiotherapy following a bad fall when my crew, with a substitute W/AG, was detailed for a supply drop. The pilot said the load was too heavy and some of it should be taken off, but no one paid any attention. On take-off, just airborne, the port engine cut and they hit the deck. In a ground loop the port propeller sheared off and slammed through the fuselage. It killed the W/AG. The aircraft caught fire. Both pilots got out, as did the navigator, but he was badly burned and hospitalized for ages. He never flew again.

My demob number came up at the end of January 1946 at which point I had completed 21 sorties of a second tour. I was sent to Mingladon, Rangoon, to get a flight to Singapore. After days and days of waiting a flight came through; unfortunately it was late on a day when a big delivery of beer arrived in Mingladon and the pilot refused to let me board. So I went to Singapore by boat and India rum. Then on by Union Castle to old Blighty's shore" and a demob suit

# ROBERT N. GOURLIE

*Bob was born and raised in Toronto, joined the RAF in 1940 and took his pilot training in Britain. He completed a tour in the Middle East with Bomber Command's 70 Squadron; then in 1942 it was back to UK as an instructor. In '43 he was back on Ops, this time with 420 Squadron, still flying Wimpeys. The squadron was transferred to Middle East in mid-tour. He later transferred to the RCAF and served on 437 Squadron. Post-war, Bob achieved a degree in law and practised in BC. Bob was awarded the DFC for his exploits.*

## Hammering the Enemy in the Middle East

This is my story; this is my song. I was attending Forest Hills High School in Toronto in 1940 when the RAF sent a board to Canada to recruit aircrew before the Empire Air Training Scheme had become effective. The RAF was desperately short of aircrew at the time. Half a dozen of us were inveigled to England, where I immediately started the arduous course of becoming a pilot. My elementary training was on Tiger Moths, and my service flying training at Grantham was on Oxfords.

A problem with flying training in England in 1941 was that during night flying, intruders would invade the circuit and fellow students would be shot down while doing circuits and bumps. This was decidedly unsporting. On the night that I went solo on Oxfords, I was on the final leg coming in for a landing when the entire flare

147

path in front of me went up like a row of geysers. A Jerry in the circuit had unleashed a string of bombs. As a student I was somewhat upset, not having been told by my instructor what do in such a case. I certainly didn't want to get back in the circuit with intruders about. I therefore landed parallel to the string of bomb holes and taxied away from the runway. I stopped engines, got out onto the grass, and stayed there until the All Clear. Fortunately neither the aircraft nor I was damaged. I was congratulated by the CFI for taking appropriate action, but disconcerted when he said, "Wizard show, Canada! We thought you had gone for a Burton."

I received my pilot wings and a commission in the RAF in July 1941 and converted to Wellington Ic's at 15 OTU, Harwell. I was then posted to the Middle East via Hampstead Norreys, where preparations were made for the long flight to Egypt. In those days we flew first from the UK to Gibraltar. And since the enemy controlled both coasts of the Med, we flew down the centre, making landfall at Cape Bon before setting course for the short hop to Malta. The objective was always to land there about one hour before sun-up because the enemy started bombing at dawn. But Malta is a pretty small place; it was always possible to miss it and find oneself over Sicily. From Malta we flew direct to Kabrit in the Canal Zone (Egypt), where 70 Squadron was based. I did this trip on several occasions, taking replacement aircraft to the squadron.

We were losing a large number of aircraft to Ju88 long-range fighters over the Bay of Biscay. Those in command therefore stipulated that we take off from UK at 0200 or 0300, be over the Bay by sun-up, and then follow the Portuguese coast to Gibraltar. From a sprog point of view this was somewhat shaky. The weather at Portreath was often rotten, take-off was over a thousand-foot cliff, the Bay was always rough, and I found it difficult to sleep before the trip.

The take-off aerodrome for the Middle East was Portreath. On one occasion, a navigational error led us to miss Portreath and land at a small fighter 'drome nearby. When we took off again, we clipped a blockhouse at the end of the runway, which resulted in the propellers slowly disintegrating. The tower at Portreath plagued us with red Very pistol flares and we found ourselves in the middle of a mass of gliders. I had to land and there was no hope of making a circuit. Fortunately the gliders pulled aside and we went up the middle, without incident except for our damaged propellers.

I joined the squadron in Egypt in December 1941. Although our main base was at Kabrit on the Great Bitter Lake, we operated from various landing grounds, LG104, LG105, LG117 etc., in the eastern part of the great Sahara desert. Accommodation was dug-in tent, canvas chair, canvas washbasin, and canvas bathtub. The food was foul, fresh food non-existent, and water scarce. But there was plenty of booze. *See map inside back cover. Kabrit is on the Suez Canal.*

Our main task was to interdict supplies on their way to the Afrika Corps, which meant continually bombing Benghazi. At other times we flew in support of the Eighth Army, raiding tank columns and enemy landing grounds from a low height. Once in a while we paid a visit to Greece.

We were involved in the seesaw battles in the desert, chaotic situations, moving to forward strips when the Eighth Army advanced and scurrying back, usually without my kit, when the army retreated. One beautiful June morning in 1942, after we had been flying all night, an army motorcycle rider rushed into the mess in the middle of breakfast to tell us the Afrika Corps had broken through and was fifteen minutes away on the coast road. We had no time to refuel the aircraft, but since we were only about an hour from Kabrit and it was necessary to save the aircraft, we dashed for them. Those of the ground crew who could make it piled in with me, and we made it back to Kabrit in one piece. The ground crew who failed to get on the plane mostly ended up in the bag.

We appeared to have a gentleman's agreement with the enemy; one night we would bomb their airfield at Halfaya Pass, and the next night play host to a Do17 whose bombs did no harm, since the holes were quickly filled in by the Africans. Now and again, on returning from a night operation, we would be plagued by intruding Ju88s in the circuit. As a result we lost many good aircraft and experienced crews. Aircrew were buried at a military burial ground at El Daba; no coffins, just a blanket. To keep from letting the funerals get us down we followed each of them with one hell of a wake.

This was unlike Bomber Command's war in Europe: we had close contact with the enemy; we flew at five or ten thousand feet not twenty thousand; and in general we fought a more gentlemanly war. The RAF had long experience in desert warfare in Afghanistan, Mesopotamia and the Persian Gulf area, but conditions were still rough.

I had completed my tour just before El Alamein and boarded a troop ship for the UK. The next day panic ensued and all pilots on board were disembarked. I returned to my squadron where I found great confusion, with a new CO and two new flight commanders with very little desert experience. We again bivouacked in dug-in tents in very primitive conditions. We had a detachment of African troops whose main job was to dig the tents in to a depth of three feet and fill the bomb holes in the runway.

During the battle the squadron was engaged day and night without respite. I was eventually shot up by a Ju88 night fighter. With one engine on fire, and the aircraft full of holes, but with the controls still working, I had no trouble making the twenty-minute flight to an RAF base at the foot of the Pyramids, where I landed wheels up. I did not realize what a narrow escape I'd had until the ground crew told me the controls would have become defunct in another five minutes

Finally I was issued with civilian clothes and a passport and sent back to the UK on a BOAC flying boat. The flight took us into deepest Africa: Stanleyville, Leopoldville, and Lagos. Unfortunately I picked up malaria (second dose) at Stanleyville, was disembarked at Lagos, put into a bed at the transit camp beside the airport, and forgotten. The malaria proceeded on its merry course, with me appearing to be in a state of extreme intoxication, and unable to walk. After a month I was found by the British authorities and taken to a hospital in Lagos, where I was given very heavy doses of the worst tasting drug (liquid quinine) in the world. It worked. I finally got my health back.

I arrived back in the UK in September 1942 and was posted as a staff pilot and instructor at 15 OTU, Wing. We had a number of very old Whitleys, Wellingtons, Lysanders, Defiants, and Ansons. Accidents and funerals abounded.

In April I was posted to 420 Squadron in 6 Group at Middleton St. George. The RCAF was busy Canadianizing their squadrons (approximately twelve) and were collecting Canadians in the RAF. I was made deputy flight commander. We were still on Wellingtons, but had an improved version, the Mk X. Losses were very high.

FROZEN OVER DUISBURG

It was the custom in 6 Group for a pilot who had been screened and was now going back on ops to be asked to do his first trip as second pilot in order to get acclimatized. Thus it was that on my first op in the European theatre, I nearly got the chop over Duisburg. Flak was intense. Searchlights everywhere, though not the radar-controlled blue "master" light. (I think they were introduced later.) We completed the bombing run. Why weren't we getting out of there—fast? We were circling the target. The navigator and W/AG noticed something was terribly wrong. The W/AG grabbed his helmet and clipped on his 'chute pack. We "spoke to" the captain. He didn't answer. He was frozen at the controls with a glazed look in his eyes. The three of us—navigator, gunner, and I—had a terrible time unstrapping him and dragging him from his seat. All the time we were coned. The light was blinding, the flak was deafening, and the stink of cordite rasped at out throats. I put the old Wimpey into a great dive so steep I didn't know if she would ever come out of it. But we shook the searchlights and the old girl held together.

I did a number of trips out of Middleton St. George to such places as Frankfurt, Stuttgart, and Mannheim—mostly to the Ruhr. Losses were very high, and just when all seemed hopeless, with most of us believing we would not see the end of it all, somebody upstairs took notice. Policy concerning deployment of Wimpeys changed and three squadrons. (419, 420, and 425) were posted to North Africa under G/C Dunlap, later to become the Chief of the Air Staff, RCAF. No. 420 went to a place near Tunis and Kairowan (a holy city of the Arabs).

Unlike the RAF, which had stations all over the world, the RCAF knew little of desert campaigning. An airstrip was just bulldozed out of the raw sand. We lived under the most primitive conditions. There was just a mess tent with bomb cases for chairs. Food was mostly fried Spam and fried bread. Water tasted foul, ice was non-existent, and liquor scarce. We ended up being lousy, as well. Unlike at the landing grounds I had known in the Western Desert, we had no African labourers. The RAF and army tried to fill in the best they could, but conditions remained austere.

Despite the conditions, we were on operations immediately in support of the invasion of Sicily. We raided aerodromes and some of the larger cities from low altitude and night after night we struck at the troops as they fled across the Straits of Messina. I didn't think we did too much damage, but we dropped flares that scared hell out of the enemy, who would jump into the water in what appeared to be panic.

We took on Italian targets: Naples, Viterbo, Bagnalio, Taranto and Pompeii. Taranto was difficult since it housed the Italian battle fleet and the flak barrages were as bad as I had seen in the Ruhr. On one trip there we took Group Captain Dunlap with us, since he made a practice of flying with each of his squadrons. We were coned. With the whole Italian battle fleet shooting at us, we took violent evasive action, and brought our Groupie back in one piece.

One night in September 1943 we had completed a raid on Naples, and by four o'clock in the morning were off the island of Pantelleria, with 'George' steering the plane toward our base at Pavillier. There was a hell of a bang. The port engine was on fire, feathering did no good, and the throttle was ineffective. My rear gunner opened up, saying he saw what looked like a Ju88, and I took evasive action. I saw nothing. Then the other engine got rough and started smoking. There was no hope of making base. Before us was a dried-up lake, about ten by twenty miles in size; if we had to make a wheels-up landing, that was the place. I could not maintain altitude on one engine. Fortunately the engine fire died, but gas was pouring out. Nobody was injured except the bomb aimer who had a bad fracture above the knee and was in agony; we broke out the first-aid kit and gave him morphine. *See map inside back cover. Bob landed in Tunisia.*

When we looked at the aircraft at daybreak, we found the port engine and wing full of holes and assumed a night fighter had done the foul deed. We were not sure if it had been that or mechanical trouble, since the port engine would not feather and the vibration was so bad bits of the fuselage were flying off.

In the morning we were surrounded by Arabs demanding what was left of the aircraft. Since we all carried sidearms, we had a quick conference. Should we fight and almost certainly get our throats cut or should we give the aircraft to the Arabs? After all, it was a total wreck with its back broken. We decided to give our goolie chits and the aircraft to the Arabs. They were grateful, and took us under their care until the Long Range Desert Group rescued us a week later. Aircraft flew over every night, and we shot off the colours of the day, but I suppose the planes were too high to see us. We also worked the emergency Gibson Girl transmitter, but it was quite ineffective.

I went on to finish the tour. As usual on every operation we were subject to flak, searchlights and sometimes fighters. On our way to bomb an airfield at Battipaglia on a beautiful Mediterranean night we

الى كل عربى كريم

السلام عليكم ورحمة الله وبركاته وبعد ، فحامل هذا الكتاب ضابط بالجيش
البريطانى وهو صديق وفيّ لكافة الشعوب العربية فنرجو أن تعاملوه بالعطف والاكرام .
وأن تحافظوا على حياته من كل طارىء ، ونأمل عند الاضطرار أن تقدموا
له ما يحتاج اليه من طعام وشراب .
وأن ترشدوه الى أقرب معسكر بريطانى .
وسنكافئكم مالياً بسخاء على ما تسدونه اليه من خدمات .
والسلام عليكم ورحمة الله وبركاته ؟

القيادة البريطانية العامة فى الشرق .

To All Arab Peoples — Greetings and Peace be upon you.
The bearer of this letter is an Officer of the British Government
and a friend of all Arabs. Treat him well, guard him from harm,
give him food and drink, help him to return to the nearest British
soldiers and you will be rewarded. Peace and the Mercy of God
upon you.

The British High Command in the East.

## Useful Words.

| English | Arabic | | English | Arabic |
|---|---|---|---|---|
| English. | Ingleezi. | | | |
| English Flying Officer. | Za-bit Ingleezi Tye-yar. | | Water. | Moya. |
| Friend. | Sa-hib, Sa-deek. | | Food. | A'-kl. |

Take me to the English and you will be rewarded.
Hud-nee eind el Ingleez wa ta-hud re ka-fa.

2672/PMEB/2,000-2/42.

This chit was issued to Bob Gourlie to replace the one he gave to the Arabs in Tunisia

We carried "goolie chits" offering rewards to Arabs who returned shot-down airmen to the British forces. If a man had no goolie chit, hostile Arabs would send him to the harem. AMEN!

saw a great Allied fleet, with battleships, landing craft and all. Before we could get out of the way we were subjected to intense flak; apparently the IFF was not working.

On another occasion we were off the coast of Sicily, on our way westward toward Cape Bon when we found ourselves in the middle of a squadron of Italian Fiat 42 biplanes flying eastward. We didn' t exactly wave to each other, but they proceeded on their merry way and so did we. Was a Wimpey supposed to assume the role of a fighter in such circumstances?

The remainder of the war was an anticlimax. I was not keen to go back to the UK in the middle of winter; I knew what to expect from the weather and the food and I liked the desert climate and the way of life in colonial Africa. The rest of the wing all returned to the UK. I went to the Senior Air Staff Officer in Tunis, and told him I wished to go the other way, something that had seldom happened before. I ended up in Habbaniya in Iraq, where the aircraft reminded me of a museum; short and long-nosed Blenheims, Gladiators, Valentias and Bombays, nothing modern at all. The officers' mess, built on the lines of the RAF stations in India, was like a palace, but empty except for our puny outfit and sundry transients.

We led a pampered life with many servants serving us good food, including fruit and eggs, which made us mindful of the comparison between the RAF stations in the UK and their Indian version.

I was involved in a major crash in a worn-out Bombay aircraft. My left arm was severely cut up, and I was rushed to the military hospital in Cairo and then back to the UK to recover. That's when I found my rear gunner had been making more money than I and decided to transfer to the RCAF.

I retired in 1947, to go back to college. I loved the comradeship of the Air Forces, the RAF, the RCAF, and the USAAF, and I am proud to have served in the finest forces ever conceived by man.

# ED HUTTON

*Ted was born in St. James, Manitoba, on 28 June 1921 and enlisted in August 1942. He graduated as a navigator/bomb-aimer in October 1943 and completed a tour of ops with 433 Squadron. He returned to Canada, and was discharged in 1946.*

## A Piece of Cake

On 15 March 1945, we are relaxing in the lounge after lunch when the skipper comes in to tell us we are going on ops that evening. He says he has seen the target and it should be a piece of cake. He couldn't tell us where, but being our flight commander he has inside knowledge of the raid and we feel he has picked another good one for us. The target is Hagen, a city in the Ruhr Valley, not far from Dortmund. As Frankie and I finish marking our maps he turns to me and asks, "What do you think, Teddie?"

"It's in the centre of the Ruhr, but our lines aren't too far away. We'll just nip in, drop the load, and get out fast. A piece of cake."

The briefing over, Frankie, Freddie and I ride out to the dispersal in the same crew bus to do our pre-flight inspection checks. The standing rule is that none of the crew can enter the aircraft until the ground crew, who are doing their own pre-flight tasks, have left.

As we are leaving the vehicle the mid-upper gunner meets us; he is ashen-faced and has difficulty in speaking. All he can do is point to our aircraft T-Tom. On the tarmac, under the open bomb-bay doors, sits a four-thousand-pound blockbuster with 1550 incendiaries stacked around it.

It is customary for crews arriving at their aircraft to walk under the bomb bay to look at the load they are carrying. The air gunner, who was the first to arrive, had walked in under the fuselage for a look and had just stepped away when the whole load crashed to the ground.

Before leaving the plane after making his pre-flight inspections, the armourer should insert an insulating strip in the bomb-selection panel. This time, however, something went wrong. As an electrician left by the rear door, he turned the 'air-ground' switch to the 'flight' position. The 4000-pounder and the 1500 incendiaries took it as a "jettison" command and the whole lot tumbled to the ground.

Wib Pierce, our skipper, had driven up in his flight commander's van to find the aircraft and the area absolutely deserted. All around had taken off for the River Swale at speeds that would have left Olympic sprinters in the dust. One of them is later reported to have said, "If blood is yellow, I'm wounded." The mid-upper said that no matter how hard he tried to run he couldn't seem to get his legs moving. It was like being in a nightmare.

Fortunately, the ten-foot fall was not enough to arm the 'cookie' or the incendiaries. A tractor pulling a train of bomb-trollies was dispatched to the bomb dump to get a new load of bombs, with Pierce calling for haste so we could make the last allowable take-off time.

The skipper drove off to perform his duties as flight commander and returned to find an armament officer busy supervising the winching of the 4,000-pounder with a battered nose back into the bomb-bay.

"What are you doing?" Wib asks.

"Putting this bomb back in the aircraft."

"I don't want it on my aircraft."

"Well, we sure as hell don't want it on the station."

Time was moving on so the skipper conceded the point; but there was not enough time to load the incendiaries, so it was decided we would take off without them.

We got airborne at 1650. The evenings are getting brighter and we have daylight most of the way down through England, but it is dark by the time we've crossed the North Sea and are over the Continent. It's a clear night as we approach the Ruhr at 19,000 feet. Judging by the fires already started, the bombing appears to be well concentrated. Happy Valley is living up to its reputation of providing a hot reception. Hundreds of searchlights are sweeping the area and the sky is well saturated with exploding flak shells. The Pathfinders are busy dropping more coloured markers.

"Bomb doors open, skipper."

"Bomb doors open."

Fifteen seconds to go. We are flying straight and level; it is the most critical moment of the operation. With frightening suddenness a Lanc off our port side is hit. Flames stream back along its fuselage until the large aircraft turns into a fireball and finally plunges to the ground. You see it and know what it is, but even at this stage of our tour it still seems unreal.

I am all set to press the bomb release, when I see the dark form of a Halifax emerging from the darkness directly below us, crabbing across the aiming point. It receives a direct hit, hurling chunks of flaming debris in all directions. The force of the explosion rocks our aircraft violently, but the skipper quickly recovers the bombing run. I press the release. "Bomb gone", I shout, watching the blockbuster tumble toward the conflagration below. It's the second time that bomb has dropped from the belly of T-Tom, but this time it has gone for good.

With the flak exploding viciously around us and the sweeping searchlights hoping to ensnare an aircraft in their beams, the skipper does a masterful job of weaving out of the area. As we head for the coast, the fires of Hagen can be seen for a considerable distance.

Not until we have crossed the Allied lines do we allow ourselves a little relaxation. Cruising over Belgium, the tail gunner shouts, "Hey, skipper, those dumb bastards are shooting at us."

Of course we think he is kidding, but when some ack-ack shells begin bursting nearby, we can't believe it. We're over friendly territory.

"Shall I fire the colour of the day?" asks Freddie. The colour of the day cartridge is fired from a Very pistol located in the roof of the fuselage. The colour is changed each day and is the signal for friendly aircraft or one in distress.

"No! Don't let them know where we are."

"Jeez, two more just shot down."

The gunner calls out the bad news and a moment later reports that another aircraft has fired off the colour of the day.

"Tell me what happens," orders the skipper.

Within seconds the aircraft that identified itself is hit by artillery shells, spirals down in flames, and explodes on the ground. "Teddie, direct me to the open spaces," shouts the Skipper. As he puts on more speed, I switch on the H$_2$S set, directing him around built-up areas, keeping to open spaces. All this time, Freddie is shoving out bundles of window. These are strips of metal foil cut to a length that reflects the radar signals to the radar-operated guns and jams them. We don't feel secure until we are back over the Channel.

Four aircraft have been shot down by 'friendly fire'.

At debriefing, we beg an extra tot of rum from the padre and tell the skipper we don't want any more piece-of-cake ops.

Flying Time: seven hours, 30 minutes.

Before concluding I would like to relate one more incident.

After some twenty raids, the Air Force promoted our skipper to squadron leader and named him Flight Commander, 433 Squadron. His new responsibilities meant he could fly only three times a month rather the normal ten or eleven, thus pushing our screening date even further into the future. Crews who had arrived at Skipton after we had commenced our tour were finishing theirs and moving on to happier times.

The skipper wanted to avoid any criticism that he favoured his own crew and therefore bent over backwards to give short trips to the newer crews. During the month of February 1945 we flew only one op.

On 11 March 1945 we flew a daylight raid to Essen in the Ruhr and took along Group Captain Rutledge, Station Commander, as second dickie.

After completing the bombing run and heading for home, the skipper, unbeknownst to the crew, hands the controls over to the Groupie. We are not long into the flight home when Frankie, the navigator, calls, "Skipper, you're off course", and gives him a correction.

About half an hour later Frankie calls again, "Skipper, you've never done this before, but you keep straying from the course I'm giving you".

"Navigator, it's not your skipper. It's me and I'm handing the controls back to him."

"You'd better," says Frankie," I want to get home to-day."

Four nights later we flew our last op. The next day we went on leave and were 'screened'. We had flown thirty-four ops on our tour.

# DOUGLAS CROWE

*Doug was born in 1924. He enlisted in the RCAF in 1942, received his Air Gunner brevet and joined 626 Squadron in September 1944. Doug ended his operational tour via parachute in January 1945 and returned to Canada. He spent the balance of the war in Prince Rupert, and was demobbed. He re-enlisted the following year and served until 1974. He then opened his own business providing aids for handicapped people. In retirement, Doug still serves the handicapped–but now as a volunteer.*

## The Last Op

On 7 January 1945, after the usual preliminaries we and the rest of 12 and 626 Squadrons were briefed for a night raid on Munich. It would be our 24th sortie; our aircraft, Lancaster Mk1 (LL961 S2), faithful old Sugar 2, was loaded with a 4000-lb "cookie" and cans of 4lb incendiaries.

Our crew comprised:

F/O R Marshall Smith, pilot
F/O J Ken Yeamans, navigator
F/O Dave Rymer, bomb-aimer
Sgt Cyril Lane, flight engineer
F/Sgt Geoff Magee, wireless operator
F/Sgt Doug Crowe, mid-upper gunner
Sgt William. McLean, rear gunner

Four were RCAF, two RAF, and 1 RAAF. Our original crew of six RCAF and one RAF had changed. W/0 Abe Kerr, Wireless Operator, had finished his second tour on 29 December 1944 and been replaced by Geoff Magee, RAAF. Our original rear gunner, F/Sgt Earl Bock, had been killed on 22 October on the way home from laying mines in the Kattegat when a pair of Ju88s jumped us. The first time we met Bill McLean was when he attended the briefing. It wasn't the best way to meet a new crew member.

After a normal take-off at 1844 hrs we set course and proceeded on route as far as the third turning point. In the vicinity of Soissons we ran into heavy cumulo-nimbus cloud; the pilot turned to course 090° and started to climb to get above the cloud, as he could see clear sky to the east. When we had been on this course for two or three minutes the bomb-aimer observed the starboard navigation lights of an aircraft very close on the port side. This seems strange to me, as I don't ever recall seeing navigation lights on an aircraft in the main bomber stream.

Immediately after the sighting, there was an orange flash and we felt a heavy bump. We were now at 15,000 feet, ten to twelve miles north-east of track; time approximately 2015 hrs. Our aircraft went into a slow diving turn to port that the pilot was unable to control. The pilot then ordered us to abandon the aircraft and all the crew responded except the rear gunner. The navigator, bomb-aimer and flight engineer left by way of the front hatch; the wireless operator and I left by the rear door.

The five of us landed in a semicircle after a long descent. By bailing out in the midst of a cumulo-nimbus cloud we were caught in the updraft and at times went up instead of down. The navigator, who was always aware of the time, took forty-five minutes to reach ground; the rest of us got down in about thirty minutes. By the time we reached ground the aircraft had crashed and was on fire. Following standard procedures we each headed away from the crash site. I had landed in an open field surrounded on all four sides by trees. On this cold January day the ground was covered in snow. I hid my 'chute in the trees and covered it with snow. I did not know exactly where I was but did know it was close to the front lines. I looked around the field for a way out and found a fence and gate. The lane led to a small village. I think it was called *Vorsges*. I met some French farmers who befriended me and invited me into their home. A short time later the village priest arrived; I had already found his church and had a look around in case I needed shelter. Shortly after the priest's arrival a US Army vehicle arrived with two servicemen who took me to a US Military traffic control point. The control point's job was to direct traffic to its correct destinations. At the control point, the navigator, wireless operator and flight engineer joined me. Our names were forwarded to SHAEF who notified the squadron that we were alive.

In the meantime the bomb-aimer had landed near another village and been taken to SHAEF HQ in Rheims, where he had been debriefed.

Following our debriefing at SHAEF we were taken to the RAF-occupied airport at Juvincourt to await transport back to the UK and our squadron. Juvincourt was an RAF advanced emergency field containing a miscellaneous lot of aircraft in various states of disrepair. The RAF technicians were repairing some to fly again and taking parts from near-useless ones to make other aircraft serviceable. We were told that a transport would arrive some day to take us back to the squadron, but there was no fixed schedule and we would just have to wait. We were there six days when a USAAF Dakota came in with a USAAF Colonel and staff as the only passengers. Our navigator met the pilot and arranged for the five of us to return to the UK with them.

When we arrived at the US Base at Stansted, we were taken to the local railway station and left to fend for ourselves. Have you ever tried to board a British train without any money or a ticket or to leave a station without one? We got to London and spent the weekend there by courtesy of the Returned Aircrew Unit.

There is a difference of opinion as to what happened to our aircraft to cause it to go out of control. What I have told so far is from the official record; however, there is another story. The US troops around the area where we came down had been firing AA guns at some aircraft thinking they were Jerries. Did one of those shots hit us by mistake?

The official record states that our aircraft was headed for the town of Laon when "a burst of power enabled the aircraft to clear the town and crash into the railway cutting (2 miles SW at 2030 hours) where it burst into flames and finally blew up at 2100 hrs." The pilot's body was found 50 feet from the wreck, still wearing his unopened 'chute.

We, his crew, tried to get an award for Marsh Smith for his selfless act, but we were unsuccessful. Not even a DFC was awarded. As for the rear gunner, his turret was not with the aircraft wreckage and as far as I know has never been found.

# CHARLES PLEWMAN

*Charles comes from County Kildare, in Ireland. He enlisted in the RCAF in 1941 and earned his Observer/Navigator brevet in early 1942. Charlie joined 98 (Mitchell) Squadron in September 1942 and completed his first tour of ops. He became an instructor at 13 OTU, Bicester, and in November 1944, after enjoying leave in Canada, he went back on 98 Squadron and completed a second tour. Charlie was demobbed in September 1945.*

## Human Error

My grand-daughter left home a couple of years ago at the age of eighteen to live with her boyfriend. When I tried to talk her out of it, she declared that she had to make her own mistakes.

Then I thought back to some of the mistakes I had made in my life. As I am now seventy-nine years old, you can safely guess that there were quite a few. But one incident in particular stands out in my memory.

I was stationed at 13 OTU, RAF Bicester. On the morning of the first thousand-bomber raid we were ordered to "sweep the seas" between England and the European mainland, searching for downed aircraft or survivors.

We flew Blenheim IVs, with a crew of three: pilot, observer, and wireless operator. We saw something yellow on the water from five thousand feet. On the way down to get a closer look, our pilot noticed his airspeed had dropped from 180 to 140 mph. He asked me for a course back to England.

"Two-seventy degrees; due west."

A few minutes later I noticed the coast coming up and asked the wireless operator to get me a radio fix. I thought this would look nice in my navigational log. Suddenly I realized we should not be reaching land so soon. I checked my bombsight (an old model even for 1942) and found that we were flying east instead of west. I told my pilot that we must be approaching the Dutch coast and that we should turn back immediately. He would'nt believe me. I handed him a landing compass that had been secured to the wall.

We were by now crossing the coast and dead ahead was an aerodrome with loads of fighters, every one bearing swastika markings. Without delay we circled the aerodrome and turned back towards England. We were very lucky. Nobody shot at us. It was breakfast time there, and I guess they'd had a busy night

We were still flying at 140 mph. The wireless operator reported his fix, and it confirmed our location over the enemy aerodrome. It also told base where we were, much to our embarrassment. Wouldn't you know, though, that the Blenheim, like a horse returning to the barn, increased its speed as we reached the coast of England. We altered course to fly to our base, found it, and landed.

At debriefing I was blamed for not checking my pilot's course quickly enough. I was also told in no uncertain terms that my life was expendable, but that the RAF could not afford to lose another aircraft. The aircraft was checked out and found airworthy.

Unfortunately the crew that took the same aircraft out that afternoon were not as lucky as we were. They crashed. The experience of this trip cemented the relationship of our crew. We went forward to complete a tour of operations on Mitchells with 98 Squadron RAF.

My granddaughter may not be as lucky as we were. She is expecting her first child in the next few weeks, and the boy friend is gone. Fortunately for her she still has family support to help her to adjust her compass heading.

Sometimes it is by making mistakes that we learn to deal with life's flak.

# RAY BARBER

*Ray was born in Yorkshire on 24 October 1916 at a time when his father had just returned to the battlefield in France. Ray joined the Bradford City police and was thus in a reserved occupation. In 1943 the rules changed and he had the opportunity to volunteer for aircrew training with the RAF. He won his navigator brevet in 1944 and arrived on 195 Squadron later that year. On 18 April 1945 Ray flew to Heligoland on the last operational sortie of the war. Ray was discharged in July 1945. He rejoined the Bradford City police force and then in 1948, he emigrated to Canada and worked with Westinghouse. Ray retired in 1979.*

## Training and Beyond

When that fateful day in September 1939 arrived, I was working on Police HQ Staff and thus in a reserved occupation. I stayed until the Pilot/Navigator/Bomb Aimer scheme was introduced and then volunteered.

Eventually I was called to ACRC in St John's Wood at Regents Park, London. After the usual shots and vaccination I was posted to Scarborough for ITS–not forgetting the route marching up and down the promenade, and being told twice a day to get a hair cut. On course completion I was posted again, this time to Heaton Park, Manchester, where I was informed I had been chosen for navigator training. That was great; it was what I'd been hoping for.

At Greenock I boarded the Queen Elizabeth for New York, thence to Moncton, and from there to 5 Air Observer School at Stevenson Field (now Winnipeg International Airport).

July 1944 was a great day for me. I graduated and was presented with my wing and a commission. The following day I was off by train to Toronto for seven days' leave before going back to Moncton. Finally I was of to the UK; I was off to the war. I should have had twenty-eight days' leave, but I received a telegram recalling me. Leave always seemed too short.

I then went to 8 AFU at Mona, Isle of Anglesey, and from there to OTU at Chipping Warden, where we crewed up on Wellingtons.

Our first op looked like being one of the tough ones, to Potsdam (Berlin). We carried a full load of fuel and thus a lighter bomb-load than our aircraft was designed for. We had just one four-thousand-pounder and a bunch of one-thousand-pounders.

The operation turned out to be nothing like as horrific as we all expected. Me109s flew across our bow but didn't appear to notice us; they didn't attack. The ack-ack was heavy, but we had been warned of that. Looking down at the fires below, I had the distinct impression we'd hit the target.

The war was nearly over and operational requirements were winding down. I had the distinction and privilege of being on the last op of WWII. That was on 18 April against the Heligoland fortress. I imagine it was in support of the Royal Navy. According to my logbook, we made two strikes on the fortress; it must have been a tough nut.

At the beginning of May my squadron and I were involved in dropping supplies to the starving Dutch people at The Hague, Holland, a pleasurable change from dropping bombs.

We then took part in Operation Exodus. This was the code-name for an operation that involved flying newly liberated POWs back to Britain. These trips were by far the most gratifying.

# GORDON THOMSON

*Gordon was born in Dublin in January 1913. He enlisted in the RAF in June 1942 and was awarded his Navigator brevet in August 1943. Gordon joined 68 Squadron. After twelve operational sorties, he and his crew were transferred to Pathfinders. Gordon was demobbed in October 1945 and returned to teaching.*

## One Good Thing

Our crew, of which I was navigator, managed thirty-nine operations–twelve in Halifaxes on Main Force, and twenty-seven in Lancasters on PFF. The pilot and bomb-aimer did a "second dickey" each and so totalled forty ops. The war ended before we could do a full PFF tour of forty-five ops.

We got shot up a few times, came home on three engines twice, and got lost once because the starboard outer engine (which operated the generator and hence the nav devices) was shot out. We came home on my astro-nav; it was pretty dicey. Fortunately our W/OP, a nineteen year old Aussie, got a radio fix way up north so we barrelled home safely, only to find that we'd been posted missing. Andy, the mid-upper, got hit by flak on his elbow. He saved the chunk, about as big as his thumb, for a souvenir.

Everything that happened to us was exciting at the time, but minor. No fires, no crashing cannon shells, no wheels-up landings, no bale-outs, no ditching. We just stooged along, dropped our bombs and flares, and got home safely.

# JOHN HOWARD

*John joined the RCAF in 1942 at age 18 and was awarded his pilot wings in June 1943. After completing operational training programmes, he joined Bomber Command in Britain. He flew the Halifax III and was awarded the DFC during his tour of ops–September '44 to April '45. After demobilization, he returned to the University of Toronto and in 1948 graduated with honours in mechanical engineering. John spent his entire career in the pulp and paper industry where he managed multi-million-dollar construction projects during his final twenty years.*

## A Lucky Tour

In July 1941, at the age of seventeen years eleven months and two weeks, I went to the RCAF recruiting office to volunteer for aircrew. They must have been flooded with applicants at the time because I was told to come back when I was eighteen. This I did, returning ten months later after completing first year Mechanical Engineering at the University of Toronto. Thus it was 1944 before I was fully trained on the Halifax and posted to 578 Squadron, Burn, Yorkshire.

We were a very young squadron, having been formed on 14 January 1944 and manned initially with air and ground crews transferred from 51 Squadron at Snaith.

Δ : *Chemnitz.*
Date: *14/2/45*
T. on Δ : *2103.06*
T.I.'s: *3① M.B.② R/G③ R④ G⑤ GR SKY*
A.B. *Brutus I+II (C)*
M.F. *Bombload.*
B.L. *2x1000, 8x CL. (500*
B.Ht. *19500.*
Taxi Out: *1653*
Take Off: *1659*

Nickel- WGI.

OSS

Great Yarmouth

Leeuwarden    Gro
Texel I.
53°                        53°

Amsterdam

Ipswich

o The Hague
Rotterdam

80

7000
20 2
3°E.                        5°E.
Duisberg
40
Ostende
Dover        Bruges        Antwerp    Dusseldorf
Calais    51°              51°              51°
20
o
Boulogne    Brussels        Aachen
100
9000
192              167
80
15000
16 2            24
7000    177              2286F
192  232 F  12000
60              12000
12000    220

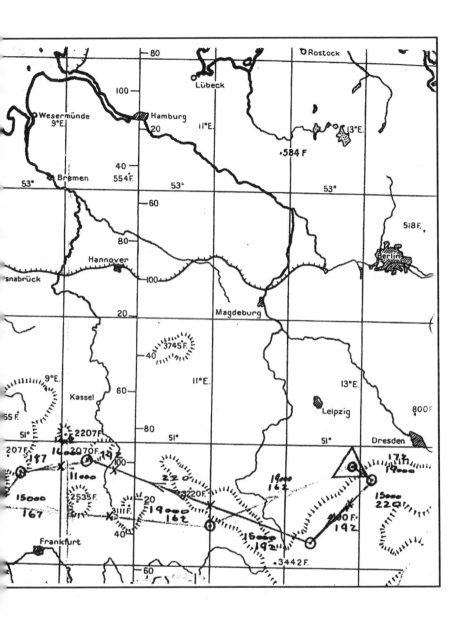

The station commander, G/C Warburton, and the squadron commander, W/Cdr "Jimmy" James, welcomed us. They told us in no uncertain terms that if we had mechanical problems such that we would not reach the target with the bomber stream, we were to turn back. Better to have one less aircraft bombing than to lose an aircraft and crew. Moreover Wingco James did not believe in second-dickie trips. My crew and I would fly our first op together.

The squadron was equipped with the Halifax III, powered by 1615 hp. Bristol Hercules engines. These aircraft were a delight to fly, light on the controls, fast, quiet, and climbed like a homesick angel. My check-out took only twenty minutes, and then we were off for a week of practising circuits and landings, bombing, and air/sea firing. We started our very lucky, relatively uneventful tour of operations with a daylight raid on Bottrop on 30 September. Not all our crews were so lucky. During the 5½ months we flew with the squadron, half the squadron was lost, twelve aircraft and crews.

**14 OCTOBER.** On our way to Duisburg in daylight we lost an engine over the North Sea. With 10,500 lbs. of bombs we could not maintain height so turned back and jettisoned part of the load. That night, same target, same aircraft, same bomb load, we lost the same engine again but were much closer to the target so carried on. There were close to 9000 tons of bombs dropped on Duisburg within 24 hours. The fires could be seen a hundred miles away.

**25 OCTOBER.** Badly shot up by flak during a daylight raid on Essen, our second visit there in two days. Nobody got a scratch but a splinter passed between the bomb-aimer and navigator, another between the arms and legs of the gunner in the mid-under turret, and a small piece came through the windshield and whistled by my right ear. After joining the circuit back at Burn I asked the mid-under gunner, a new addition to the crew, to have a look at the undercarriage. He reported the port tire flapping and undercarriage damage. We then proceeded to the emergency landing ground at Carnaby, which, as I recall, was the width of three runways, about two-miles long with a half mile undershoot area and one-mile overshoot area. I touched down as gently as possible on the starboard side of the triple width runway and swung to port, coming to rest on the port side of the runway and facing in the opposite direction. Following us in was a Lancaster with its hydraulics shot away (no brakes or flaps). It was lined up on the port side of the runway and as we swung there was some swearing on the R/T and the pilot had to make a steep turn to the starboard side. Well, it turned out that the Lanc pilot was Ken Wallace, one of my best friends in high school in Toronto. We had joined the RCAF together, gone through Manning Depot together, and here we were meeting again almost 2½ years later. Our Halifax was riddled with holes but repairable. I received a green endorsement in my logbook for "Exceptional Flying Skill and Judgement".

I do not now recall having seen any aircraft shot down, but notations in my logbook confirm otherwise. Night of 2/3 November, Dusseldorf. "Saw several A/C shot down." Night of 6/7 December, Osnabrück: "Several aircraft seen destroyed."

Our intelligence officers told us that during a bombing attack the Germans would intersperse the flak with pyrotechnic shells (Scarecrows). When the pyrotechnics exploded they looked like an aircraft blowing up. Did these things really exist or were they bombers exploding? Were Scarecrows invented by RAF Intelligence to boost our morale? On the other hand, at night, quite often below the bomber stream a pinpoint of fire would appear on the ground, swell rapidly, then slowly subside. One of our aircraft burning on the ground? Probably.

**17 DECEMBER.** I spilled the Elsan can during violent evasive action over Duisburg. The slop ran back and out by the rear turret making it most unpleasant for the tail gunner; I hoped it had rained down on some Germans below.

My navigator, Chuck Wilschke, had almost completed his pilot training when he was washed out after injuring his knee falling down a flight of stairs on a drunken 48-hour leave. (That's what he told us!) Anyway, he was a very good pilot, probably the best second-pilot in Bomber Command.

**14 February 1945.** While returning from Chemnitz, well out of enemy territory, I had Chuck relieve me while I visited the Elsan. As I returned to my seat the harness of my bulky experimental backpack parachute caught the release lever of the pilot's escape hatch. The hatch flew off into the night, making the remainder of the trip home very cold and draughty. Leaving my seat had been an idiotic thing to do, yet I did it again on a beautiful clear afternoon returning up England from a daylight op. Chuck used to complain when I got a little off course; so I put him in control while I went back and replaced the tail gunner in his turret. A few swings of the turret showed Chuck why it was sometimes difficult to maintain a heading.

While on the subject of second pilots, I should mention that we were required to give our bomb-aimer a little flying training so that he could fly the plane back to England if something unpleasant were to happen to the pilot. Well, my bomb-aimer wasn't cut out to be a co-pilot. He couldn't even ride a bicycle. I don't know how he mastered the bombsight but we had our share of aiming points show up on the target photos. Bud Smith was, I am quite sure, the oldest aircrew member of the squadron. He had changed his birth certificate from 1907 to 1909 in order to squeak into aircrew.

**21 FEBRUARY.** Worms. A stream of tracers crossed over our port wing near the fuselage. I saw it; Derek Watts, the flight engineer, saw it, but the gunners didn't. On return to Burn we found the insulator which attached an antenna to the port fin had been shot away.

**24 FEBRUARY.** We had just taken off for a daylight raid on Kamen when the starboard outer engine failed. The cowling was bouncing up and down. I feathered the prop, shut down the engine and we proceeded out over the North Sea to jettison much of the load. Upon inspection of the engine it was found that one of the top cylinders had blown.

**5 MARCH.** While flying over the Channel in a new Halifax en route to Chemnitz (a nine-hour trip) there was a bang from the starboard inner engine. All instruments showed normal readings so we continued on to the target. On our return we were diverted to Bovington, a US B17 base with a strange runway lighting system. A strong crosswind was blowing. As soon as we touched down we knew what the bang had been—the starboard tire. We swung violently to the right into the middle of a large patch of gooey mud where we shuddered to a halt facing the opposite direction. While we were being debriefed, another 578 Squadron Halifax swung off the runway in the strong crosswind and ran into our kite. Nobody was injured but both Halifaxes were destroyed in the ensuing fire. Our wireless operator, Australian Lin Francis and I, each have a piece of mud-spattered Perspex from the nose of our new LK-K.

I did not record the date of my worst moment at Burn. We had returned in darkness from an op over Germany and I was instructed by the tower to orbit while earlier returns landed. Instead of watching my instruments and flicking a glance occasionally at the nav lights of the other aircraft in the circuit, I did the opposite. Suddenly my navigator spoke up.

"You're getting a little low, aren't you, Skip?"

Before his words were all spoken, I had yanked back on the yoke, glanced at the altimeter (150 feet), flicked a glance out the port window, and saw a tree go past the wingtip. Chuck's words are burned into my memory. I close my eyes and I can still see the tree. If Chuck had not been watching his altimeter, or if he had waited a few moments more to speak, all would have ended there. Over-confidence is a condition most pilots face sooner or later. I was much more careful after that near fatal mistake.

Between ops we did some training, practice bombing, air/sea firing, fighter affiliation. I was never prone to low-flying, but finally got tired of hearing my crew complain that other pilots took their crews low-flying, so one day after air/sea firing I flew for a few moments so close to the water that spray was hitting the Perspex nose. There were no more complaints. On the other hand, one day after a practice bombing flight we came back with a seagull in one of the oil coolers. Nobody would believe we hadn't been below 1000 feet.

While on ops, we got a week of leave every five weeks. Early in February, some of the crew went to London; on the first day I went to my Canadian bank for some money. In the queue in front of me was an officer in the British Columbia Dragoons, my brother's regiment. I asked him if he knew Ben and he told me my brother was trying to contact me. The BCDs had been in Italy with the 5th Division, were on their way to Holland, and some of the officers had come to London for a week, the same week that I had. An hour later my brother and I were having a drink at B.C. House. What was an officer from Toronto doing in the BCDs? During the Italian campaign Easterners replaced most of the original officers from the Okanagan. You won't find the reason in the regimental history.

As the European bomber offensive was starting to wind down, our squadron was reduced from three flights to two, then on 15 March 1945 it was disbanded. In its short fourteen-month existence it had flown 2721 sorties and lost forty aircraft in 155 bombing raids. Among the many decorations won by its aircrew was one posthumous Victoria Cross. Our crew was transferred to 78 Squadron at Breighton where we completed the final five ops of our tour.

A few weeks later we were on board the Louis Pasteur, heading for Halifax. I volunteered for the Tiger Force, but then the Bomb was dropped, the Japs capitulated, and I went back to university, but this time at government expense. The chart on pages 168-169 was prepared and used by John Howard for the attack on Chemnitz.

# HUGH McMILLAN

*Hugh was born in Claresholm, Alberta, in 1923 and enlisted in the RCAF in 1942. One year later he was awarded his Bomb-Aimer brevet. In July '44, after advanced training,, he arrived on 434 Squadron, 6 Group.. Hugh completed his operational tour in May 1945 after 20 operational sorties on Halifaxes and 13 on Lancasters. After demobilization, he obtained a law degree and established his practice in Victoria.*

## Down in the Drink

After ITS at Regina, I was posted to Dafoe, Saskatchewan, for Bombing and Gunnery flying. There, the mosquitoes ate you alive and the alkali water gave you the 'screamers'. A petition deploring the living conditions was signed by just about every airman on the station. The Air Force considered this mutiny, but they moved G/C Holmes and brought in G/C Mosley, a remarkable, if unorthodox, officer who improved conditions greatly.

On to Rivers Central Navigation School, where I graduated as a sergeant bomb-aimer. Instead of receiving the bomb-aimer's B, I was lucky enough along with five others to receive an Observer wing, the old esteemed O.

After four days at sea on the Queen Elizabeth, we docked at Greenock, to be greeted by Scottish hookers announcing their prices and specialities in a most engaging manner.

Canadian aircrew were billeted in luxury hotels and apartments in Bournemouth, a resort city on the south coast. I was in an apartment in Bath Hill Court with two other bomb-aimers, Howard Cathrae and Wilf Bouvier. Cathrae had the amazing ability to fall asleep at the drop of a hat, at the dinner table or standing up on the train. It was only after completing thirty-nine trips as a Pathfinder bomb-aimer that the Air Force discovered Howie was an epileptic, and these frequent 'naps' were the petit mal. To the best of my knowledge he's alive, living rich in Alberta.

In the spring I went to an Operational Training Unit at Long Marston. We picked up an entirely NCO crew:

W/O Jack Bell from Toronto, pilot
Sgt Wilf Odegaard from Saskatchewan, navigator
Sgt McMillan from Calgary, bomb-aimer
Sgt Hank Kaufman from Windsor, W/AG
Sgt Des Burke from Newmarket, Ontario, mid-upper gunner
Sgt Jack Archibald from Montreal, rear gunner.

We were on Whitleys that were not equipped with Gee and navigation was difficult. We finished OTU with flying colours before most of the other crews and only had to show up for an 0630 parade. The skipper and I spent two weeks at Stratford on Avon in glorious debauchery before reporting to Dalton, in Yorkshire, for 'Battle School' and then on to Topcliffe Heavy Conversion Unit for conversion to Halifax aircraft.

Jack couldn't seem to handle the four engines. It didn't help that he had a flight lieutenant flying instructor who had a boil on his neck and another on his butt and a disposition to match. Things went from bad to worse, the abuse from the instructor increased, and finally Jack Bell had so little confidence he couldn't even taxi properly. They washed him out and posted him. None of us ever saw him again. The rest of the crew were posted back to Dalton Battle School to await a new skipper and take another battle course. What were we, aircrew or commandos? Finally the Air Force posted the crew to Topcliffe again, where F/O Johnny Wagman was appointed to skipper our crew.

Wagman was a different type entirely; where Bell was big, dark and good-natured, Wagman was big, blond, tough and bad tempered. He was saved from being a complete disaster by his sense of humour and the fact that he was a superb pilot.

We went through Heavy Conversion Unit at Topcliffe, this time with John Wagman as skipper. Unlike Jack Bell, Johnny had no trouble converting to the four-engine Halifax; we completed Conversion Unit and on 6 August 1944 were posted to 434 (Bluenose) Squadron at Croft.

Running out of petrol was always a worry in the Halifax; on many ops we couldn't make it to Croft and had to land at lameduck and diversion 'dromes because we were short of fuel. Croft was the most northerly squadron in Bomber Command, which made for longer trips and aggravated problems of gas shortage.

Ten days and four operations after reaching our squadron we were briefed to attack Kiel. When we took off for Kiel we had 1600 gallons, but after I dropped the bombs on Kiel we had only 380 gallons. We knew right at that point we didn't have enough to get back to England. We hoped to make it to the coast and bale out.

To conserve gas we flew low and slow. When we realized we weren't going to make it to the English coast we broke radio silence and the W/AG (Hank) sent out an estimated position of ditching.

In a Halifax there is a rest position between the front and the rear spars which are about six feet apart, located about the fore and aft centre of the fuselage. Back of the rear spar there is about forty feet of fuselage, with the mid-upper turret and the rear turret.

The ditching stations for the bomb aimer, W/AG and navigator call for them to lie stretched out at full length with feet braced against the front spar. Immediately behind their heads the two gunners and the flight engineer sit braced with their hands clasped behind their heads and their backs snug up against the rear spar. Ditching instructions called for remaining stationary in your position until the aircraft has stopped. The theory is that the aircraft will skip along the water like a flat stone and that if you get up too soon, you'll be thrown around and injured at the next impact.

So much for theory. When we ditched in the North Sea at 0245 we were about twenty-eight miles from Scarborough. We hit the water at an angle without levelling out and hit very hard. So hard, in fact, that the plane broke completely in half right at the rear spar and the two gunners and the engineer were thrown into the sea.

After we hit we remained stationary, waiting for the second impact. I decided I'd better get out before I was sucked down and drowned. Odie, Hank, and I climbed out through the hole in the fuselage. We didn't see the back half of the fuselage nor did we see Des, Jock, Archibald or Johnny. We thought they were drowned. We inflated our Mae Wests, jumped into the water, and swam away so the plane wouldn't suck us down when it sank.

It was a hopeless feeling. We knew even in the summer one could only last about two hours in the cold water of the North Sea before one died of what was then called *exposure* and now *hypothermia*. This was a feeling that lawyers seek to establish when they're trying to introduce a dying declaration into evidence. It is described as a 'settled and hopeless expectation of impending death'. The courts presume that at this time a man speaks the truth. This was our state of mind when the three of us, miracle of miracles, heard the voices of the rest of the crew.

They saw the half-inflated dinghy out of the wing, but not the emergency supplies that contained a bellows for manual inflation.

Hank, Odie and I swam back and climbed into the dinghy, which rode so low in the water that the bottoms of our legs were in the water. It was cold but infinitely better than being totally submerged. Water slapping around in the half-inflated dinghy made it difficult to move. Paddling as best we could with our hands and flying boots, we managed to get a safe distance from the aircraft.

We hoped that as soon as it was daylight an Air Sea Rescue plane would spot us. Daylight came at about 0500. At about 0700 what was left of the Halifax rolled over, leaving one wing sticking up fifty feet in the air like a church steeple. No Air Sea Rescue or any other plane came to look for us. We became depressed and discouraged, fearing that we would not be spotted or rescued. Someone started the Lord's Prayer, and we all joined in with the exception of Hank, who was an atheist or an agnostic. So much for the dogma 'There are no atheists in fox holes.'

Time dragged until we spotted four Halifaxes and, better still, one spotted us. A Very cartridge was fired off, and the Halifax dropped a smoke float so close that we had to push it away to prevent it setting fire to our dinghy. The four Halifaxes stooged and circled about us so they wouldn't lose us. At about 1300 an Air Sea Rescue Hudson dropped a fully inflated dinghy that contained milk, food, cigarettes, waterproof matches and four dry flying suits. Four of the crew including the skipper got out of their wet clothing and into the dry suits.

A few minutes later the Hudson dropped a message in a container on a rope float. Johnny said, "I'm the skipper so I guess I'll have to swim out and get the message". He shed his cosy flying suit, stood up stark naked, and stuck his toes in the water. Then he said,

"To hell with it!" and jumped back into his warm suit. The message may still be floating around out there.

At about 1600 an Air Sea Rescue launch from Grimsby picked us up. We got dressed in civilian clothing, white turtle neck sweater and checked pants.

One of the crew of the launch got out a big tin of mock turtle soup with a wick down the centre to heat the soup. He lit the wick, and then realized that he hadn't punctured the tin. He threw the tin overboard; it exploded before it hit the water. Wouldn't it be ironic to survive a night ditching only to be done in by shrapnel from a tin of mock turtle soup?

We slept at Grimsby. Early the next morning a Halifax flew us back to the squadron. The principle was to get you back in an aircraft as soon as possible so you wouldn't think about it and get squeamish about flying. The squadron adjutant reported the ditching to the Lindholme Dinghy Company and the crew were appointed members of the Goldfish Club, with a membership card and a small goldfish patch that could be worn on the battle dress.

Johnny was awarded the DFC and Hank the DFM. Only 13 percent of aircrew survived a ditching; consequently the Goldfish Patch is scarce and respected by other aircrew. So despite the fact that we were a sprog crew we acquired a reputation and status from that point on. Shakespeare wrote of a soldier as *'jealous in honour, sudden and quick in quarrel, seeking the bubble reputation even in the cannon's mouth.'*

After two weeks survivors' leave we completed twenty trips in Halifaxes and fourteen in Lancasters before we finished our tour.

Life on the squadron was good in the sense that there was no petty discipline or parades and aircrew were pampered in relation to other airmen.

At Croft, also known as Croft-in-the-mud, twelve sergeants shared each Quonset hut, with no hot water in the washrooms. When over the Tannoy (loudspeaker) came the call, "All aircrew report to your sections immediately", you rolled out of bed, sloshed through the mud and rain to the mess. If it was an 'ops' day you were served one fried egg with your meal. If the op was called off so was the egg. Aircrew didn't bathe at Croft; they had a quick wash under the taps with cold water in a cold washroom. They shaved in cold water or water heated in a mess tin. I'm speaking now of the sergeants' huts; the officers had it a little better. When I was commissioned, I didn't move out of the sergeants' Quonset hut, nor did any of the other newly commissioned officers.

Right from day one we had trouble functioning as a crew. Johnny had a lot of flying experience flying LAC students around in Canada. Instead of treating us as equals he started trying to treat us as students. After his DFC came through before Hank's DFM this gave him a swelled head. He was also a bully and like all bullies if you took it he would dish it out.

I had it out with him before we left Conversion Unit. On a training exercise he refused to do an orbit on a simulated bombing run. I told him, or rather screamed at him, that if he didn't do the orbit and bombing run I would never fly with him again. He did the orbit and I got my target picture. When we landed he apologized. I accepted it and from that point on we got along famously and became good friends.

The next lesson in Johnny's education came shortly after he'd received his DFC. We landed at a diversion 'drome. When we were outside the Halifax prior to take-off the next day, there wasn't an external battery cart, and so one of the ground crew came out to wind the props. Before any of us could go and help him Johnny said, "Archibald, go help him wind the props". Archibald replied, "What's the matter with you, Wagman, you paralysed?" So Johnny walked over and helped wind all four props while the rest of the crew sat and watched.

Jock Cameron, our Scottish flight engineer, never did stand up to Johnny, and was bullied for the entire tour. They hated each other.

On operations, fear of being shot down and killed is constant with you. It is not something that you talk about but it is there in the back of your mind until you finish your tour and are 'screened'. The trick is to keep this fear under control and not let it develop into panic. Some airmen tried to push this fear into the background with booze, some with sex, and most with both. Aircrew never talked about an airman being killed in action. If you enquired you were told, "He went for a Burton".

Poor Jock Cameron was in panic most of the time he was in the air. Because of this he was the weak link in the crew. I can still see him the night we ditched, hunched over the petrol cocks trying to make sure he'd drained the last drop of gas out of a tank before he switched to another. He was so frightened his eyes were bugged and he was spewing his guts out. To his credit he never shirked.

The authorities recognized and tolerated this fear up to a point, which was 100 hours logged in operational time. Before getting 100 hours if an aircrew member refused to fly on operations he was branded LMF (lack of moral fibre) and whisked away from the squadron and never heard from again. If you had more than a hundred hours you were allowed to bow out. The usual excuse was unbearable back pain when you flew. This was not only a pain in the back to the airman involved but also a pain in the butt to the crew, who had to break in a new man (a spare) to complete the tour.

The fact that so few quit after a hundred hours was due to crew loyalty. You felt you were letting the team down, and each crew was indeed a band of brothers.

Duisburg was not our lucky city. On 14 October, on a daylight raid, we were hit by visual-predicted flak that knocked out the port outer engine as well as the rear gunner's intercom. The fuselage was riddled. I got rid of the bombs, and the skipper put the aircraft into a screaming dive. We escaped the flak. A Halifax behind us was shot down.

Against Duisburg again on the 14th at night we had a runaway prop over Reading, and couldn't maintain height on the remaining engines. I was ordered to jettison the bombs over the sea and we made an early return to Croft.

Ditching so early in the tour was a highlight, but there were a number of other scary incidents. On 18 December 1944, returning from Duisburg, we were attacked by a night fighter. We took evasive action and returned his fire, shooting down one Me109F. This kill was officially confirmed by Group Headquarters about two weeks later.

On our second last op, on Hagen on 15 March, a fighter we hadn't seen attacked us. Fortunately he shot slightly above us. Johnny, when he saw the tracer, threw the Lancaster into a violent dive. The gunners returned the fire but missed and the German night fighter didn't renew the attack.

Almost all bombers lost to night fighters were shot down by fighters they hadn't seen. Time and again you'd see a burst of tracer and a bomber would explode. If your gunners sighted the fighter before its attack, the odds favoured the bomber because the gunners could rotate their turrets and fire at the fighter, but the fighter could not bring his guns to bear on the bomber when it was taking evasive action.

There were some funny incidents. One night the code word to call off a raid was 'Lemon'. About two nights later as we approached a target a guttural voice called over the Master Bomber's frequency:

"Lemon! Lemon!"

If he'd left it at that he'd probably have caught some of the crews. But he went on.

"Lemon! Lemon! Close your bomb doors and go home."

That's when the Master Bomber chimed in indignantly in his obviously Australian accent:

"Don't listen to that bastard! He's a Jerry."

There was a certain squadron leader who seemed to be favoured by the high brass. This favouritism was noted and resented by the other crews. One night when the bombers were stacked up circling and waiting to land a call came over the RT: "Can you tell me or do you know if Squadron Leader Harvey is the illegitimate son of Butcher Harris?" Click! (Name altered). There was a big investigation, but the culprit was never identified. S/Ldr 'Harvey' was screened after 25 operations; F/Lt Wagman was screened after 34.

Our crew split up. I saw all five in 1950, but after that we didn't keep in touch. I always assumed that if anything happened I would hear. I was wrong. Some time ago I discovered Hank Kaufman, Johnny Wagman, and Jack Archibald had all died from cancer. Our mid-upper gunner is still alive. I had a nice letter from Hank's widow Joyce, with some photos of her and Hank, and also a group picture of their wedding in Pontefract, Yorkshire, showing Johnny, Archibald, Mel Isenberg and Percy Mandrell (Isenberg's W/AG) along with the bride and groom. I thought to myself when I looked at the photograph:

"Were we ever that young?"

# ELLIOTT F. NICOLLS

*Elliott was born in Brantford, Ontario, in 1921 and joined the RCAF in early 1942. He was awarded his navigator brevet in 1943 and arrived in Bomber Command, serving with both 425 and 420 Squadrons. Whilst on 425 (Alouette) Squadron, his pilot and two gunners were killed in a training accident. He transferred to 420 (Snowy Owl) Squadron. It was on 420 that he did most of his operational flying.*

*Elliott completed his operational tour in the late summer of 1944. The targets allocated to him included the V1 launch sites, fuel-oil tanks, bomb dumps, and troop or armour concentrations. In the days following the Normandy invasion he flew on operations in support of Allied ground troops, and it was one of these operations that is the subject of this memoir. Elliott returned to Canada to serve in AFHQ until demobilized in 1945. He moved to Victoria and worked for the BC government until his retirement in 1983*

## Mistaken Markers

As navigator of a Halifax bomber, I flew thirty-one operations. The saddest flight of all was as part of an operation that killed some of our countrymen in what euphemistically has been called "friendly fire."

Our 29th op, on 14 August 1944, was an early afternoon take-off; in just four hours and forty minutes we would return to our base in Yorkshire. Our target was Bons Tassilly, in France, an area that was part of the Caen-Falaise gap, which the ground troops were attempting to close and thereby trap a large concentration of German troops and armour. We were one of a number of squadrons involved in the operation.

At the briefing before take-off we were told the operation was in support of our ground troops and that it was up to us to avoid hitting them. To do this we were given the appropriate courses to follow in leading up to the target and returning home.

The final course to the target was an approach over water. Our bomb-aimer would report to me the moment the coastline passed through his bombsight and again a short time later report when a prominent land feature near Caen passed through the sight. Based upon this time interval, so many units of time would be required to elapse before it was safe to release our bombs.

While we were still short of the safe release time, our bomb-aimer indicated some bombs from other aircraft were already falling and I warned him it was too soon. The Pathfinder directing the bombing from an aircraft below indicated the yellow target markers as being the aiming point. What caused the early bombing confusion, we were to learn years later, was that the ground forces were also firing yellow colours and some aircrews mistook them for the yellow Pathfinder target markers.

We were on a southerly heading with a tail wind. The speed of our aircraft over the ground was approximately one mile every fifteen seconds, and time was of the essence. Given the desire of aircrews to successfully complete the mission and get away from the target areas as quickly as possible, these and other factors all contributed to the sad situation that evolved.

It was reported later by the troops on the ground that the smoke and dust they generated caused them to fire the yellow colours to guide their own movements.

The enemy activity around the target area was minimal, and we returned to base some two hours later. By then the word of early bombing by some crews reached the station and the "boom was lowered" on those guilty of it.

Each of our aircraft had a camera directed and timed to take a photograph of the area where the bombs struck. The films were part of the record, along with the extensive de-briefing by the intelligence staff, of our activities during the flight. Although the photographs confirmed we did bomb our target, it was of small consolation when we learned later that many losses on the ground had occurred among

Canadian and Polish units who suffered the brunt of the errors. Many heads were to roll before the investigations were over.

On 25 August we flew our final op (number thirty-one for me) and we were sent off for a rest and some leave.

*Marshal of the RAF Sir Arthur Harris had this to say in his book "Bomber Offensive" first published in 1947:*

*When the use of heavy bombers in the battlefield, very close to our own troops, was first put forward I expressed doubts; it seemed to me that the army had no idea of the risk that the troops would be running. In the event, by extremely careful planning and the extra-ordinary skill of the crews, we brought down that risk to much less than the soldier ran in the last war when his own guns put down a barrage. The main safeguard was the use of a double check, a carefully timed run by each bomber, and a very careful assessment of the position of the target-indicators by a Master Bomber. In one out of eight such operations there was, in point of fact, a small number of casualties among our own troops. An investigation afterwards discovered that some crews had omitted to make timed runs, in spite of the orders that had been given to them, and aimed their bombs at pyrotechnic signals, which were no markers at all, but were being displayed by the army for some purpose of its own although it had been agreed that such pyrotechnics would not be used when we were bombing. The army commanders were on every occasion completely satisfied by the way in which the bombing had been carried out.*

# CONTRIBUTORS
## MARITIME OPERATIONS

**ASV:** Air-to-Surface vessel. The early (200 mc/s) ASV II radar could detect a surfaced sub at 6 nm or more. The Kriegsmarine fitted "Metox", which intercepted the ASV transmission and gave the sub enough warning to dive to safety. In the spring of '43, Coastal Command fitted ASV III (centimetric) radar. Metox could not intercept this and German subs were ordered to submerge by night and surface by day only long enough to charge batteries. Admiral Dönitz ordered crews to fight it out on the surface if there was not time to dive. Ed Miskiman, Ned Stanley, and Monty Williams all attacked surface subs. Frank Laughlin used both the Mk II and the Mk III.

**Loran:** A system similar to Gee, but working at a lower frequency (2 mc/s) and thus having a longer range. Loran is still in use today.

**M/Vs:** motor vessels

**Ten-tenths.** Refers to cloud. Ten tenths is totally cloud-covered.

**White flashes:** white cap flashes as worn by aircrew trainees

**Lat and Long.** Latitude and longitude

**ETA:** Estimated time of arrival

**nm:** nautical mile

# MARITIME OPERATIONS

During WWII maritime operations encompassed a wide variety of over-water activities. Primary duties were convoy escort and anti-submarine patrols, but there were also air-sea search and rescue; meteorological flights; anti-shipping strikes with torpedoes, cannon, and rockets; mine laying sorties; and operations from aircraft carriers.

Areas of operations included the North Atlantic, both Canadian coasts, all around Africa, Madagascar, India east to Australia and New Zealand, and wherever water and an enemy were to be found.

A variety of aircraft were used, from single engine biplanes, amphibians, land planes from one to four engines in size (often converted bombers), to fighters, torpedo planes and flying boats. The pilots in particular were given extra training. After receiving their wings they were posted to General Reconnaissance School (GRS) for additional courses in navigation: dead-reckoning; astro, and radio and forty hours in the air as trainee navigators, as well as other subjects such as advanced compass theory, meteorology, and ship recognition.

GRS was followed by OTU (Operational Training Unit) where crews were formed, learned to work together, fly operational types and learn about their special aspect of maritime flying.

Because they made extended patrols of eighteen hours or more, long-range aircraft carried a crew of nine: two pilots, one of whom could give the navigator an occasional break; two engineers; two wireless operators and a wireless mechanic to operate and maintain the radio and what is now called radar; and a rigger who with the engineers could maintain the aircraft when away from base. All crew members received gunnery training and the rigger, apart from his maintenance duties, was in charge of cooking and keeping a steady supply of coffee available.

*Walter Wickson*

# BOB BROWN

*Shortly after he was born in 1916, Bob's family moved to Seattle. He returned to Canada in the 1930s and enlisted in the RCAF in late 1940. Bob was trained as an Aero-Engine Mechanic, a non-aircrew trade, yet flew for over 2000 hours getting his job done. Not until mid-1943 was he awarded a Flight Engineer brevet. He was commissioned in 1944, by which time he was doing 16-hour patrols over the Atlantic*

## Western Atlantic

My flying began on Stranraers, a strutted and wired flying boat that looked like a refugee from the First World War. I flew in them for only 39 hours, until the squadron converted to Catalinas. The CAT was known to the Americans as the PBY; it was an extremely long-range, twin-engined monoplane with a 104-foot wingspan. In October 1941, when I became first engineer of a Catalina, I was promoted to the dizzy height of corporal. *Later in the war I flew in Cansos, the amphibious versions of the Catalina.*

Starting a Catalina's engines was easier, since an electric motor ran an impulse starter. If a start failed three times I had to change twenty-eight spark plugs on the twin-row engine.

In flight the engineer monitored the engines, controlling temperatures and pressures, and he spent much time looking for submarines. The engineer and one wireless operator shared the cooking duties on the long, often 16-hour, trips. With auxiliary tanks the Catalina could fly for thirty hours. Five-gallon milk cans were used to fill the fifty-gallon oil tanks of a moored aircraft.

On 1 February 1943 I was promoted to sergeant. On 14 February, I was sent to Bombing and Gunnery School and reverted to corporal.

After Bombing and Gunnery it was off to Aeronautical School in Montreal to teach me about aircraft on which I already had some two-thousand-hours flying time. I got my third hook back when I completed the three-week course.

On 1 December I was promoted to flight sergeant and in January 1944 was awarded the E wing. Now I was officially aircrew. I was commissioned as a pilot officer on 24 August.

The Catalinas were employed mostly on anti-submarine patrols, with some mercy trips thrown in. On one of these trips we carried a lady with meningitis from the Magdalen Islands to hospital in Charlottetown; the family was most appreciative.

We also did transportation trips to various outposts.

Anti-submarine patrols, especially in the early stages of the war, were not without stress. The Atlantic convoys started forming up in Bedford Basin, Halifax Harbour, assembling later outside the Halifax Gates, screens that could be opened and closed. Convoy escorting usually started well out to sea: we made rendezvous with the naval escort and stayed with them for four or five hours as time permitted.

Escorting by air was done in a box formation. The Navy was in charge of the operation, communication was in Morse code on Aldis lamps, radio silence being observed at all times. All our crew members could both read and transmit in Morse and all were involved in submarine detection with binoculars. Convoys differed; varying from five ships to fifty, but usually comprising twenty to thirty vessels carrying mixed cargoes.

One aircraft would cover one convoy, patrolling the area considered most favourable to submarines. Weather was always a factor in their or our success. At times of heavy ice our patrols tracked and reported on the size and location of floes for the safety of the convoy. Our armament consisted of four 500-lb depth-charges, and four .50-calibre Browning machine guns.

Most of our operational time was spent escorting convoys. We usually did this at 3000 feet on patrols lasting up to sixteen hours. The waves looked like picket fences to me. Our job, of course, was to keep the submarines submerged in the vicinity of the convoy.

On one anti-submarine patrol we lost oil pressure in the port engine, south of Northwest River, where Eastern Air Command had a fuel and oil cache. We shut down the engine and landed. The first job was to find the cause of the trouble; it turned out to be a rag left in one of the oil pipes. We drained the oil and flushed out the engine, then refilled it and started it. This required someone to get out on the main plane and engage the impulse starter manually. I completed the job and started down into the fuselage; but the pilot forgot about me. The aircraft had reached 35 knots taxiing on the step before someone realized I was not aboard. When this contretemps was sorted out we resumed our patrol.

When I first began flying on Catalinas I belonged to Crew 5, whose pilots were P/O Hodge and W/O Nicholls. The team was not working out and it was decided to split the crew and form Crew 13, with crew members making up their own minds which pilot they would fly with. I chose to fly with P/O Hodge in Crew 13. All went well for some time, with both crews flying steadily. In the spring of '43, the squadron moved to Goose Bay, where it stayed for six and a half months.

The other half of my former crew went out on patrol, far out from Goose Bay to the north-east, where they encountered foul weather and were forced down. A Lindholme survival gear was successfully dropped, but contact with them was lost. The squadron was frantic and we wanted to send out a skeleton crew to attempt the rescue, for which I volunteered. Ottawa turned us down because they did not wish to risk another aircraft. The weather turned worse and all were lost. We took the order to abandon the rescue pretty hard.

Six days after I received my commission we left Goose Bay to pick up a ship 150 miles off the Labrador coast. There was no visibility, and the temperature was -5°C. Suddenly we encountered propeller icing; the ground crew had filled the de-icing tank with water instead of alcohol. The first call I heard on the intercom was "Bob! Where to from here?" The captain said, "Prepare to ditch!" We broke radio silence. Knowing our chance of survival was poor, I replied, "Increase boost pressure steeply, start a slow spiral climb, and the ice should disappear." The pilot did what I told him and as a result the seven men of crew 13 survived.

*Readers will note that Bob's story ends abruptly with much obviously left unsaid. He had been in declining health for some time and died with his story unfinished. We include it here to honour his memory. Ed.*

# WALTER WICKSON

*Walter was born in Stettler, Alberta, in January 1920. He enlisted in the RCAF in June 1941 and was awarded his pilot wings in early 1942. He completed nine hundred hours of operational flying with 202 and 262 Catalina Squadrons in Africa before heading back to the UK in September 1944. He flew with auxiliary squadrons after he was demobilized and returned to the RCAF to complete a further thirteen years' service.*

## Flying Boat Pilot

I had been an airplane nut since the age of eight and decided in mid-1941 to join the RCAF as an airframe mechanic. When I informed the recruiting officer of this he said that was fine and put me down as a pilot trainee. So I learned even before I was sworn in of the weight carried by personal decision in the RCAF.

At Initial Training School in Edmonton, being an optimist with a short memory, I decided that I would combine my love of the water with being a pilot and become a flying boat pilot.

By the time I completed Elementary Flying Training at High River, I knew I had made the right decision and asked for flying boats. I received a recommendation for fighter pilot. Not even close.

So I went on to Service Flying Training at Dauphin where I worked hard, asked for flying boats, and was posted to Charlottetown for the General Reconnaissance Course, the way to Coastal Command and flying boats. My delight was somewhat tempered when my next posting was to the OTU at Debert to fly Hudsons. When it transpired that I was surplus to the course, I suggested to the Chief Instructor that I go to the Hampden OTU at Patricia Bay, eighteen miles from my home in Victoria. This brought rapid results; five days later I was on HMS Strathmore en-route to the UK.

After a delightful sojourn of two months in Bournemouth, where I reminded those in charge that I wished to fly flying boats, I was posted with two others to Invergordon, a flying boat OTU. The adjutant asked why we had come, there being no place or a course for us. This was discouraging. Before we returned to Bournemouth, he told us he had good news, a requirement for two second-pilots with a Catalina squadron at Gibraltar. The three of us flipped coins for the two slots. I lost and returned to Bournemouth.

After a month–it was now November–I was again posted to Invergordon. At last I was to be a boat pilot. My enthusiasm for flying helped offset arriving on a cold Scottish winter day to move into a typical Nissen hut complete with knot-hole air conditioning and a central stove with a one-foot heating radius. Things weren't helped by my laundry, including all my pyjamas, being still in Bournemouth. Many months later my flying kit was located in Ireland, which is why I flew all winter in my dress blues and great coat.

My new flying instructor F/Lt Boyd inquired of my experience and didn't seem impressed, as I was still at the two hundred and thirteen hours completed eight months earlier. He merely looked resigned, turned around and sat down in the dinghy which was to carry us to my first flight in a Catalina.

I remember my first solo in a Cat. The drill was to lift off at 66 knots indicated. At about the right speed I glanced at the Air Speed Indicator to find it was one o'clock. I forget where I found the ASI but I still have a clear impression of that clock. The placement of instruments in US built aircraft was casual at best and often inconsistent.

A month into the course I was given a crew consisting of RCAF P/O second pilot and P/O navigator, and six RAF sergeants: flight engineer, flight mechanic engines, wireless mechanic, two wireless operators, and an airframe mechanic (rigger). The second pilot and the navigator were fresh from training. The flight engineer had grey hair and had been a gunner in the Royal Flying Corps in WW1; the FME (flight mechanic, engines) had seen the pioneer Grahame-White fly way back when; our wireless mechanic had done a tour on Wimpeys; and the rigger had been a glider pilot.

The Catalina was great fun. Water handling was a real challenge. There were no brakes and no water rudder. A pair of conical canvas drogues helped reduce taxiing speed, along with intermittent cutting of the master switch to keep the revs to about 200 while closing to a mooring buoy. As the Cat refused to stay pointed in the right direction during slow taxiing, differential use of drogues and of switches, as well as using rudder and ailerons (if there was any wind) kept one busy in confined areas and while mooring up. Take-off and landing had varying degrees of excitement and technique depending on wind velocity and water surface. A light four-to-six-inch chop was best. High winds and seas required a full-stall landing, dropping onto the water with minimum speed. No finesse here. Flat calm and night landings were pure instrument approaches onto the water.

After three months came a posting to Ferry Training Unit (FTU) at Stranraer where I signed for a brand new Cat (27 hours on it) and many pounds worth of equipment. As well as being given a new Cat, we were each issued with tropical kit, including the peacetime style RAF topees. Life was getting interesting.

Winter gales were a common facet of flying boat life at Stranraer. Gales demanded a "gale crew" of pilot, engineer and wireless op. One dark night I remember sitting in the cockpit with both engines running at 2000 rpm to ease the strain on the mooring cable and watching the airspeed indicator registering gusts of up to six knots below our take-off speed of 92 mph. The idea of going to the tropics was becoming even more appealing.

Near the end of February 1943 we were told to go to RAF Mount Batten, Plymouth. Our squadron was 209 but no one seemed able to tell us where it was and obviously we wouldn't need tropical kit at Plymouth. The 310 nautical mile flight seemed uneventful until after an hour or so I was informed that the fire from our stove (flames licking around the gasoline to the Auxiliary Power Unit) was now out. Nice of the crew not to cause me unnecessary worry.

Having been assured by Ops at Stranraer that the balloon barrage at Plymouth would be down for our arrival, I was starting a pre-landing survey of the harbour at about 1000 feet when the second pilot pointed out the balloons were up. It seemed appropriate to get out of the air right away. This is how I discovered that a Cat would not stay on the water at 150 mph, although each time it touched it slowed some. I retain a vivid recollection of the rapidly approaching docks across the harbour. However, we made it.

After five days enjoying the peacetime mess at RAF Mount Batten, we were told the swell at Gibraltar had subsided and we were to go there. That sounded OK and we took off in a gale around dusk on 1 March on what was to be my first solo night cross-country flight. To avoid possible Ju88s in the Bay of Biscay, we flew out to 10° west longitude before turning south. After several hours our ASV operator picked up another aircraft. We manned the guns, a 0.303 and a couple of 0.5s, and peered into the dark; the bogey eventually drifted off our scope. We emerged from the gale at the north-west tip of Spain and followed lighthouses to Gibraltar, landing after 14½ hours in the air and having covered a distance of 1168 nm.

The aircraft at Gibraltar were moored in a rather small rectangular basin with an entrance at the end of one side. I taxied through the entrance with drogues out and called for the starboard one to be dumped so as to turn us lengthwise down the centre of the basin between the two rows of moored flying boats. When I asked for the drogue to be released, nothing happened–the trip rope had fouled. This was when I discovered that whatever the taxiing speed, one drogue exactly offset the thrust of one engine. I will never forget thundering between the two rows of Cats with full throttle on the port engine, straight for the concrete wall at the end of the basin. Luckily the vacant mooring buoy was at the end of the left row and as I yanked off the throttle, we swung into the vacant space. Adrenalin deluxe!

Later, at breakfast, we were chatting with another crew who had passed Biscay during the night. They too had picked up a Ju88 on their ASV at the same time and place as we had!

When we left Gibraltar the next evening, I had a dinghy tow us, tail first, slowly and safely out of the basin.

The take-off was interesting in that I'd never before had the opportunity to fly with full fuel (1460 imperial gallons) which we carried along with some cargo, human and otherwise. All went well and we were off to Bathurst, Gambia, 1628 miles south. We kept clear of Tangier and Casablanca because of people with guns. During the night the ASV operator reported we were over mountains. We thought that strange as we were supposed to be on the seaward side of the coast. After a fair bit of intercom activity and dropping a flare, it turned out we were indeed over water. We had never been as high as 10,000 feet and the time-base line on the scope pulled up at that height and just looked like mountains. Another lesson learned.

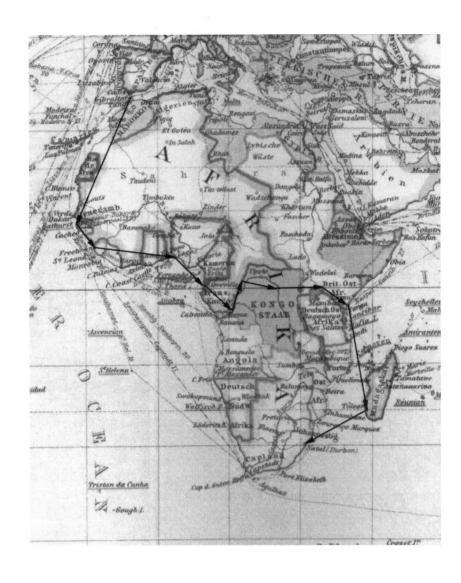

Map of Walter's flight across Africa.
Flight paths were not as straight as shown

The other lesson learned on this leg concerned headwinds. I was experimenting with the effect of lower airspeed on a long haul. A headwind developed and we arrived at Bathurst mid-afternoon instead of around 9 am, after 21 hours and five minutes in the air. So I learned to use a higher speed into a headwind. I also learned that commanding officers get upset at people arriving six hours late.

At Bathurst everything tasted and smelled of peanut oil. We swam and fished off the Cat. Great. It seemed we weren't posted to Bathurst but were to go to RAF Jui at Freetown, Sierra Leone. This was a pleasant five hour and 25 minute flight in hot sunny weather. At 29 inches of manifold pressure and 1900 rpm, our true airspeed was 101 knots at 1000 feet using 32 gals per hour each engine. Our weight was less than gross and we carried no external stores.

Freetown was not large. There was an open-air market. The local women did their washing in nearby streams. The harbour was full of ships. We wore our topees (the only time) and explored the mangrove swamps. After maintenance we were sent off to Lagos, a port in the Gulf of Guinea, a day flight of 1130 nm. and nearly eleven hours along the Gold Coast and Ivory Coast, past Abidjan and Accra and at one point past a water spout a mile to starboard. The weather was perfect, with hot sun, light winds, and 2/10 cumulus casting royal-purple shadows on the powder blue water.

At Lagos we were sent to the BOAC operations to pick up maps and learn the route to Mombasa on the other side of Africa. We finally knew our eventual destination. From Lagos we headed across the Gulf of Guinea en-route to Libreville in French Equatorial Africa. Part way along the 511 nm. leg to our landfall we passed Principe, a tiny island that the ASV operator announced was twenty miles to starboard. The navigator corrected him, saying the distance was 19½ miles. He was using dead-reckoning only and he was right; our landfall was perfect and within a minute of ETA. BOAC took us ashore and on a twelve-mile drive through lush jungle (and a man-powered cable ferry) to Libreville.

The Free French Commandant, a naval captain, entertained us with drinks and then we went on to our hotel. Our seven-course dinner was served in the open-air dining room. Pretty nice. Breakfast the next morning on a second-story patio was great. The one problem was that when consuming the last third of my coffee I found it contained a large spider and some loose legs. I still hope there were eight legs left.

Our next destination was Leopoldville, on the Belgian Congo across the river from Brazzaville. The 528 nm flight took us six hours. We flew over jungle for a hundred miles—we could see antelopes and water buffalo in open spaces—before cutting down towards the coast to Pointe Noire and heading east inland through 9/10 cumulus at 4000 feet to Leopoldville. The Congo between the coast and Leopoldville was full of rapids and red in colour but when we got to Leopoldville the river was wide and placid with a nine-knot current that made mooring up into it slow and easy. A dug-out canoe tied up astern to carry the hose from the Shell fuel barge. I signed for 1200 gallons and hoped Shell had some other source of payment.

The beer here was excellent but deadly. The city was civilized with up-to-date American cars and no gas rationing. We made a five-hour return trip to drop an unfortunate squadron leader off at Banana at the mouth of the Congo. We were lucky to find the place.

Our next leg took us north up the Congo (the 50 ft ceiling hid the tops of the river banks) to Coquilhatville, on the equator, then east over the tall tree jungle to Stanleyville. We were entertained by local residents and billeted with BOAC. We logged 7¼ hours for the 739 nm trip. The next morning we were off to Kisumu, on the north shore of Lake Victoria, heading 077° true and climbing (always laborious in a Cat) towards the wireless station at Irumu. The vegetation became sparse, the ceiling went up to 10,000 feet, the ground came up, and we went to 7000 ft. The air was very rough; at one point the rising air took us up 5000 ft at 700 ft a minute. Along the north shore of Lake Victoria we passed circling vultures at 10,000 ft. At Kisumu we were billeted by an RAF detachment.

I discovered several things the next morning when taking off for Mombasa. The combination of altitude at 3726 ft above sea level and the lower buoyancy of fresh water have a marked negative effect on the take-off run. Unless there is a reasonable headwind, don't take off towards land when the shore is out of sight behind you. And, also important, if the nose is raised only slightly above normal, drag and power become equal at 60 knots indicated. However, full throttle, floats up while still on the water and a slightly lowered nose (at times like this one tends to learn quickly) combined with a depression in the approaching shore enabled things to work out.

A circling climb to 8000 ft and a climb on course to 11,000 feet cleared the Kenya Highlands. Mt. Kilimanjaro, over 19,300 feet high, passed to our starboard shortly before our descent to a sea level landing in the harbour at Mombasa, a four hour and twenty minute hop from Kisumu and 93 hours from Stranraer.

I reported to the CO of 209 Squadron to be told I was posted to 262 Squadron Durban, South Africa, without my crew or boat. I was to take over an experienced crew. Their captain had been killed when the port propeller hit solid water and came off. The crew had kept the bloodstained parachute bag. The disappointment of leaving crew and boat in Mombasa was tempered by reports of the delights of Durban.

After a few days in Mombasa I left with a 262 crew and Cat on a midnight takeoff for a six and three-quarter hour hop south along the Mozambique Channel to Tulear, Madagascar and the following day another eight-hour-fifty-minute leg to Durban.

One might say my first three ops trips were educational. Three days after arriving I was off with my new crew to pick up an eastbound convoy. The take-off was my first with full load including eight depth charges (each 250 lb) hung below the wing. Later on my boat and contents were weighed to find we were flying at 37,000 lb. instead of the maximum of 34,500. We disposed of two depth-charges and were then only 2000 pounds too heavy. I did not realize until later the risk involved in an instrument take-off in the dark with a heavy boat. This required hauling off the water at 66 knots indicated (the power-off stalling speed), then lowering the nose to get flying speed, without hitting the water. As the crew had done ops, I felt it wise to fit in with their routine. A mistake. After a couple of hours the ASV operator announced he had lost the convoy. We never did find it again. It seems that the 15-knot wind from the south had shifted to 15 knots from the north so every hour we searched we were 30 nm farther south. The lightning storms that seemed to be everywhere provided entertainment value during the ensuing ten hours. At dawn we gave up and headed for base but, as the navigator still hadn't picked up the 180° wind shift, when we made landfall and turned south, we were already south of Durban.

We finally came upon a town with the name East London painted on a large roof. Without enough gas to make base, we landed in the narrow, shallow, S-shaped harbour after fifteen hours and forty minutes in the air, and anchored. It was April Fool's Day 1943. Appropriate. After getting gas from a bowser belonging to a nearby South African Air Force station, and a somewhat hairy take-off, we headed north to Durban and some positive discussion about navigation and other procedures between my crew and me.

I made my second op three days later, escorting a north-bound convoy about 200 nm east. This job required a night take-off and a night landing. All went well until dusk when the airspeed indicator went unserviceable. We used astronavigation for ground speed and made base OK. However, a night landing in a boat was strictly an instrument affair. The flarepath consisted of three lighted dinghies, each about half a mile from the other, to show where the landing area was and the wind direction. The procedure was to fly downwind at 1000 feet until it appeared time to turn crosswind, then throttle back and reduce height to 800 feet and then turn upwind onto the flarepath while descending to 400 feet. At this point the nose was raised and as the airspeed reached 75 knots indicated, about 17 inches of manifold pressure was set (the exact amount depending on the weight of the boat) to give a rate of descent of 200 ft a minute. This would give the precise landing attitude needed for touch down, when the throttles were smartly closed. The ASI was vital to maintain rate of descent and attitude. Luck was on my side and we touched down, with a small hop, just above stalling speed. Scary in retrospect.

My third op, about a week later, was to escort an outbound convoy several hundred miles from Durban. Not long after an 0345 take-off, lightning appeared ahead, stretching from horizon to horizon. I told myself "line squall" and planned to ease through at 500 feet between build-ups. Not a good decision. We hit violent turbulence, were at 1000 feet then 10 feet. Lightning was all about and St. Elmo's fire decorated the windshield frame, ASV aerials, props, etc. The second pilot finally got my safety harness done up. A wireless op in the port blister caught the 0.5 Browning as the plane dropped, the blister opened and he almost floated out.

After a couple of hours that seemed much longer, we emerged into the eye of the hurricane. We circled towards the patch of blue sky high above, located the convoy about 10 miles away on our ASV and dropped back to 500 feet to pick up the ships at 0800 hours. The ships' crews must have thought we were crazy out in that weather. I know we were. A few hours into our escort we received a message to return to base because of poor weather. What a time to tell us!

# ED MISKIMAN

*Ed joined the RCAF in Vancouver in 1941 and was awarded his pilot wings in Saskatoon. He completed fifty-two ops on 86 and 53 Squadrons in Iceland, and Northern Ireland. Subsequently, he flew in Transport Command between England and India, until leaving the RCAF in 1946. After the war Ed's career took him to the position of President and CEO of Quaker Oats of Canada.*

## The Day the Pigeons Nearly Froze

The day began early at 86 Squadron, Ballykelly, in Northern Ireland, darkness, and the usual cold, duff weather. It was our twelfth op. The lorry picked up the crew; flight breakfast, met and intelligence briefing, and the usual gourmet lunch boxes. We also carried two live pigeons. The idea was that if we had to ditch in the North Atlantic, we could write down our message together with our lat. and long. and attach the message to each bird's leg. The faithful birds would home to base in Ireland and help would be sent. It all seemed somewhat improbable and made us wonder if this was why aircrew were called pigeons.

The trip was to be the usual RAF 15 Group convoy escort and anti-submarine assignment. We cruised at 160 mph at 3000 feet under a ten-tenths overcast grey sky on our way to intercept "ONS 20" convoy somewhere in mid-Atlantic. To maximize our range, two 670-gallon fuel tanks were mounted in the front bomb bays and our fire-power was reduced to one 0.5 calibre that the navigator could fire through a peek hole in the nose; four .303s in the tail turret and a 0.5 that could be swung into place after opening the beam window. We also carried six depth charges.

Because of the severe weather, we mistakenly first contacted the "ON" convoy, which was some distance from our assigned job with the "ONS" Group convoy. We were en route from "ON" to "ONS" when we spotted a blip. A vessel of some sort lay dead ahead. It turned out to be a 640-ton U-boat.

We increased height into cloud cover thinking the U-boat may not have seen us. When we broke cloud just over them, with bomb doors open to begin our attack, we were greeted with heavy flak. It was one of the newly fitted U-boats armed with high-angle 37-mm AA and four 22-mm AA guns. They had obviously picked us up on their radar and were ready to fight it out on the surface rather than dive. Later in the war, Germany abandoned that tactic.

After corkscrewing down from 2000 feet to 200 feet, our first attack with two depth charges was a straddle. We pulled away with our rear gunner trading fire with the U-boat gunners.

Smoke was swirling up from the U-boat, but she didn't go down. We decided to have another go, first eating our chocolate ration so that if we had to ditch, Jerry bloody well wasn't going to get his hands on that.

The second run was similar to the first; the sub tipped on end and sank; we saw survivors on life rafts.

We advised the Senior Naval Officer of the convoy but we never found out whether those survivors were picked up.

We completed our line-ahead escort job and headed for home. The trip had lasted 17¼ hours. In the excitement of winning the game, we had forgotten to feed the pigeons. They were shivering and nearly dead in the pen aft of the bomb bay. We had all survived to live another day, crew and pigeons.

As the only Canadian in the crew, I was directed to go to London and give an account of the sinking on the BBC Home News Broadcast to Canada. On arriving at the BBC, I asked the receptionist how long this would take, as I had other things to do in London. We all did. When she informed me I would be paid a guinea a minute while on the air, I took time to describe the crew's derring-do in some detail. I received a handful of five-pound notes that I dutifully shared with the receptionist at lunch.

*The map on pages 254-255 shows the operational area covered by Ed in 15 Group. A circle to the west of Ireland marks the spot where he sank U-boat U964.*

This submarine, seen surrounded by depth-charges, sank soon after the picture was taken.

# SABO LANTINGA

*Born in Fort Macleod, Alberta, Sabo joined the RCAF in March 1941 and was awarded his pilots wings in May 1942. He was posted to the UK in December. In October 1943 Sabo joined 14 Squadron RAF in North Africa, moving with the squadron to Corsica, Sardinia, and Italy. By September 1944 he had completed an extended tour of 295 hours, flying Marauders (B26). After discharge in August 1945, he worked as Airport Manager in Ft. McMurray and then with the Dept. of Transport. He added another 3500 hours to his log book before retiring in 1975.*

## Med, Yes—Club Med It Wasn't

When I joined the RCAF, aged 29 and with a university degree, I expected to be selected for navigation training but was told I was to be a pilot. After receiving my wings and completing operational training, my crew and I were posted to Algiers to await allocation to a squadron.

It was 5 October 1943 when we arrived at 14 Squadron (RAF) and were introduced to the Marauder, the B26. With a long body and short wings, the Marauder was known as "the flying prostitute" because it appeared to have no visible means of support. The Americans also called it "the Widow-Maker". With the highest wing loading of any aircraft in service, it took off at 150 mph, and landed at 120 mph according to some records, but 150 mph according to me. With its two 2000 hp Pratt and Whitney Double Wasp R-2800-43 engines, it had a good turn of speed. I got one up to 325 mph in a dive to wave height during a combat with Me109s. It was also heavily armed with 0.50-calibre machine guns, two in the nose, two in the dorsal turret, one in the tail turret, and one in each beam location.

Seats and controls were Cadillac-style, in contrast to the Spartan design of British aircraft, but pilots found them hard to fly. We carried a pilot, a co-pilot, a navigator, a wireless operator, a turret gunner, and a tail gunner. The co-pilot had the secondary duty of photographing shipping with a 14-inch camera. There was no automatic pilot.

The squadron's duties included anti-submarine patrols, shipping strikes, and coastal and harbour reconnaissance; aircraft always flew singly. Most of my trips were reconnaissance, photographing enemy shipping. We had no radar and so all the reconnaissance had to be done with the eyeball. The pilot and co-pilot did most of the reconnaissance, since the navigator was busy all the time and the gunners were constantly on the lookout for enemy aircraft.

In November we moved to Blida, near Algiers. I made my first operational flight on 16 December and my second on the 23rd when we went to Marseilles to fly into the harbour to check on the shipping there. En-route we flew at fifty feet, which resulted in the rear gunner complaining that his feet were getting wet. On 12 January the squadron moved to Ghisonaccia, in Corsica. From there we flew sorties into Genoa and Spezia in Italy, and Toulon, Nice, and other ports in France. We also flew sorties to Barcelona to check what shipping would be leaving there to supply the Germans.

All sorties were carried out at fifty feet, where we could sense the cushioning effect of the air between the aircraft and the water. Flying lower than fifty feet, the aircraft left a very visible wake for enemy aircraft above. Above fifty feet we could be detected by the enemy's coastal radar-controlled guns, which were extremely accurate.

On 11 May three Me109s attacked us while we were shadowing enemy shipping off Marseilles. I headed for the waves and levelled off–still taking evasive action–so close to the water that the shells from enemy fighters were bouncing off the water and striking the bottom of my aircraft. Drill called for the co-pilot to slide out of his seat to man the front guns, but as my co-pilot did so, his Mae West caught on the back of his seat and he hung there. I grabbed him, pushed him back into his seat, and told him to stay there. During the attack, the enemy pilot tried to manoeuvre into a nose attack, but as soon as he indicated a right turn toward me, I countered with a steep turn to the left, and flew under him. In the meantime the upper gunner found his gun was jammed, apparently a common occurrence. The rear gunner kept firing all the time even though enemy fire was striking the deflector plates on either side of his sight. My gunners sent one of the aircraft away pouring out smoke; the other two disappeared, probably damaged. When I landed, we had eighty-eight holes in the aircraft, including damage to the port aileron, one hole through a propeller, and holes in the self-sealing fuel tank. This meant we lost of forty gallons of fuel; when we landed red lights were showing on all fuel tanks.

On another occasion I was flying over a rough sea when just as we passed over a high wave we found ourselves above a Seibel ferry loaded with German troops being evacuated from Greece. The ferry seemed to explode with anti-aircraft fire coming straight at us. I had no choice but to fly through the flak and came away without a scratch.

Trouble happened on test flights too. On one occasion, a main wheel broke off and bounced against the aircraft, tearing off the pitot head and port aileron; this left me without an airspeed indicator or any aileron control. The control column was jammed. Using engine power, my co-pilot and I kept the aircraft level and made flat turns. We managed to maintain control and landed. I didn't know the wheel had gone. As soon as our speed fell off, we did three magnificent ground loops and collapsed into a heap of scrap. The aircraft was a complete write-off, but nobody was injured. I received a commendatory endorsement in my logbook for it. Our crew gained a reputation for always coming back, and so getting volunteers to fill a vacancy was never a problem. Quite a morale booster.

From Corsica we went to Sardinia, and then to Italy. Our sorties from Italy were mostly over the Adriatic Sea, with flights taking us as far away as the island of Corfu. I got to know all the little islands along the Yugoslavian coast. We also checked on places like Venice and Trieste. On my second-to-last trip we were directed to photograph the Italian luxury liner Rex, in harbour in Trieste. We did get the picture, despite a hot reception from flak guarding the ship, and the next day a group of Beaufighters hit it with dozens of high explosive rockets; the beautiful thing turned over and sank. That was my last operational mission.

# J. MURRAY COOK

*Murray was born in 1921, joined the RCAF in August 1940, and was awarded his Navigator wing in March 1943. He began his operational tour in June 1944 and completed it in May 1945. After the war, Murray joined the Department of External Affairs and served in Ottawa, Peru, Italy, Egypt, Germany, Kenya and Uganda, retiring in 1974 to his own business in Sooke. He lives now in Victoria.*

## What did you do in the war, Daddy?

I've never forgotten the distinctive smell of the Underground stations in London during World War II. It was, I assume, a by-product of the trains and the people. Thousands of Londoners spent their nights sleeping on the platforms sheltering from the raids by German bombers and, in the last year, from the Vls and V2s. Some had nowhere else to sleep, their homes having been destroyed, while others rushed in when the alert was sounded by the eerie sirens. Very sad it was—but the Londoner was a strong minded cheerful person who rolled with the many punches the metropolis suffered in six years of war. But I am ahead of myself.

About two months after visiting the recruiting office I was called up in August 1940, and reported to 1 Manning Pool on the grounds of the Canadian National Exhibition. Our first pay parade took place in the ring normally used for judging cattle, much to the surprise of two English actors who had come up from Hollywood to join the RCAF. And we had a lot of recruits from the USA, all of whom seemed to be called Tex no matter their origin.

In due course, suitably outfitted as an AC2, I joined a group posted to No. 1 Wireless School in Montreal. The school was situated in a former home for the blind and had no mirrors. After several months I graduated as a Wireless Operator Ground (WOP/G) with the rank of AC1. My first posting was to the Army Co-op School at Rockcliffe on 1 March 1941. The School folded within six weeks, following the destruction of two of its three Lysanders. I was then posted to the Army Co-Op Detachment in Dartmouth, Nova Scotia, alternating as the wireless op in a Lysander and at one of the shore-based heavy artillery sites. Two months later I was helping to load a ship which was to transport a group of us to Labrador to establish weather and wireless stations on the coast. We set course in mid July and, although it was technically summer, we had to battle ice and dodge icebergs for most of our journey.

Our first stop was Cartwright where we were immediately engaged in carting supplies from the boat, digging holes and ditches, mixing cement and what have you in order to erect a tower for the aerial and accommodation for the four-man detachment—two wireless operators, one wireless mechanic and one cook. Our next stop was an Eskimo Village at Hopedale, where we repeated the labour and I learned new trades such as building frames, laying floors, and roofing. Leaving Hopedale we battled our way up to Cape Chidley, only to find the terrain too steep to land and construct a base. We turned south for Hebron where my team was slated to stay. We had the usual work to erect a tower but inherited three "model homes" which the Eskimos had refused to live in. In addition to the Eskimos there was a Moravian mission, a Hudson Bay post, and a Newfoundland Ranger. (Newfoundland was not part of Canada at that time.) We were supporting a couple of Stranraer flying boats and the occasional PBY. Since we had only one hour of instruction in meteorology and were issued with only a few instruments, our weather reports must have been fairly rudimentary. The four of us got along well and enjoyed the company of the aircrew from time to time and the friendship of the Missionary and his wife and that of the Ranger. We were asked if we would stay the winter, but our Corporal declined. The powers at Eastern Air Command must have realized it would have been difficult to keep us supplied, and we were not reprimanded. The first snowfall was on 10 September; by the end of the month we were airlifted out to North West River. It looked like an oasis after the starkness of the Coast.

A PBY had crashed and sunk in the inlet and efforts were being made to raise it. I spent the better part of a day pumping air for a diver in one of those old fashioned suits. The craft was eventually raised. By this time Macnamara Construction Company was set up in a camp called Happy Valley, now a town or city, in preparation for the building of the aerodrome at Goose Bay.

In mid-October a group of us went to the Goose Bay site to construct and establish a wireless station. We lived in tents until after Christmas and until we had constructed some "Bluebird Honeymoon Special" prefabricated cottages. Someone in Halifax had a sense of humour. They had also sent us a variety of dehydrated vegetables–all tasteless and unrecognisable except for the beets. Happily our cook was a pastry chef and managed to present us with appetising meals. He also preferred vanilla extract to Scotch. We had a busy work schedule but found time to relax on skates or at the bridge table. In March 1942 the first DC3 arrived to use the huge runway and some of us were flown out to Halifax for leave and reassignment. By now I had reached the dizzy height of LAC at $1.35 a day. Wealth and status at last. I could also proudly say I was in Goose Bay before the runways.

In April 1942 I was posted to No. 2 Air Navigation School, Pennfield Ridge, New Brunswick, as a staff wireless operator. This involved flying in Ansons and helping the trainee navigators. One important chore was to wind out, and more importantly wind in, the trailing aerial. Towards the end of May we moved the school to Rivers, Manitoba. We had good weather for the four-day trip, flying relatively low to enjoy the scenery. The Ansons were operational the day after we arrived and there followed a summer of flying over Manitoba and Saskatchewan. Our average flight was 3½ hours day or night and by early September I had logged over 400 hours—not bad for a wireless operator, ground.

In early September I was remustered for training as a navigator. After ITS in Toronto our training was at Malton, site of today's Pearson Airport. On graduation in March 1943 as a pilot officer I enjoyed embarkation leave and was at last on my way to the war and the UK. Our convoy sailed on 13 April; it took fifteen days to make the crossing. I have only two interesting memories. One was a talk by the ship's doctor on Lenin, and the other was waking each morning to find our ship in the middle of the convoy. Our prudent captain probably saved our lives with this manoeuvre: two ships were carrying aircrew, ours and one other. The other was torpedoed with the loss of 99 of the 100 aircrew on-board. We did not hear of this tragedy until three weeks after we reached UK. The lone survivor, a classmate from Malton, reported his experience to us.

We had arrived in Bournemouth during a temporary surplus of aircrew and were seconded for ten days to the army in Kent and for the better part of a month to an RAF Regiment school in Sidmouth, Devon.

By the end of August we were pretty fed up and somewhat embarrassed by our inaction. When volunteers were called for to take a course for wireless-navigators to replace British Nav/Ws on Canadian squadrons, I jumped at the chance. By mid-September I was at RAF Cranwell with twenty-four others. It was a damp and cold winter in Lincolnshire; I remember the steam coming out of my uniform when standing in front of a fire. We worked hard but also tried to field an ice hockey team for a Canadian Forces league. We were not very skilful which was just as well since we were eliminated before having to play a team with the NHL Kraut line.

In January we were posted to No. 3 School of General Reconnaissance, Lytham St. Anne's for further training. The high point was playing golf at the famous club where Bobby Jones won one of his championships. His wooden-shafted mashie was displayed in a glass case in the clubhouse. Next stop was an OTU near Carlisle where I was crewed with F/Lt Chris Wilson, a Canadian who had joined the RAF before the war. We did a lot of training on Beaufighters and were posted to RCAF 404 Squadron at Davidstowe Moor, near Tintagel, King Arthur's legendary castle in Cornwall.

Chris and I did our first familiarisation flight on the squadron on 24 June 1944. Chris was starting his second tour on 404 Squadron, while I had finally reached an operational squadron 22 months after beginning my training for aircrew.

No. 404 Squadron had been formed in April 1941, the second RCAF squadron to be formed overseas, the first Canadian unit in Coastal Command, and the only one of its type in the RCAF. During its four-year wartime history the squadron was primarily involved in anti-shipping operations. Originally flying Blenheims in a fighter reconnaissance role, it converted to Beaufighters in 1942; from 1943 its principal weapon was the rocket projectile (RP). It often operated in support of torpedo squadrons. Early in its career and again at the time of the invasion of Normandy the squadron engaged German

Attack on German troopship off Askvoll, Norway,
by S/Ldr Robert Schoales, 404 Squadron, 19 September, 1944

Photograph courtesy of DND

warships successfully. During the course of the war 404 operated in the North Sea, the Bay of Biscay and off the coasts of France, Holland and Norway. For much of its time the squadron was involved with other strike squadrons in an attempt to disrupt the shipment of vital supplies from Sweden and Norway to Germany. Merchant ships and their armed escorts were, for the most part, forced to travel only at night. The Beau was a sturdy aircraft that flew well on one engine. Three times S/Ldr Schoales brought back a damaged aircraft; on one occasion he did this despite having been wounded. The squadron was disbanded on 14 May 1945 but re-established in 1951 as a maritime reconnaissance squadron flying Lancasters from the East Coast of Canada. *To the best of my knowledge the squadron is still active. There is good coverage of its war time experience in Volume 3 of the official history of the RCAF.*

When we joined the Squadron the Commanding Officer was W/Cdr Ken Gatward, RAF. He had joined the squadron several months earlier and took over when the CO was shot down and taken prisoner. He had quite a reputation for derring-do. In 1942 he flew a Beaufighter to Paris, dropped a fleur-de-lis (or was it a tricolour?) on the Arc de Triomphe, and went on to shoot up the Kriegsmarine headquarters. He had great leadership qualities and a keen sense of humour; he was well liked by everyone on the squadron. He finished his third tour in August having been awarded the DSO and DFC and bar.

Shortly after we joined the squadron it was transferred to Strubby in Lincolnshire and on 15 July Chris and I had our first operation. It was a reconnaissance flight alongside the Frisian Islands but we did not sight any targets. I remember having some difficulty with my Gee box (position finder) but Chris had had a similar problem before and was able to suggest the solution. Our second operation resulted in a strike south-west of Heligoland at last light. There were several aircraft involved and my principal recollection is that the attack on the ships was very impersonal and the flak slightly unreal. Had we been hit I am sure my recollection would be quite different. We had two more operations, neither of which resulted in strikes, and some training exercises in July. In August we were transferred back to Davidstowe from which base we flew ops over the Bay of Biscay. In ten days we had five operations, three of which involved strikes on shipping or dock installations. Twice we had to land at an aerodrome near the coast as we were running out of fuel.

At the end of August we returned to Strubby, packed our gear, and moved to Banff on the Moray Firth. In September we managed three Rovers with Mosquito protection. The purpose was to get to the Norwegian coast at first or last light in hopes of finding a target. Sometimes we did, but not in September. In October we had even less action, due in part to bad weather, and to our transfer to another base at Dallachy, also on the Moray Firth.

The weather in Scotland during the fall and winter often kept us grounded for several days and even when we got off, the weather on the Norwegian Coast could prevent useful operations. Quite often one or two aircraft would do a weather recce to determine whether an operation should go ahead. We usually flew to our target area in formation at about 50 feet to keep under the German radar; navigation was by drift and windlane more often than not. We spent a lot of time on standby waiting for the weather to clear or for word of a possible target.

We also did jobs such as paper navigation exercises, studying ship and aircraft recognition, or simply shovelling snow off the runway. We would also practice formation flying or gunnery. On one occasion I hit the drogue with two bullets out of a hundred. Perhaps it is a good thing I never had to fire in anger. I also remember that the butt of the swivel-mounted machine gun used to bug me by getting tangled up in my parachute harness.

Chris and I had six trips from Scotland before he became ill and was sent off on sick leave. This left me as a spare navigator. From early November until almost the end of January I flew with six different pilots on ten flights, six being operational. A tour of duty was two hundred hours, so experienced crews were leaving regularly and new ones arrived to replace them. In my case I was crewed on 23 January with F/O McCallan who rejoined the squadron for a second tour without a navigator. He had been instructing on Mosquitos in Canada and was disappointed to find that we were still using Beaus.

As a spare I had had a couple of interesting experiences. Just before Christmas F/Lt Cummins and I were despatched to Ireland to collect turkeys for the Squadron dinner. We had a Beaufort and also took our Irish nurse for a holiday at home. Unfortunately we ran into a post when taxiing and bent one propeller. Another crew came for the turkeys but left us to wait for the repairs. As this was Christmas the repairs were slow and although we had a good dinner and too much Irish whiskey it was not the most enjoyable week. I returned to base in time to do a last light Rover with F/O Lee on new year's eve. I note in my logbook, "Feisten Light to Christiansend–no flak–saw four neutral motor vessels." Then on 4 January I was sent to an RAF station near Londonderry for a Loran course. This was a new position-finding system and my job was to determine whether it would be of any use to us. I had one day trip and two night trips in Wellingtons and some training on the ground. On return I reported that in my view it would not help us over the North Sea since there were not enough stations to give us a fix.

In early February some of us were sent to Leuchars for a gunnery course. The remarkable thing about this posting is that I did not think of playing golf at nearby St. Andrews. Perhaps the weather was unsuitable. Let's hope I had some reason. Back in Dallachy, Mac and I had our first op together on the last day of February. In March we had four operations on the coast of Norway, bad weather for three of them and a nil sighting on the fourth.

On 22 March we were posted back to Banff to convert to Mosquitos and Mac was one of the few able to help the pilots make the conversion. We did our first Mosquito operation a month later–a recce from the Naze to Lerwick–nil. On 3 May we went to the Kattegat and back across Denmark at tree top level. The weather was so bad there was no action, but people on the ground waved sheets at us. That was rewarding in a way.

We had one more operation–a submarine recce–on the 16th. That was eight days after "D-Day". The squadron was officially disbanded on 24 May at 2359 hours.

During its four-year wartime duty, 113 members of the squadron were killed and three taken prisoner. There were seventy awards for gallantry. The worst day, 9 February 1945, became known as Black Friday. Eleven aircraft from 404 took part in an attack on several ships at the end of a narrow fjord, met a barrage of Ack-Ack, and ran into strong opposition from Fw190s. Six of the eleven were shot down. Only one pilot, Roger Savard, survived. He became a POW. I was not flying that day.

My two best friends on the squadron were Jack Tomes and Don Burns. Don was 32 and called Dad since he was our oldest member. Another English navigator, called Uncle Don, had a lucky escape. Having broken a finger he was grounded for a few days and his pilot, Maurice Baribeau, flying with a replacement navigator, was shot down off the coast of Norway. The navigator was killed and Maurice managed to reach the shore. He was picked up by the wrong Norwegian and turned over to the Germans. He told us later that he and his guard arrived in Hamburg just after a devastating raid. Some angry citizens wanted to get at Maurice but his guard held them off. *Maurice and I spent a happy year together in the 60s at the National Defence College.*

Jack Tomes was awarded the DFC for helping his wounded pilot to fly back from the Norwegian Coast and land the aircraft. The pilot's windscreen had been shattered and the pilot badly wounded. Jack, who was over six feet, managed to get up to the front of the Beaufighter in record and lifesaving time.

I have mentioned flying to Ireland with John Cummins. At an earlier time his plane had crashed and caught fire. He was trapped and unconscious but his navigator, Red McGrath, managed to rescue him. The squadron doctor unaware of the rescue plunged into the burning aircraft in search of John. Both men were given awards for bravery. John was badly burned and after treatment fitted with a wig. One night at Davidstowe Moor he was returning from a night in town when he decided to take a short cut through a farmer's field. On climbing over the stile John said he lost his wig and tried on four or five before finding the right one. A likely story.

My favourite bit of squadron memorabilia is a battered pewter mug donated by John when he left for home.

Not all our activities were in the air. From time to time we had various ground duties. I was on duty one day; in some way I was connected with the take-off for an operation. We used to take off in quick succession and form up in a V behind the leader. This time two of the aircraft crashed in the circuit and all four men were killed.

There were other non-flying activities on and off the base. At Dallachy a group of us put on a minstrel show. We even tried soccer and rounders and many an hour was spent playing bridge and poker for small stakes. In Scotland we discovered we could cycle to nearby farms and buy eggs. Most of us had a carton in the kitchen. But when we were flying we were entitled to two eggs from squadron rations. One before we took off and one if we returned. The black joke was to ask your friend if you could have his egg if he didn't return. I suppose this type of humour helped to relieve the tension in the briefing room.

I have not mentioned the non-flying members of the squadron. We had a doctor, Grant Beacock, who was a psychiatrist; a nursing sister; a dentist from the Army Dental Corps; a padre or God-botherer, as they were affectionately known; an adjutant; and an Intelligence Officer. But the mainstays were the groundcrew: the mechanics, fitters, electricians, and armourers, who kept our planes in good order; and, of course, the WAAFs who were parachute packers, wireless operators, cooks, drivers and sometimes our dates.

Looking back on my eleven months on 404 Squadron, during which I took part in twenty-eight operational sorties including five strikes, I realize how fortunate I was to come away with no really scary memories. I must have been anxious when we had to turn back with engine trouble a couple of times, and when Mac and I were turned upside down one "dark and stormy night". On that occasion all loose equipment was on the ceiling briefly and then on the floor when Mac quickly righted our Beaufighter.

This leads me to the different accommodations for navigators in the Beau and the Mosquito. The navigator in the Beaufighter was several feet behind the pilot, separated by four boxes holding the cannon shells. There was a large Perspex cupola and a rear facing .303 machine gun with a 180° radius, a desk, and a swivel chair.

The Mosquito was faster and lighter, being made of plywood–rumoured to be an innovation pioneered by a Czech refugee in BC, if my memory serves me well. It was essentially a pilot's aircraft with barely enough room for the navigator to sit beside him. There was either a Gee or a radio on a shelf behind and a board on the knee for chart work. Although a less convenient working space, being next to the pilot meant the navigator was closer to the action.

Although the squadron was officially disbanded in May, we stayed in Banff for the better part of a month until posted to a transit camp in Norfolk and subsequently to Torquay to await a ship home.

On 3 July I married a VAD from Yorkshire. We had a brief honeymoon in Torquay; I had to go on parade at 0800 and 1400 each day until boarding a troopship for home. I was discharged on 13 September 1945 and my young war bride joined me in Toronto in April 1946.

I was officially on the Reserve until my posting to the Embassy in Peru in 1948 when my military career came to an end.

# FRANK LAUGHLIN

*Frank was born in Summerland, BC. He joined the RCAF in January 1941 and received his Wireless Operator/Air Gunner brevet in September. He received further training in Britain and was posted to Egypt—first to 38 Squadron and later to 221 Squadron. Then he was sent to Malta to join 69 Squadron, Special Duty Flight. Frank returned to Britain, where he was an instructor at OTU before going back on ops with 423 Squadron in Northern Ireland. He was demobbed in October 1945.*

## Anti-Shipping Patrols
### The Early ASV Radar

Before being sent to the Middle East, I was trained to operate the ASV (Air to Surface Vessels) radar equipment fitted to the Wellington Mk VIII, an anti-shipping torpedo bomber. We spent a short time at Moreton-in-Marsh getting issued with khaki uniforms and doing fuel consumption tests with overload tanks, in preparation for flying to Egypt.

Our first leg took us to Gibraltar, then on to Malta to land there in darkness; the island was still a hot spot and short of everything, especially fuel, armament, aircraft, and crews. Two of our group were hijacked to stay there for operational duty. On reaching Egypt, all our crews were split up with some of us posted to Shallufa on 221 Squadron. For two months, we did no flying and enjoyed ourselves swimming in the Suez Canal.

Eventually we flew back to Malta. One aircraft had engine trouble and had to ditch. They were fairly close to Malta and were soon picked up by an Air Sea Rescue (ASR) launch. This was early November 1942, and the constant enemy bombing of the island had ceased, although there was still a lot of rubble everywhere.

We were now on 69 Squadron, Special Duty Flight (SDF). Our job was to operate at night, searching for and destroying enemy shipping on the way to supply Rommel's forces in North Africa. The Wimpy could carry two torpedoes but we operated with just one and some flares. On some of our trips, we carried only an overload fuel tank and flares; when we sighted any shipping we would home in the torpedo-carrying Albacores or Wellingtons and illuminate the target for them. We would also work with the navy using the same tactics, then fall back and watch the annihilation of the enemy. After one of the occasions, when landing back at the base, we discovered enemy fire had almost severed our port tailplane.

We were tasked with making strikes on the Italian fleet. We had an escort of Spitfires and Beaufighters until dusk and thus had some protection. We didn't find the fleet; perhaps that was fortunate for us.

We never fired a torpedo in anger. Night fighters occasionally stalked us but they never attacked. Our problems were with the engine and the ASV; because of this we did airtests just prior to each operational trip. The ground crews did their best given what they had to work with.

Due to illness, I was grounded for about a month, so when my crew's tour expired I joined 458 Squadron, which was just taking over the duties of our Special Duty Flight. This Squadron was Australian with many Canadians on it.

On one of our tests with this new Squadron, and flying with only a crew of three plus two ground crew, we experienced engine trouble on the way in to landing. We skidded across a grassy field and ended up against one of the many low stone walls in the area. Because the flares in the bomb bay ignited and because the Wimpy was a fabric-covered aircraft, we were a mass of flames in an instant. I removed the astro hatch and shot out, running a few yards to safety. No one was following me and because of the intense heat I could not get back to the plane. It seemed like ages before the two pilots, obviously injured, slowly climbed out through their hatch. Then one ground crew member came out of the astro hatch, and at last the second man exited through a fiery break in the fuselage. We all hurried as best we could to take cover behind another stone wall as the ammunition was starting to pop off and we knew the torpedo would explode. It soon did, leaving a large hole in the ground and a broken, twisted, skeleton of the aircraft. An ambulance soon found us and conveyed us to sick bay.

Soon after that incident, I was tour expired with the mandatory 250 hours. I had made thirty-seven operational trips.

After home leave in Victoria, I was back on ops with 423 Squadron on Sunderlands, operating out of Castle Archdale, Northern Ireland. These aircraft were powered by Pegasus engines of the same type as on our Wellingtons in Malta but were better maintained.

Our crews consisted of ten or eleven members: two or three pilots, observer, two flight engineers, three W/AGs and two A/Gs. Our pilots were trained in navigation and gave the observer a helping hand. Our ASV was an improved system that covered the full 360 degrees. In lieu of the dipoles of the earlier ASV, the new model had an aerial (a scanner) installed under each wing.

The Sunderland carried 250-pound depth-charges (eight of them) that ran out of the bomb bay on rails attached to the underside of the wings.

In all the fifty trips our crew completed doing anti U-boat patrols and convoy escorts, operating off the coast of France, the Bay of Biscay, the Western Approaches, mid-Atlantic, Iceland, the Shetlands, and the Irish Sea, we never saw or made contact with the enemy. We were required to do 650 hours for a tour. I had almost accomplished this when the war in Europe came to an end.

In 1992 the Maltese government issued "The Malta George Cross Fiftieth Anniversary Medal" to mark the 50th Anniversary of the award of the George Cross to Malta by King George VI. All military personnel, merchant marine, and civilians who had served in Malta or in connection with the defence of Malta between 10 June 1940 and 8 September 1943 were eligible for this medal. In September 1993 I received this award from the Consul General for Malta, in Vancouver, British Columbia..

# N. O. (MONTY) WILLIAMS

*Monty was born in 1922 in Cardiff, South Wales. He joined the RAF in April 1941 and was awarded his pilot wings in February 1943. After completing OTU, he arrived on 210 (Catalina) Squadron, Coastal Command (April '44.) Monty was demobilized in July 1946 and emigrated to Canada to work in the lumber industry. He retired in 1989 as Vice-President & General Manager of a wholesale lumber company in Vancouver.*

## From Bicycle to Bomber
### The recollections of one who flew aircraft for five years, but couldn't drive a car

In August 1941 I reported for duty and after the usual run around in transit camps, the Air Ministry started me off on my world cruise aboard the Empress of Russia. We were bound for South Africa in company with the battleship Prince of Wales and the battle cruiser Repulse. I may have been the most widely travelled airman in the Commonwealth Air Training Plan, not by air, but by water and rail. During the war I spent almost six months travelling on six different troopships, visiting the outposts of Empire.

I was walking along a street in Cape Town with a friend when a large black limousine stopped. A chauffeur asked us where we were headed.

"To the opera house."

"Step in. We are also going there."

In the back was an old gentleman with a goatee and dressed in formal clothes. He did not volunteer his name but he did ask us a number of questions. At first we thought we were meeting an enemy agent, but none of his questions were of a military nature. As we stepped from the car on arrival, we asked the chauffeur the name of the gentleman. He replied, "Do you not recognise him? He is the Prime Minister, General Smuts".

The Prince of Wales and the Repulse headed for Singapore to be sunk by air attack and we headed to Bulawayo for air training.

Skipping over ITW, we arrived at 27 EFTS Induna and started our flying training. This brings me to my second dubious possible record. I believe I hold the record for taking the longest time to go solo of any pilot in the Commonwealth Air Training Plan. It took me 34 hours and 15 minutes.

After I had flown for sixteen hours, the Chief Flying Instructor took me up for a wash-out test. On landing, he stepped from the plane. I'd failed.

"I don't know why you haven't gone solo long before now; there is nothing I can do about it at this point; you'd better return on the next course, and try again."

Perhaps the fact that he was a fellow Welshman influenced his decision. So, back for another try. This time I had flown for another eighteen hours and was awaiting my second wash-out test, when the instructor stepped from the plane.

"Take her up. If you want to kill yourself, do it without me."

I don't know why they persevered. Perhaps the Chief Flying Instructor was trying to save face. If he is still alive I would like to let him know he is not responsible for my death. I survived the war.

I finished EFTS and came the time to decide the direction I wished to take in my career. My last instructor was an ex-fighter pilot and, since I had so many hours on Tiger Moths and had become proficient in aerobatics, he suggested fighters but as I had no desire to kill myself quite so quickly, I opted for Coastal Command.

Off to Kumalo for SFTS on Oxfords, where I redeemed myself somewhat by going solo quite quickly. On receipt of my wings as a sergeant pilot, I was off on my journey again, stopping at George for a course in navigation.

Thence to Durban to board an American troopship, the Sibone, bound for New York—carrying German prisoners of war that we had to guard—and further training.

In January 1944 I was posted to 131 OTU on Loch Erne in Northern Ireland as a second pilot on Catalinas. On completion, we were sent to Sullom Voe in the Shetlands to join 210 Squadron.

On about our third patrol, we headed out over Muckle Flugga light. We had been in the air for approximately eighteen hours and were nearing the limit of our endurance. We were flying at about 300 feet, with a cloud base at about 500 feet and visibility was not much more. I was half asleep in the second pilot's seat with the automatic pilot in control and the skipper behind the bulkhead talking to the navigator, when we sighted a submarine on the surface. By the time I had taken over from the automatic pilot and the skipper was back in his seat, we had passed right over the U-boat. The skipper circled around and went in to attack. We dropped our depth charges, with no sign of damage, so we went in again at the breakneck speed of eighty knots with all our guns blazing (one .303 gas-operated Vickers machine gun in the nose). We then tried to drop the only armament we had' left, our cache of house bricks, down the conning tower and onto the white German faces staring up at us. We used to load up house bricks from a construction site in case of such an emergency.

Having sent out a sighting report earlier, we circled around and awaited the appearance of the relief aircraft. We couldn't understand why the sub stayed on the surface for so long, but learned later it was a flak submarine stationed there for the specific purpose of enticing aircraft in to be shot down. The old spider and the fly concept. We were lucky to escape unscathed, considering we passed over it three times at a height of 50 feet. See map on pages 244/255.

The relief aircraft arrived, piloted by F/Lt Cruickshank, and we headed for base. He went in to attack and was gravely wounded. He was taken back to the bunk and made as comfortable as possible, while the second pilot flew the aircraft back to base. For this action, F/Lt Cruickshank was awarded the Victoria Cross. I was pleased to hear later that he fully recovered from his wounds. *(F/Lt Cruickshank was well and active at the Aircrew Association Reunion in Dundee in October 1997.)*

In the course of half a tour of ops (400 hours) we sighted one other submarine but since it was off Scapa Flow, we were not allowed to attack it; this was the Royal Navy's domain. We were required to send out a sighting report and then shadow the submarine until the navy came out in full force to destroy it. Something, apparently, they never failed to do.

I then sailed to Canada on the New Amsterdam and went by rail to Pat Bay, arriving there in early September 1944, for a captain's course on Cansos. While at Pat Bay we heard reports of a number of Liberators blowing up on the circuit at Comox and Abbotsford. It was thought this happened because the auxiliary tanks were empty but not purged and a spark from the wireless or the bomb bay doors closing caused the gases to explode. This problem was solved later, I understand, by ensuring that the auxiliary tanks were kept filled at all times. The irony of this will become apparent later in my narrative.

I arrived at Pat Bay as a flight sergeant and left there as a flying officer in late January 1945, heading back across Canada by rail to join the new Mauritania. On arrival in Britain we set sail for India on board the Winchester Castle.

I joined 240 Catalina Squadron in Madras. After a few patrols with them, they decided I did not fit in with their plans and shipped me off to Kolar, in the Central Provinces, for a conversion course on the dreaded Liberator. I was a little apprehensive about this move, partly because of the reports we had received at Pat Bay, partly because I hadn't landed on solid ground for almost two years, and partly because of a rumour that wings would fall off Libs in extreme weather. I have talked to a number of Liberator pilots since that time, and none of them had heard of, or experienced such a problem. Fortunately, I didn't have such an experience either. I did, however, have one chance to prove or disprove it.

Despite my misgivings, on the first day of flight at Kolar I had two flights with an instructor in the morning and went solo in the afternoon of the same day.

When the course was completed I found myself posted to a Dutch naval Liberator squadron, 321 RNNAS at Trincomalee, Ceylon. The Dutch Air Force in the East consisted of two squadrons, one army and one navy. The pilots were all very experienced, most of them having flown eight to ten thousand hours. A second pilot could not become a captain until he had clocked five thousand hours. As a result of this I, with my meagre eleven hundred hours, would on occasion, when my own second pilot was indisposed, have a second pilot with more than three thousand hours experience sitting in the other seat. I have explained this to try to justify what happened to me later. Incidentally, the Dutch pilots on the squadron were receiving, if I remember correctly, about fifteen dollars an hour flying pay. As a result of this largesse, we did not pay mess fees, nor did we ever buy a drink in the mess; every night one of the officers would have a birthday party with free drinks all around. Each of the officers must have had a dozen or more birthdays a year.

While I was in Ceylon, our war ended and the squadron was moved to the Cocos Islands in the Indian Ocean, to assist in the ongoing Indonesian war. Our duties consisted of flying medical supplies from Ceylon to Java, using Cocos Islands as a staging post. We would return to Ceylon carrying internees, mostly children. The distance was twelve hundred miles from Ceylon to Cocos, and eight hundred miles from Cocos to Batavia.

When we left Cocos Islands, headed for Ceylon, the weather report had told us of a front close to Ceylon. We flew into heavy cloud soon after take-off, and I decided to climb over it. We broke cloud at about 10,000 feet and could see the anvil of a cumulonimbus at 30,000 to 35,000 feet. We didn't carry oxygen, but we had on board a pet pi-dog, we used to call our third pilot. When we were getting too high he would start frothing at the mouth. He was frothing and so I decided to turn into the cu-nim. It was so violent I was thrown up and hit my head on the ceiling. When the noise of the hailstones hitting the aircraft drowned out the sound of the engines, I chickened out and did a 180-degree turn out of there.

The Cocos-Keeling Islands

I am sure a lot of pilots have a vision of hell, especially those who flew over enemy territory. My vision is of having dropped down to about 300 feet over a very angry sea, with a cloud base at 400 feet, almost dark, lightning flashing all around, dodging water spouts that were all around us like pillars of doom. Then, reaching the eye of the storm, checking with the engineer on the amount of fuel left, and learning there was barely enough to reach Ceylon–and with another front ahead of us, I decided to turn back through the maelstrom to base. Fortunately, we had not quite reached the point-of-no-return. And the wings didn't fall off my Liberator.

We Coastal Command pilots did not experience the prolonged, intense emotions or dangers of bomber or fighter pilots but we did have our moments. Flying for ten hours over nothing but water, with one engine out of commission and thirty children as passengers, was no picnic. We didn't carry parachutes, just dinghies to accommodate the crew, and knowing that even with a perfect ditching the Liberator would float for only thirty seconds, this gave one cause for anxiety. I must admit that after landing in Ceylon with only twenty minutes fuel left, my knees gave way as I stepped from the aircraft.

Since the runway at Tan Jan Preok airfield in Batavia was only twelve hundred feet long, we were instructed to fly in low over the fence, touch down immediately, and jam on the brakes. This of course was not a problem for the Dutch pilots, as they could land on a postage stamp, but since I was a first pilot, I too had to land there.

I managed to land in Batavia twice, without breaking the aircraft, but on the third try I had problems. I was instructed to fly the squadron CO and his wife to Batavia, to attend a reception for Lord Louis Mountbatten. I made my usual approach and touched down, but when I looked ahead, something had changed. Without my knowledge the runway had been extended that day by three hundred feet of new blacktop. There were no markers showing the extension, and I ran on to the still soft blacktop. Since it was a very busy airfield and there were no other taxi strips, one had to sit and await instructions from the tower before taxiing back down the runway to the far end. When I received the go-ahead I tried to turn to port and discovered that my nose wheel was stuck in the tar at an angle to starboard. I decided to turn to starboard over the grass. It had been raining heavily the night before and the ground was very soft. When I had managed to turn 180 degrees my port wheel sank into the mud and jammed against the side of the runway. My port props were turning just above the ground so I switched off the engines and waited for assistance. A bulldozer was sent to pull me out.

While this was going on, I received word that Lord Louis Mountbatten and the station CO were observing the action and were asking to speak to the pilot. Since I had no desire to meet the great man under such circumstances, I made myself scarce and I too became an interested observer at the back of the crowd on the other side. They never did catch up with me.

*You may well wonder why I would tell a story of an event that possibly happened often in those days, a simple runway accident. Well, forty years later, I was living in West Vancouver and my youngest sister came out for a visit from Wales, bringing her new husband to meet us. (Her first husband, whom I had met, died some time before and she remarried.) We were sitting in the den one evening having a drink, and Geoffrey was relating some of his war experiences. He was in the Indian Army during the war, and in 1945 had been in charge of maintenance at Tan Jan Preok. I told him I had landed there on Christmas Eve that year. That was when one of war's co-incidences came to light.*

*"You weren't the fellow who got stuck in the mud, were you?"*

*"Yes I was."*

*"I was the one driving the bulldozer that pulled you out."*

*He also told me something I had forgotten– that he'd pulled off my nose wheel.*

Hoping to get a better Christmas dinner than the tinned turkey and isinglass eggs at Cocos, I refused to take off until the undercarriage had been tested. They had to fly in jacks from Ceylon, so we had several enjoyable days in Batavia. It was a bit dicey driving in to Batavia from the airfield as the taxi driver made us lie on the floor to avoid being shot. There were opposing troops on each side of the road firing at each other.

Flying back to base, I noticed a pronounced vibration in the rear of the aircraft. So the next day we were sent off to Ceylon, where we spent six glorious weeks in a Dutch bungalow, working only one day a week, air testing the aircraft. All good things come to an end. Someone must have reported the RAF airmen having a good time at the Galle Face Hotel, and we were posted to 203 squadron at KKS in northern Ceylon. When we arrived we were asked where we had been. They had lost track of us.

A few weeks later we were on our way home, this time by air landing at Leuchars in Scotland. Apparently, 203 squadron was to convert to Lancastrians, but since we had ended our usefulness, we were sent to Oxford to await demobilization.

I was sitting in the mess at about 0200 on my last day doing a crossword puzzle. The station CO and the squadron CO were playing crown and anchor at the bar. Suddenly one of them called to me.

"Come on, Williams, we have cleaned out everyone else, and no one is allowed to leave the mess with money in his pocket except us."

"But sir, I cannot play crown and anchor and in any case, I have only ninepence in my pocket."

"We will teach you."

When it came time to go in for breakfast, I had all the money, and everyone else was broke.

Most of this story has been told in the first person, so at this point, I would like to acknowledge the bravery of the other eight members of my crew for flying with me for eighteen months, and bearing it stoically. As I said to them on parting: "I may not have been the best of pilots, but I have managed to bring us through safely and uninjured".

The next day I picked up my pin-stripe suit as a reward from a grateful government, and went home to await passage to Canada. It was virtually impossible to obtain passage to North America in those days, but after trying for six months, a friend in Victoria, through a friend on the board of directors of BOAC, managed to get me a seat on a Constellation bound for New York. Since the war emergency was still in effect and as I was still subject to recall, I had to obtain permission from the CO of my last station to leave the country. This permission was forthcoming and in his letter, he asked me to stop in at the station on my way to London to pick up my passport, to give them a chance to win back their money. Unfortunately for them, I was in too much of a hurry.

Back in Canada, my mother-in-law taught me to drive a car, and one of the first things I did was to hit a telegraph pole.

# NED STANLEY

*Ned joined the RAF in late 1940 as a young man of nineteen. He was awarded his Observer brevet (navigator/bomb-aimer & gunner) in April 1942. He completed operational training and in 1942 he joined Coastal Command. Ned served with 86, 220, and 120 Squadrons in Ireland, Iceland, and Scotland and was demobilized in July 1946. He emigrated to Canada and later joined the RCAF. He retired to Vancouver Island in 1971.*

## The Arnold Scheme and the U-Boat War

Little did I realize when I volunteered for aircrew in late 1940 that my immediate future in the RAF held an ocean voyage across the North Atlantic to Canada, followed by a period of training in the southern USA.

Following the passing of the Lend-Lease Act by the US Senate in early 1941, General Hap Arnold, Deputy Chief of Staff US Army, and Chief of the US Army Air Corps, visited the United Kingdom to discuss with the British Government a plan under which the United States would provide facilities and instructors to train RAF pilots. This meeting was eventually formalized with a plan whereby pilots would be trained in the south-eastern states of the US at civilian-contracted Primary and Basic and Advanced military flying schools. It was formally named "The Arnold Scheme".

After initial indoctrination at Babbacombe and ITW at Newquay, our group of LAC airmen, complete with "white flashes" in their caps, was posted to Padgate where were we kitted out for overseas and, surprisingly, issued with lightweight grey civilian suits. This was a real puzzler until we attended a "secret" briefing at which we learned our overseas destination was the USA. In mid-1941 the US was still a neutral country and we would be going as civilian trainees.

In Toronto we settled in for a few days at the Manning Depot in the CNE grounds on the lakeshore and enjoyed the welcome sight of a city ablaze with lights and all the pleasures of food and drink. We were made most welcome by everyone except the SWO in the "bullpen", who received us with much joy as a bunch of new recruits for his circus.

Our brief stay in Toronto ended and the order came to dress in our civilian suits the following day for the train journey across the border to the USA. I'm sure the RCAF lads must have wondered what kind of an air force the RAF was that dressed its airmen in grey civilian suits to go to war.

We arrived at Arcadia, Florida, the last day of September as RAF Course 42D and joined with USAAC Class 39 at the Riddle Aeronautical Institute, a civilian contract flying school at Carlstrom Field. Here the RAF and USAAC cadets were kept in separate academic classes but otherwise lived together. Carlstrom was quite a new facility and our quarters were superb compared with RAF barracks. We did have to observe and respect the US service routines and procedures, many of which were strange to us. Our rooms had to meet a rigid daily inspection by the senior cadet captain and were judged with the "white glove" procedure for testing for dust and the "coin bounce" for bed-sheet tightness.

Discipline was enforced with a system of demerits, and "gigs" were handed out for misdemeanours or infractions of the rules. More than five demerits led to punishment in the form of a tour or march, kitted out with parachute on back, round the perimeter at weekends—one hour for each "gig" over five.

Starting time for the student day was 0530 hours, when rooms were readied for the morning inspection. This was followed by flights lining up before the flagpole for reveille every working day, and at seven we were in "formations" for academics or flying.

Dining room etiquette was a bit of a shock to us at first as we had to learn to sit on the first couple of inches of the chair at attention, eyes down, until permission to eat was given. After the first week or so, some of the rules were relaxed for RAF students; however, the beautiful board of the dining room with its never-ending supplies of wonderful dairy products, meats, southern fried chicken and fruits in abundance more than compensated for all the odd rules and regulations. We were happy in our paradise.

Tea with ice cubes and lemon or sugar seemed a bit foreign to us Brits at first though it soon became a favourite hot weather thirst quencher for most of us, along with bottles of ice-cold Coca-Cola, a beverage which hadn't then reached Britain.

Flying training was carried out in the Stearman PT17, possibly the finest primary training aircraft of all; they looked so great in the USAAC markings of blue fuselage, yellow wings, and red-and-white striped tail. Our instructors were all US civilian pilots, with a senior instructor for all check rides. Conditions for flying over the flat Floridian countryside were near perfect, with the weather CAVU (ceiling and visibility unlimited) ninety-five percent of the time, blue skies and fair-weather cumulus.

As can be imagined, we had our troubles initially with the southern accents of most instructors, but soon were used to hearing such warnings as "Watch your co-ordination, mister" or "Y'all better get that right next time, mister, or it's a lil' ol' check with the CI". Check rides were flights with the Chief Instructor to demonstrate your suitability to continue training or to be "washed out", the US term for ceased training. Apparently the Air Ministry were advised at the start of the scheme that the programmed failure rate at the US Flying Training Schools was about 50%. This was borne out by the final figures for RAF trainees in the Arnold Scheme: 7885 cadets input and 4370 graduate pilots.

The Primary Flying course at Carlstrom was for 60 hours with approximately half these hours solo. There was quite a pleasant ceremony attached to your first solo, a ceremonial throwing of the intrepid flyer into the base swimming pool, followed by an ice-cold coke poured over his head.

All too soon our time at the Riddle Aeronautical Institute came to an end. Our flying was over and academics almost completed when, on 7 December, Pearl Harbor was attacked and the President announced a State of War. We put our civvies away and were back in uniform full time.

After graduation from Primary Flying School at Carlstrom, our course was posted to Gunter Field, Montgomery, Alabama, for Basic Flying Training on the Vultee BT13, a similar aircraft to a Harvard but with a fixed undercarriage. At Gunter we were now on a USAAC base with standard West Point cadet procedures and routines, though the peacetime standards were slowly eased with the USAAC changing to a wartime regime.

We were slightly in awe of the more advanced single-wing BT13 aircraft and its increased performance, but we continued to learn. It wasn't too long before the dreaded check rides became part of the course. My turn came with the start of night flying when I had trouble with landings and had one real hard one. I didn't do well on my check ride, met the Washout Board, and was classified "Cease Training".

Life continued as I departed the "Land of the Free" and returned to Canada, where I was selected for training as an Observer. Following navigation, bombing and gunnery, and astro courses, I graduated with the coveted "O" wing given to observers. I was then shipped back to the UK.

On operations I flew with 86, 220 and 120 Squadrons of RAF Coastal Command operating from bases in Iceland, Scotland, and Northern Ireland. I won't say I wouldn't rather have been a fighter pilot, but I always enjoyed the challenge of being a navigator able to bring home the aircraft and crew after long ocean sorties over the North Atlantic, Denmark Strait, Norwegian North Sea, or Bay of Biscay. Navigation over these waters during the early 40's was carried out mostly by dead-reckoning and astro, and of course that homing ability all navigators are endowed with during their training.

The operational tasks of these particular squadrons were reconnaissance, search, and surveillance, which necessarily included the primary job of convoy escort. Success lay in preventing enemy submarines from reaching their attacking positions relative to a convoy and thus ensuring the survival of the convoy with its vital supplies for Britain.

On 16 October 1943 we took off in Liberator F120 from our home base, Reykjavik, in Iceland, flew across to Meeks Field (now Keflavik) where we fuelled and bombed up with depth charges. We then set course to convoy "ONS 206" at 1510 hours. We had been briefed to intercept this convoy, then carry out sweep searches for submarines that were gathering to attack it. We met the convoy approximately 380 nautical miles south-west of Iceland and after firing off our "colours of the day" to confirm our identity, received our orders from the Commodore, and commenced our square search, flying at our usual 150-foot altitude.

On our outbound flight, in accordance with normal operating procedures, we had checked our guns, depth charges, armament circuits, and low-level bombsight had all been checked.

After about half an hour on our search pattern, the radio operator reported a blip on the ASV radar. We homed on the blip and sighted a surfaced submarine at the two o'clock position at about three nautical miles. As we flew in on our attack run, letting down to fifty feet, the U-boat remained on the surface and let go with a barrage of anti-aircraft cannon fire. In reply our gunners sprayed the deck and conning tower with fire from our 0.5 calibre machine guns. The bombsight, being in the glass nose of the aircraft and operated by the navigator in the prone position, was immediately below the 0.5 gun operated by the front gunner. It is not difficult to imagine the noise and confusion of the moment.

We dropped four depth charges on the initial attack; they straddled the U-boat and exploded, noticeably slowing the enemy. The sub's cannon shells hit our tail plane and rear fuselage. The skipper swung around for a quick second attack, which we made with very little reply from the U-boat, which was now listing heavily and dead in the water.

Because of the damage to our aircraft, we deemed it advisable to return to base and did not see the U-boat sink. However an aircraft that had come over from another search area confirmed the sinking and we were later to learn that U-boat U470 went to the bottom, leaving fifteen survivors who were picked up by one of the corvette escorts and landed in Londonderry. The captain was not among them. He had been killed on the conning tower together with most of the gunnery crew during our initial attack.

It is quite a coincidence that, following my initial flying experience in the USA, all my 540 hours of operational flying as a navigator were carried out in American aircraft: Lockheed Hudsons, Flying Fortresses and Liberators.

The map on pages 254-255 shows some operational areas of the Battle of the Atlantic. The north-west corner was covered from Iceland.
On 16 October 1943 Ned attacked and sunk U-boat U470. A circle to the south-west of Iceland. Shows the approximate position of the sinking

# CONTRIBUTORS
## TRAINING

For student-pilots, training from Manning Depot to graduation from SFTS and the award of wings might take the following form.

Manning Depot (4 weeks)↦ITS (10 weeks)↦EFTS (8 weeks)↦SFTS (12 weeks)

The award of wings or brevet did not mean the man was ready for operations. There still remained AFU for fighter pilots, OTU for most crews, HCU for crews destined for the heavy bombers (Halifax, Lancaster, and Stirling), and GRS for crews destined to fly maritime missions (Stranraer, Liberator, Catalina) Other aircrew categories went through a comparable series of courses.

**ITS**   *Initial Training School: ground school preparation.*
**EFTS**  *Elementary; flying Tiger Moth trainers: small biplane.*
**SFTS**  *Service; flying Harvards (single) or Oxfords (twin)*
**OTU**   *Operational Training Unit*
**AFU**   *Advanced Flying Unit*
**HCU**   *Heavy Conversion Unit*
**GRS**   *General Reconnaissance School*

# TRAINING

Instructors and trainees in all the aircrew categories tell stories. The ones that follow are those of the men who were flying instructors and those who were u/t pilots–(pilots under training). They taught and learned those things that would often mean the difference between life and death in the skies; how to dodge and weave and throw a fighter plane around to elude the enemy; how to bring a multi-engine aircraft home on one engine; that take-off and landing is a rush; that a spin doesn't always happen as described in the manual; and how to react when lives were threatened by the expected awful and the awfully unexpected. In short u/t pilots learned how to survive.

Every man who volunteered for aircrew duty had a vision that was glamorous, exciting, thrilling, and, yes, courageous. Few chose to be an instructor, most wanted to go overseas, but they all learned that the air force sent you where *it* wanted not where *you* wanted.

Who taught us how to fly? Who transformed our airmen into the most powerful airborne weapon in the world? When they were killed, did they give any less than an operational man? Those who were killed died in the line of duty just as surely as did fighter, bomber, coastal, and ferry aircrew.

On 17 December 1939, Canada (Mackenzie King) and Britain (Lord Riverdale) signed an "Agreement Relating to the Training of Pilots and Aircrews in Canada and Their Subsequent Service". This was the start of the British Commonwealth Air Training Plan (BCATP). By mid-May 1940 the scheme was fully operational in Canada and soon afterward in Southern Africa. Other crews were trained in the U.S. under the Arnold Scheme Throughout the European war the BCATP trained 72,835 RCAF and 42,110 RAF & Commonwealth airmen. The Arnold Scheme trained a further 4000 pilots.

A few of our authors were trained in the UK. That was in the early years. The others were trained under the BCATP or Arnold Scheme.

*Ken Pask*

# BERT KEMP

*Bert joined the RAF in June 1939 and shortly after graduated as a Fitter II (engines). He re-mustered to aircrew and was trained in South Africa. He received his Navigator brevet in August 1944 and returned to Britain for operational training, in which he narrowly escaped death in a low-flying accident. He was demobbed in February 1946.*

## Just the Beginning

It's March 1941. I'm stationed at RAF Station West Kirby, a transit camp from which we are being posted to some place overseas. Don't know where, don't know when (lyrics of an old song). After dozens of parades and hundreds of rumours we are confined to camp. This is it–maybe.

Friday night and pay-day, a bottle or two of McEwan's Ale and a sausage roll, and for dessert an air raid. The sirens are wailing and we wander back to our huts. The Luftwaffe seems to know when ships are in dock and whether their sources of information are wrong by a day. There are always the cities of Liverpool and Birkenhead with their residents on which they can unload their cargo. We soon hear the unsynchronised throb of the planes and a little later the distant bang of something going up (Ack-Ack) and the crump of something coming down, a bomb, not too far away. We get inside and sit under the table. The stuff making the noise on the roof of the hut is pieces of anti-aircraft shells; what goes up must come down. It tinkles on the path outside. After a couple of hours the "All Clear" sounds and we go outside to have a look. There is a glow of a fire in the sky over Birkenhead and a large one just north that must be Liverpool. Confined to camp; there's nothing we can do but wait.

Wakey! Wakey! Rise and shine! Full pack in two hours. Get your breakfasts and be back here in arf-an-ahr, which in English means eat and return to this spot in thirty minutes. We're on our way and pull into the docks an hour or so later, where we are lined up and shouted at:

"You over there! You move to your left over here. The rest of you stay where you are."

Suddenly everything calms down and up the gangway we go. We're dispersed below deck and given a couple of minutes of instruction on how to sling a hammock, but not how to get in it or stop falling out of it. Butland, Doig and I go on deck and smoke Woodbines. We gaze at the oily water and wonder if we'll ever see this place again. Something floats past and almost disappears under the stern of the ship before we realize it's a body with scraps of clothing still on it. Jack informs one of the seamen who appears nonchalant.

"Bodies float in and out with the tide. They could be sailors from the sunken ships or men, women, or children from the dock area. Someone will get it out of the water eventually."

We're below decks for the night. There's another short raid and then the "All Clear". The thumps in the night are not bombs; they're mostly bodies falling from hammocks.

Breakfast. Then lifeboat stations with us looking like large-chested opera singers. The most important thing to remember is "Muster at this spot when the order is given". This is mastered after several practice runs and meeting faces wondering "Are you in the wrong place or am I?"

Still in dock. Doig thinks the powers that be are taking too long to make decisions and we should get out of here right now. Butland reminds him that ACI means Aircraftsman First Class and not Air Commodore and when we sail will be decided by the driver of the ship.

Afternoon and a break. We are looking over the rail again and watch some men in a boat with long poles with hooks on the end pulling things from around the pilings of the dock. We're shocked to find that the objects are bodies and parts of them. Most do not look as if they're complete, except for a very small one that is obviously a child. We thought children had been evacuated from port areas.

We leave the rail and join the line of volunteers. Having both served engineering apprenticeships, we're sure we'll land a job in the engine room, but no such luck—we finish up as volunteer Lewis gunners. However, anything would be better than peeling tons of spuds after carrying them up from the bowels of the ship. As we walk the deck, we take a look at the gun platforms; they seem to be quite substantial steel-sided boxes. We'll be on split watches, dawn till dusk and report for duty at 0600 hours the following morning.

We start our first watch and notice with a shock that the boxes we're in are not made of steel but of three-quarter-inch plywood painted grey. At least this should keep the wind off us. Doig says Robin Hood could put an arrow through both sides and kill a whale on the other side of the deck. This interests me. What would a whale be doing on deck? Doig points to a huge officer of the Merchant Service on our deck; twenty-stone, that's two hundred and eighty pounds.

The officer glances up at us and we scan the horizon for periscopes. Yes, periscopes. The U-boats can be anywhere and every little white foam pattern looks like a possible sighting.

We get under way during the night. As we move into the Irish Sea we pass wrecks and debris and oil slicks everywhere. We wonder how many ships lie under the water with no visible signs above.

We sail unescorted up to the south end of the Firth of Clyde and join a large convoy of troopships, merchant ships, two destroyers, a couple of corvettes, and what looks like a light cruiser. There is a lot of activity as we enter the North Atlantic; a special lookout for U-boats is ordered. The convoy steers a zigzag course to elude the enemy or at least make him rethink his strategy.

We sail north-west then west and the informed wizards on our deck decide we are going to Canada or the USA. But what about the sun helmets and baggy khaki shorts? Ah, that's to fool the spies. This thinking prevails until we're aware the sun is rising on the port side and setting on the starboard side. Interesting, since it had been rising over the blunt end of the ship and setting over the sharp end. We hear nothing from the experts and we don't disturb their quiet conversations and calculations. They are on average bigger than we are and they've been in the service longer, some as much as five weeks longer. Doig says we are on our way to the south pole and will be issued with mukluks and portable igloos when we arrive. I feel my education is far below average–I've never heard of an RAF station down there.

Day and night the destroyers are busy racing around and through the convoy. Sometimes we hear a dull thumping sound that, according to our informant, is caused by depth charges. One morning we see a dark cloud way back of the convoy. Our informer says it's a cargo ship. We press on and the cloud disappears over the horizon.

The Walrus from the cruiser is hoisted back onto its pad, and one of the destroyers appears astern. We have lost a ship and we don't know how many seamen. It's a sad day. This zigzag sailing and navy ships racing around continues until we sight land. We are told it's the Azores. We don't stay long and are off again.

There seems to be more activity by the navy as we sail south, more depth charges, and the Walrus is working overtime. There are dolphins and flying fish; Joe the crewman says there are sharks there too. We don't see any, but if this ship went down (or any of the others) we think we would. A sobering thought.

This I should mention: the NAAFI bloke pours beer into a small bath and drops a block of ice in it. Cold beer for a hot climate. By closing time what is in the bath is straw-coloured water and the less knowledgeable of us still drink it. Doig and I imbibe early as we don't like our beer too cold.

Land ahoy! This time it's Freetown, warm and muggy. The experts say this is it. Someone disembarks with a pile of packages and big sacks that could be mail for some poor bastards stationed at a place called Takoradi. We are escorted in by a Sunderland, causing Doig and me to put our tin hats on ready to do battle with the Hun; then we recognize it as one of ours. Thank God!

The local youth are around the ship in bumboats selling fruit such as bananas. Others dive in the water for coins, a bit risky since it is said there are sharks in the harbour.

Morning comes, with lots of comings and goings of launches ferrying people between the ships. We sail again to open water. The Sunderland flies over and disappears, probably on a routine patrol; we felt a lot safer when it was around. The convoy seems smaller, although we have no idea if it's because of casualties or some ships sailing off to another destination. We are moving faster, and soon we cross the equator. There is a small ceremony with King Neptune and his Court initiating the few selected for the soaping and flouring and other strange acts. All great fun. It takes one's mind off other things.

As we travel south we see strange stars in the sky, the Southern Cross and Canopus. The climate improves, but it's still hot in our Lewis box. The sailor tells us it's a bloody sight hotter in a steel one. He could be right, too.

The great minds have decided we're on our way to India, round the bottom of Africa. All this comes from a round potato with strange markings on it. We have seen them looking at this object intensively and muttering. Doig says he thought they had resorted to black magic. It seems the marks and inked-in areas are certain lands, islands, and such; the triangle was Great Britain and the shape like a fried egg was Ireland and what looked like dried spots of jam was the Azores. Africa is the lower limb with housemaid's knee.

A few days after we know the truth; we're wallowing in Table Bay off Cape Town. A good job too; the grub is getting worse and the old sweats tell us the more seasoning in it means it's going off. We take that with a pinch of salt.

Soon we are at dockside parading in baggy shorts and sun helmets; then we board a train bound for the Transvaal as trainees in the British Commonwealth Air Training Plan. Some people remember the Boer War and express their views in certain ways, but the majority are OK.

Some of the chaps that pass through the Air School do not survive; others do.

I am instructed by South African and RAF types, all of them excellent. Why did I remuster to aircrew? Even now I can still see that boatman lifting the little body from the oily waters at Liverpool and placing it in the boat.

We didn't join to kill women and children; we joined to bring the whole sorry tragedy to an end.

# KEITH MacKINNON

*Keith was born in Burdett, Alberta in 1919. He enlisted in the RCAF in October 1939 and qualified as a Senior Armament Instructor. He instructed on several units until remustering to aircrew training in September 1943. Keith was awarded his pilot wings in 1945. He stayed with the RCAF postwar, serving with No. 1 Air Division and at AFHQ in various staff positions. He retired in October 1968.*

## Flying Against Nature and the Dollar Watch

The January I spent at 17 Service Flying Training School, Souris, Manitoba was a terrible month for flying training. The weather was awful: snow, blizzards, and an unexpected mixing fog. This latter claimed the lives of an instructor (new to the station) and his student when he mistook a road with a telephone pole on its border for the live runway. Fortunately for me I was not scheduled to fly on the morning of the fog and fatal crash; I was in ground school.

A session of bad-weather flying with one of my instructors on 27 January when the weather was indeed bad probably gave me a false confidence in my ability to fly in foul weather. Two days later the experience may have saved my life and the life of my fellow student.

The day dawned clear and sunny, and our flight commander decided to send the student pilots off on a sealed-envelope navigation exercise. One student was detailed to be the pilot, the other the navigator. The navigator was given an envelope he was to open after take-off. The envelope contained a three-course navigation plot. The navigator was instructed to direct the pilot to fly each course for the time given, at a specified height and airspeed. The final course would terminate back at base.

I was the designated pilot.

Following the instructions the navigator gave me, I climbed the Anson aircraft to height, turned onto course, and set the throttles for the speed at which we were to fly. I did not know how long I would continue on that heading; the navigator was to give me a course change at the end of the time shown on the instruction sheet. I continued to fly the course given for what I began to feel was too long. We were flying into a snowstorm, which added to my concern. My navigator insisted we had to continue on course for a few more minutes.

The storm was getting worse and I was flying on instruments. I decided we shouldn't wait for the course time to end but must get back to our station as quickly as possible. It was only then my navigator realized we had indeed flown too long on our first course: his dying one-dollar pocket watch had finally died.

The prairie blizzard was getting worse, and we were becoming aware that neither of us had the experience to cope with the terrible situation we were in.

Before I remustered, I had spent many hours in the nose of Anson aircraft, looking down on the prairies while teaching students the mysteries of the bombsight. Being familiar with prairie geography, I sensed we were somewhere north of a railway. I asked my navigator to move up into the co-pilot's seat and be prepared to help me locate the railway. I turned south and descended to a lower altitude. We found the railroad and followed it at low level to the first elevators that loomed out of the snow. I don't remember the name of the town, but believe it was near Regina. My navigator set a course for the base. It was wrong. Had we followed it we would have flown into North Dakota!

As the storm was getting worse, we wondered if we should climb to height and bale out. However, we knew if we did that, we would probably freeze to death on the ground or, if rescued, would not graduate as pilots. Nor would the abandonment of our aeroplane be appreciated by the authorities.

I had a quick look at our topographic map and gambled on a

course to fly at low level. After flying the course for what seemed an eternity, dimly through the blowing snow we could see 17 SFTS ahead. By this time, the windscreen and aircraft were becoming layered with ice. I opened the side window and stuck my head out into the blinding storm hoping I would see the live runway. I couldn't, the runways were blanketed in snow. But I did get a glimpse of a building I recognized as the maintenance hangar and knew that if I could make my approach to the right of it, I could land without hitting any buildings.

I flew the downwind and crosswind legs, which put me into wind for my approach to the right of the hangar. I had changed the prop to fine pitch, put on rich mixture, and lowered the wheels and flaps. On final I could see faint glimpses of the hangar, but I wasn't sure where the runway was. There was also a danger of flying straight into the ground or rounding out too high, stalling and crashing.

With my head stuck out into the stormy slipstream, I caught a glimpse of the perimeter fence ahead. I pulled my head back into the cockpit, looked at the instruments for the last time, rounded out, pulled off the throttles, and stalled–plunk, into deep snow, but on the runway.

Because of the deep snow I couldn't taxi. A tractor came out to tow the aircraft to H-Flight hangar. We were met by the flight commander and his deputy who gave us an emotional greeting and congratulated us for our safe arrival We arrived back long after all the other aircraft had landed and I'm sure they feared that as we were overdue, we must be casualties somewhere out on the Prairie.

The fact that we were not able to produce a completed plot and log didn't seem to matter. We were given credit for having completed the exercise, the only ones to do so that day. All the other crews, including instructors, had returned to base when the blizzard started. Without the modern day advantages of radio contact and runway lighting it was wise to do so.

After I had shakily signed the F17 and made the appropriate entries in my flying logbook, I was instructed to report to the squadron commander's office. Expecting to be congratulated for not losing one of his aircraft, I was surprised and humiliated to have him tell me that we had been reckless and foolhardy. I did not disappoint him further by admitting that we had also relied on a dying one-dollar pocket watch to time our courses.

The Spitfire MkVIII armed with two 20-mm cannon and four .303 machine guns. There were many versions of the Spitfire, adapted as high-level, low-level, dive-bombers, fighter-bombers, and photo-recce etc. Tet Walston recalls his love affair with a Spitfire MkXI

Photograph courtesy of D.N.D.

◆ Farnborough. Site of the memoir by Bryon Sims and the crash of the Whitley.

✈ Hugh McMillan's Halifax ditched in the North Sea just off Scarborough.

▲ Jack Hughes's story of The Dunking describes a major air battle in which he scored hits on an Me109 and an Fw190. He was downed by another Fw190 and baled out over the Channel.

■ Alec Uydens' Spitfire was damaged during a Rhubarb attack on railways and other targets of opportunity. He got back to the Allied lines before crash landing.

● Harry Pilkington tells the story of Daddy Dale who was lost somewhere in this area. Daddy's Mosquito would have been able to get home on one engine; so there must have been other damage to his aircraft.

→ Perry Bauchman tells the story of returning from a Rhubarb and losing his engine. He made a dead-stick landing at Bolt Head in the south-west of England

The map shows radar coverage as of 1940, the time of Mike Cooper-Slipper's gripping memoir. The outer boundary shows coverage of the early radar, Chain Home. The inner boundary shows the shorter-range coverage of Chain Home Low. In later years, the UK introduced Chain Home Extra Low to detect enemy planes comes coming in just above sea-level. German radar had similar limitations and is the reason our authors talk of flying "under the radar".

Photograph courtesy of Salamander Books.

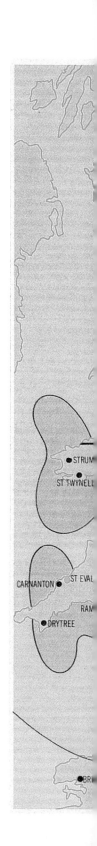

DREM
COCKBURNSPATH
DRONE HILL
SE

BAMBURGH

ACKLINGTON

LUFTLOTTE 5
FROM NORWAY AND DENMARK

CRESSWELL

ERCOPS MOSS

NEWCASTLE
USWORTH
SHOTTON

NTER COMMAND GROUP 13

CATTERICK

DANBY BEACON

RANGE OF LOW-LEVEL RADAR        RANGE OF HIGH-LEVEL RADAR

STAXTON WOLD
FLAMBOROUGH HEAD

LECONFIELD

CHURCH FENTON

EASINGTON

KIRTON-IN-LINDSEY
MANCHESTER
STENIGOT

DIGBY
INGOLDMELS

WATNALL

WEST BECKHAM
HAPPISBURG
COLTISHALL

COMMAND GROUP 12

WITTERING
STOKE HOLY CROSS
NOPTON

GLAND
HIGH STREET
DUNWICH

AMSTERDAM
SOESTERBERG

DUXFORD    MARTLESHAM
DEBDEN
BAWDSEY

NETHERLAND
ROTTERDAM

MMAND GROUP 10

FILTON

STANMORE
NORTHOLT
BOX
UXBRIDGE

NORTH WEALD    WALTON
HORNCHURCH    CANEWDON
LONDON
GRAVESEND    SOUTHEND
WHITSTABLE    FORENESS
DUNKIRK

BROMLEY

EINDHOVE
ANTWERP

DDLE WALLOP

CROYDON
KENLEY    BIGGIN HILL

FIGHTER COMMAND GROUP 11

TANGMERE
THULEIGH    PEVENSEY
POLING
VENTNOR
WORTH
BEACHY HEAD

LYMPNE    HAWKINGE
RYE    AUDEMBERT
FAIRLIGHT    WISSANT
MARQUISE

MANSTON
DOVER

MARCK    YPRES    COURTRAI
GUINES
TRAMECOURT
CAFFIERS    LILLE
ST OMER    ARQUES

ST TRUIDEN

ALOST
RENAIX

BELGIUM

AMER
ARRAS
ABBEVILLE

CAMBRAI

ENGLISH CHANNEL

AMIENS
LUFTLOTTE 2

CHERBOURG
ROSIERES-EN-SANTERRE

CARQUEBUT
LE HAVRE
BEAUVAIS    MONTDIDIER

CREPON
CAEN    PLUMETOT

CREIL

PARIS

BEAUMONT-LE-ROGER
EUREAUX
ST ANDRE
ST MALO
DINAN    LUFTLOTTE 3
DREUX
CHARTRES

ORLY
MELUN
ETAMPES
ORLEANS

Hurricane IIc armed with four 20-mm cannon. The Hurricane is sometimes said to have won the Battle of Britain. This may be an exaggeration but certainly there were more Hurricanes than Spitfires involved. Story by Mike Cooper-Slipper

The Beaufighter TFX was designed for Coastal Command and was one of the most effective aircraft used by the Strike Wings. It could carry torpedoes or eight rockets (visible in this photo) as well as four 20-mm cannon and was flown with devastating effect against enemy shipping. The Beau was supplied to the USAAF under reverse lease-lend and was known to American flyers as the Bristol

Photograph courtesy of D.N.D.

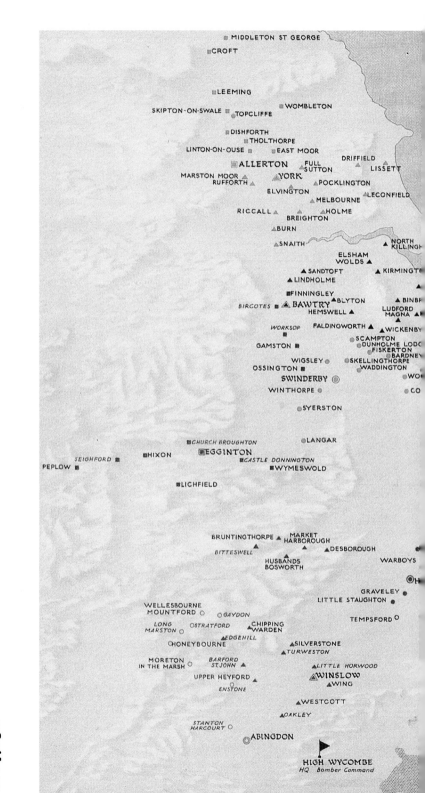

MIDDLETON ST GEORGE
CROFT

LEEMING
WOMBLETON
SKIPTON-ON-SWALE   TOPCLIFFE

DISHFORTH
THOLTHORPE
LINTON-ON-OUSE   EAST MOOR
DRIFFIELD
ALLERTON   FULL SUTTON
LISSETT
MARSTON MOOR   YORK
RUFFORTH   POCKLINGTON
ELVINGTON
MELBOURNE   LECONFIELD
RICCALL   HOLME
BREIGHTON
BURN
SNAITH
NORTH KILLINGH
ELSHAM WOLDS
SANDTOFT   KIRMINGT
LINDHOLME
FINNINGLEY
BIRCOTES   BAWTRY   BLYTON   BINBR
HEMSWELL   LUDFORD MAGNA
WORKSOP   FALDINGWORTH   WICKENBY
SCAMPTON
GAMSTON   DUNHOLME LODG
FISKERTON
BARDNE
WIGSLEY   SKELLINGTHORPE
OSSINGTON   WADDINGTON
SWINDERBY   WO
WINTHORPE   CO

SYERSTON

CHURCH BROUGHTON   LANGAR
SEIGHFORD   HIXON   EGGINTON
PEPLOW   CASTLE DONNINGTON
WYMESWOLD
LICHFIELD

BRUNTINGTHORPE   MARKET HARBOROUGH
BITTESWELL   DESBOROUGH
HUSBANDS BOSWORTH   WARBOYS

H

GRAVELEY
LITTLE STAUGHTON
WELLESBOURNE MOUNTFORD   GAYDON
LONG MARSTON   STRATFORD   CHIPPING WARDEN   TEMPSFORD
EDGEHILL
HONEYBOURNE   SILVERSTONE
TURWESTON
MORETON IN THE MARSH   BARFORD ST.JOHN   LITTLE HORWOOD
UPPER HEYFORD   WINSLOW
ENSTONE   WING

WESTCOTT
OAKLEY
STANTON HARCOURT
ABINGDON

HIGH WYCOMBE
HQ Bomber Command

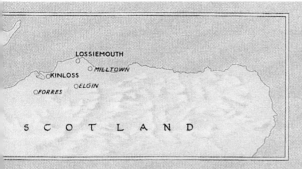

LOSSIEMOUTH
○ MILLTOWN
○KINLOSS ○ELGIN
○FORRES

S C O T L A N D

Map 2

# BOMBER COMMAND
## 25th September 1944

○NORTH CREAKE
○LITTLE SNORING
FOULSHAM ○OULTON
○
○ ○WEST ○SWANNINGTON
RAYNHAM
◎ BYLAUGH HALL

MARKET
LD

NHALL
DENHAM

HEDBURGH
DISHALL
G
N

Legend

| 1 GROUP | H Q | ▲ | AIRFIELDS | ▲ |
|---|---|---|---|---|
| 3 | " | ◎ | " | ○ |
| 4 | " | ▲ | " | ▲ |
| 5 | " | ◉ | " | ● |
| 6 | " (RCAF) | ▣ | " | ▣ |
| 8 | " (P.F.F.) | ◉ | " | ● |
| 91 | " (OTU) | ◎ | " | ○ |
| 92 | " | ▲ | " | ▲ |
| 93 | " | ▣ | " | ▣ |
| 100 | " | ◎ | " | ○ |

OTU Satellite Airfields are shown in Italic type

Scale of Miles
0    10    20    30    40    50    60    70    80    90    100

The Vickers Wellington, affectionately known as the Wimpey, was anything but. The first production aircraft flew in December 1937 and these aircraft formed the mainstay of Bomber Command until the arrival of the heavy bombers. Although it had to be

Photograph courtesy of D.N.D.

The Catalina (the PBY-5 of the U.S. Navy) was introduced into Coastal Command early in 1941. Although slow it was reliable and could stay airborne for up to 27 hours when fitted with extra fuel tanks. Stories by Bob Brown, Walter Wickson, and Monty Williams

Photograph courtesy of D.N.D.

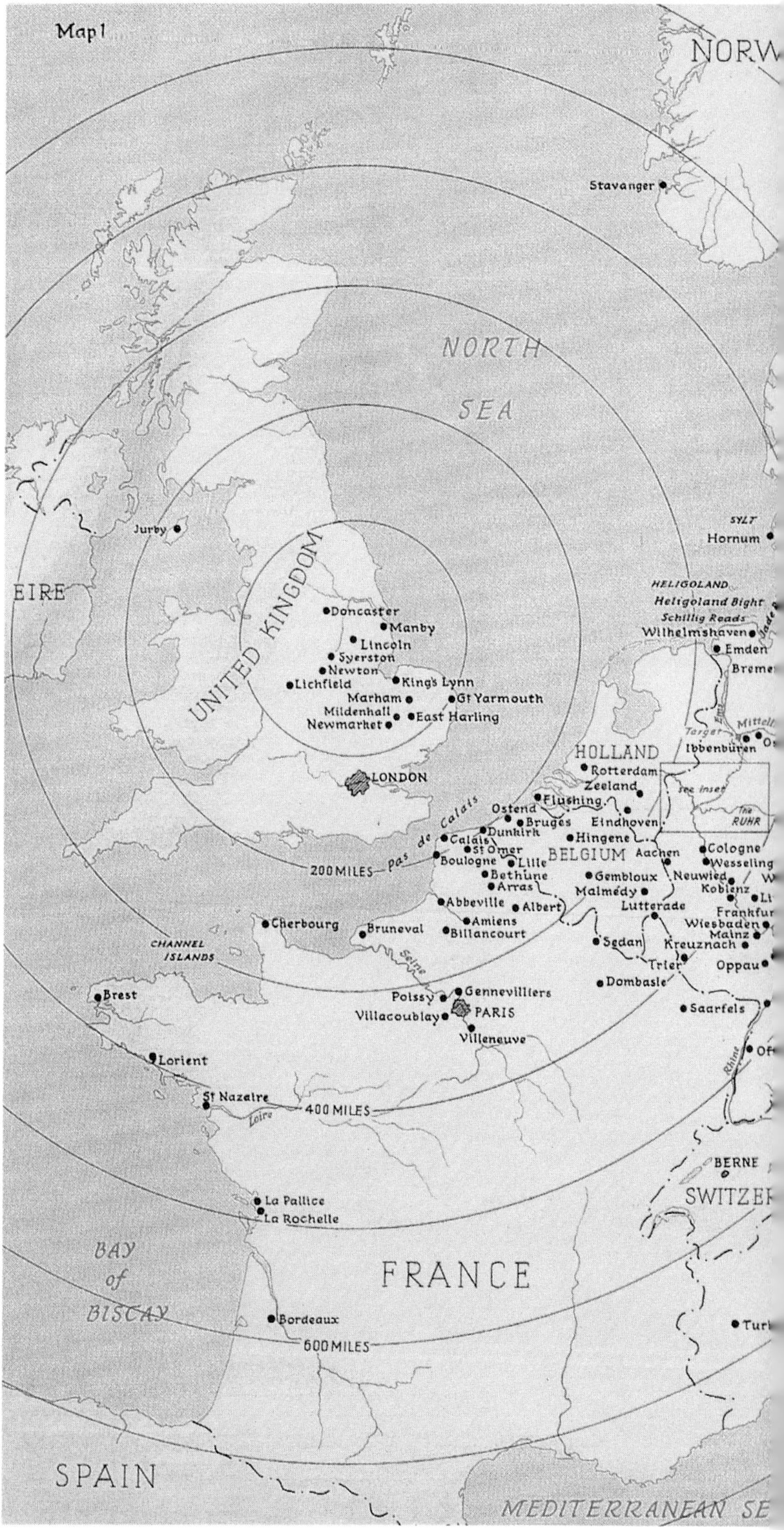

Map 1

HOLLAND GERMANY

Target

Münster

Dortmund-Ems Canal

Rhine

Hamm

Huls
Kamen
Castrop Rauxel
Soest
Rheinberg
Bottrop
Gelsenkirchen
Dortmund
Hamborn
Oberhausen
Homberg
Essen
Schwerte
Duisburg
Mulheim
Huls
Krefeld
Ruhr

Wuppertal
München
Gladbach
Düsseldorf
Remscheid
The
RUHR

Maas

Miles  0    10    20    30    40    50

Range Circles are measured from Lincoln

International boundaries shown as they
were at the outbreak of war.................

BALTIC
SEA

EAST
PRUSSIA

ndie
ck

Danzig
Marienburg

Poelitz

U.S.S.R.

RMANY

BERLIN

Wistula

WARSAW

urg
e

Posen

Oder

Ruhland

POLAND

pzig
len
Dresden
Chemnitz
Schkopau
Bruex

Upper Silesia

PRAGUE

n
z
Weiden

CZECHOSLOVAKIA

ensburg

Danube

VIENNA

AUSTRIA

BUDAPEST

RUMANIA

HUNGARY

Ploesti
BUCHAREST

BELGRADE

Danube

YUGOSLAVIA

BULGARIA

SOFIA

ADRIATIC SEA

The Lancaster III. Lancasters first entered R.A.F. service in December 1941 and before the end of the war,

Photograph courtesy of DND

Halifax II bombing-up. Early marks of the Halifax were unpopular with aircrews but the Halifax III, with Bristol Pegasus engines, proved to be a great bomber. By end 1944, No. 6 (RCAF.) Group of Bomber Command was operating nine squadrons of Halifaxes

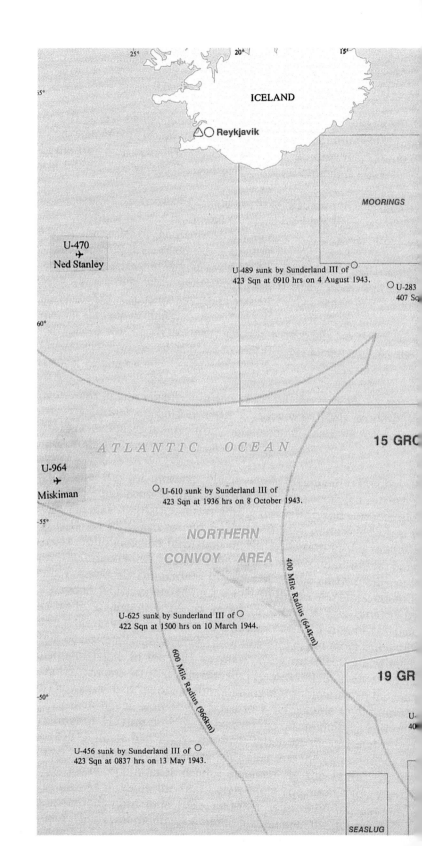

ICELAND

△○ Reykjavik

MOORINGS

U-470
✈
Ned Stanley

U-489 sunk by Sunderland III of ○
423 Sqn at 0910 hrs on 4 August 1943.

○ U-283
407 Sq

*ATLANTIC   OCEAN*

**15 GRC**

U-964
✈
Miskiman

○ U-610 sunk by Sunderland III of
423 Sqn at 1936 hrs on 8 October 1943.

NORTHERN

CONVOY AREA

400 Mile Radius (644km)

U-625 sunk by Sunderland III of ○
422 Sqn at 1500 hrs on 10 March 1944.

600 Mile Radius (966km)

**19 GR**

U-
40

U-456 sunk by Sunderland III of ○
423 Sqn at 0837 hrs on 13 May 1943.

SEASLUG

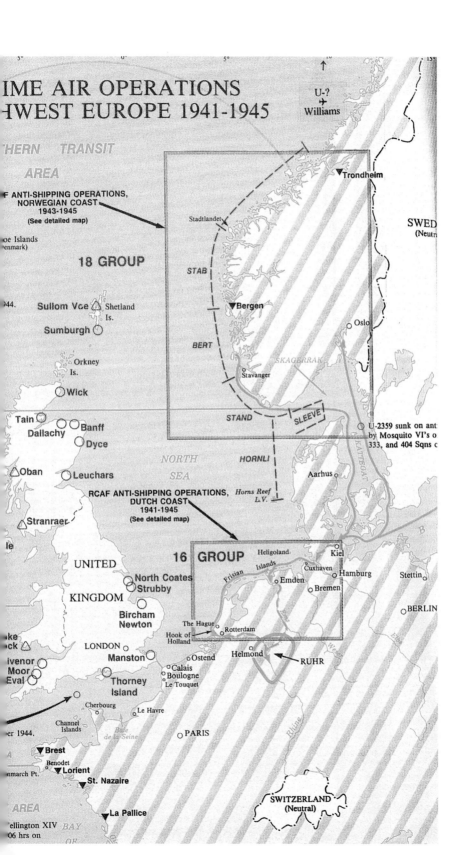

# IME AIR OPERATIONS
# HWEST EUROPE 1941-1945

U-?
Williams

HERN TRANSIT

AREA

F ANTI-SHIPPING OPERATIONS,
NORWEGIAN COAST
1943-1945
(See detailed map)

oe Islands
enmark)

18 GROUP

▼Trondheim

Stadtlandet

SWED
(Neutr

STAB

044.   Sullom Vce △ Shetland
                    Is.
       Sumburgh ○

▼Bergen

○ Oslo

BERT

Orkney
Is.

Wick

SKAGERRAK

Stavanger

Tain ○
Dallachy  ○ ○ Banff
          ○ Dyce

STAND

SLEEVE

○ U-2359 sunk on ant
by Mosquito VI's o
333, and 404 Sqns c

△ Oban    ○ Leuchars

NORTH

SEA

HORNLI

Aarhus ○

△ Stranraer

RCAF ANTI-SHIPPING OPERATIONS,   Horns Reef
DUTCH COAST                       L.V.
1941-1945
(See detailed map)

le

UNITED

16  GROUP   Heligoland
                              Kiel

○ North Coates
○ Strubby

KINGDOM

Frisian  Islands  ○ Cuxhaven
                            Hamburg
○ Emden            ○ Bremen

Stettin ○

Bircham
Newton

The Hague ○
Hook of    ○ Rotterdam
Holland

○ BERLIN

ke
ck △

LONDON ○

ivenor ○
Moor ○
Eval ○

Manston ○

Thorney
Island

○ Ostend
○ Calais
○ Boulogne
Le Touquet

Helmond ○

▼ RUHR

Cherbourg
○       ○ Le Havre

er 1944.

Channel
Islands

Baie
de la Seine

○ PARIS

A

▼ Brest

Benodet
nmarch Pt.  ▼ Lorient
         ▼ St. Nazaire

SWITZERLAND
(Neutral)

AREA

▼ La Pallice

ellington XIV  BAY
06 hrs on

The CF-100 all-weather fighter. The first flight of the prototype CF-100 was on 19 January 1950. It was powered by two Rolls-Royce Avon jet engines. Later marks were powered by two Avro Orenda jets.
Story by Hugh Young. Photograph courtesy of Chris Pike

# DON KERLEY

*Don was born in 1923 at Brock, Saskatchewan, and moved to Victoria for his high school education. He joined the RCAF in July 1942, received his pilot wings in September 1943, and went to the UK. He spent the next two years training members of the Glider Pilot Regiment, towing and training glider pilots. He returned to Canada in 1945 and studied at Victoria College and UBC. He began his teaching career at Sooke, BC, where he became Principal, a position he held until retirement*

## Towing For Victory

It was springtime 1942 and I, a Grade 12 student at Victoria High School, had come home after school to find a young, handsome, RCAF sergeant pilot sitting in our front room. He had only recently earned his wings and was on his way to Alaska to take part in the action against the Japanese invasion of some of the islands. I was fascinated. He loved to talk about flying and I loved to listen. I knew then what I was going to do as soon as I graduated from High School. Right after graduation I joined the RCAF

We did our Initial Training in Edmonton, Elementary Flying at High River, and Service Flying at MacLeod, Alberta, which is only a hoot and a holler away from Lethbridge. Right after "Wings Parade" we were ordered to sew "Canada" flashes on our tunic sleeves. We were on our way overseas.

While I was on the Queen Mary travelling from New York to UK, I met Eddie Kent. Eddie was from Guelph, Ontario. We two nineteen-year-old sergeant pilots were off to join the air war against the Nazis. We were both slated for fighters and proud of the prospect. We didn't earn that distinction because of our flying skill or our daring. We were so classified because of our height–or lack of it–sixty-six inches. Eddie was better qualified for fighters than I; he had trained on single-engine Harvards, whereas I had trained on twin-engine Ansons and we didn't do aerobatics in the Anson. We became fast friends and stayed together throughout our time overseas.

After a stay in Bournemouth we were sent to RAF Elmdon, (Birmingham Airport) for the month of December to fly the delightful Tiger Moth and get acquainted with flying in wartime England. I loved the little trainer, no brakes, no coupé top, no starter, no heater, and no steerable tail wheel. I loved it. In it I felt I was very close to Billy Bishop and the Wright brothers. But I hated the weather.

*What a change it was from the previous summer in Alberta. That summer it seemed the sun shone all day long every day. All the roads ran due north and south or due east and west and the Rocky Mountains formed a solid wall along the western boundary. Navigation was easy. At night you could see the lights of Lethbridge and Calgary and all the towns in between. If you did get lost you could always nip down and read the name of the town off the grain elevators.*

While flying Tiger Moths at RAF Elmdon, we never saw the other side of the airfield; the green grass just disappeared into the smog. Every so often a Stirling bomber would take off, emerging from the stuff and disappearing into it again. Someone told me these enormous aircraft were equipped with heavy-duty windshield wipers to brush off any "Moths" they encountered. The area around the airfield consisted of smoking factories, blast furnaces, and roads and railways that twisted and turned like spilled spaghetti. I was too terrified to leave the local circuit. I was sure that if I lost sight of the airfield I would never find it again. Was this the land of Wordsworth, Keats, and Shelley? This dull, dismal, dreary, sunless clime? I felt those surly bonds of earth holding me down and how I longed for the time when I could climb high above those clouds into the sunlit silence.

A few months later Eddie and I were at Advanced Flying Unit, RAF Ternhill, flying Miles Masters and Hurricanes. One day, it must have been a Sunday, I think it was Easter Sunday, I was low-flying over the Shropshire countryside and discovered the England of the poets. The lush greenery of the landscape sparkled in the morning sunshine and beneath my wings I could see people in their Sunday best gathering in churchyards and in front of the pubs. It was like one huge enchanted park with hedgerows running wildly across verdant fields where sheep and cattle paid little attention to the noise as I came roaring by. It gave me a thrill to wave at the people below and see them wave in return as I did a steep turn around the steeple. I can't honestly say I noticed the daffodils but I'm sure they were there, fluttering and dancing in the breeze. At last, this was the England I had read about back home in Canada. I had found it. And I had also found a young girl in Shrewsbury who was to become my wife.

With the arrival of spring we began to look forward to the next phase of our training, an Operational Training Unit on Spitfires, Mustangs, or maybe Typhoons. But this was not to be. All the K's went to Glider Towing, Kerley, Kent, and Keatley. We were training men for the Glider Pilot Regiment, towing Hotspur gliders with Miles Masters. Our dream of being fighter pilots would have to be put on hold. Our disappointment was huge but we soon found that our new situation did have some interesting moments.

*Actually, my first ride in a glider had taken place at an airfield near Bournemouth shortly after we arrived there from Canada. The glider was a Horsa and the pilot was an army type, in a brown uniform. It didn't seem proper being a pilot and not wearing blue. I began to suspect his flying ability on our approach to landing. We crossed the boundary of the field at 500 feet. It was obvious to me that we were going to overshoot badly. Our pilot then yanked a mighty lever and two flaps, each the size of a barn door, flopped down from the wings. The glider went into a steep glide and with a gentle round out at the bottom we landed as sweetly as could be just where we ought to be. Little had I foreseen that gliders would be such a large part of my future military career.*

Before being qualified as glider-tug pilots we had to learn to fly gliders by day and by night. Overshoot procedure was the usual thing, more flap, sideslip, and zigzag; undershoot procedure consisted of a burst of no flap. For night flying and cloud flying there was an instrument in the cockpit called the Angle of Dangle. It looked very much like an artificial horizon and was connected to the towrope in such a way that the angle of the rope controlled the instrument. The glider pilot could follow the tug in thick cloud using the instrument as an artificial horizon. For night flying the tugs had rear facing blue lights on the wing tips that gave the glider pilot an indication of the tug's attitude. The towropes were 300 feet long and some included wires used for communication between the tug and the glider.

The Miles Master was a crank-wing aircraft made of wood and fabric and, in the original design, was powered by a 600-hp Kestrel engine. The engine was replaced by a 850-hp Bristol Mercury engine that gave the machine some of the characteristics of the more powerful fighters, particularly at low level. One result of the alteration was that it had a pronounced tendency to swing to the right on take-off; this could be a problem if we had a strong cross wind and an inexperienced glider pilot in tow. During take-off the glider would always become airborne while the tug was still on the ground. If the glider pilot let his craft be carried to the left by the crosswind it increased the swing to the right for the tug. It was not a big problem but once in a while it made for some interesting moments. The gliders had two choices, to fly above the slipstream or below the slipstream. The usual position was above the slipstream. One day I took a glider on a low-level exercise. I wasn't sure how low they wanted me to go. I took a conservative position and looked back to see how things were going behind me. The glider was in the low position, beneath the slipstream, with his wheels just inches off the ground and the tow rope was actually dragging along the ground for much of its length.

The life of a glider tug pilot wasn't as exciting or dangerous as that of an operational fighter pilot but we did have a few interesting experiences. One incident involved my chum Eddie. The tugs threw off a lot of oil as they struggled to pull the gliders around. In the flight hut we had a rag-bag that supplied us with the wiping cloths we used to clean off a patch of the windscreen prior to landing. On this occasion Eddie reached in the rag-bag and pulled out a pair of dark blue WAAF-issue bloomers. There was a chorus of hoots and hollers as he displayed his find prior to tucking it into the top of his flying boot. Eddie had to take up a WAAF passenger who was doing some testing of the radio equipment. As they flew around the airfield the transmit-receive button stuck on transmit and every word of their spicy conversation was broadcast to all the other tugs and gliders. As I recall, Eddie was trying to learn whether or not WAAFs actually wore these garments or did they prefer the two-button camiknickers style he had heard about.

On another occasion, Eddie and I were enjoying ourselves with a little bit of dual low flying. We were really low, skimming along over the hedges and fields, when there was a sudden loud bang; a strong smell filled the cockpit and the engine faltered. My first reaction was to gain as much height as possible and look for a soft spot to land. I thought the engine had ingested a chicken or something. Fortunately the engine picked up power again and we managed to get back safely to our field. It turned out that the fire extinguisher had gone off accidentally. The mechanics told us this usually stops the engine completely.

I spent three months in Night Flight, towing gliders up to about 800 feet on the downwind leg where they would release their end of the rope. I would swoop down and drop it at the edge of the field before coming around to land. One night I did over forty such circuits; not that I counted them, but the ground crew who picked up the ropes told me so. (I think it was some kind of local record.) For some strange reason I enjoyed this assignment. Not all the flights were enjoyable, however. One night, I had just got airborne with a glider in tow when the rocker box on top of one of the cylinders blew off. There was a great shower of sparks and flames coming back in my face and a decided loss of power. Somehow I managed to get the glider back to the field and land safely myself.

"Grampa, were you ever afraid while you were flying in the war?"

That's easy to answer. Yes. I remember one time when I was really afraid; but as it turned out, the thing that frightened me never came about. I was scared for no good reason. There were other times when I should have been afraid and didn't know the peril I was in until later or events took place so suddenly that fear didn't have time to develop. Fear seems to need time to grow; it seems to breed in a period of inactivity. If you are busy and active, your mind doesn't have time to brood and fear doesn't take hold.

The time I was really afraid was a dark and stormy night. I was at one end of the runway, sitting in my aircraft and waiting for a signal from the control tower. A red light would mean stop and wait, a white light would mean return to the flight hut, and a green light would be the signal to go, to take off. As I sat there waiting, it began to snow and my mind began to wander. *What's going on in the control tower? Why am I sitting here alone and cold and waiting? They aren't going to send me out on a night like this, are they?* I could imagine the officers and the WAAFs sipping champagne and dancing around in the control tower. I grew impatient. *Don't they notice it's snowing?* I was scared, really scared. This could be dangerous.

It seemed to me to be a long time before the light came. It was green. At last I got to do something. I was roaring down the runway when Saint Elmo's fire struck. The propeller disc was lit up by this strange bright blue dancing light and sparks flew everywhere. I kept telling myself this was perfectly safe and it wouldn't hurt me. I think I had read that in Initial Training School. As I passed the control tower someone must have looked out and decided the weather was unfit for flying and I was recalled. I had been afraid for no good reason.

An example of an incident when there was real danger but not enough time for fear to develop would be a near miss in a potential mid-air collision. We've all had several of these. Suddenly there is another aircraft, as big as a house, right in front of you. I remember one such meeting when a strange black, ugly, square looking aircraft suddenly appeared. It looked like an Me110, but I couldn't identify it. I didn't stay around for a second look; I nipped back into the clouds, and headed for home. It turned out to be an American Black Widow, a new aircraft not covered in our aircraft recognition classes.

Then there is the incident where there is real danger and the pilot is blissfully ignorant of the peril. I was involved in such an event while towing gliders at night. The gliders landed on the grass to the left of the runway. The gliders and tugs took off on the lighted runway; and the right side of the runway was used for the tow planes to land. Most dangerous incidents occur as a result of a combination of unusual events. In my case one of the tugs did a wheels up landing on the right side of the runway, blocking that strip for landings. I was low on petrol and my radio transmitter went unserviceable. I flashed out a message in Morse code that I was nearly out of fuel and that the RT was u/s. I could send Morse a lot faster than I could receive it. They flashed back that I should land on the centre strip. Somehow I read this as the 'glider' strip. They had moved all the gliders off the centre runway onto the glider area. In my blind faith in my ability to read Morse code I landed in amongst all the gliders and the tractors used to move them. Luck was with me but I sure scared a lot of people on the ground. One of our pilots, sitting as a passenger in a truck with the motor running, claims that he prevented an accident by jamming the truck into gear at the last moment as I came barrelling in. According to his account, the truck jumped out of my way. I was happily ignorant of the danger.

There was one tragic event that made a deep impression on me and made me a much more careful pilot. It happened one night when several of us were getting ready for some night flying. We all left together, taxiing to the end of the runway. As we got close to the take-off point a thick fog came rolling in, swallowing up each of the runway lights in turn. We had to return to the flight hut where we were all laughing and joking and looking forward to a night in the pub. Word came down that one of our group did get airborne and had pranged at the end of the runway. We got on our bikes, still laughing and joking as we made our way through the thick fog expecting to find F/O Brentnal sitting there after a wheels-up landing. Our fun ended abruptly when we found that the aircraft had crashed in the bushes outside the airfield and the ambulance crew couldn't find it. We all joined in the search immediately.

As we groped our way through the woods in complete darkness I began to feel lots of little short twigs and sticks underfoot and soon stumbled over something metallic. It was the propeller. From this I was able to guess at the direction to go to find the rest of the wreck. In a few minutes I heard the moaning of the injured pilot. He was lying on the ground and I did what I could to comfort him. As I held him in my arms I called out for help. Soon others came and took him away. He died that night in hospital.

What I remember most of all about that night was the smell of the petrol and oil and the absolute darkness. We couldn't strike a match with all the fuel soaking the ground. They say that the faculties of smell and memory are located close together in the brain and that a particular odour can evoke distinct memories of certain events. That certainly worked for me. For months after that incident, every time I buckled myself into the cockpit and got a whiff of the particular aircraft odour, my mind flashed back to that tragic night. I think it made me a much more careful pilot and finally made me accept that we were not immortal.

I count myself an extremely lucky person. I volunteered for war service and came home alive. The Department of Veteran Affairs helped me get a University education and the Department of National Defence provided me with some interesting experiences. The best thing of all is the friends I've made along the way.

# THE TIGER MOTH

The de Havilland 82 or Tiger Moth: wing span 29 feet 4 inches; tare weight 1115 pounds; colour yellow; engine: a gravity fed inverted engine Gypsy Major producing 145 horsepower.

Endurance? My log book discloses that I signed a pilot's log book endorsement form as having been told it would fly for 2 hours and 30 minutes; at which time it was out of fuel. And, presumably, should I run out of fuel while flying on a training exercise it would be <u>all my fault</u>.

It was not fast (I recollect about 85 or 90 mph) but it was built for loops and rolls and spins. It was a great training aeroplane. We under-training pilots were delighted to be learning to fly on an aircraft that out-performed the First World War combat machines; or so we led ourselves to believe.

At #7 Elementary Flying Training School in Windsor, Ontario, the civilian line staff, who refuelled the Tiger Moths and hand swung the propellers to start the engine, (no electric starter on this trainer) were young women about our age, i.e., in their teens or early twenties. The lovely summer weather and the socializing that took place on the flight line in between training flights made for a great time to be young and in the RCAF.

Doug McLaughlin

# MURRAY RYAN

*Murray was born in Winnipeg in November 1923. He joined the RCAF in 1942 and completed his pilot training at 12 SFTS, Brandon, Manitoba. Murray was demobilized in October 1945 and began a teaching career. He retired as Secondary School Principal and Director of Instruction at Peace River South School District twenty-nine years later.*

## There are Landings and there are Landings

This is the story of three aircraft crashes in which I was involved during my three years of RCAF service in the 1939-45 war. Two occurred when I was piloting the plane and one when I was a passenger.

The "passenger" crash occurred when I was at 4 SFTS at Saskatoon. (I had finished Initial Training School in that same city and was temporarily engaged in tarmac duties whilst waiting for the next stage in my training.). It was here at 4 SFTS that I had my first flight. I caught a flip in a Cessna Crane; I sat in the back seat and an instructor with a student-pilot in the front. It was a beautifully sunny though cold day in January 1943 and the air was very smooth indeed. The flight ended abruptly and ahead of schedule when the aircraft was dumped by the instructor in a snow-covered field near Langham, eighteen miles north-west of Saskatoon. I have on the wall of my computer room an official RCAF picture of that rather forlorn looking aircraft lying on its back in the snow.

The instructor and student were partially ejected through the windshield and I had to help them get out of the fix they were in. I remember using my hands to scoop the snow from around their heads so they could breathe. The aircraft was snapping and crackling and we wanted to get out in a hurry in case it caught fire. I was nearest to the door. I tried to open it but it wouldn't budge. I put both my feet on the door and kicked it right off its catches and hinges.

After we extricated ourselves from the inverted aircraft we walked a very tough mile and a quarter to a farmhouse we could see across the fields. We had struggled through waist-high snow and discovered later that just a few feet from the crash site there was a sleigh track leading right up to the house. The authorities at our station in Saskatoon sent a snowmobile to pick up the instructor and student-pilot right away. They also sent out an AC2 with a rifle and tent to guard the aircraft. The poor fellow must have been pretty cold in that tent. He later got into trouble for expending a cartridge firing at a coyote. There wasn't room for me on the snowmobile; before they sent transportation for me, I'd spent three days and nights in that farmhouse sleeping on a cot by the kitchen stove to keep warm,

The farmer and his family butchered a turkey to help feed me. I was treated regally and thought they were just doing their patriotic duty in helping a stranded airman. But the accounts officer told me later, when he asked me to confirm I had stayed there and eaten the food, that the farmer had presented a bill for $37.10 for my room and board for three days. The RCAF paid.

To this day I can't believe the stupidity that led to that crash. I learned afterwards that the instructor was showing the student how to find out the depth of the snow. He put the wheels and flaps down and tried to touch the ground beneath the snow with the wheels. Unfortunately, just below the surface of the snow was a layer of ice. It caught the wheels and dumped the aircraft onto its back.

When I returned to the station I was a pretty grubby sight in my tarmac overalls and big rubber boots. I hadn't shaved or had a shower for three days and imagine my arrival could be sensed well ahead of my appearance.

To add insult to injury, I was put on a charge for being Absent Without Leave. I had a terrible time tracking down the officer who had authorised that flight for me; I didn't know his name. I finally found him; he certified that I had his permission for the flight and the charge was dropped.

Being in that crash proved fortunate for me. When the time came to be assigned to an aircrew category there was little demand for pilots and I sorely wanted to be a pilot. My chances seemed slim but when the examining officers on the selection board read about my being in that crash and learned from me that I was still keen to be a pilot, they acceded to my request and I was sent for pilot training.

The second crash was in May 1943 on my second session of solo circuits in a Tiger Moth at Elementary Flying Training School in Virden, Manitoba. On my round-out to land, not recognising the sensations in my stomach as a warning of a very sudden descent (sensations which I certainly recognized once I had more flying experience) I "landed" the aircraft in a three-point attitude while I was still fifty feet in the air. When the plane hit the ground, there was a loud thump and a tearing sound. The Tiger Moth was severely damaged to say the least. The engine dropped out of its mounts, the wings folded along the fuselage, and the landing gear strut pushed its way up through the front cockpit.

I crawled out in considerable confusion and embarrassment and shambled across the grass field to the flight shack. My instructor asked me why I had come back so soon.

"I pranged Sir." I pointed to the pile of yellow and black Tiger Moth parts out on the field.

"Well, so you did", said the instructor and immediately took me out for another session of dual circuits. Fortunately I had no further trouble in landing aircraft during the rest of my flying days.

The following is the story of a successful landing, or should I say arrival, during training on heavy bombers; it was successful in that the whole crew of six walked away from it.

In October 1944, after completing operational training on Wellingtons at Finningley and Worksop, my crew and I were posted to Conversion Unit at Lindholme. We trained on Halifaxes and later on converted to Lancasters. The maintenance was not too great; in fact it was worse than anything I encountered at any other flying station. One day we tried starting up three aircraft before we found one that didn't a have coolant leak in at least one of its engines. Other crews had similar experiences.

On 12 November 1944 we set out on what was expected to be a

routine daytime cross-country which turned out to be anything but. Our crew numbered seven, but on this day there were only six of us flying. My rear-gunner was in the station hospital with a cold and Moose, my very large mid-upper gunner, occupied the rear turret.

For some unknown reason the port outer engine caught fire. This was not unusual; it happened all too often with the poor maintenance on that station. I shut down the affected engine and pressed the fire extinguisher button. Out went the fire and I feathered the prop. I had no problem at all in continuing the cross-country; most crews returned from such trips on three engines.

When we got back to our Lindholme base there was a slight fog or haze in the air, but I could see the field just fine and we made our preparations to land. I was instructed by the tower to divert to Carnaby, an emergency field just north of The Wash. I protested rather vigorously that I could see the field all right and would like to land, but I was instructed to divert. Although we all had dates in Lindholme that night I pulled out of the circuit to divert and set course for Carnaby. As it turned out it was the wrong decision; I should have intentionally lost another engine, declared an emergency, and landed at Lindholme.

We arrived at Carnaby which had one runway about half a mile wide and ten miles long—well perhaps not quite that large but it was certainly very big and extended inland from the sea. Although I knew better I did a normal left hand circuit, which put my duff engine on the inside of the turn. This is not a recommended procedure and turned out to be a particularly poor decision.

As I turned into final approach at about 500 feet, the left wing kept dropping rather disconcertingly. I had a terrific fight on my hands trying to get the wings level. I remembered something from my Tiger Moth flying and used the rudder to increase the lift of the left wing. This worked. I was deathly afraid of hooking a wing on landing. Cartwheeling was the last thing I wanted to do. With the wings level the chances of our survival would be much improved.

All this was accompanied by a frightening loss of power in the remaining engines and I suddenly realized we were not going to be able to make a one-engine-out landing and would very likely pile in. On closer inspection I could see that after all the struggling to get the wings level I had missed the runway completely. Here I was approaching the widest and longest runway in all the British Isles and I had managed to miss it.

While we were in the circuit I ordered the crew into crash positions. Poor Moose got stuck in the turret and the bomb-aimer went back and helped haul him out. They had just got back and down into their crash positions behind the main spar when we struck the ground.

When we hit I shut my eyes. There was a bloody awful roaring noise as we shuttled and skidded across the ground for what seemed to be an interminable period of time. I expected to be hit by something large and lethal at any moment. I had definitely missed the largest runway in England and possibly the world.

We finally came to rest; I reached up for the escape hatch; there was nothing there. I reached for the side of the aircraft; there was nothing there either, just a big hole. I stepped out through the hole, caught my foot in a radio antenna, and suddenly was dangling upside down. When I finally kicked myself free I fell on my head on the ground and just about broke my neck. I got to my feet and took off my oxygen mask. It was full of blood. I thought I had internal injuries and was going to die. I discovered later that the blood came cuts inside my mouth and some loosened teeth. One of the ambulance fellows told me they found me wandering about in circles in a daze mumbling, "Thank God I've got my scarf, thank God I've got my scarf". It was an air-force-blue scarf about six feet long that my mother had knitted for me. Evidently I placed great value on it.

They took us in ambulances to the station hospital and put us into beds with heat lamps on us to treat us for shock. They also administered a couple of large tots of medicinal rum poured from a gallon jug. The attendants made the serious error of leaving the rum where we could reach it. That helped to speed our recovery. At least I don't think it impeded it.

When we went out to inspect the crash site the next morning we could hardly believe that we had escaped alive. The scene was one of utter devastation. That poor Halifax was a complete mess, its wreckage scattered over the countryside. When we first hit, the landing gear broke off. We carried on, broke through a stand of large trees, and cut them off so cleanly a few feet above the ground that it looked as if a saw had been used on them. The left wing broke off here but carried itself up and over the fuselage where it dropped an engine just behind where the crew had been in crash positions. We came to a stop near a Nissen Hut where one of the shift crews was sleeping. It was a good thing for them we'd stopped where we had.

The Station Commander told me that if he'd had a movie camera he could have made a fortune out of pictures of that crash. It was the most spectacular one he'd ever seen there even though it was an emergency field. He was sure I had lost the port inner engine on my turn on to the final approach. That would explain why I had trouble getting the wings level, turning into two dead engines. It explained also the impression of that loss of power beyond that of the dead engine which I had shut down on the cross-country.

On our walk about the crash scene I found my oxygen mask tube at the place where we went through the trees. Something must have torn it off and it occurred to me that it might easily have been some part of me that was ripped off.

Our rear gunner, left behind in the base hospital, was told we had crashed at Carnaby and all been killed. The poor guy got up from his sick bed and in dressing gown and pyjamas went over to the sergeants' mess where he sat drinking coffee and crying. He was upset over our deaths and knew he might have been with us.

Back to the crash. When we came to a final stop our navigator got tangled up in some wires inside the fuselage and couldn't get out of the aircraft for quite a while. There was a red sunset and some of the practice bombs we had aboard detonated. With all the smoke and sand from the practice bombs and the red glow from the setting sun the poor fellow thought we were on fire. Quite understandably he panicked and practically tore his leg off trying to escape from the crashed aircraft. We took him for one more flight later, but he shook so much he couldn't hold a pencil let alone do any navigating. He was sent back to Canada.

The wireless operator, Bill Lowes, had recently joined our crew as a replacement. He had been in a crash at Lindholme where he and the rear-gunner were the only survivors. Bill thought as we were ploughing in that surely it couldn't happen to him twice. It could and it did. The engineer was the luckiest of all for he could have been severely injured. He had insisted on staying with me to help me handle the engines on our approach. He was standing beside me until we hit and was thrown into the nose only a split second after the nose caved in. He landed on top of the wreckage. If he had been thrown forward before the nose smashed in he would have been killed. A very lucky guy.

We continued our training on Halifaxes. Very shortly after the crash I heard a rumour that we were going to switch to Lancasters. I went to the Commanding Officer and suggested, tongue in cheek, that since my crew and I had survived the crash, could we be given two weeks survivors' leave. Sure enough he gave us fourteen days leave and we went on our merry way. When we returned we finished the rest of our conversion training at Lindholme on Lancs.

As an indication of how young, ingenuous and, yes, dumb we were, my crew printed in large red letters "Crash Ryan's Crew" on their bicycles, kit bags, and anything else that was visible. They appeared to be quite proud of the name. Mind you, one benefit was that nobody stole any of their property.

The rear gunner in this story is Gordie Albright, a member of our branch of the Aircrew Association. He is in poor health and now lives in Ottawa. After years of searching for our mid-upper gunner John (Moose) Cameron, I wrote to the newspaper in Barrie, Ontario, his home town. The newspaper published an item and found his family. He was the youngest of our crew, and it was sad to learn he had died of a heart attack in 1984, about six years before I finally found his family.

The crew spent many years searching for our first navigator Ron Austen who returned to Canada after our Carnaby crash. I found him through the internet in 1995. He was overjoyed to hear from me and contacted the other three members of our crew who were in Canada. He was planning to come out to British Columbia to a reunion with the remaining four of us in the summer of 1996, but he died of a stroke that June before we could meet with him.

Bill Nelson, the engineer whom we called "Pop" because he was an old man of 30, died some years ago in England. Our bomb-aimer, Bill Dean, golfs and lives in Garden Bay, BC. Bill Lowes golfs and lives at Cobble Hill. Our replacement navigator Noel Read, with whom I now correspond, lives in Middlesex, England. This all happened so long ago that these incidents, in fact all of my service experience, seems like a dream. I really doubt that any of the four of us still alive will ever forget that very eventful day in November 1944 when we were diverted to Carnaby. That was no dream!

# BILL PEARSON

*Bill was born during WWI. He enlisted in the RAF in 1940 and was awarded his pilot wings in mid-1941. He served as an instructor in Britain and Canada. Early in 1944 he returned to the UK and served on 233 and 187 Squadrons. Bill was demobilized in 1945.*

## An Instructor's Life

When I left high school in 1932 during the depression in England, jobs were scarce. I thought of joining the Air Force but what put me off was the number of pilots that were being killed, as often reported in the press.

At the time of the Battle of Britain there were placards displayed everywhere: Aircrew Wanted. My father had served in WWI and had often told me of the horrible conditions in the army, which I was determined to avoid. I went into the RAF recruiting office; I had only gone in to enquire but was told "Go to the end of the line and we will check your hearing". I was wondering how this would be done, but it was very elementary. I was told to put one finger in my ear; they did not say which ear nor how far. So I did as I was told and put a finger in my deaf ear. After passing this first hurdle I did six years in the RAF without anyone knowing I was deaf in one ear.

I did my flying training in Canada and when we were awarded our wings we were asked our preference for the next stage. I put down "Fighter Command" but they told me I was too old - at 26! So I returned to England and was selected for training as a flying instructor.

I flew Airspeed Oxfords and Avro Tutors. It was on a Tutor, during my training, that I made my shortest precautionary landing; it was about 20 feet. I had underestimated the effect of landing uphill and landed on the wrong side of a wire fence, which acted as a very effective arrester. Things seemed to happen in slow motion. I saw a hole go through the port wing and then a post made a hole in the starboard wing. I was flying with another trainee pilot and we were seeing who could make the shortest landing. I guess I won.

While waiting to be picked up we saw another aircraft knock down one of the remaining posts with one wheel. It turned out to be a high-ranking officer; perhaps that was why I was never reprimanded.

I instructed for a year in Calgary, Alberta. What a change! Night flying with lights everywhere. Then I was transferred to Swift Current. This was like being a civilian instructor, yet it was there that I came nearest to being killed.

One snowy day it was dual flying only. I thought I might demonstrate low flying since it always had to be a dual exercise, but the weather was too bad for that. So we climbed up to about 2000 feet just below the cloud base. I banked left and pulled back on the elevator control, but the control column collapsed into my stomach and the aircraft dived away. We were halfway out of our seats. I began to fear we would never make it but managed to control the dive with the elevator trim. Once we were flying reasonably straight and level it gave us time to think.

I was confident I could land using the trim provided nothing else went wrong, such as loose wires becoming tangled. But there was a risk that things could go very badly. I decided to instruct my pupil to bale out; there was no need for him to be at risk also. He asked, "Is this an Irvin parachute?" Maybe he knew he would get a "caterpillar" for an emergency bale-out, or perhaps he needed assurance that his 'chute was reliable. I assured him it was and gave him instruction on what to do.

He removed the door and placed it in the rear. I told him to sit on the edge of the doorway with his feet hanging outside, to make sure he knew where the ripcord was, then fall forward and release the 'chute as soon as he was clear. I told him to follow these instructions carefully to make sure he wouldn't be hit by the tailplane. After he left I circled to watch him float down and land safely. Then I felt horribly lonely; I was tempted to follow him.

I flew back to base. We had no radio so I flew down the runway and waggled my wings. It could easily be seen that something was wrong because the door was missing. I then made what appeared to be an easy landing.

I was commended for landing safely with broken elevator controls. It was discovered that this aircraft had at one time nosed over in deep snow at the side of the runway. In repairing the damage, aluminium (instead of duraluminum) rivets had been used to connect the wires to the control column. Subsequently all Oxfords had to have five rivets instead of three to make that connection.

While at Swift Current I did a few loops and rolls in an Oxford. This was not recommended, since the aircraft was not designed for aerobatics and there was little margin for error. *The main thing is to avoid the negative G that can occur if the loop is done too slowly. If the loop is too tight the extra G from centrifugal force can result in an inverted spin.* I did not broadcast what I was doing but another instructor must have decided to try a barrel roll. He got negative G and although strapped to his seat he went through the Perspex roof. I never did find out how he explained that accident.

Many instructors, and I was one, were posted to England in the summer of 1944 only to find out the RAF was not sure what to do with us. Finally, we were attached briefly to 233 Squadron at the time of the Arnhem Operation Market Garden in September 1944. The Allies had underestimated the strength of the German Army in Holland and an anticipated unimpeded advance by British and American airborne divisions supported by the British Army turned into a costly battle. We flew night and day bringing back wounded troops. On one occasion we brought back a load of German prisoners.

There were still several pockets of German anti-aircraft emplacements on the French coast. We had to fly between them as best we could. On one trip I saw about six Lancasters nearby being pounded by Ack-Ack. At last I was able to say that I flew over enemy territory and saw some enemy action during the war

# DON SHAW

*Don was born in Manitoba in August 1925 and enlisted in the RCAF in 1943, when he was little more than 17½ years old. He was awarded his pilot wings in April 1944 and sent to join a Lancaster squadron at Topcliffe. He was demobilized in 1946, became an academic, and was later named Dean of the University of Regina. Don retired in 1988 as Vice-President.*

## Yesterday's Teenager

In early Spring of 1943 the RCAF lowered the minimum recruitment age to seventeen and a half years provided that the applicant had parental permission. Having for three years yearned to become an Air Force pilot, I was able to persuade my parents (after much weeping and their great reluctance) to allow me to apply for aircrew training. Earlier, I had arranged with a family friend to have an RCAF Medical Officer give me an Air Force medical, unofficially, at the Brandon SFTS.

Everything appeared to be going well until I applied at the Winnipeg recruiting office. A new hurdle was placed in my path. I was just finishing lst Year Science at Brandon College and discovered that people who were taking a science program at a Canadian university or college were not allowed to enlist in the Canadian Forces without a special release from their academic program, such release to be authorised by the Minister of Labour. What to do now?

I sought the advice of the President of Brandon College about how I might gain his support for my release. Fine and patriotic gentleman that he was, the President suggested that my failing to pass one of my current classes would provide him with strong evidence to recommend to the Ministry that I be released from my academic program to enlist in the RCAF. I decided it would not be difficult for me to fail first year chemistry. I did, and my release to join up was granted almost immediately.

*An interesting human sidelight in relation to the release served me well when I went back to university after the war. My chemistry professor knew the circumstances; he suggested that he should give me a supplemental examination in the laboratory section, so that my re-entry to university would be easier without having to repeat all the experiments from first year. In the event he was right, although I was more than a little put out when I discovered that the tutor assigned to help me remember my first year chemistry theory had been in my 1943 class and evaded the war by remaining at university.*

I was accepted for aircrew training on 30 April 1943 and sometime in May went to Brandon Manning Depot, where all new recruits were confined to barracks for the first fourteen days. Since I had been brought up in Brandon, I knew most of the sneaky ways of getting into and out of the old Arena and its attached cow barns. Moreover, my then girlfriend, Adele, now my wonderful wife of 53 years, lived not far from the Arena. My partners in suffering, who were as loath as I to be so confined, soon noticed that I was not around during most evenings. From about the third day, I attracted a band of followers most of the fourteen evenings on my way out; a meeting place and time was designated for the nightly re-entry.

From Manning Depot I went to ITS at Saskatoon, EFTS at Regina–a city in which I later spent many years–then to 11 SFTS, Yorkton on Cessna Cranes. There are undoubtedly as many flying stories as there were student pilots. Two of my experiences come to mind.

The Air Force had a Central Flying School (CFS) at Trenton, Ontario. Part of its mandate was to pay unexpected visits to Service Flying Training Schools across the country to monitor the quality of instruction and the flying skills of student pilots. When the CFS team visited Yorkton I was asked to fly with a CFS flying-officer instructor. When we were airborne, the instructor asked me to perform several manoeuvres, ending up at the low flying area. I stuck to the rule of 250 feet minimum. He then took control and dropped us down to contour flying, including steep turns around haystacks. He passed control to me and told me to do steep turns around some haystacks with the tip of the "down" wing about twenty feet from the ground. I started with some trepidation but quickly began to enjoy the whole thing. His comment was simple; "This is low flying".

On 3 March 1944 I was assigned a low-level cross country from Yorkton to Carlyle and back. Having flown to the Carlyle destination at the prescribed height, my instructor told me to fly around Carlyle to return home, I did so–at about fifty feet off the deck. The instructor said nothing as we headed back toward Yorkton; I carried on at about the fifty-foot level. A town named Kennedy (like many Prairie towns it had few residents but two grain elevators) appeared about two miles ahead. The instructor finally spoke, saying something like, "Shaw, if you're so good let's see you fly between those two elevators".

Well, I estimated the distance between the elevators at about 70 feet, and, as I recall, the Crane's wingspan was 52 feet. The elevators were getting closer and I quickly decided that my judgement was not good enough for the few feet of difference. The only solution was to drop the port wing and hold on top rudder, which I did and slid through, then returned quickly to straight and level, still at almost the same height. The instructor was clearly shaken but had the grace to say, "OK. Now fly us home".

I had visions of his reporting to the CFI and its effect on my Wings Test. However, I got my wings a couple of weeks later and am confident the incident was helpful in my later flying. I assume that either the CFI or the shaken instructor felt my action was appropriate for a fledgling service pilot.

We were winter flying on the prairie. Another trainee and I were out on separate solo cross-country exercises east from Yorkton. Earlier flurries turned rather quickly into blowing snow and a ceiling of about a hundred feet. I was returning to base when the ceiling dropped, and I "inched" my way toward the deck to investigate a darker mass and confirm the direction to Yorkton. As it turned out, this was also an elevator story. The dark mass was a grain elevator, and I was able to get close enough to read the name of the town: Bredenbury. The problem was solved, as long as the ceiling held at a hundred, since it was easy to follow the rail line to Yorkton, the north road to the airport, and catch the east-west runway. My power-on wheel landing was one of my best yet. Luckily my flight instructors were out on the tarmac listening and watching for their two missing aircraft.

# SPECIAL OPERATIONS

World War II saw many forms of Special Operations: SD (Special Duty) squadrons were formed in all theatres. The most publicised special ops were those conducted by the Special Operations Executive. Winston Churchill formed SOE when France fell and there was little opportunity for Britain to take the offensive. SOE was the model upon which America's OSS (transformed in 1947 into the CIA) was built. To provide transport for its agents and to drop supplies, SOE had its own airfield at Tempsford, near Bedford. Two of our authors, Peter Corley-Smith and Arnold Dawkins, flew on these SOE missions. Arnold was shot down and his memoir appears under "The POW Experience."

Another of our authors, Norman Reid, flew from Foggia Main with 40 Squadron, a unit of the Mediterranean Allied Strategic Air Force. We include Norman's story here because he baled out (into Yugoslavia) and landed in the Balkan political cauldron at precisely the time SOE Cairo was succeeding in having Britain withdraw its support from Mihailovich and instructing British officers attached to the Mihailovich forces to quit their posts and make their way to the Partisans. SOE Cairo alleged that Mihailovich was handing Allied airmen over to the Germans. Norman tells how he was cared for by Mihailovich and eventually flown out to Italy.

Our third and fourth authors flew unusual operations although not strictly "Special Ops." in the clandestine sense of the word.

Tet Walston flew Spitfire aircraft on photo-reconnaissance, flying at heights in excess of thirty thousand feet–and sometimes as low as thirty feet–in what could be long and lonely missions.

Bob O'Brien. flew DC3 aircraft in support of the army in Burma, dropping or landing supplies and evacuating wounded.

# CONTRIBUTORS
## SPECIAL OPERATIONS

# PETER CORLEY-SMITH

*Peter joined the RAF in January 1942, was awarded his pilot wings in early 1943. He served with 138 squadron. The squadron came under the administrative control of 3 Group, Bomber Command, but was under the operational control of SOE. For the most part its aircraft operated from Tempsford, in Bedfordshire. Peter flew Stirlings, dropping agents into France or wherever SOE sought to operate. This is Peter's story.*

## Special Operations Executive

The first two years of my career in the RAF during the Second World War were, quite simply, undistinguished. I believe one was allowed to volunteer for aircrew at 17½. Much against my will I was persuaded to finish the school year, meaning another six weeks to wait. I volunteered as soon as school was out in 1941. Six long months passed before I was called up in January 1942. I finally presented myself on hallowed ground, the Marylebone Cricket Club pavilion at Lord's, and emerged with the heady title of AC2, but with that oh-so-distinguished white flash in the cap.

After all the usual frustrations, designated "exigencies of the Service" by our lords and masters, I was one of the lucky few elected for pilot training, and I was off to Greenock for passage to Canada. On a grey, drizzly day, we were ferried out in lighters to a vague but large ship anchored about a mile away. As we closed on it we recognized that it was Queen Mary, but there was something wrong with the bow. In fact, there was a huge, gaping hole in it. We heard a little later something of what had happened. As the QM steamed slowly into the Firth of Clyde, the Royal Navy captain of a light cruiser had decided to play chicken and cut across her bows. He misjudged and the QM went right over the top of the cruiser. It sank in a few minutes and I believe very few of its crew survived. The official history of the Admiralty provides this account:

*On the 2nd of October, just after the Western Approaches escort had joined Queen Mary, she rammed and sank the anti-aircraft cruiser Curaçao. This old ship was slower than the liner, and the accident happened while she was escorting from ahead on a steady course, with Queen Mary zigzagging across her wake. Unhappily 338 lives were lost. The inquiry finally held that the blame was attributable to both ships in proportion of two-thirds against the Admiralty and one-third against the Cunard-White Star Company.*

They had built a bulkhead and plugged the hole with concrete, which made us all a trifle nervous; sailors know best, however, and the voyage was uneventful. Just under five days later, we were in Boston—Boston because it had the only dry-dock on the east coast large enough to accommodate the QM for repairs. We were there just for the one day before climbing on a train that evening to go to Moncton, New Brunswick.

Moncton was pleasant enough. We were there about three weeks I think, but we were so eager to get to our flying training at last that time dragged. Then I experienced another disappointment. I had been looking forward to a posting to somewhere romantic like Moose Jaw or Medicine Hat. Instead, at the beginning of November, I had to go to Clewiston, Florida, a civilian training school, one of those run by the Embry Riddle Company. It was located on the Tamiami Trail, halfway between the east and west coasts of the peninsula, just south of Okeechobee Lake and just north of the Everglades. We had civilian flying instructors, but ground-school instruction and administration was provided by the RAF.

Florida, of course, was a joy. Beautiful weather and, at that time, almost Utopian: good food, no crowds and far more young women than men in the towns. As well, because the demand for pilots had slowed, there seemed to be no pressure to shovel us through. We did our elementary (primary) on Stearman PT-17s and we started our advanced on North American AT-6As (Harvards) in January 1943.

The instructors I had for primary and advanced were both experienced and relaxed–not above chasing farmers off haystacks for a change of pace. We were there until mid-May, six months of the prime winter weather season in Florida, and when we reached the last thirty or so hours of training we were allowed to go off with a friend and play. We would take off in formation and then play fighter pilots to our heart's content.

For me the flying training went without too many bumps. The weather was so benign it was a joy to be up there. Cool but not too cool mornings, with some build-up of cumulus in the afternoons; a little bumpy but unthreatening and great fun to dive in and out of when we were chasing each other. One thing that I appreciated was that, except for check rides, I had the same instructor right through primary; then another right through advanced. The one bump I ran into was for me at the time very, very scary.

It was the last check before the final one, this with a Canadian flight lieutenant who, we learned from gossip–because he never spoke to us except to give commands–had been soured because he had wanted active service but been diverted to instructing. He was an unhappy warrior even after a plum posting like this one. Naturally, I did my walk around on the ground very conscientiously. The care I took didn't seem to please him.

"Took a long time, didn't it?"

"That's what I've been trained to do, sir."

He grunted then climbed up onto the wing and into the front cockpit; I followed into the rear. His attitude seemed to be 'let's get this over with' and was discouraging.

In the air, he said very little except to give me the next exercise. We did turns and steep turns, figure eights, a couple of spins and recoveries, followed by a couple of loops. Finally, he asked for a slow roll before we did the practice forced landings I knew were to come. The roll seemed to start reasonably; I kept straight and kept the nose up with top rudder. Then, as we rolled right over and I pushed the stick forward to keep the nose up, the intercom suddenly blared profanities in my ear–language one can't repeat in a family publication like this one. I had no idea what the problem was. The slow roll seemed reasonably competent as I came out of it.

"What did I do wrong?"

"Take me back to the field." His voice was distinctly snappy.

After we'd landed and taxied back to the apron, he jumped out before I had time to cut the engine and stalked off. I was bewildered and scared. The dreaded name Trenton (where washouts were sent to be reclassified) came all too easily to mind. It turned out that two trainees had done a cross-country that morning and left an empty Coca-Cola bottle in the front cockpit. It had nailed the Flight Lieutenant two or three times on the way round.

When we finally had our wings pinned on us, towards the end of May, there were only four commissions out of the whole intake. Apparently there was an oversupply of aircrew officers as well; so I became a sergeant. We began the long train journey back to Moncton and from there, after another week or two of inaction, on to Halifax, where we embarked on the Louis Pasteur. This was a far cry from the roomy and comfortable QM. This time we had to sleep in the dining area in hammocks practically touching each other, and on the dining tables. There were three sittings for every meal and the sanitary conditions were atrocious. Fortunately, this too was a fast boat and we docked in Liverpool five and a half days later.

I was posted to Shawbury in Shropshire early in August for conversion to twins, flying Oxfords. This was pleasant enough, though I found the density of buildings, roads, and railways, made the map reading tough after Florida. Fortunately, there was a large, distinctive hill called the Wrekin that stood out over the low, rolling hills of the country in general. If the visibility was half decent, you could see it for miles and home on it. Night flying was another matter because there were training airfields all around and, when the DREM lighting systems were on, it could be very hard to pick out your own. A story that is usually dismissed as apocryphal but I know to be true occurred while I was there.

An instructor took off with a student to do some night circuits and bumps. After a few, they landed, taxied up to the tower and the instructor told the student to do one solo circuit, land, and pick him up. The student took off, did his circuit, landed, then taxied back to the tower, but there was no sign of the instructor. The tower called him and told him to park the aircraft at dispersal; they would send a lorry to pick him up. Evidently, they had just learned that the instructor was at another airfield—but the student had landed back at the right one. I suspect the unfortunate instructor heard about this for some time.

More frustration was to come.

Confident that I would at last get to OTU I was infuriated to learn I had been posted to a wireless operators training school at Yatesbury, near the village of Calne in Wiltshire. This was a gruesome posting and I was there for about six months, from October to April 1944. We were flying Percival Proctors, little single-engined, low-wing monoplanes. The student wireless op sat next to you facing the back and did his thing while you literally swanned around for about two-and-a-half hours at time. It was profoundly boring and, to add to your disgruntlement, students were frequently airsick.

At last my exile ended and I was posted to No. 26 OTU at Wing, in Buckinghamshire, early in May 1944. This helped to restore some measure of self-confidence. Now, as we went through the curious ritual of sorting ourselves out into crews, I began to feel as though I belonged. I remember that I thought the navigator the most important choice, and I think I made the overture to Dennis Somper. In any event it was very much the right one. The bomb-aimer was Bob Boyle, a New Zealander; the engineer, Taffy Card, was Welsh; the mid-upper gunner was Ben, a roly-poly, cheerful Cornishman; the wireless operator was Jack Wheilden, an Australian; and the rear gunner, Jim Colbert, was a cheerful Cockney with a sharp wit.

We appeared to be compatible and in the eighteen months we were together I don't recall any friction. I found the Wellington a solid aircraft to fly, with no tricky bits, but heavy on the controls. Things went smoothly at OTU; we did well in things like navigation, practice-bombing and fighter affiliation. At any rate, when we moved on I earned my first above average and moved up from flight sergeant to pilot officer.

The next move was to 1651 Conversion Unit at Wratting Common, a little disconcerting when we found we were to fly Stirlings. We knew that the Stirling had not turned out to be a success as a bomber and to us at the time it looked huge and rather ungainly; with the tailwheel on the ground the pilot's head was some twenty-five feet above the runway. The conversion was quick and relatively painless, especially when we learned that we were going to 138 Squadron on Special Duties. We felt that this was definitely a mark of distinction though, as with most RAF postings, it probably came out of a hat.

At Tempsford, not far from Bedford, there were two squadrons: 138, which flew only Stirlings—though they had converted fairly recently from Halifaxes—and 161 Squadron, which flew mostly

Hudsons and Lysanders. To my mind, the pilots of 161 were the brave ones. They delivered and retrieved Resistance people, landing at night in fields with only the most rudimentary of runway lights to guide them–and in the Lysander, the pilot, of course, had to do all the navigating. It must have been a nerve-wracking business.

We were at Tempsford about a year and then only completed twenty-six trips. The reason was simple: we could fly only when there was a decent measure of moonlight, which amounted to about ten days a month; but when the moon was with us, the weather very often wasn't, and vice versa. We did a good deal of practice low flying in the dusk to accustom us to staying low when visibility was limited. Our task was to deliver supplies to Resistance movements in Europe and, occasionally, more Resistance people. We would fly low to the dropping zone—which was called a Reception—but with a good deal of variation of course and track to avoid signalling our destination. The Reception would consist of a variety of patterns of lights— perhaps an L or a T—together with a Morse code flash of two or three letters. These would only be confided to us just before take-off.

A typical operation would start when we were advised where we were going, usually in mid-morning. The navigator and bomb-aimer would go off to meet with one of the two WAAF intelligence officers who had the latest on anti-aircraft gun emplacements; together they would work out a suitable course to follow, with recognizable pinpoints for map reading. In the afternoon, all crews who were on that night would assemble for a briefing: the latest meteorology, new tactics by the enemy, and a pep talk by the Station Commander.

After an early supper we would put on flying gear and collect the other paraphernalia: an escape kit, with its silk maps and appropriate currency for our destination, flasks of tea, and so on. After picking up parachutes from the packing shed we would be driven out to the dispersal a little before dusk, and stand around trying not to look nervous. Finally, if we were to carry a live one, he or she would turn up at the last minute and we'd all climb in.

As a rule we would fly out to the coast at around 2000 feet and then, if we were crossing the English Channel, drop down and fly at around 100 feet. We had a radio altimeter, so this didn't require too much concentration. If we were over the North Sea, we might stay up at 1000 feet until about thirty miles from the coast and then let down to try to keep out of radar. The trick before reaching the coast was for the navigator to try to get a bearing on at least one of the shipping navigation lights along the coast, which would stay on until we were heard. This would give us a nice secure crossing of the coast on course, for the most part safe from flak and easier for the bomb-aimer, who now took over the map reading until we reached the Reception.

The difficulty for the rest of the way was, of course, to keep on track in the half light, a task shared between the navigator and bomb-aimer. Depending on the topography, we would try to keep within two or three hundred feet above ground. This was the big safety factor because few people on the ground heard you, much less saw you, in time to get a shot at you. We picked up only three bullet holes on all our trips.

While the Stirling may have failed as a bomber, it was ideal for our purposes. The Bristol Hercules radial engines had sleeve valves, which rendered them much quieter than the Merlins on a Halifax or a Lancaster. Apart from that, they were roomy, both in the cockpit and the fuselage. The mid-upper turret had been removed. There was a large trapdoor hatch in the floor, used for dropping objects too big to fit into the canisters in the bomb bay, and to drop personnel. Ben, the mid-upper gunner, had become a dispatcher and it was his job to shove the loads out. There were occasions when dispatchers had to give reluctant parachutists a friendly nudge to get them through the hatch as well.

The Stirling was comfortable, clipped along at a good 180 mph and was delightfully light on the controls, which made quick turns when needed easy to accomplish. This was one of the safety factors. If enemy fighters did happen to pick us up, they seldom tried to hang on our tail for long in the half light. We only saw night fighters twice during our tour. The first upped the heart rate quite a bit. We had pulled up to about 700 feet to let the bomb-aimer pick up his pinpoints when I saw a Ju88 flying across from left to right and about 500 feet above us. I thought he hadn't seen us but, just after he passed in front, he turned steeply towards our tail. I poked the nose down and the rear gunner said the fighter was turning to follow us down. When we got down and he started to close, I went into a steep turn. The fighter started to follow but then suddenly broke away and climbed out. The Germans simply didn't have the experience we had in low flying in moonlight. The second fighter we saw on another flight, an Me110 passed us almost from rear to front, about 600 feet above and obviously never saw us. Once again, I think the low flying defeated them; they weren't expecting to see anything below them at 1000 feet.

The critical time on these trips came when we neared the Reception. Between them, the navigator and bomb-aimer would have picked out a clearly identifiable turning point about twenty miles from the Reception. I would get a course to the Reception and stay down until we were about five minutes away, then climb up to our standard dropping height of 800 feet. If the gods were smiling we would pick up the prearranged lights and the code, slow down, drop some flap and open the bomb doors. The speed was about 100 mph for the drop, and if things went smoothly we would be able to make the drop in one run which, of course, gave comfort to the people on the ground because, if we had to circle back, it would obviously raise suspicions with any German troops around, making it much harder for the Resistance people to move our "drop" to safety.

These last few minutes before the drop were known as pucker time. We were aware that the Resistance people had sometimes been infiltrated by the enemy, in which case the Reception would be anything but friendly. In our case, good fortune remained with us and although we occasionally found no Reception, we would usually learn afterwards that there were too many Germans around for safety. We had to abort occasionally because of weather. In the end, though, it is difficult to describe the vivid feeling of exhilaration after a successful drop. Unlike bomber crews, who could seldom see the immediate results of their efforts, we knew we'd clicked and made a very tricky connection work.

One of the biggest difficulties sounds a little absurd now. Some of our trips were long ones—the longest around ten hours. When we had crossed the coast on the way home, perhaps at 0400, and still had another two hours of flying over the North Sea, the steady drone, even with the engines well synchronised, induced drooping eyelids. There was no one to spell you at the controls and it became an agony to keep awake: a mixture of a fierce desire to let yourself drift off, and an equally strong fear of the consequences. As well, one needed to be on the alert when reaching the vicinity of our base because German night intruders were fairly active at the time.

If we had to divert because of weather, there was another complication. The intelligence officer at the base would insist on a debriefing. We were under the strictest orders to refuse and it was often tedious to have to drum this into an intelligence officer's head. He (in one case she) would threaten all sorts of outcomes, mostly courts-martial, while we waited irritably to go and get something to eat. One particularly green and eager debriefer demanded to see my log book. I explained the obvious: that I never carried a log book on operations and that, in any case, he would learn nothing from it because we were not allowed to enter anything but the time of the flight and "Operation as Ordered"–which was logged when we got back as either DCO, for duty carried out, or DNCO, for an aborted operation.

For this reason my log book tells me little and I can no longer describe most of the individual flights. I flew over France, Belgium, Holland, Denmark, and Norway and, on one occasion, dropped someone just inside Germany. Our Receptions were invariably anonymous locations in secluded areas. One trip, for a reason that will become obvious, does stay in my mind, though none of our crew felt it necessary to share our experience with anyone else at the time.

We were on our way to a Reception north-east of Oslo, Norway, and we ran into cloud near the coast. Unless you detoured well up the west coast, entry into Norway was tricky because you had to climb fairly high to get over the mountains. The southern tip was well protected with flak emplacements. Flying up the Skagerrak didn't work either because the ridges on either side were heavily defended; instead of firing up at you, the flak fired down at you, so we usually went a little way to the west coast before penetrating. In this case, we ran into cloud at the coast and, after flying over it for what seemed an awfully long time, breaks appeared and I dropped down. Before long the bomb-aimer picked up a lake he recognized. He was satisfied we were only a few miles off track. If I altered course 10 degrees to port, we would very shortly pick up our recognizable run-up point to the Reception. In a few moments, there it was.

I swung onto the course the navigator gave me and, as we spotted the lights, lowered the flaps and opened the bomb doors. A minute or two later I turned a few degrees to line up with the lights. Thirty seconds later, I had to make a second correction, then a third. This time I muttered about navigators who couldn't plot a simple course from A to B. The navigator responded testily, something about pilots who couldn't hold a course for two minutes without wandering all over the sky.

At about this time quite a few other lights began to appear on the ground. There was an animated burst of commentary from the whole crew. I had to shout for silence so that the bomb aimer, the navigator, and I could discuss this phenomenon. Eventually, the truth dawned on us–we had crossed the border into Sweden. The lights of the "Reception" I had been trying to line up on were those of a moving train.

At this discovery, the rest of the crew felt free to comment again. They waxed sardonic, but it was Jim Colbert, the rear gunner, who was most outspoken. He proposed that the bomb-aimer should bale out while we were still over Sweden and allow himself to be interned for the duration. Then the rest of us could return to base and find a replacement who could at least tell from the map what country we were flying over.

As it turned out, we ended up with a DCO that night. Feeling safe over Sweden, I climbed up to about 3000 feet, the bomb aimer got his bearings and we let down over the border again into Norway. The Reception was up towards the drainage of a heavily forested valley. By now the weather was clear and there was very nearly a full moon so we had good visibility as we flew up the valley. The problem was that the Reception, though admirably remote, was in a clearing less than a mile from the end of the narrowing valley, where the ground rose fairly steeply. If we tried a drop in the reverse direction, we'd never get low enough and slow enough for any sort of accuracy.

I nearly chickened out, but finally kept going at about 1000 feet. I warned the crew we were going to have to do a split-arse turn to get out and, the moment I felt the canisters go, whipped up the bomb-door lever, opened the throttles wide, did a sharp turn to the right, then reversed and went into a really hairy steep turn the other way. We came uncomfortably close to the trees on the hillside but, with some heavy breathing, we made it. Jim, in the back, watched the 'chutes landing and reported that it was a pretty fair drop.

At the debriefing, as I mentioned earlier, we didn't feel it necessary to give too detailed an account of the trip. Instead, we emphasised the difficulties of the drop and the splendid airmanship with which we overcame them.

By the end of 1944, as the Allied forces moved steadily northward, our activities began to dwindle. One unusual trip we made was to the Ardennes, the area where what later became known as the Battle of the Bulge took place. The Germans had mounted an unforeseen and serious counter attack. We were loaded with a hundred or so miniature dummy paratroops. We had been on standby for two nights, waiting for weather. Finally, it cleared on Christmas Eve. It was a crisp, clear, moonlight night. The ground was a blanket of snow and it was illuminated by countless gun flashes and the occasional curve of tracer bullets, seemingly coming from every direction. I remember thinking how lucky I was to be where I was and not on the ground. As far as we knew nobody fired at us; presumably they were too busy firing at each other. We turned to have a look after we'd dropped the dummy 'chutes. I think the figures were less than a foot tall and they looked very convincing. We never heard whether they deceived the Germans into moving troops in the wrong direction.

Finally the news came that the squadron was going to convert to Lancasters and join the bombers. The conversion went smoothly and we did two bombing trips. The second I remember well because it was a daylight attack on Bremen. The cloud cover was broken and now, for the first time, we discovered what it was like to keep flying into visible flak. We had been told that there would be very little. From our perspective, there was a great deal and it seemed disconcertingly accurate. In the event, we didn't suffer any damage and that was our last operation. The next sorties, the first on May 2, several days before VE Day, were bread runs. Some sort of truce had been worked out with the Germans in the area because the local population was starving, and we dropped food and supplies. We made three of these in Holland, two to the Hague and one to Rotterdam.

Our last trips with the squadron, however, began on VE Day to Juvincourt, near Rheims, to repatriate prisoners of war. The runways were steel mesh but the weather was fine and dry and we had no difficulties, except that the number of people we had to pack into the cramped space of a Lancaster was a little scary. I can't remember how many people we carried now, but we were afraid that somebody would jam the control cables running along the inside of the fuselage. It didn't happen and, while we missed out on the VE Day celebrations, it was very satisfying to bring these troops home, some of whom had been in POW camps since Dunkerque.

By May 7 1945 several of us were posted to do yet another course; this time it was conversion to Yorks in Transport Command.

When we were halfway through our conversion, I was told that if I completed the course satisfactorily, I would be eligible for a permanent commission. If I didn't want it, I should say so.

I said I didn't and was posted to Transport Command Headquarters in Bushey Heath, where I served out my time as a clueless staff officer.

# NORMAN REID

*Norm enlisted in the RCAF and subsequently transferred to the RAF He flew 40 operational sorties as a navigator with 40 Squadron, 205 Group. Subsequently he earned his pilot wings. He was twice the recipient of a Caterpillar Club badge, awarded to aircrew who 'hit the silk'. Norm is a director of the Royal Air Forces Escapers Society. Post-war he pursued a career as an engineer and founded Reid Crowther and Partners, Consulting Engineers. His story is of a fascinating episode of WWII*

## The Betrayal of an Ally

**C**ATERPILLAR ONE

The beachhead at Anzio had turned sour. A constant 24-hour air attack was laid on. Fuel needs were low for a short run over the mountains from our base at Foggia, and so our Wellingtons were loaded up with nearly 6000 lbs. of anti-personnel fragmentation bombs. These we dropped on armour and troop concentrations in a night operation at low level, each aircraft flying a different given track fanning out from lights in the form of an X placed on our side of the bomb line. Light flak, unpredicted 20-mm stuff, was hose-piped up at us and we caught an unlucky hit. It wasn't too serious but the resulting power loss combined with severe icing—both carburettor and jammed flying controls–as we tried for height to get back over the mountains, caused the aircraft to become uncontrollable, necessitating the order to bale out.

I landed in the mud on our side of the lines. My flying boots had flown away in the slipstream and I was sloshing around in stockinged feet with my parachute draped over me. I wandered around in a general southward direction until I came to a farmhouse. I banged on the door, not thinking about how I must have appeared. An elderly Italian couple took one look at this apparition in white in the pitch black midnight darkness, panicked, and in a barrage of screaming Italian slammed the door. If I'd raised my arms and said, "I am the resurrection" there'd have been two new saints canonised in Italy that night.

By dawn I came across an American Advanced Medical unit and ultimately got back to my squadron by surface transport a few days later.

## CATERPILLAR TWO

We of the RAF were doing our usual night raids on Ploesti and tactical ops to impede transportation of oil products to Germany. We mined the Danube at the Iron Gates where the river cuts through the mountains. To get at barge traffic, we ran the gauntlet at 200 feet. The German 88-mm guns had to point down instead of up at us. It was easier for them than shooting fish in a barrel; crashed aircraft were burning all over both sides of the Danube and in it.

The target that won me a free trip to the Balkans was a railway bridge over the Jiu River in Romania near its confluence with the Danube, which we attacked at night at low level. After locating the target using a timed run from Tumu Severin, a port on the Danube, we made a dummy run at 1500 feet. Not a murmur came from below, we seemed to have taken them by surprise and it looked like a piece of cake. On the bombing run at about 200 feet in the moonlight we must have been beautifully silhouetted and all hell broke loose from rail flak that had been moved in a few hundred feet up-rail of the bridge. The first bursts hit the nose of the aircraft and killed our bomb-aimer instantly--the starboard wing tank was hit and streaming petrol; the port engine's constant speed unit went crazy; and the racing engine threatened to pull out of its mounts. Two of us battled adverse yaw and tried to find a pitch and throttle setting for the port engine that might help–but to no avail. The fuel gauge for the starboard tank dropped steadily to near empty. I changed the P-8 heading from homebound to somewhere south of Belgrade. It was doubtful that we would even get back to the Danube let alone make a return to base, but with the gentle gradient of the railway to follow we did just make it to the west side of the river where I and the three other surviving crew members managed to bail out.

In the darkness of the wee hours of 8 May 1944, 1 once again found myself hanging under the canopy of a parachute. This time I was over Serbia some forty miles south of Belgrade just west of the Danube. I hit the ground in open country and sooner than I had judged—perhaps a problem of depth perception in the faint light of a partial moon—or was it due to preoccupation with what might be waiting for me below? Was it a case of out of the fire into the frying pan?

I wasn't going to have to wait very long to find out. The first chapter in an adventure and an association with a people was about to open, the related events of which continue with me to this very day. To say the least it has given me a peek into the merciless world of international power politics, a world in which the very essence emerges from diametrically opposed political ideologies inflamed by the emotions of religious conviction and inseparable from ethnic nationalism.

The usual pre-flight briefing had included advisories from intelligence officers who indicated that if we survived, if we came down in Yugoslavia and evaded capture, our chances of escape and repatriation in areas where Tito's Partisans were active would be good, but in the areas controlled by Chetnik guerrillas our treatment might be different–and at best an unknown.

As it turned out, Intelligence (whose information originated with SOE) was no more accurate on that count than in its advice that our target would be undefended.

It was my 40th operation and one that would have marked the end of an extended tour, and been the last for a while. I would be screened and do a spell of duties as an instructor. Somewhat traditionally a tour-expiring trip was expected to be a " milk run".

I landed in a pasture of hard turf, once again losing my flying boots to the slipstream.

After burying my 'chute and harness at the field's edge,–à la training film prescribed style–I stayed concealed by some wild brush. It did not seem that my presence was known, although I still distinctly recall hearing the barking of dogs while I was descending.

Chetniks who helped rescue Norman Reid

I waited some hours in the partial darkness. In the early dawn, four figures appeared on the nearby dirt road; as they drew nearer I could see they were heavily armed with automatic rifles, Sten guns, bandoleers of ammo, grenades and knives. They were not in German uniform. Sooner or later it was imperative to risk seeking help and this looked as good as it might get.

Moments later I was looking into the wrong end of four automatic rifles and wasn't so sure. The skull and cross bones hat badge provided no comfort either. (Years later I was presented with one and made an honorary Chetnik). Luckily they didn't *open fire and investigate later*. Even more luckily, I had stumbled onto a Chetnik Underground Resistance patrol. Through sign language and from my flying clothing I convinced them of what I was and how I came to be there. This incidentally was not always easily done, since the Germans used the ruse of planting fake allied flyers into occupied areas hoping to infiltrate and expose resistance groups in their role of helping escaping airmen.

I was concerned that the Germans might find my recently buried 'chute and harness, so we went back to get it. I mention this because the 28-foot circle of white silk later made me an instant hero with the peasant ladies, who made it into a wedding gown for a Serbian bride and countless babushkas thereafter.

From initial contact and until my ultimate escape months later, I was protected, hidden, fed and clothed, receiving nothing but the utmost kindness from the Serbian people. The term *Serbian* can be taken as synonymous with the term *Chetnik*—a very important point, critical to understanding the difference between Mihailovich's allegiances and objectives compared with those of Tito.

## THE CHETNIKS AND MIHAILOVICH

The name *Chetnik* derives from *Ceta* or band. For centuries villages had formed armed bands for their own protection from foreign invaders—a sort of home guard or militia in our terms. Drazha Mihailovich was born into a Serbian military family and had himself entered the service at age fifteen to fight in WWI. In that war he was twice wounded and acquitted himself with distinction, receiving the country's highest decorations.

He has been described as a brilliant officer and military theoretician, with an uncanny knowledge of his country's intricate topography. Having been privileged to meet him on more than one occasion, I was impressed by his modest manner, humble relations with the peasants, and abstemious personal habits. Most revealing to me, however, was the effect he had on the Serbian people. They literally revered the man. Their name for him in Serbian was *Chicha*, which means uncle.

## THE PARTISANS AND TITO

Tito, a nom de guerre, was born Josip Broz, the son of a Croatian blacksmith. He was drafted for service with the Austro-Hungarian army on the Russian front where he went over to the Russians. When the revolution came he volunteered for the Red Army and fought in the civil war. He stayed in Russia marrying a Russian girl. He studied Communism and returned to Yugoslavia and eventually became the unchallenged leader of Yugoslav communism.

## MAY 1944. THE LONG WALK

With the majority of British liaison officers by now withdrawn from the Mihailovich forces and the British having dumped him, it was Mihailovitch's Chetniks who were risking their lives to save mine. Since bailing out on the $8^{th}$, I had been travelling, first hidden, covered by straw in an ox-cart, then partly on horseback but mostly on foot, from eastern Serbia where I had landed, toward Mihailovich's headquarters in the mountains of central Serbia. There were many hold-overs in peasant safe-houses along the way.

The journey was long, tiring, yet fascinatingly interesting. While we dodged German columns, the Chetniks took out sentries (they were silently effective with bailing wire and a knee in the back). One evening as we approached the outskirts of the village of Svilajnac we proceeded cautiously; Chetniks cleared the way in a leapfrog-like manoeuvre. The signal to proceed was a light placed in the window by friendly Serbian villagers. We thus made our way to a restaurant where the owner, himself a Chetnik, accommodated us near the back of a large dining room. We had just got nicely settled and were looking forward to a drink and food after a hard day's march when a commotion of vehicles outside the front of the restaurant occurred. The owner came running back to us screaming "Idi idi" and something that meant 'hurry, hurry, get out of here Germans, Germans'.

We dashed out the door behind us and ran a fair distance into a field of tall maize where we scattered and hit the ground. The Germans knew something was going on, re-entered their vehicles, and drove into our field using overhead spotlights in an effort to find us. One came within a few feet of where I was grovelling in the dirt.

Eventually they grew impatient, doubtless enticed back to the restaurant by the promise of food and drink. We ultimately regrouped and got away in a wood-burning truck brought by a Serbian friend. The Germans got the food and drink that night. We went to sleep hungry, but happy to have avoided capture once again.

During later days we saw from the daylight raids many American planes being shot down. We watched the blossoming of parachutes of the "luckier" airmen. German eyes were also watching them. Often a firefight broke out between Germans and Chetniks over who would recover the fallen flyers. I'm guessing but believe the Chetniks rescued at least a third of the survivors. Our group was joined by some of these, many of whom were badly wounded or had broken their legs on landing. I helped a Serbian doctor, who had been smuggled out of a nearby German occupied village, pull three broken legs into position while he applied splints. This was all done without morphine. I can still hear the screams as I held on for dear life to keep the limbs in position as the doctor had warned me I must do.

For reasons of concealment, the airmen who were fit to travel were broken up into small groups of four or five, always accompanied by heavily armed Chetniks. Eventually, and not without further incident, we reached Mihailovich's headquarters. My first meeting with him along with two or three other airmen was at a delightful large outdoor picnic table. It was now July 1944. The food was good and the Slivovic and Rakia were plentiful. Drazha told us of his dreams for a free Yugoslavia and his frustration at receiving no more supply drops. He asked if we knew what had happened and when could he expect more. We couldn't tell him. We knew only what the intelligence officer had told us: that we might not be able to trust the Chetniks, and we could hardly mention that to Mihailovich.

WHAT TO DO NOW?

The number of shot down airmen rescued by the Chetniks and scattered all over the Balkans was climbing into the hundreds, the vast majority being American. *Over 270 B24 Liberators were lost on Ploesti, to say nothing of like numbers of B17s and some escort fighters.* Unlike central Europe there were no "lines of escape" organised by the underground resistance movements. Most of Yugoslavia, the mountains of Montenegro and the Adriatic Sea separated us from the nearest allied forces in Italy. There appeared to be no means for any of us to get back home. Some of us considered walking to the Adriatic coast hundreds of miles away, through German occupied and hostile mountainous terrain. And even if we reached the coast, how to cross the Adriatic Sea? Despite all these odds against succeeding, some made the attempt. Two of us, RAF types and one American, took off but battle-and-terrain-wise Chetniks forcibly dissuaded us after we had made only a few miles westward.

A lieutenant in the US Air Force, Tom Oliver, then persuaded the General to let us use one of his transmitters and a Chetnik operator to send out messages. We didn't know the "letters" of the hour and could not give the correct response to the challenge of the Allied receiving station. SOE advised that our transmissions were a German trap.

We couched our messages in Air Force slang to veil them from the Germans. They intercepted the signals and a Fiesler Storch observation plane came snooping around in low flight. This was followed one day by Ju52s, which the Germans used to carry paratroopers. I thought once again it was game over—but the Germans did not commit themselves.

THE WAY OUT

One day weeks later I was thrown into a state of euphoria, when standing beside the Chetnik wireless operator I watched him type: *Help will arrive.* Persistence in sending out a constant stream of slang and jargon filled messages had finally convinced a D/F station in Italy that they were not just an enemy ruse. Our trust in Mihailovich took a meteoric rise.

I had another meeting with the General and obtained maps so we could advise Italy of our precise location. We devised a code giving the name and service number of one of the Americans but added our latitude and longitude. Once an Allied intelligence officer checked the serial numbers . from records, deciphering became simple. One interesting problem remains in my memory. The maps had been obtained during the course of a Chetnik raid on a German stronghold. The origin of the meridians of longitude was Berlin. It took a little figuring to convert this to Greenwich.

We lighted fires at night and after several abortive attempts an American Air Force DC3 in a night operation dropped an officer agent of the OSS (Office of Strategic Services, forerunner to the CIA) with two operators and radio equipment, medical supplies and C-rations.

The climax to all this was the arrival of DC3 transports to a small grass strip at Pranjani, prepared by the peasants while Chetniks stood guard. The first attempt was at night with a single aircraft and ended up in near disaster as it brushed treetops on take-off. We paced the field again to measure its length. The debate then raged as to whether or not a risky, brazen daylight attempt should be made.

Finally four DC3s came in low at dawn over the mountains with a P51 Mustang fighter escort. While the transports landed on the all too short grass strip keeping their engines running, we airmen scrambled on board. The P51s circled around providing top cover and shooting up German installations, while the Chetniks provided a surrounding cordon for surface protection. There were German units, including a Luftwaffe base, a few miles away.

I'll never forget the take-off in that lumbering transport from that oh-so-short, tiny pasture and then the feelings of exhilaration in the DC3s as the squadron of P51 fighters closed in protective formation around us. We flew across central Yugoslavia, over the mountains of Montenegro, across the Adriatic Sea and into Bari, Italy. We were at last on our way home!

This was an All-American mission and was repeated many times throughout Yugoslavia in the late summer, fall and winter to the very end of 1944. During that period some five hundred American airmen were rescued, as well as my three surviving crew members. I know personally of three other RAF personnel who were brought out, and there were probably as many as twenty more. Mihailovich got no official recognition until after it was too late for him. The rescue operation was code-named "The Halyard Mission."

THE SAD ENDING

One of the OSS agents directing the mission "hands on" in Yugoslavia was Captain Nick Lalich of Baltimore, an American of Serbian descent. He remains a close friend to this day. He was the last American officer to see General Drazha Mihailovich alive. He tells of the tearful parting in late December 1944. When he told the General that the American government had granted permission for him to be vacated to safety by plane, Mihailovich replied, "No! I will stay and share the fate of my people, whatever that may be. These are my people, this is my land, and I will stay to the very end."

In the closing months of the war the Chetniks were trapped between the Russians coming in across the Danube from the east and Tito's partisans from the west. Accounts now tell of massacres by the thousands of the Serbian people. Tito was taking war material dropped to him by the western allies and using it against the Chetniks.

General Drazha Mihailovich was eventually captured by the Russians and turned over to Tito's Partisans for "disposal" as they saw fit.

He was thrown into jail in Belgrade and brought to trial in the spring of 1946, charged with being a collaborator and war criminal. I and other rescued airmen, as well as former British and American liaison officers, offered to testify on his behalf. Many of us travelled to Washington and in my case also to Ottawa, seeking intervention at government level. We were denied the right to testify by Yugoslavia. In desperation evidence was given under oath at the U.S. State Department. In answer to charges of collaboration with the Germans, not a single airman of the over five hundred or more rescued by the Chetniks (who protected them and enabled them to return home safely) saw any collaborative act whatsoever by the Chetniks. Whether such and other supportive evidence was read into the trial I cannot say. It would not have mattered; the judgement was a foregone decision.

We pressured our governments to have the trial moved to Nuremberg. We argued that as he was charged with being a war criminal he should then be accorded the rights of due process.

Belgrade refused or ignored this plea.

Nazi criminals responsible for the most heinous of crimes against humanity received trials in a court of free society. Our ally who had done so much for the cause did not. The verdict in communist style "justice" was a foregone conclusion. General Mihailovich was found guilty and sentenced to death.

General Mihailovich's words, spoken at his trial, were so honest, so wise, so mild:

> *"I wanted nothing for myself. I never wanted the old Yugoslavia, but I had a difficult legacy. I had against me a competitive organisation, a party that seeks its aims without compromise.*
> *I believed I was on the right road and called on any foreign journalist or Red Army mission to visit me and see everything. But fate was merciless to me when it threw me into this turmoil and whirlpool.*
> *I wanted much, I started much, but the gale of the world carried away me and my work."*

General Drazha Mihailovich was taken to a golf course in Belgrade and executed by firing squad on 17 July 1946.

On 29 March 1948, he was posthumously awarded the Legion of Merit-Chief Commander, the highest military honour that can be conferred by America on a non-American. The citation is signed: Harry S. Truman, President of the United States of America.

## POSTSCRIPT. NORMAN REID'S CASE FOR GENERAL MIHAILOVICH

In assessing the campaign against Mihailovich, one factor must be clearly appreciated: The scope and success of Mihailovich's early resistance was unexpected and unacceptable to the Germans. When their numbers of dead began to climb, Hitler announced that for every German soldier wounded or killed, 50 or 100 Serbs would be put to death. Every home from which shots were fired would be razed. No respect for gender, age, or members of the Cloth was shown. Hostages were even held in inventory so that immediate reprisal executions could take place. In the village of Kraguyevats during the second week of October 1941, thousands of innocents were rounded up, dragged out of homes, schools, shops, churches, or wherever they might have been. General thinking was that it was a check for those without identity cards. Like sheep the arrested went to the slaughter, in groups of forty, one group after another. All day and all night long the machine-guns rattled

The exact number of the murdered is not known, but counts range from a minimum of 4000 to as high as 6000. Details of this reprisal are well and authentically documented. Hitler's orders were carried out with Germanic precision.

Against this background it is understandable that Mihailovich, as a patriot endeared to the Serbian people, would begin to exercise caution and selectivity in his operation. In fact this was exactly the role advocated to resistance groups throughout Europe; to remain at silent alert until support to Allied military operations would bring liberation.

# A.B. (TET) WALSTON

*Born in Morley, Yorkshire, in June 1922, Ted enlisted in the RAF nineteen years later in 1941. He was awarded his wings in Canada in April 1942 and joined 541 (PR) Squadron in October. He moved to 543 (PR) Squadron the following month. In March 1943, he was posted to 682 (PR) Squadron and finished his tour of operations in September of that year, He was demobilised in October 1946.*

## Alone Above All

That is the motto of 541PR (Photo-Reconnaissance) Squadron RAF, my first squadron. The crest is unusual in that the badge motif is a wild flower, the bird's-eye (speedwell), cleverly selected by somebody who knew all about us. We flew blue Spitfires, as speedily as we could. Our cameras were the bird's-eye, and we flew even higher than the USAAF.

At a recent Battle of Britain Sunday Parade, a lady guest asked what my blazer badge was and wanted to know how I managed to collect all my campaign stars. I explained the meaning of the badge, then answered her other question–by surviving.

The following is a brief account of some of my years in the RAFVR, and I lay claim to having been a skilful survivor, and I can prove it. I'm still here.

I was born and raised in Yorkshire, England. My nickname

comes from one of my family names, Tetley, famed all over the world for beer, and very good beer at that.

In August 1939, I was already a member of the RAF Volunteer Reserve, and eligible to apply for a Short Service Commission. I had passed the preliminary tests and was due to go to Ad Astral House, London, for my final interview on 5 September 1939. Britain declared war on Germany on 3 September and I received a telegram cancelling the interview and stating: "All recruitment will be through usual channels." As a pupil-apprentice mechanical engineer, I was in a reserved occupation. Eventually, however, I found a way to join the Armed Forces and was selected for training as a pilot. I had the good fortune to be sent to Canada, where I got my wings. That was in early 1942.

Back in UK I volunteered for PR because of a rumour that members of my AFU Course were to be posted to twin-engined aircraft. My burning ambition was to fly a Spitfire as a fighter pilot, and since this was not now possible, I joined the photo-recce business. Had I known PR work would be lonely, cold, miserable, and boring, I would not have joined. Serves me right.

I was sent to the photo-recce OTU in Scotland, first at Fraserburgh, then later at Dyce in Aberdeenshire. The fourteen pilots who began my course were a typical mixture. Eight had trained under the Arnold Plan in the USA, and the others, like me, had trained in the British Commonwealth Air Training Plan.

We were mostly about nineteen years old, all NCOs, all enthusiastic, and all very competitive. I was the first to fly a Spitfire. It was a clapped-out ex-Fighter Command Mark IA but to my naive mind the most desirable plane in the world. That flight was the most memorable of all. The Spitfire had no vices and if handled gently could be coaxed into making a straight stall, just like a Tiger Moth. The long nose gave poor visibility when landing, so we overcame this by landing at the end of a curving final approach.

The training for PR work took a lot of practice; the Spitfire was never designed for this purpose. Since we could not see our target at the time of the photo run, we had to learn how to align our aircraft properly over the target. The technique was to approach the target, turn (usually) left and watch it disappear under the leading edge of the wing, about halfway to the tip, then straighten up. We trained using a single 14-inch camera and had to be exact. Good training for the future operations.

We also flew Spitfire XIs fitted with an oblique camera installed on the port side behind the pilot. We were encouraged to make low level photo-flights on suitable targets–and boys will be boys. When it came to low level obliques, the battle was on. My friend Bert Gardiner brought back a photo taken looking up at the wing of a parked Lancaster. He'd found one parked on the raised edge of an airfield and flew a little lower with the camera looking upwards. "Beat that", said Bert, and I did, with a photo taken below street level in Aberdeen. Our favourite watering hole was the Caledonian Hotel on Union Terrace, just off Union Street. The railroad ran under Union Street, parallel with Union Terrace and in a deep cutting. There was probably enough space to fly over Union Street, dip down after the bridge, take one shot of the Caledonian, and then pull up before the next bridge. There was lots of room across the cut, but not much between the bridges.

On my next suitable flight I approached Aberdeen from the sea, flew along the rail tracks at 500 feet until just before the Union Street bridge. I dived into the Park cutting, tilted my port wing up towards the Caledonian, and pressed the camera button once before I pulled up to safety. I had a fleeting glimpse of the Caledonian doorman staring at me in amazement and the deed was done. I was very proud of my efforts; no one beat my shot.

One day Bert Gardiner went missing. I was the last person to see him alive as he roared past me on the perimeter track giving me the V salute. Years later, I learned that his body had been found off the coast of Norway, though his duty had been a high level cross-country to North Wales and Northern Ireland. Another Bert "initiative" that went wrong? The previous course had one scrubbed and two killed.

On completion of the course, we were told that our marks were the best yet and our "initiative" pictures, vertical and oblique, set a new standard. When I was handed my logbook, the CO asked: "How the hell did you chaps do so well?" Of the twelve who completed the course, we had one average and nine above average. Two of us were classed as exceptional.

From OTU I was posted (October 1942) to 541 Squadron at RAF Benson, the main base for PRU. We flew Spitfire Mark IVs as we had done at OTU. This was the unarmed and unarmoured version of the Mark V. Instead of guns we carried 67 gallons of petrol in each wing. Together with our main tanks this gave us a duration of four to six hours (compared with 90/120 minutes of the Mark V).

The cockpit was not designed for comfort. The high-altitude performance was excellent. At 30,000 feet an indicated airspeed of 180 mph gave us a true airspeed of 295 mph. In the Mk. XI an indicated airspeed of 200 gave 330 true. These were our optimum cruising speeds, giving us the longest duration.

Most of our flights were at 30,000 feet or above. The outside air temperature was minus 50°, the air pressure was 4lb per square inch, and we were on oxygen from take-off. The cockpit was only barely heated, our feet were almost frozen, and our hands were little better.

The one redeeming feature of our duty was that we expected to return from each op. Because of the height at which we flew and the speed of the Spitfire, we were unlikely to meet enemy aircraft–but we had better bring back some pictures. From Benson I flew to French, Belgian and German targets.

In November 1942 I was seconded to 543 Squadron on detachment and was able to work with the PR Unit in the Middle East. These were shorter sorties, usually on more tactical targets.

When I returned to Benson I stayed with 543 Squadron until I was posted to 4 PRU at Maison Blanche, Algeria, in late March 1943. I was given a brand new Spitfire XI, the latest PR type, with the 2-stage supercharged Merlin 61 series engine. There were still only a few of these wonderful planes in existence, so I was very fortunate. Having tested my new mount, EN 422, I waited for orders. Then on 4 April 1943 I flew to Portreath in Cornwall for onward dispatch. The Operations Board in the ops room listed all the aircraft and crews who were to fly to Gibraltar and from there to their destinations. There were Wellingtons, Beaufighters, Hudsons, Blenheim, Liberators, and right at the bottom of the board was my plane, Spitfire EN422, destination Algiers. While standing there reading the list, I overheard a Wellington crew casting doubt on my chances of getting to Gibraltar. I butted in, told them even though they would take off two hours before I did that I'd be there before them and would have a table booked for dinner at the best hotel.

The route I was given took me out into the Atlantic in order to avoid the Brest hot spot, then south down the coast of Portugal. Since I intended to fly in relative safety at 30,000 feet, and Gibraltar was 180° true from Portreath, this was the course I took–but I did not tell the dispatcher. I took off at dawn in overcast and drizzle and climbed on course, breaking cloud at 12,000 feet. I crossed the north coast of Spain dead on track and all was going well. Some 2½ hours after take-off and a few miles west of Madrid, the engine spluttered, coughed and almost stopped. I changed tanks back to the main, pumped the priming pump, and the engine picked up. After a few minutes the engine showed signs of quitting again, and so I repeated the pumping. By now I knew that I was in deep trouble. My options were to attempt to reach Gib. or to head towards Portugal where I would be safe. I decided to try and make it and called Gib. on my VHF radio. They asked me to transmit for a bearing, and when they gave it to me, I knew I was spot on.

I flew and pumped and flew and pumped, all the time losing altitude, but my right arm was getting tired and I'd worn through my gloves to the flesh. Finally I flew through the mountains in southern. Spain and over the harbour of Algeciras. Dead ahead was the only runway. A Hudson was on the runway but there was little I could do about it, since I was now essentially making a dead-stick landing. Suddenly a loud message from Flying Control just about made me deaf.

"Get that *something* Hudson off the runway. Now."

The Hudson roared into the air and I landed in its slipstream. The detached PR unit at Gib took care of my aircraft while I was debriefed. Apparently, this was the first time a bearing had been given to an aircraft that far inside Spain.

I was there to greet my Wimpey friends, though with a bandaged hand. We dined at the Bristol Hotel and had a good booze-up.

The next day the mechanics who had examined EN422 said they couldn't find anything wrong with the engine, but agreed with me the trouble was probably an air lock in the fuel system.

I joined my new squadron the next day. On my first operational flight over Sardinia, the engine quit after about two hours, and I repeated my get-home antics. This fuel problem showed up on other Mk XIs and eventually it was found advisable to vent the wing tanks to the atmosphere to allow the trapped air to escape as the outside pressure decreased.

"Lizzie" (as I called EN 422) served the squadron well. Together we once flew from Tunis to the Franco-Spanish frontier, along the South coast of France, to Italy, Genoa, Spezia, across to La Madalena, Sardinia, and back to Tunis, photographing targets all the way. That was my longest flight, six hours and forty minutes. For me "Lizzie" would fly on the memory of the smell of a rag dipped in petrol, or so it seemed.

One of my memorable flights was taking pictures for the bombing of Rome and photographing British gliders in the sea off Sicily, dropped short by Allied towing pilots.

Our job was to fly out, take the ordered photos, and return to base. Most of these photo-reconnaissance flights were flown for strategic analysis of enemy shipping movements and cargoes, aircraft movements, beaches, gun emplacements, military buildings, and radar sites. Many were before-and-after photography.

Our two 20-inch focal length cameras were tilted to produce stereo pairs, operated through a Type 33 camera control mounted high on the instrument panel. This gave us an "On", an "Off", and a time interval between exposures. Simple gadgets for simple people. We were briefed in the evening before the actual sortie, so one went to bed with a mind actively working out the best way to carry out the duty. In my case it did not lead to a restful sleep.

A typical PR sortie started with a full briefing giving details of all targets to be photographed. There were usually several, and priorities were stressed. Sometimes a required scale was needed, involving flight at calculated, specific altitudes. In most cases these photos were printed as a map or copied by a mobile offset printer.

Our function was to provide pictures for strategic intelligence reports compiled by the photo interpreters. Their skill was the interpretation and cataloguing of intelligence garnered from our pictures. If PRUs had been operative before the Germans invaded Norway, photographs showing shipping activity in the Baltic would have made the German plans obvious. The Bismarck was sunk because a pilot on a routine PR flight over Norway saw that the battleship was on the move.

One important aspect of PR work was bomb damage assessment. Early in the war PR photos showed that claims to have bombed a target were not always substantiated. Sometimes the closest bombs were five miles off target. As the war progressed new and better navigation and bomb-aiming equipment produced markedly better results.

Many sorties were routine coverage of targets of interest. Our photo interpreters could follow a ship from port to port, often gaining a fair idea of the cargo carried. Constant monitoring of airfields exposed any significant changes and activity. Just before the invasion of Sicily, increasing numbers of fighter planes moved to airfields around Foggia in south-east Italy. Evidently Sicily was going to be heavily contested by the Germans; air losses of 10% were anticipated. Large numbers of Allied aircraft assembled in North Africa, the Foggia airfields were heavily bombed, and the Germans pulled back. Air losses were less than 1% partly because of warning by PR.

PR activity was sometimes carried out for no apparent reason. This anomaly is perhaps explained in the "Ultra" books which suggested the Allies wanted the enemy to believe that intelligence was gathered by PR; they must not suspect that their coded signals were being "cracked".

PR crews had a lot of leeway in many flights. When briefed for a sortie we were usually given several targets but the order in which they were to be photographed was up to us. Wind velocity was always a factor that we must check out. We were all "GR trained" so our DR navigation was of high standard; the Dalton DR computer was a great help. Anti-aircraft guns and/or fighters usually defended targets, so we usually flew above all that at 32-35,000 feet. Targets known to be less diligently protected could be overflown at 10,000 feet or less. The discomfort of high altitude unpressurised flights under freezing conditions was simply one of those things we had to bear, but we flew fast and were trained to avoid combat so this was the price we paid for comparative safety.

The PR Spitfires had engine exhaust heating to the cameras and some heat was ducted off into the cockpit, aimed at the abdominal regions; but at any height above 10,000 feet it was not noticeable. Several types of heated suits had been tried and rejected for various reasons. Experience taught us to wear loose-fitting, multi-layered, clothing and loose-fitting multi-pairs of gloves. Despite all that it was bloody cold; there was little feeling below the knees and our hands were not too dextrous either. We could operate our camera control and carry out some scrawled note-taking, but not much more.

Combined with my civilian-looking clothing, hidden passport photographs, silk "escape" maps and escape money and other aids, I was well equipped for most eventualities. I also had two water bottles attached to my Mae West when flying over the sea for long periods. We had been trained well in evasion tactics should we be shot down over land but survival in the drink would not be an easy matter. Moreover a Spitfire did not ditch well–I know of only one successful ditching. We flew on oxygen from take-off because of our relatively rapid climbs, but the lack of air pressure became evident after a short time at high altitude. The smallest exertion such as using the hand to bang open the frozen wing tank fuel cock made one gasp for oxygen. There was also the chance of nitro-embolism (the "bends") and despite our previous testing to 40,000ft. in a decompression chamber, there was no guarantee that our bodies would continue to be resistant over time. We had occasional twinges in sites of old injuries, not dangerous, but painful at times. A badly filled tooth could be agonising, and a blocked sinus almost unbearable.

All in all it was a very uncomfortable occupation, but we had volunteered and couldn't un-volunteer. As they said: "Serves you right: you shouldn't have joined!"

We avoided too much liquid intake or gas-producing foods before going on a long trip. I only had to "go" once in the air, and it was quite a job. To get into my layered clothing I had to stand up as far as the hood would allow, unbutton, reach in and make sure that the urine would not wet my clothing, and this at 31,000 feet. It was also essential to avoid frostbite in the exposed member.

When we returned with exposed film in our magazines, we were permitted to "beat up" the airfield, and we were past masters at the extreme low pass. *Remember the line-shoot: I prefer Rotol props to de Havilland. They're three inches shorter, so I can fly lower.* Unlike the fighter and bomber boys, we did not have the satisfaction of a heartfelt *"Take that you bastards"* as we fired guns or dropped bombs–we were almost non-combatants. I realize that today these sentiments are considered unseemly, but the modern day moralists do not appreciate that we were fighting for our freedom and theirs. Our masters told us that our work was of great value to the war effort and just as important as the fighter and bomber sorties. We just didn't get the glow from a successful combat.

During my time with 682 Squadron we lost six pilots: we buried three, one has no known grave, and two became prisoners-of-war. I survived sixty-seven trips, every one *Alone Above All.*

# BOB O'BRIEN

*Bob was born in 1921 and joined the Canadian Army in 1941, serving as a gunner with the Royal Canadian Artillery. He transferred to the RCAF and was awarded his pilot wings in 1943, serving in Transport Command until 1946 when he was demobilised. Over the next sixteen years, whilst an academic at the University of British Columbia and University of Alberta, Bob continued flying in the RCAF Auxiliary Squadrons in Vancouver, Lancashire, Ottawa, and Edmonton. In civilian life, He achieved an engineering degree and a PhD in metallurgy and followed an academic career until retirement*

## Liberating Burma with DC3s

I was too late for the dangerous missions in World War II that were attended by the RCAF transport command in which I served. I was trained at Comox OTU for the Arnhem drop but was on a boat in the Clyde waiting to disembark when that one happened. We were whisked down to Bournemouth anyway, as the administrators appeared not to know it was all over. At Bournemouth they sent us on up to Morecambe Bay, the Transport Holding Unit, and we were given leave but told to stay close. Then the siege of Kohima required drops so they whistled us out to Karachi by private aircraft. We arrived just as the siege was lifted and bummed around Karachi for a month or so. Then up to 436 (RCAF) Squadron; the two Canadian Squadrons 435 and 436 were then forming at Gujurat, in what is now Pakistan, for further training and finally to Imphal for operations.

This left us with nothing to do until the Japanese could be driven out of the Imphal Valley. After a few lazy weeks we went from Karachi to Gujurat to join the two RCAF Transport squadrons 435 and 436 that were forming there. We trained a bit more, towed some gliders up at Fatajang at the mouth of the Khyber Pass and at Rawalpindi. At Pindi we met some of the troops who were just out of Burma with Wingate's first sortie.

One night on a night flying exercise after only two daylight flights from the old fighter field at Gujurat I was assigned a co-pilot. I assumed he was familiar with the kite, and as we had no ground crew available, I told him to go in and start the engines while I took off the control locks. He started the starboard at about half throttle and blew me over with the slipstream. I quickly ran to the door in case he started the port at the same setting which would prevent me from getting into the a/c. I got in safely, throttled down, noted the hydraulic pressure was up and got out to pull the u/c pins, forgetting that I had not taken the last lock off the rudder. Anxious to have a well-trained co-pilot, I told him it was his first take-off and landing and to do the taxi check and taxi out. The runway was 3000 ft. and the flare path was twelve hurricane lanterns erratically spaced on either side of the narrow runway. We had no cockpit lights but were issued with a flashlight (torch) to be held by the co-pilot (in this case me) on the airspeed indicator during take-off.

At about 40 mph a swing started to the right, I asked him to check it. At 50 or 60 mph we went off the runway and he shouted, "You have control." I immediately found the problem, tried to break the locks, couldn't, then closed the left throttle and opened the right through the gate, but no joy. By this time I was worried about obstructions so elected to fly, bouncing the aircraft into the air off the tail wheel, calling for quarter flap and getting it and initiating a climb while pedalling away on the rudders and using gentle aileron to stay level and in the air. On the downwind leg I asked the tower for permission to land. The co-pilot asked if we should ask for the crash truck and I said I'd try to land once then call. At about 100 ft. with a 30 degree light breeze cross wind I made a 30-degree bank turn, landed on one wheel slightly hot and got control with the brakes, stopped, got out and got the rudder lock off and taxied around for the next circuit, which was flown by the co-pilot uneventfully. He was an excellent pilot and remained in aviation after the war. We did not file a report of the incident.

About three years later Grace Moore and many others died in a DC3 crash on Danish Airways. I was sitting in the ready room of 442 Auxiliary RCAF Squadron on a Saturday afternoon listening to the news. The commentator said that the cause of the fatal crash was that the rudder control lock had been left on, and that the most senior pilot had tested another DC3 with the rudder control lock on and confirmed the DC3 cannot be flown in this configuration, even in the daytime with lots of experience and much runway and no crosswind. Am I lucky or just too dumb to recognize a serious problem?

In early 1945 we flew down to Kangla, near Imphal, and arrived around midnight after about eighteen hours of flying. I jumped out of the aircraft and was nearly bayoneted by the Gurkha guard who had hurried up to the aircraft. The guards allowed us to sleep under the wing of our kite. At 5 am we were aroused, went to a briefing and were assigned to an aircraft for our indoctrination ops trip. We drew a captain I had flown with at Comox. We had landing loads for the three trips and were returning well after dark. I was diligently map reading to be ready for ops the next day and informed the captain he was about twenty miles north of track as we approached the Imphal Valley. He did not agree with me. We were flying at about 8000 feet and this was sufficient to clear the local mountains, which had a few peaks up to about 7500 feet, but the captain said we had about twenty minutes flying before we came to the valley. I could see we were over the valley already and heading across to mountains at 9000 feet. After showing the captain the map, reiterating my view a couple of times, I strapped on a chest pack parachute and asked his permission to jump. He did not give it to me. I then said I would jump anyway if he did not alter course within two minutes, estimating that I would come down in the foothills and be able to walk to a road I could dimly see. I also told him I would encourage my crew to join me. After about a minute of standing by the open door (we always flew with the doors off) the aircraft banked onto the course that would take us down the valley to our aerodrome, which we reached in about fifteen minutes. Nothing else was said about the episode, no thanks from the captain or his crew and I asked my crew not to mention it.

One day at an airfield in Central Burma we had a landing load aboard and I was teaching my W/AG to fly. He was sitting in the co-pilot's seat, as I did not have a co-pilot at that time. There was a sudden "twister" over the field and we could see American tugs dropping Waco gliders, which were landing backwards and on top of one another in a real shambles. On the approach I realized we had a very strong wind directly down the runway; when I rounded out at about five feet, we just hovered with some throttle still on. My W/AG, who thought he was being helpful, threw down quarter flap, as we would have done in a normal landing. We ballooned to about fifty feet. And, remembering that there was a stream of DC3s coming in behind us and this wind might not last long, I elected to land anyway. It turned out to be slightly backwards. On touchdown with still some throttle on, it was yoke forward, flaps up, more throttle to get out of the way of the landing stream and on to the end of the runway. At the end of the runway with throttle on and no chance of taxiing at 90 degrees to the wind and with the tail still up, my crew jumped out and ran for the nearest bushes, leaving me to wait for the wind to drop. Fortunately for my slacks, it took less than ten minutes and comfort of a sort was restored.

My aircraft was shot at by ground fire at least five times and once by our own gunners. We dropped a priority load of gasoline to our tanks just in front of Rangoon. They were firing steadily and as we went down the downwind leg of the dropping zone at about 250 feet, it seemed they always fired right at us and we could feel the shock wave of the shells passing underneath us. My crew, busily throwing out the load, came up and complained, saying it's all right for you up here in the cockpit but we're standing in front of an open door. I pointed out that we were flying the civilian version of the Dak and that it had less than an eighth of an inch of duralumin at the cockpit, which was easily dented by a parakeet and would not be much help in stopping a 4.5-inch shell. We never got a hole in us, but we had numerous tangles with jungle birds at less than 50 feet, one close encounter with trees, and a near miss with an elephant's trunk. It was a grounding offence to fly above 50 feet until you got to the DZ or the forward strip. This kept us in the "grass" in the Japanese radar and thus did not bring the fighters on us. Besides, before the monsoon it kept our ground-galloping shadow under us and gave our camouflage a chance to work.

One day, when the 'little monsoon' was upon us but without the continual rain of the real monsoon, I had been having trouble with dusty carburettors all during the day. I had thumped the designated spot on the 1200-hp. Pratt & Whitney radials with my trusty six-shooter (6-inch blued-steel, Smith and Wesson) till the wood on the stock was beginning to splinter. On the last trip, the trouble had been such that I was the last to taxi out onto the forward strip about one hundred miles north of Rangoon when a man in American uniform (followed by several officers in pressed uniforms in contrast to his clothing) waved me down. He came up into the cockpit and said I must go south sixty miles and pick up our prisoners who had walked out of the Japanese prison at Rangoon. I told him I would have to have authority since my kite had to be ready on the line in the morning and it was then that he revealed himself to me. He was Colonel Terry Cochrane, CO of the Cargo Task Force, 436 Squadron was a Canadian squadron in an RAF Wing attached to the CCTF.

He briefed me, and I found about one hundred and thirty-five men–foot-sore because they walked barefoot up the cinder covered railway right of way for about 60 miles in two days, skinny because they had had little food for months, wet because it was gently raining–men with no baggage at all. The designated leader was a British Army colonel of the Medical Corps who had been beaten by Japanese soldiers into a vegetable-like state. I spoke to him to no avail, he could not reply or did not understand that a reply was necessary. The Second in Command was an American major, U.S. Army Flying Corps pilot of about 6 ft. 4 in. height and I guess about 120 lbs., the heaviest of the entire group, except the MO. He was about standard weight as he had been given part of the rations of the others since they felt they owed their lives to him and his now-vanished medical skills. The major persuaded me to take thirty-five of these skeletons though twenty was the usual number of seats and passengers. I argued against this citing my engine trouble, but it was really futile in the circumstances and the old bird flew like a bird should with the proper weight aboard.

By the time we were loaded and off, the weather had deteriorated so much that I was sure I could not get back over the Arakan Yomas. These mountains along the coast rise to 7500 feet in some peaks and are a continuous range, getting lower as you go south, and, subject to the most savage of Chota monsoon cumulonimbus, Dakota-wrecking clouds. So I headed slightly south to an area where the Yomas petered out, then out to sea so as to sneak up the coast to our base on Ramree Island. A close look at the map showed mud volcanoes inshore. Having no idea what a mud volcano was–and I still don't–we went fifty miles offshore and encountered such heavy rain that with the cowl flaps on the radials closed and the oil coolers shut, the cylinder head temperatures decreased to the point that had we been on the ground, we would be below take-off temperatures. I could see water about a quarter of an inch deep rolling into the air intakes when I had time to look from scanning the sea ahead for waterspouts, and worried that the engines might quit. It was soon so dark that maintaining 50 feet above the waves on the radio altimeter was really the only consideration.

We had a radio compass and the radio beacon on the end of the runway as navigation aids. The drill was to fly out to sea at least 10 miles, turn in to the island until the radio compass showed 128° and fly that course until you saw the first buoy to lead ships into the harbour, at four miles from the runway, drop wheels and quarter flaps here and throttle back to 120 to 100 mph, then watch for the next buoy at one mile. At this buoy, start a rate one turn and throttle back further and watch for the shoreline and a couple of deadly palms. Then straighten out and land. In the rain we had, the spray off the nose obscured vision ahead so with the side window open it was possible to see within about 10° of dead ahead. In this dark night it was still difficult to pick up the buoys. After landing, I took the major to the ops tent and phoned the CO to tell him what I had done. While waiting for him to arrive, the major went over to the Intelligence table and asked me to read some of the dispatches to him as he could not, even with a 60-watt bulb hanging three feet above the table. I went to bed and never heard any more about what happened to the prisoners, except that I did ask our MO if the major, who was spitting fire, would ever fly again. The MO said after more than a year on the rations he'd had it was almost certain he never would.

On about 20 August 1945 we drew straws to see who would be in the first wave of five aircraft to fly back to Britain. I was lucky enough to be in the first wave that was led by S/Ldr Frank Smith. We had to wait a few more days because we were to exchange aircraft with an RAF squadron that was going to use ours to go on to Indonesia. We also got held up in India while the medical people debated how many holes to put in our arms. They finally settled on none. So we flew off through Arabia, Palestine (stop at Tel Aviv for a swim), Egypt, Libya, Sicily (where we were robbed—the lock on the aircraft forced while we were at a dance in Catania, and this with a guard on the kite) and on to Istres, which is the military aerodrome at Marseilles. By then Frank and I were the only two still flying. The last to leave just made it over the cliffs in Libya on one engine after throwing out everything but their shoes. All the aircraft had unserviceabilities. I was lucky enough to have the ground crew on board who had looked after my kite on ops and they kept me informed of what I must do to limit the effects of the unserviceabilities and prevent deterioration, we were that keen to get to England. We had begun to call it home.

Frank and I went to a briefing and were told we must fly a certain route through France to Britain. We asked why and were told that we might get lost (and this with good maps after dead reckoning over the Arabian desert, the Mediterranean Sea and the Indian Ocean) and that there was bad weather on the direct route. We asked how bad and were told there were cb's above 10,000 feet. We were used to monsoon cb's of 50,000 to 60,000. Frank and I began to laugh and nearly had to sit down. Frank told me to get control or these people would send for the men in the white coats. So we flew straight to England. I said I'd race Frank there and in fact was in the downwind leg at Down Ampney when I saw Frank just joining the circuit, so I went around again thinking that though we were now on a first name basis, we were back in Limey Land and one should not annoy a senior officer unnecessarily. Then the six-month wait for a boat to get home began.

Post-war in my first year at UBC (Chemical Engineering) the RCAF started 442 Auxiliary Squadron, designated Fighter. For about seven years, through BSc and MSc and a year as a steel-maker and then as a research assistant in the Physics Dept. at UBC, I happily flew Mustangs and Vampires as well as Harvards. One year with few lectures, I got to fly flying boats at last, co-pilot on Stranraers for Spilsbury's Queen Charlotte Airlines. When I went to the UK for a PhD, I got transferred to the Royal Auxiliary Air Force (at a great reduction in rank) and flew Meteor VIIs and VIIIs with summer camps at Malta and Celle (on the end of the Berlin Corridor–1955), then back to National Research Council at Ottawa and on as a Fighter Controller on a Dew Line station on weekends. Then to U of Alberta and being held for one and one-half years against a flying position on Beechcraft Expeditors (and possible helicopters) in the Edmonton Auxiliary Wing, as the clock ticked and they finally said they'd like someone younger. So the end of military flying. See map on page 56.

True mud volcanoes are small cones that eject mud, water, and dust. Burmese mud volcanoes are eruptions of mud caused by escaping gases. Ed.

# CONTRIBUTORS
## The POW Experience

**DulagLuft**: transit camp, probably from du(rch) lag(er). Dulagluft was situated north-west of Frankfurt. Downed Allied fliers were interrogated there before being moved on to a stalagluft.

**Goon-baiting**: making fun of prison-camp guards.

**In the bag**: in a prisoner-of-war camp,

**Man of Confidence**: A POW, usually selected by the prisoners, who would represent the prisoners' complaints to the prison authorities and often take the lead in POW affairs.

**Terrorfliegers**: Terror fliers. German name for Allied bomber crews.

**Wurzburg**: a German radar working on 570 mc/s and the basis of the enemy GCI (ground control of intercept).

**Big blue one**: the master searchlight.

# THE POW EXPERIENCE

Perhaps the least-known aspects of the POW experience are the forced marches. We reproduce here extracts from the diary of Arnold Dawkins who was marched from Stalag VIIIb (344) to Ditfurt, shown on the map on pages 360-361 as a straight line although it was far from being that.

24 January Wed. Our boots were frozen. It was difficult to put them on. We started at 8. a.m. another hard grind today. To keep us moving the guards encouraged us with their rifle butts. At 7 p.m. we stopped and were pushed into a barn. It had electric lights and lots of straw but no room to stretch out. If you had to go outside you would step on someone. We were so exhausted after 23 Kms we fell asleep sitting up.

2 Feb Fri. Up early, this is a windy, sunny, spring-like day. We were very tired as Gerry had pushed us hard for 25 Kms. At dusk two hundred of us stayed at a farm. We waited in line for hot water. Our feet were cold and wet. No rations issued.

5 Feb Mon. I slept fairly well on the bench. 5 a.m.-mint tea issued. 8.30 a.m. parade on a wet field, our boots are never dry. 11 a.m. black bread issued. In the next compound there are Russians. Their wounds haven't been treated and their clothing is filthy. The German guards keep them in control with whips and dogs

12 Feb Mon. Up early but we didn't get kaffee as we were in the loft. Rations-¼ loaf and one-sixteenth tin of meat. Off at 8.00 a.m., the roads are wet and muddy, our feet are wet and cold. At one stop civilians gave us hot kaffee and onions.

13 Feb Tuesday. We had milk and beer given to us by some Panzer soldiers. We travelled uphill to an RC church. We have a choice of sleeping on the floor or on a pew. We travelled 34 Kms today.

17 Feb Sat. Robbie and Geordie helped themselves to an officer's cake. They were chained to a tree at night. Barley soup issued, then a mad scramble to get seconds. The guards settled the problem with rifle butts.

23 Feb Frid. Someone stole my bread. Being hungry, I ate purple cabbage from the scrap pile. I never thought I would eat garden compost.

27 Feb Tues. No rations today. Prisoners passing out all along the route. After dark a thin swede soup was issued.

25 March Palm Sunday. The Russians wanted our soup. The fights that started caused the keebles to tip. The Russians ate the soup off the ground. We didn't get any. The guards beat the Russians with their rifles, then attacked us. My ribs took quite a beating.

The march started on 22 January 1945 and finished 12 April.

# ARNOLD DAWKINS

*Arnold was born in Vancouver in 1913, joined the RCAF in January 1941, and graduated from Air Observer School later that year. Following a brief spell with Pathfinders, he joined 138 Squadron (1942) and flew Halifaxes on Special Duty missions until he was shot down on 14 February 1943. This is Arnold's story of evasion, capture, life as a POW, forced marches, and eventual release.*

## A Change of Address

The difficulties of navigation for the special duties crews were increased by the need for pin-point accuracy on a small and often ill-defined target after hours of flying across enemy territory. The navigation on the journey and on the approach to the target had to be of a high order. Reception committees were instructed to choose sites for their dropping grounds that could easily be seen from the air. This was not always possible for them and even after finding the target area, we might have to search for some time before discovering lights obscured in a valley or hidden by woods.

The navigator nearly always had to rely on map reading and dead reckoning. To help him do this the pilot flew at a low altitude across enemy-occupied Europe.

Researchers in SOE, co-operating with other scientists, created a navigational device, a type of mobile radar in two halves called Rebecca/Eureka. Rebecca, the interrogator, was operated by the navigator. Eureka, the ground beacon or responder, was set up in the reception area. When interrogated by a signal from Rebecca, the Eureka responded and thereby gave its position. Range could be seventy miles or more if the aircraft had sufficient height. Eureka weighed about 100lb; the weight and the life of its batteries often being a problem for the people who had to carry it around in enemy territory. Rebecca and Eureka were equipped with devices to blow them up if anyone tried to open them up and examine them.

To drop agents and supplies the pilot of a heavy aircraft had to fly just above stalling speed, flaps down, at an altitude of about six hundred feet.

The front gun turret and the mid-upper turret had been removed from our aircraft. In the floor aft of the bomb bay, a round hole about a metre wide was cut and fitted with a removable cover. Near this hole was a rail to which parachute static lines could be clipped. A signal light operated by the pilot or the navigator shone red when the drop zone was near. The dispatcher then removed the hatch cover. When the signal shone green he checked to see the static lines were attached to the 'chutes. Then the agent jumped through the hole, his 'chute being opened by the static line. The dispatcher retrieved the static lines when all jumps had been made.

What with navigation difficulties in the air, police difficulties for the reception people on the ground, and the unpredictable weather that might cloud over a dropping zone in a few minutes, it was not surprising that quite a number of sorties flown by special duties dropping aircraft were abortive.

On the night of 19 February 1943 we flew from our base to a drop zone in France. Our pilot Jack Doy was in hospital; we carried another pilot and a co-pilot who was making a familiarization trip. We had one male agent to deliver and some cargo; we were never told what cargo we carried. We were flying at about 500 feet when we ran into ground fog in the Loire River valley. The pilot took the plane above the fog and a short time later we were hit by anti-aircraft fire. We lost altitude very quickly and the pilot told us to prepare for a crash landing. I had no time to get into a safe or crash position so I fastened my seat belt and hoped for the best. The first impact produced a sound of metal being torn apart. My seat was ripped out of its fastenings with me still in it. I hit various parts of the fuselage before losing consciousness. I woke up on my back and still strapped to the chair; one knee and leg were injured and my face was bloodied. I crawled out of the aircraft and joined the rest of the crew and the agent; they were not injured. As the overload tank was leaking fuel, we were able to set the aircraft on fire and destroy the charts, maps, and other material that might identify us or our destination. The agent suggested we go north to avoid Germans who might be searching to the south of the burned out wreck for the crew.

Eventually we came to a river and found a rowboat, but no oars; we used our hands to paddle across. When we reached the other side we walked some distance to an empty barn. While we rested the agent went to a nearby farmhouse to obtain food for us. He then left and continued his journey on foot to reach his contact. We stayed in the barn till the next night and then split up in pairs. Eric Ramm, the wireless operator, and I headed in a southerly direction. Later that night we crept through a village without disturbing anyone. We went into a wooded area to sleep during the day; no one came near us. The following days we slept in woods, or barns if we could get into them. Night travel was across vineyards, on roads if there was no traffic, or along the edge of woods.

Because of my knee and leg injuries, we made slow progress. Some farmers gave us food. One evening we knocked on the door of a house on the edge of a town and were invited in by the owner, who spoke some English. While he obtained civilian clothes for us to wear over our battle dress his wife prepared a meal for us. He suggested we take a train to Marseilles where we could make a contact. This idea was abandoned because I was limping so badly that we would be questioned and our knowledge of French was poor. I hoped that by walking and resting, my leg might improve.

On 25 February after walking all night, we stopped at a farmhouse to get food and water. The farmer and his family were having breakfast and invited us to join them. As we sat down, one of the sons left on the pretext that he had to attend to the cows. We'd barely finished breakfast when a French policeman walked in. He spoke some English and greeted us in a friendly manner. We were given the impression he would help us and left with him.

After walking a short distance we were surrounded by six armed policemen. So this was the help. We must have been considered important to have seven policemen escort us from the farm. We were taken by truck to the jail in the village of St. Senach. The cell doors were open and we were free to walk in the walled courtyard but an armed policeman prevented any attempt to escape. At mid-day we were given what looked like bottled beer but turned out to be a very, very dry wine. This was lunch.

Later in the afternoon a car with three German policemen arrived to take us north to the prison in Tours. Here we were put into separate cells. My cell was small; the window at the end wall had no glass, just iron bars. Standing on a chair provided a view of stone walls and nothing else. The bed was an iron frame with two-inch iron rods set on edge and covered with a blanket, a no sag bed. A small table hinged at the wall and held level by two chains was useless as the chains were broken. By the door was a toilet bowl with a tap above it, no paper, no soap, and no towel. The door had a peephole with a sliding cover on the outside. Periodically a guard would slide the cover up and look in. The temptation to poke a finger into his eye was considered but not attempted, as I might have been shot. However when an eye appeared I put my eye close and stared back. The result was fewer peeps by the guard.

Food for the day consisted of a tin containing about half a litre of hot water with a few slices of turnip. The guard opened the door and pushed the tin in with his boot. During the last week of our stay, the nearby Luftwaffe station sent some crackers and a small round of Camembert cheese. The cheese had a hard crust and a liquid centre. You applied the cheese to the cracker with a finger; that meant you had to live with a stinky finger for the rest of your stay. We never did find out the Michelin rating for our accommodation. On the second day Eric and I were ushered into an office occupied by a steno and a civilian who stated he was Gestapo. He spoke with an American accent and said he had lived in New York before the war. He asked if we had been on a four-engine aircraft; we were noncommittal and he then assumed we had been on a twin-engine aircraft. He told us we were lucky the German army did not have us. A truckload of soldiers had been looking for the crew of a large aircraft when a twin-engine aircraft had strafed them, killing many of the soldiers. He asked no more questions and we returned to our cells.

The next day we were back in the interrogation room. We were given a cup of ersatz coffee; it tasted as though it had been made from roasted acorns and was certainly a change from turnip soup. The interrogator tested our knowledge of German and when he was satisfied we were ignorant of the language, he spoke to his steno. She left the room and reappeared later with a guard and Harry Long the trainee-engineer. Harry said nothing to us, but the expression on his face told the interrogator what he wanted to know–that we belonged to the same crew. No more questions were asked. However, he said the crash had spread a supply of Sten guns on the field. There were no more interviews during our stay.

On 4 March 1943 Doug Robinson the rear gunner, Joe Davison the dispatcher, Ron Jerome the flight engineer, Harry Long, Eric Ramm, and I were taken from the prison in handcuffs and put on a train to Paris. In Paris the handcuffs were removed and we boarded a train to Frankfurt. We shared a compartment towards the rear of the car with two German soldiers, our guards for the trip. Doug Robinson went to the toilet; his guard put his foot in the doorway to prevent the door being closed and the occupant escaping out the window. When Robbie returned he seemed amused about something. Later there was a lot of angry shouting by a German officer at the rear of the car and Robbie burst out in uncontrolled laughter. He had taken a bottle of water from the table, emptied it in the toilet and refilled it (though not from the sink tap) and put it back on the table.

On arriving in Frankfurt we were taken to the Dulagluft interrogation centre and put in small cells, electrically heated, with locked windows. Although there were bars on the outside the guard would not open the window; if you complained that the cell was too hot, he turned off the power, and then it was too cold. However, the bed was softer than the one in Tours prison.

A wall of my cell had anti-Nazi remarks scratched into the surface. One day a painter painted along the scratches; when the paint dried it was darker and the messages were more noticeable.

One day I had a visitor wearing a German uniform with a Red Cross armband. He told me was a Red Cross representative from Switzerland. I asked why he was wearing a German uniform. He said it made it easier to visit prisoner of war camps. I had been warned that Red Cross people travelled freely and wore civilian clothes; this had to be another interrogator.

During the conversation he asked if he could locate any friends for me when he toured the camps. I gave him the name Thomas

McRoberts and said I had a lot of things to discuss with Tom. He looked in his book and couldn't find the name, but he made a note of it and said he would try to find Tom. Thomas McRoberts was my grandfather; he died in Belfast, Northern Ireland in 1920.

After a few days my crew and I were taken from our cells and put in the compound with all the other prisoners. Here we were greeted by a man who claimed to be the British man-of-confidence or some such title. He was too friendly and asked too many questions. I considered him to be yet another interrogator and avoided any conversation with him.

Our next move was to Poland. We travelled in a passenger car on a troop train going to the Russian front, an uneventful journey through forests and prairie land. We left the train at Lamsdorf (21 March) and walked to a large building about a mile from the village. In the building we were ordered to remove all our clothes and put them into some large containers. The doors of the building were then locked. We could see nozzles set at intervals in the ceiling. Was this a gas chamber?

Soon jets of cold water hit us from the nozzles in the ceiling; this was our first shower since leaving the squadron, but there was no soap and no towel, and so we air dried. Our clothes had been deloused and were returned to us. After we had dressed, the guards marched us a short distance to the gates of Stalag VIIIB, an army work camp with a compound for air force prisoners. By 1943 there were 97,000 prisoners attached to the camp.

After passing through the main gates, we were marched to the RAF compound. Here we were allotted a bunk each that had bed boards instead of springs, a thin straw-filled mattress, and two blankets. Some of the windows had been broken and the glass was replaced with cardboard from the Red Cross parcels. Our compound also had some Canadians caught at Dieppe.

At Dieppe the Germans claimed to have discovered dead Germans with their hands tied or handcuffed. In reprisal they used string to tie up the Dieppers and airforce people whom they considered to be "luft gangsters". After they had collected enough handcuffs they used these instead of the string. The Dieppe compound was across the road from ours and inhabited by an active and cheerful group of men in spite of the hardship they endured.

We were issued our chains prior to morning parade. During summer after parade we would open the handcuffs with a key that came with the bully beef cans from Red Cross parcels, take off all our clothes to sunbathe, and then replace the handcuffs. We would turn up at evening parade fully clothed and wearing our handcuffs. The guards never understood how we could take our clothes off and put them back on again while still wearing handcuffs. The handcuffs were taken away after evening parade.

During the colder weather we wore the chains with our hands in our pockets. The guards didn't realize our hands were free, as the cuffs were resting in our pockets. If we were caught without the cuffs they would wrap our wrists with chain, using a padlock to keep the chain tight. We wore handcuffs for many months; then one day they were not issued.

We learned that the two pilots of our aircraft had been captured in March 1943. Eric Ramm received a letter from his parents in May telling him that Jack Doy had been killed in action. If our aircraft had made it back to base we would have been with Jack on his last trip.

Joe Kessel, the German in charge of our compound, kept a close watch on our crew; we never found out why. Joe was a strict disciplinarian. If, after morning parade, he saw any blankets not folded properly, he would take them away. One day I left a blanket unfolded on my bunk, Joe picked it up and was walking out of the hut when I caught up to him. After some discussion he gave the blanket back saying an old man like me might freeze during the winter with only one blanket. How true, except I was not that old.

The German ration was a few small potatoes, a slice of black bread, and a ladle of turnip soup. We existed on Red Cross parcels; Canadian parcels were the best. The small bag of coarse ground coffee (in a Canadian parcel) could be boiled at least four times, dried and put back in the bag. It was then traded to a guard for something we needed. Not all guards would enter into trading. Klim tins were flattened to cover broken windows. We made cooking stoves, used bed boards for fuel, and even built a still to distil the German version of jam into some thing more palatable.

One of the English soldiers worked at a Philips radio plant nearby. Each night he smuggled parts out of the plant until there was enough to build a radio set. Thereafter we were able to listen to the BBC news and follow the progress of the Allies.

We remained here till January 1945 when we were marched for three months to western Germany, ahead of the advancing Russians.

The weather hit a new low of minus 45 degrees. The guards shot many of our comrades; others died from the cold or starvation.

On 11 April about fifty of us were put into the barn of a large estate in the town of Ditfurt. Our bedding was a pile of dried bean and pea vines. Our meal for the day was dry peas and beans we found amongst those vines. We had seen Allied fighter-bombers flying low and knew the end must be in sight.

Next morning was Liberation Day, the glorious 12th. The guards were gone and the gates were open to the street. While other POWs were touring the town looking for food and drink, John Porteous and I found a bakery, where we obtained some bread. The owner was a woman whose husband was a POW in Florida. She was helpful to us, laid a table with food, and sent her German customers packing.

She gave us bread and honey. Sitting at a table with cutlery and plates was a real treat for us. Later we investigated a train that had been shot up by allied aircraft. At the train we filled a sack with boxes of cigars, not Havanas, and an assortment of alcoholic beverages. We borrowed an Opel car, much to the annoyance of the owner. Our first stop was an American army supply depot where we were given some cans of real gasoline; the car then ran better. Our plan was to cross the Rhine and tour France. After travelling some distance we were stopped by US military police who advised us that we could not continue our journey as there were no bridges available into France. They guided us to an aerodrome. Here our clothes were deloused while we had a shower. It was the first time since leaving Lamsdorf that we had removed our clothes We hadn't realized we were so thin, no extra flesh, just skin covering our bones. No wonder it was painful sleeping on straw. Until other POWs arrived we sampled K rations and other US army food. We also had a good opportunity to examine the German aircraft in the hangars. On 16 April we were flown back to England. I spent some time in the Bournemouth RCAF hospital. Then I went to London just in time to celebrate VE day.

# LLOYD KIDD

*Lloyd was born in 1918 just as one war ended, only to grow up in to another war. He joined the RCAF in June 1941 and completed his training as a W/AG in February 1942. Lloyd left for Britain and after OTU in Scotland, he joined 78 Squadron (RAF). That was August 1942. Less than two months later, his aircraft was shot down and he spent the next two and a half years in a POW camp.*

## Why Me? Why Not Me?

When I joined the RCAF on 4 June 1941 at Saskatoon, Saskatchewan, I already had my private pilot's license (earned in 1939 flying a DH 60 Moth) and was sure I'd not have any problem being selected for pilot training. Yet after completing ITS at Toronto's Hunt Club, I was selected to be a W/AG What a jolt!. "Oh well", I thought, "I can remuster at a later date." Haw!

March 1941 found me in England, posted to a Whitley OTU at Kinloss, Scotland. After completing the course I was posted to 78 Squadron at Middleton St. George, still flying Whitleys. On 10 October 1941, I flew on a practice bombing flight in Whitley 26640. *I found out many years later that it was the only Whitley used in operations to have survived the war.*

On 16 October I was assigned to Whitley 26646 to do my first night flying operation on 78 Squadron. There were two pilots and two of us W/AGs. I asked Jerry Dufors if he wanted to go in the gun turret or on the wireless set. He said he would like to listen to some music, so I went into the gun turret. On our first take-off run we lost an engine, the pilot couldn't control the aircraft, and we spun in. When we hit the ground there was an eerie silence and then "poof" as the petrol exploded into flames. The gun turret was partially torn from the aircraft's fuselage and I was able to squeeze out. As I approached the aircraft to see if the other crew members got out, the ammunition and flares began to go off all around me.

Eventually I saw the others crawling out. They were terribly burned. I led them to a road beside the field, saw the dim lights of a car approaching, flagged it down, and asked the driver if he could take us to a doctor. He said he wasn't going that way: I told him he was and we all piled in. He drove us to a large house where a doctor lived. The doctor put something on the burns to relieve the pain. He handed me a bottle of Scotch and told me to pour some drinks, which I did. He then called the aerodrome. Soon an ambulance picked us up and took us to the station hospital. I never saw the two pilots again, but I did visit Jerry Dufors in the burn unit in London.

There were other traumatic experiences during the Whitley operations. One was observing two Whitleys collide at midfield. One Whitley was taking off; the other taxiing back for a second take-off attempt; both were fully loaded with bombs and incendiaries. Miraculously, both crews managed to get out of their aircraft and run like hell before the bombs started going off. We didn't fly again until the craters were repaired. Another day as I was walking up to the mess for lunch I heard a loud rumble in the sky. I looked up to see a Halifax bomber and an Anson trainer spiralling straight down into the ground—a mid-air collision. I was kind of hardened by that time and continued to the mess for lunch.

I continued flying on ops from 22 May. These operations included the first thousand-bomber raid on Cologne on May 30 1942 piloted by my good Canadian friend Bill Lunan. Bill did not survive the war. I took part in the thousand-bomber raid on Essen on 1 June. Between 8 July and 26 July I completed six operations, all to the Ruhr, known ironically as "Happy Valley." Other than getting awfully tired, returning to base on three engines, or being holed by shrapnel, the operations were uneventful.. One of the most nerve-wracking was a leaflet raid to Lyons, in southern France. It lasted seven and a half hours, all in bright moonlight. No relaxing, as we had to be on constant lookout for night fighters.

On the night of 2 October 1942 we were scheduled for a raid on a place called Krefeld. It was not a routine day. Before the operation I tidied up my room, getting rid of things and putting everything in order, nice and neat. Then I took my parachute to the parachute room for checking. It was found to be wet and unserviceable. I was issued a dry one marked "Return in 48 hours"; they never did get it back but generously didn't charge me for it. Finally, the Gee failed and had to be taken out. The other aircraft took off some fifteen or twenty minutes ahead of us and we were a sitting duck for night fighters.

About a half-hour from the target I noticed a stream of incendiaries whipping past the turret and into the starboard engines. It was a Ju88 night-fighter. I tried to call the pilot but the intercom was dead. With two engines on fire and no hydraulics left, there was nothing to do but crank the turret around by hand. I went out backwards, forgetting to remove my helmet and oxygen mask. When they were ripped off, they almost took my head with them.

What an eerie sensation drifting down in total darkness from 15,000 feet. My descent was rudely interrupted when I hit a tree and fell to the ground. After burying the parachute I started walking. When daylight came I took cover in a bluff and was almost stepped on by a couple of farmer's kids.

As night approached again I started walking down the road. All of a sudden a Jerry soldier appeared. He said, "Heil Hitler!" and gave the Nazi salute. I raised my arm and replied, "Heil Hitler". I guess it didn't sound right to him, for he turned around, pointed his rifle at me: "Halt!" We went off to the village jail where I spent the night, a lonely one.

Next morning a couple of Luftwaffe unter-officers picked me up in a car and drove me to a fighter station. They offered me a German cigarette; it was awful. They gave me a black bread and sausage sandwich: one bite was enough. Later on in POW life, when I was starving, I thought of this waste. Next, I was put on a train for Frankfurt am Main, the infamous interrogation centre. They didn't find out anything despite their threats.

I was eventually sent by train to Stalag VIIIB, near Lamsdorf. This was close to the Polish border. The camp had several compounds housing the Canadians captured at Dieppe. We found that they all had their hands tied with twine from Red Cross parcels. It wasn't long before I suffered the same fate. The Jerries said they were retaliating for similar treatment of German POWs. The Germans eventually replaced the twine with metal handcuffs. After several months they tired of the game and it was over.

We managed to survive OK as long as the Red Cross parcels arrived; when they didn't we were in trouble. You couldn't survive long on German rations. Life in Stalag VIIIB was quite harsh for me in October 1942. Red Cross parcels were scarce. I had no cigarettes to barter with. We received a fifth of a loaf of black bread per day, some mint tea which most Kriegies used for shaving, and cabbage soup at noon. That was it when we had no Red Cross parcels. There were some quarrels over food between POWs who had paired off to share parcels, but nothing too serious.

When we weren't too cold and hungry, we played bridge or chess. I was taught chess by an Englishman who really knew the game, but I was much better at bridge. I teamed up with a Welsh W/AG who had been shot down on his 46th operation. In one particular bridge game he (Taffy McLean) bid a grand slam in diamonds; it was doubled and redoubled. He then laid down his hand, showing thirteen diamonds. I don't expect to ever see that again.

Periodically the Germans used to march us out of the camp and into the surrounding fields. We were covered by several machine guns. They then searched all the huts, looking for the radio they knew we had. As far as I know they never found it.

January 1945 was cold with a lot of snow, and the Russian army was closing in. The Germans didn't seem to want us to fall into Russian hands. We were issued one Red Cross parcel each and away we went. We marched until dark each day. The first night I spent lying on a huge pile of coal. I shouldn't have taken off my wet boots–they froze in the shape of an arc and I had a hard time getting them on again. Other nights we spent in huge haylofts.

I developed dysentery and was soon down to 120 pounds. When I was deemed by a German medical officer to be too ill to march any further, I joined a group in a railway boxcar of WWI vintage. It was designed to hold forty men or eight horses. There wasn't enough room to lie down no matter how ill you were. There was one small tin to defecate in, for forty-odd men. Things got rather smelly as there were no windows and the sliding door was kept closed and locked until such time as the train stopped at a siding.

It was at one of these stops that we were strafed by our own Mustang fighters. I jumped into a ditch by the tracks. A shower of 0.50 calibre shell casings dropped all around me. About twenty or so

POWs–some in the bag since Dunkirk–were killed by this "friendly fire". They'd almost made it home!

Finally, we arrived at Stalag IXc near Kassel. It was there that General Montgomery and his Desert Rats liberated us. We were led to an 8th Army kitchen where I gorged on the most delicious meal I have ever eaten, or so I thought at the time. Montgomery addressed us in a building used as a theatre. He arrived on the stage and just as he was about to speak, we heard a loud crack and the floor collapsed under the weight of the POWs, hundreds of us. In a stony silence the general watched the waving limbs until the hubbub died down, and calmly proceeded with his speech. We were then loaded into lorries and taken to a small village where we showered and put on army battle dress before resuming our lorry trip to the Brussels airport. There we found DC3s to fly us to London, but before we could board we had to unload drums of gas destined for tanks and other army vehicles When one DC3 had been emptied, about thirty-nine of us climbed in. There were no seats, but who cared? We were off to London, where we were met by a number of WAAFs who directed us where to go next. "Next" was Bournemouth and, after a month of fattening up, HOME!

Many times I've asked myself, "Why me?" I was the only one of four to escape unhurt when we crashed on a training flight. Twenty-one times I returned safely from ops. When we were shot down, only two of a crew of eight lived. I survived a strafing by our own aircraft. I ended the "death march" in a boxcar instead of on the side of the road.

My only answer is, "Why not me?" I guess somebody had to survive.

# ROBERT L. MASTERS

*Bob was born in Nelson, British Columbia, in 1922. He enlisted in the RCAF in November '41 and was awarded his Air Gunner brevet in December '42. He was shot down while serving with 51 Squadron and spent the rest of the war as a POW. He was liberated in 1945.*

## Roadrunner '44

This story is seldom talked about and written about even less. It is being submitted in order that some brief record be kept before opportunities to do so slip away.

In July of 1944 the Russian advance was bearing down on East Prussia through Lithuania. The Germans decided to abandon Stalagluft VI near the Lithuanian border and move the Allied airforce prisoners to camps in a more central part of Europe. The bulk of the camp was to go to Thorne in Poland and the remainder to a new camp at Grosstychowo in Pomerania, Stalagluft IV. It is with the latter group that this narrative is concerned. *See map on pages 360-361.*

On the morning of the July 17 the prisoners in K Lager were told to be ready to evacuate the camp by 1800 hours. The men were to take only what they could carry as there would be no transport.

Some of us had been in prison camps since September of 1939 and over the years had accumulated personal treasures from Red

Cross parcels and personal parcels from home. This sudden order was an unwelcome development because it meant leaving so much behind. The portable gramophone and collection of records sent into the camp by the YMCA would be the first items to be forfeited.

Several months earlier three men had escaped and although the Germans knew of the escape they never really knew how many men had gone. As a result they were anxious to get an accurate count of the number of men being evacuated. Prisoners did not co-operate in anything that would make life easier for their captors. The manufactured confusion, although subtle, was totally effective. The German count indicated more men were leaving the camp than had ever arrived. When resourceful men are given all day to think up ways of driving other people to distraction, they can be masters of the art; the Germans should have realized that they were on the wrong end of the equation.

As soon as some semblance of order was established, the column moved out. The boxcars were waiting and loading did not take long. The journey to Memel in Lithuania ended around 2200 hours. The men were lined up on the rail siding on a wharf where a small coastal freighter was tied up. It was the SS Insterburg. *See page 368.*

The vessel was 1500 tons with well-decks fore and aft and a large wooden structure erected on the forepeak. The structure was to serve as a postern box for the guards. The men were ordered aboard with much hustle, which was aggravated by the order to leave all personal kit on deck. Everyone was directed to a manhole leading to the hold. The 'tween-decks were removed so that the hold was empty. By the time all the men had been boarded the complete floor of the vessel was covered by men sitting with their knees under their chins. The ship sailed as soon as loading was completed and the beginning of what was to become for more than 650 men the centre point in the misery of their captivity.

As soon as the ship got underway there began a great settling in of bodies. There was not enough room for everyone to lie stretched out and as the men started to fall asleep they inevitably infringed on someone else's space. The claustrophobic effect on some caused rumblings of annoyance from their neighbours who had stretched their legs over the poor man beneath. This game of patti-cake continued through the night.

The weather was fair and the hatch remained open for most of the voyage. This was a blessing for it provided ventilation and, even more important, a glimpse of the sky. One meal was provided. A large kettle of lukewarm water lightly laced with small bits of cabbage was lowered into the hold. Since all kit was left on deck no one had a billycan and we had a ship full of very hungry men. But this unfortunate situation was offset by the knowledge that the soup kettle was the same one that had been lowered during the previous night and used by those who could reach it. That was not many, however, since it was not possible to walk forty or fifty feet over an uncooperative sea of bodies.

During the day men were allowed on deck for the more serious calls of nature, but only one at a time. Needless to say few were able to avail themselves of this privilege. There simply were not enough hours in the day.

As that first day wore into the twilight of the second night of the voyage, the discomfort became more acute. It was more of the first night only worse.

The ship docked mid-morning on the third day, 19 July, at the naval base at Swinemünde at the estuary of the Oder River. The disembarking took place with the same rush and impatience that the embarkation had. No one was allowed to sort out his own kit. Each man was told to take the first one he came to and the sorting out would be done at the camp upon arrival.

By this time uneasiness was beginning to settle in. These men had been subjected to all manner of Nazi indignities over the years of their imprisonment, but this movement of a whole camp had some decidedly sinister overtones. Ordering us to leaving the kit on deck was understandable on boarding because of the lack of space. There was plenty of time once the ship was along side upon arrival to have organised an orderly regrouping. Although no one spoke of it the murder of the fifty men by the Gestapo, after the Great Escape a few months before, was still fresh in everyone's mind. The usual joking was replaced by an air of apprehension.

The next leg of the journey was to be by the time honoured 40 or 8 boxcars. In this case the 40 were put in one end of the boxcar with a wire fence across it, leaving both doors and the other end for the guards. July on the Baltic coast can be very hot indeed.

The sun beat down on the roof of the unventilated car. To further aggravate the situation the air raid sirens started and guns of a light cruiser began firing. A smoke screen was laid over the port. When the all clear sounded, the train pulled out. Conditions on the train were as bad as they had been on the ship. No water had been issued since we had left the camp three days before: Thirst now replaced hunger.

In mid-afternoon the train pulled into the village railroad station of Kiefueide in Pomerania. We were all tumbled out onto the platform and immediately formed into a column in preparation for marching out. The German officer in charge, Hauptmann Pichardt, walked up and down the ranks shouting unintelligible oaths and invective. The meaning of this longwinded outburst was translated shortly after by the Senior Man of Confidence, Vic Clark. It did not bode well for the next leg of the trip.

We were to be force-marched. Vic told the men at the front of the column were told to keep the pace down as much as possible. The guards at the front were Kriegsmarine sailors in their mid-teens and dedicated Nazis; the rest were Volksturm first war veterans, old enough to have had enough themselves and lacking the viciousness of their young counterparts.

Until they ran out of handcuffs, we were handcuffed together in pairs. Then the order was given to march double time.

It took time to get the column moving. As the rear started to catch up to the front a surge effect was produced. This made it difficult to conserve energy when stopping and starting. The road was narrow and built of uneven cobblestones. This made for unsure footing, but things were about to get worse.

The route turned off onto a dirt road and the urging of the guards became more determined. Rifles, hand-wielded bayonets, and guard dogs were employed with vigour. The road led through a treed area that appeared to go nowhere. At the turn off point in the road there was a small sign tacked to a tree which read "ZU STALAGLUFT IV". Very few men actually saw that sign. Those who did knew they were actually going to a camp. The others could only guess.

The teen-aged Kriegsmarine were vicious in their goading, beating us with rifle butts and repeatedly inflicting bayonet wounds. In the excitement the dogs went wild even attacking the guards. McNamara, the camp bandleader, smashed his guitar on a dog's head breaking its jaw. The dog was shot; McNamara had a rifle butt broken over his head causing a wound that took months to heal.

There were cases of men helping others when they were in danger of collapse. One in particular, a large powerful man, struggled up the road supporting a man under each arm. Those who witnessed it could only wonder at his strength and dedication to his fellows.

To avoid the strain of the surging, some men side-stepped the column and ran with the guards. The older guards for the most part carried only bayonets because the weight of the rifle proved too much. In total, more guards collapsed than prisoners did, some even being trampled.

Machine guns were positioned in the woods beside the road, as were movie cameramen. Kit bags were discarded before long and only a few men had actually retrieved their own kit on the ship. Some had even been able to hang on to it until the end of the run. Finally the woods opened up to a large clearing where the familiar barbed wire and postern boxes stood. It looked almost a welcome site as opposed to endless rows of open trenches, as those who had missed the little sign on the tree had envisioned.

Water was finally issued in limited quantities and every man sprawled out on the sunburned turf in complete exhaustion. The next day and a half was spent in the open field still in the clothes in which we stood, but that didn't seem important. The three-day trip, terminating in the three-kilometre run, was over.

EPILOGUE

*The events of this story are true. There may be errors with regard to times and even dates. Although memories fade, certain experiences remain clear when less important occurrences become foggy by comparison. The departure date from Stalagluft VI has been placed at both the 17th and 16th of July for example, but is of little consequence when the events themselves are considered. The author has relied upon notes from various ex-POWs who made this journey as well as his own recollections. Therefore it should be noted that this is only one account; there are over 650 others that may not be recorded.*

*Stalagluft IV was a new camp holding American airmen only recently shot down. The senior man was arbitrarily chosen by the Germans and was a man who represented the Germans to his fellow prisoners instead of representing the prisoners to the Germans. Importing hundreds of long-term prisoners who were past masters of escape, manipulation, and goon baiting in general, was the last thing the Camp Commandant wanted. This was the reason for the run up the road, the kit-bag shuffle, and the attempt to demoralise the new arrivals. In spite of the fact that most of us lost almost 80% of our possessions, we saved the radio. As the mail was censored, the radio was our only link to home and to the progress of the war.*

*A memorial has been erected at the site of camp; this was made possible by the Polish government and the support of many of the survivors.*

*It has been reported that Hauptmann Pichardt was captured when the Russians overran the camp at Stalagluft IV and was summarily executed.*

# ALBERT MCMULLEN

*Albert was born in October 1923 in Empress, Alberta. He enlisted in the RCAF in January 1943, received his Air Gunner brevet the following November, and he left for Britain in March 1944. He joined 424 Halifax Squadron in June and was shot down on his 23$^{rd}$ sortie, ending up as a POW in Poland. He returned to England in May 1945 and was demobbed in Canada in September.*

## A Day to Remember

My twin brother, Archie, and I joined the RCAF on 7 January 1943. Both of us were accepted for aircrew training. Archie earned his pilot wings and I was awarded my Air Gunner brevet. In February 1944 we boarded a train for Halifax.

The train ride in old rickety cars with slatted wooden seats, wood and coal stove in one end of the car, was no picnic; but finally we were in Halifax boarding the Andes for our trip across the Atlantic. We slept three deep on the ship, one under the table, one on the table, one in a hammock above the table, and got two meals a day. The sea was rough and the weather cold; we arrived in Liverpool early in March 1944.

After two weeks in Bournemouth we were posted to a training station in the north of England. We got more training in gunnery, turret function, and other military knowledge. Here we met other aircrew and crewed up. Art Keeping and I stayed together as we had become friends since Regina, two farm boys, Art from Codette, Saskatchewan and me from Alberta. Art had the biggest voice of anyone I knew; it must have been from calling hogs.

Our crew was:

pilot Bill Bonar, Sedgewick, Alberta

navigator Albert Cayer, Quebec

bomb-aimer Jack Lambert, Montreal

wireless operator Jimmy Cote, Montreal

flight engineer Jock Galbraith, the oldest crew member.

Jock was a Scot who had been a London bobby. Quite a crew: three English Canadian farm boys, three French Canadians and a London bobby. We got along very well.

We were posted to 82 OTU and after some ground training, we got down to flying bombers. My logbook shows 20 April 1944 as the date of our first flight in a twin-engined Wellington bomber. Art Keeping and I drew straws to see who would get the privilege of being the tail gunner (if you can call that a privilege). He won–and little did we know that he wouldn't come home.

On 31 May we went on leave and then reported to 1660 Heavy Conversion Unit at Wimblington for training on four-engine Mark II Halifax bombers.

On 23 July 1944 we flew our first operation as a crew, to Dongen in the south of France. On the way back to base we were running out of fuel and our airfield was blacked out for fear of German raids. After calling Darky for help, our old OTU airfield at Ossington opened up and we landed safely. We had a 500-lb bomb hang up and they didn't like that. Then they got the aircraft stuck in the mud and pulled off the tail wheel. We returned to Skipton the next day.

Our next operation was on 30 July. We were briefed to attack an armour concentration at Villers Bocage, in Normandy. This was a daylight flight. We experienced fire in an engine just after take-off but managed to feather the engine and put the fire out. Being fully loaded with bombs and fuel we couldn't land so we agreed to keep going. We couldn't keep up but went in to what we thought was the target, bombed at 2000 feet, just below the cloud, and headed home. We had a few bullet holes in the aircraft from rifle fire.

The next few flights were into France, troop support, P Plane site, Tasselly airfield, Brussels. We always ran into a lot of flak, resulting in damaged hydraulics and a few holes here and there. In August 1944 all but two of our ops were flown in daylight.

In September we had only five missions, one a night flight to lay mines near Kiel. The other daylight raids were into Germany with fighter cover. There was moderate flak, once causing us to return on three engines.

In early October we were assigned to D, a new aircraft, as up to now we had flown anything available. On 6 October we had to abort a long mission because of a prop that automatically feathered. Then we did five missions in October to Bochum, Essen, and Hamburg. On one occasion we saw an enemy night fighter with its nose-light illuminated. We laid mines in Oslo Harbour, experienced bad icing, and landed away from our base. We finished the month with a trip to Cologne and once again landed at away from home.

November saw us on a trip to Oberhausen to start the month. The next night we were called in as spares. Things didn't go very well as our own D-dog was in for inspection. We had to try three different aircraft before we got one we thought would fly. As a result we took off late and couldn't catch up on the time; moreover our engines were overheating and we couldn't reach our designated 22,000 feet. Just as we were about to start our bomb run on Düsseldorf, I spotted a fighter below and behind. We took evasive action and seemed to lose him, but a few minutes later we were hit by cannon shells. The inside of the aircraft was on fire, the intercom non-functioning, and the aircraft out of control. I climbed out of my turret, put on my 'chute and moved forward to the engineer. He indicated we were to bale out. I decided to follow him out through the front hatch. The aircraft then went into a dive and a spin, and we were forced to the floor with my head on his back. There was a mighty flash that I assumed was the aircraft blowing up. I found myself free of the plane, pulled the ripcord, and felt my 'chute open. I had no idea how high I was or when I would hit the ground. I never did see the cultivated field before I hit it with a hefty thump. No broken bones; just a few bruises.

I think this is when shock set in. One of the worst feelings I have ever had is to be all alone in enemy territory and not know the fate of the rest of the crew. But this is also when my training took over. I gathered my 'chute, buried it in the closest grove of trees, and started to get away from the area.

For the next six days I holed up in haystacks or under haycocks trying to dry out from the night before of tramping through wet fields and swamps and falling over wire fences. My diet consisted of cabbage and sugar beets. I was very discouraged. Dark nights left me unable to read the compass or maps. That night I started to walk west on the first road I found, through villages, rubbing shoulders with the population, but making time. After a while I found myself all alone and in the dark. I walked right up to two German Guards who, I suppose, were enforcing a curfew. I heard the rifles click and the "Halt, Halt!" and I was a prisoner.

I guess they figured out what I was and marched me what seemed like 1½ to 2 hours to a military post where I was questioned and searched. I was forced to remove a large cabbage I had under my blue sweater. They had me break the piece of bone that contained a saw blade from my survival kit.

I would give only my name, rank and serial number. I was put in a cell with a slanting bed that could be observed through a window in the door. This was where I had the first indication that the bomb-aimer was alive, as his name was written on the wall. Jack Lambert remembers nothing of the explosion and found himself and parachute swinging from a tree. He hid in a barn but on the second day he was discovered by farmers with pitchforks and was really afraid for his life until the authorities arrived. So Jack was passing through the system ahead of me. In about two days I was moved to a civilian prison which had a great bald-headed keeper. I was starting to feel a little better and as the keeper always opened the door and came in with food I loosened a heavy wooden leg of a stool and lay in wait. He never opened the door again.

In about three days I was picked up by a tall army sergeant and taken by train down the Rhine, past all the bombed out cities to the Interrogation Centre at Frankfurt. Here I learned that both Jack Lambert and Jimmy Cote had survived. Jack was unhurt and captured by farmers; Jimmy had a broken arm and was turned in by other civilians who found him.

The Red Cross equipped me with a greatcoat, cap, towel, and shaving gear. With other POWs I was sent by train to StalagLuft VII, Bankau, in what used to be Poland. See map on pages 360-361.

I think there were about 1300 prisoners, all aircrew including some glider pilots. The food was very poor. We received some Red Cross food parcels and they made a world of difference. They had tinned Spam, powdered milk, chocolate, butter or margarine, cigarettes and a few other items, Not everyone could have a Red Cross parcel to himself; we formed into small groups and shared them between groups of two or more people. The German food would be a ration of black bread and maybe some kind of watery soup with barley and a little horsemeat in it or some kind of dried vegetables that we named "whispering grass". There was a row of wash basins and toilets–mostly cold water. Once a week we had a shower with a shot of warm water and then cold; what a heart stopper. Soap was scarce, so washing clothes or shaving in cold water was a chore.

I think there were about twenty POWs in a room in these wooden huts; we slept on very thin mattresses of wood fibre or straw on the floor with two thin blankets and a greatcoat. There was a small wood or coal heater but very little fuel.

POWs worked in the main kitchen and delivered the soup to each hut to be rationed out. The garbage detail was a big four-wheeled farm wagon pulled and pushed by several Russian POWs who were barely alive. They would run their fingers around the inside of every empty can and lick them off.

Parade was called night and morning and everybody was counted. If you went out after dark or during an air raid, you would be shot. I lost one buddy that way. In the daytime we could walk, play games, or exercise outside, weather permitting. I believe that at times the temperature dropped to 25 degrees below. There was a kind of library and the odd stage show. We also had an English army padre.

When new POWs arrived we looked for familiar faces. In early December 1944 my bomber-aimer Jack Lambert showed up but two weeks later was gone. *I learned later Jack was taken to Berlin where he was interrogated, kept in solitary confinement, and put before a firing squad. He wasn't shot, however. He stayed in prison until the end of the war. No wonder he had a nervous breakdown when he got home.*

Christmas was a lot of make-believe and I assure you there were no turkeys or trimmings. Life dragged on until midnight 19 February when we were rousted out with what we wanted to carry on a march to keep ahead of the Russian Army. What a shock: snow, cold and no shelter. We marched for nearly two weeks on a small ration of black bread, a little watery soup, and what remained of our Red Cross parcels. We were herded into farm compounds and slept in barns or haystacks each night. By the end of that time we were a sorry looking bunch and this is where the buddy system paid off. Four of us banded together to support each other and one of our party would not have survived without the emotional and physical support we gave him. We wouldn't let him quit.

How many fell by the wayside, I have no idea. Dysentery, starvation, 20-30 km per day, the loss of body weight and energy–all took their toll. We had walked west across the Oder River with the sound of war at our backs. After this we were herded into slatted cattle cars and locked in. I think there were about two square feet per person. When you sat down somebody was between your knees; when you lay down, it was in layers. A black bread ration was about all we got.

After a week of this we ended up at Luchenwald, a town near Stalag IIIA, about 75 km south of Berlin, and 75 km from the Elbe crossing where the Americans and Russians linked up. Stalag IIIA had some 30,000 POWs, American and Commonwealth aircrew together with French and Irish soldiers, some of whom had been captured at Dunkirk and in the bag for nearly five years. We were skin and bone when we arrived. I don't think I weighed much more than a hundred pounds and I was in pretty good shape compared to some. We were supported by the other prisoners as much as they could, and finally our Red Cross parcels started to arrive. Spring came early and we never looked back.

I was pleased to discover that my wireless operator was in one of the officers' compounds. Three weeks before VE day they moved us again and marched us the three or four miles to the railway and assigned us to cattle cars. We were allowed the freedom of moving around the rail yards and the weather was beautiful.

It was the best 48-hour pass I ever had.

The guards were mostly old men, older than our fathers. They had very little to eat; we practically turned them into slaves by bribing them with cigarettes. They couldn't even climb into the boxcars; we would take their rifles and lift them in. There was no thought of escape; we knew the war was drawing to a close. After two days we were marched back to camp.

One week before VE day our guards disappeared. Later that day the Russian tanks rolled through the camp. The next day the fences were put up and we were interrogated and were Russian prisoners. Some of us were allowed to go with the truck downtown searching for food. The Americans sent in several of their trucks to take out the sick, but the general population had to stay put.

On VE day the six or eight American trucks had sat outside the compound overnight, not being allowed to load. At daybreak I was one of the bunch that went through the fence, filling the trucks and away. The first one I was in had too many flat tires so we had to squeeze into others. The next one got hung up in barbed wire and by the time we freed it we were all alone. Every bridge, every intersection was blocked by Russian soldiers who had no authority to let us through.

After a few hours of this we started to run the blockades, the Russians leaping aside too frightened to fire on the American White Stars. At six that evening we crossed the Elbe River on a pontoon bridge with the Russians on one side trying to hold us back and the Americans on the other beckoning us forward. Germany was two countries right then; the very old and the very young pushed wheel barrows or pulled little wagons with what they could bring, trying to get to the Elbe river and across.

The American side was like a new world. There were showers, delousing, clean clothes, and a mess hall with food. White bread looked and tasted like cake. We had beds to sleep in. Another week passed before the Russians allowed rest of the POWs to walk to freedom.

I was trucked to an airfield from which we were flown by DC3 to Brussels. I was told that from time to time aircraft were leaving for England and if we wanted a ride to get out there and wait. I stayed the night in Brussels, managed to find an RAF battle dress in stores, and enjoyed a little taste of freedom. Next day I was sitting at the end of the line on the airfield and, luckily for me, the next DC3 loaded from my end. I don't know where we landed in England but we were treated to a hearty meal with a pretty waitress behind every chair.

Soon we were in Bournemouth, where I found out I was a flying officer instead of a flight sergeant. I had to buy uniforms and was given two weeks leave. Soon Jimmy and I were on the boat heading home. I think it was early in June when we landed at Halifax. Then we went by train to Montreal where we were sent on leave. I think I was to report to RCAF Calgary some time in August of 1945. There I took my discharge and became a civilian again.

In June 1997 we attended a dedication of a Memorial Book and Plaque in memory of my pilot, W. S (Bill) Bonar, at the Vermilion School of Agriculture, now known as Lakeland College, Alberta.

# JAMES H. SMITH

*Born in Saskatchewan in 1920, Jim joined the Canadian Army in March 1941. Nine months later, he was accepted for transfer to the RCAF for aircrew training. He received his Navigator brevet in September 1942 and joined 432 Squadron in the UK. A short three months later, Jim was shot down on a Hamburg raid, captured, and detained as a POW until the war ended. Jim returned to Canada in 1945 and was demobbed. He had flown four trips to the Ruhr Valley before that fateful trip to Hamburg.*

## Kreigsgefangener

**O**VER HAMBURG 0115 HOURS 30 JULY 1943
We had just dropped our bombs when the searchlights got us–first the big blue one and then fifty or more white ones. We couldn't see anything but corkscrewed vigorously for ten minutes. Just as we were turning onto the first leg home, an Me109 strafed us, killing F/0 Bennet and P/0 Jewell and mortally wounding our pilot, W/Cdr Kerby. The Wellington went straight down, on fire. I passed out due to a lack of oxygen trying to get to the escape hatch. We were flying at 22,000 feet at the time.

I found myself falling; pulled open my 'chute, and hit the ground hard. My clothes were all cut and torn and I had multiple cuts and bruises, but nothing was broken. I guess the Wimpy blew up

I landed in a meadow full of cows near a Wurzburg radar site. A searchlight swept the ground and I could see Germans running toward me. I took off, ran a couple of miles, and hid in a hedgerow. It was the loneliest feeling imaginable hearing the last of our bombers going home as I awaited an unknown fate in enemy hands. I was found early next morning by a couple of elderly civilians (one of whom said, "For you the war is over") and taken to a small village jail.

In the jail a civilian searched me. On finding a bible (my Dad had carried it through the Boer War and WWI) he exploded in rage and kept it. A Luftwaffe officer came for me and we walked a couple of miles to the Wurzburg site. All morning Luftwaffe personnel brought in loose equipment from three downed aircraft. When an orderly brought the officer his dinner, he ate half and offered me the rest. I ate my first food in eighteen hours—rather decent of him I thought. This officer spoke very good English; one of his comments was most interesting.

"Eventually the Allies will side with the Germans against the Russians; the war is a long way from ending."

I was locked in a small shed with windows and became the object of interest to Luftwaffe personnel. It was a strange feeling being on public view.

Early in the afternoon I was interrogated by a civilian who said he was from the Red Cross. We had been briefed for such an event and I refused to answer his questions. He ranted, raved and threatened to hand me over to the Gestapo, but finally he left. Later that afternoon a Luftwaffe corporal with a rifle and fixed bayonet marched me through some woods to the autobahn where, to my relief, I saw a German staff car and large truck and three other NCO aircrew. Two were suffering from eye injuries, (one was Canadian Sgt Demcoe) and rode in the officer's staff car. Sgt Fenton (RAF) and I rode in the back of the truck with fifteen dead bodies.

Some three hours later we arrived at a Luftwaffe Me110 night fighter base at Lüneburg, where Fenton and I unloaded the bodies, all properly tagged as to crews. Four of my crew were among the dead–I was the sole survivor. Quite a shock! There were also six bodies from Demcoe's Halifax and five from Fenton's Halifax. We spent the next three days in the base jail, served only black bread and water. I was interrogated again by the base CO, who told me the dead would have a proper military burial. There were now five of us including a flying officer RAF navigator who was already in jail. We were taken under armed escort (a Luftwaffe sergeant and two airmen) by train to Hanover. The train was standing room only with civilians fleeing

Hamburg–we were not popular. When we changed trains at Hanover, a German Unterzeeboot captain rushed over asking to speak to the senior person. He shouted and ranted about us "Terror fliegers" but the RAF officer yelled back about bombing London, Coventry, etc. They both calmed down and saluted each other; the submariner went back to his train.

We arrived next day at DulagLuft, Frankfurt am Main, the Luftwaffe interrogation centre for all Allied aircrew prisoners. I spent two weeks, in solitary confinement, interrogated by a Luftwaffe major who was the same "Red Cross civilian" who questioned me when I was first picked up. He said, "I see you recognise me. Well, I was up to Hamburg getting my family out, which I did, or you would not be talking to me here now, do you understand that?" I said I could but that such treatment wouldn't be in accordance with the Geneva Convention. He just shrugged.

I was interrogated about every third day for two weeks before he let me out into the main holding area, where I received my first good meal and a new pair of pants (US Army). The interrogation was very interesting. Sometimes I would be taken to his office; sometimes he would come to my cell. He varied between ranting and raving and being very polite. He showed me photos of my CO's wedding as the couple were coming out of the church. Luftwaffe files had the names and squadron details about a lot of our aircrew. Two or three days later, along with fifty or sixty RAF NCO prisoners, we went by box car to Luft 1, Barth, on the Baltic coast, not far from where I was shot down. *See map on pages 360 and 361.*

**DECEMBER 1943**

The whole camp was moved by freight train through Berlin to Stalag Luft VI at Heydekrug near the East Prussia/Lithuania border. The camp (some five thousand prisoners) was divided into four separate compounds: two Commonwealth, one American, and one Russian. The Russian camp had no buildings, just a field, presumably because Russia did not ratify the Geneva Convention. POW life was a real mental shock, primarily because of complete loss of freedom, anxiety about the future, thoughts about family and loved ones so far away, inadequate food and sheer boredom. The Red Cross was our lifeline, not only supplying food parcels (although not on any regular basis) but books, athletic equipment, etc. They also made camp inspections about twice a year.

Soccer, rugby and softball were played by some and everyone

walked and walked inside the wire. Most managed to cope in some manner, but a few cracked up. It was called "*going around the bend*".

There were two British doctors to look after everyone. Our dentist was a flight sergeant New Zealander. The medical facilities provided by the Germans were primitive.

## CHRISTMAS 1943

Our camp leader, F/Sgt Dixie Deans of the RAF, asked the German Commandant if he would permit us to send some Red Cross Parcel food to the Russians as they were starving. He approved the request. Some months later we received a note from the Russians: "Comrades in Arms, Knights of the Sky, have you any more biscuits?"

## JULY 1944

Due to the Russian offensive, half the camp was again moved by freight train, this time to a British Army camp, Stamlager 357 at Thom, Poland, just west of Warsaw. The other half went by ship to somewhere in the Baltic.

## OCTOBER 1944

Because of the continuing Russian offensive, Stamlager 357 was moved. This time to a large camp at Fallingsbostel (near Hanover) close to the infamous Belsen concentration camp.

Since being shot down I had now travelled full circle and been in five POW camps. I estimate that between this new camp and the one about two miles away, there must have been twenty thousand POWs of all nationalities.

The British Airborne prisoners captured at Arnhem were all spit and polish and couldn't believe how scruffy looking we had become; nor could they understand our mindset. But some of us had been in the bag for nearly five years, two of us shot down in the first week of the war.

The Airborne RSM tried to take over the administration of the camp from F/Sgt Dixie Deans (Army RSM vs Air Force F/Sgt mentality). F/Sgt Deans spoke fluent German, was a commercial salesman in Germany before the War, knew the German psyche, and understood the POW nuances between captor and prisoner–he had been shot down in 1940. A camp vote was taken and F/Sgt Deans won hands down. After the war, the British Government decorated him for his great leadership and administrative abilities in the face of the enemy.

As the Allied offensive crossed the Rhine into Germany,

conditions in the camp got worse and worse. Food was turnip and potato soup and one slice of bread per day; we were all slowly starving. Red Cross parcels did not arrive. We were all in very poor physical condition and got dizzy if we sat up too quickly. The medical officer told us we were too run down to have cold showers, and so we became even grubbier.

**APRIL 1945**

All prisoners were marched eastward, away from the advancing Allies, in groups of about a thousand men. After two weeks on the road we returned to Fallingsbostel and on 26 April were liberated by the British Eighth Army, the Desert Rats.

Two weeks later we were transported to Holland (those who were POWs longest got out first) and flown to an airdrome north of London some time after VE Day. At Bournemouth I found I was a warrant officer and I was then commissioned in the exalted rank of pilot officer. I had weighed 180 pounds when I was shot down and was now only 115 pounds. I stayed in Bournemouth for six weeks, gaining back my health,

I went to London on leave and ended up in Hospital #23 Canadian General. The body couldn't stand the pace. The whole ward was full of POWs with similar health problems.

I finally went home on the troopship Ile-de-France and landed in Halifax, Nova Scotia, on 13 July. From there, on to Lachine then Saskatoon and finally, in August 1945, home to Chilliwack, British Columbia. 1 was released from the RCAF at Jericho Beach, Vancouver on 10 October.

I attended the University of British Columbia from 1946 to 1949 and rejoined the RCAF in 1951, serving until 1971.

# JACK WARNOCK

*Jack is a Scot, born and educated in Glasgow. At the outbreak of war he was in high school and a sergeant in the Air Cadets. He joined the RAF in 1941 and on new year's day 1942 arrived in Halifax for flying training in Canada. He completed EFTS at Oshawa and SFTS at Aylmer, Ontario. After the war, he flew for a while with the Scottish Division of British European Airways and then emigrated to Canada.*

*For many years Jack was in Sales and Marketing with British Overseas Airways (BOAC) in Toronto. After retirement, he came to the west and has enjoyed living in Victoria for the past three years.*

## Story of an Escape

In May of 1944 1 was posted from the Mustang OTU to 168 Squadron, RAF, based at Redhill in Surrey. Together with several RCAF squadrons, we made up the 39th Reconnaissance Wing, part of 2nd TAF. On D-Plus-10 the wing transferred to a prepared airstrip in the beachhead in Normandy.

My story starts on 19 July in the early evening when Ali, my colleague, and I were on a recce trip to cover enemy-occupied territory as far as Lisieux. As junior pilot I provided protection for the other aircraft while he concentrated on noting and photographing anything of interest on the ground. Two aircraft were always sent up on these sorties.

In minutes we had crossed the Allied lines and levelled out at our cruising altitude of around 6000 feet. We were met by bursts of flak that we soon left behind. About three-quarters of an hour into the flight Ali started a wide turn. I glanced down and noticed a town with a large cathedral-like building gleaming in the evening sun. I realized this must be Lisieux and that we should soon be heading back to base.

Shortly after that everything changed. As I manoeuvred behind Ali, searching the sky in all directions. I looked down and my heart jumped: three Me109s in loose formation were climbing towards Ali's aircraft.

I yelled the usual Bandits! warning and threw the Mustang into a dive to intercept them, firing bursts as I closed in. Ali did what he was supposed to do–get away and try and return to base. Months later I was to learn they chased him out over the Channel before giving up.

As I moved to engage the 109s, I found there was a fourth enemy aircraft behind me. I realized this when I felt bullets tearing into my aircraft. I broke off my attack and sent the Mustang into a climbing turn to avoid other bursts. There were none; he made only one pass at me and continued on his way.

Suddenly my engine began to misfire and sputter. I knew where I had been hit. I levelled off and eased back on the throttle, trying to find a power level at which the engine might operate smoothly. In achieving this, I found I could not maintain height, so my first plan was to stretch my powered glide back to the Allied beachhead and crash-land my aircraft on any field I could find. I kept an eye on my altimeter; I was at just over 3000 feet. My chances were slim.

Then things got worse. The engine began to shake quite violently, oil sprayed out over the windshield, black smoke poured out, and the oil pressure dropped to near zero. There was no doubt in my mind: I would have to bale out.

I jettisoned the hood, went through the other emergency procedures, and started to roll the aircraft onto its back. It wouldn't go. At this point I had feelings of near panic. The ground seemed very close. I figured I was at about 1200 feet. I had to get out any way I could.

Managing to get my feet up on the other side of the aircraft, pulling with my hands and pushing with my legs, I finally got out and pulled the ripcord without waiting to the count of ten. After a few seconds I felt a pull on my shoulders. The 'chute had opened, thank God!

After struggling to get out of a noisy, crippled aircraft, drifting downwards seemed very quiet and peaceful, even pleasant. But not for long; looking down I saw a large chateau with red crosses on the roof. Out of it were running German soldiers armed with rifles. They pointed and shouted and I became aware of a "zipping" sound through the air close beside me. Some of them were firing at me. I waved my hand to show I was reasonably friendly, then I drifted over some tall trees and out of their sight toward a field where, with fascinated horror, I watched my Mustang crash and explode. I landed not far from the burning aircraft and quickly got rid of my 'chute. Sprawled on the ground I could hear German troops pounding along a road nearby shouting hoarsely.

Bushes surrounded the field, but as I tried to run for cover I fell flat on my face. Looking down I saw that my right leg was covered in blood. I had hit the tailplane and the impact had ripped off my flying boot and torn my battledress slacks open at the knee. I remembered a thud I'd felt on leaving the aircraft.

The shouting voices were much closer now. I crawled on all fours to the edge of the field where the bushes grew out of a ditch. I rolled into it and lay still, hoping I might not be found. If I could lie there till after dark, perhaps I could make a getaway.

It was a forlorn hope.

Within half an hour they discovered me. I was hauled unceremoniously out of the ditch and was a prisoner. There were about twelve to fifteen of them, all armed. They seemed excited, as though pleased with their capture. As for me, I felt rather strange, not exactly scared, but certainly apprehensive.

They brought me back to the chateau I had seen from the air. I couldn't walk properly. I proceeded slowly, sometimes hopping along on one leg and sometimes being helped by two of the soldiers. A medical orderly cleaned up my blood-caked knee and bound it in a bandage. I took off my remaining flying boot and pointed to my feet.

"Shoes? - Shoes?" I had to repeat the words and gesture several times before he got the message and came back with a pair of rope slippers, such as might be used in a hospital. These were to be my only footwear for quite a while.

I was escorted by a couple of guards to a farmhouse about a mile away and turned over to a German NCO. The farm was occupied only by a platoon of Wehrmacht soldiers. Shortly after midnight I was taken out, put into a small truck and driven through the night.

It was now around 5 am on 20 July. We arrived at a building that appeared to be a brick-works, and I was placed in a room with about ten other prisoners. We were given breakfast: black bread and ersatz coffee. Our group was made up of English, Australians, Americans, and me, a lone Scot, all aircrew.

By 24 July my injured knee was acting up. The bandage was covered in blood and I had difficulty in hobbling around. I was taken by truck to a German field hospital and left for a while in a small, open-sided shed behind a large tent that formed the hospital.

At this stage I was not thinking of escape–I couldn't move quickly enough. It was a warm, sunny day. I studied my surroundings. I thought at first that I was alone, but soon I noticed someone else nearby. About 15-20 ft away was a man in the uniform of a British Army private. He was lying on the ground, eyes closed, absolutely motionless. There was something odd about him.

As quietly as I could I moved over beside him. His battledress was singed and his exposed skin lightly browned (not tanned) as though he had been exposed to flame. There was no breathing and I was sure he was dead. I pulled his Army paybook from a pocket so that later I could report who he was. He was Gunner P.A. McGrady of the Royal Artillery.

Soon after, a medical orderly cleaned up the wound on my knee, applied a dressing, and bound everything up in a paper bandage. Then it was back to the truck and to the brick-works.

In the early morning hours of 1 August we were taken by truck to the outskirts of Falaise and locked up in the stable of a chateau. A few hours later, about 0800, other trucks arrived and after a trip of about two-and-a-half hours we arrived at Alençon. Nearby the town was a fair-sized POW camp totally surrounded by barbed wire with wooden sentry towers at intervals. This was the largest camp I had been in so far. It had several huts with sleeping accommodation on the floor. I estimated it contained about 500 prisoners.

There was nothing to do here except talk to others, walk around, and wait for the two meals per day. I found it very frustrating and remember one morning looking out through the barbed wire at a narrow paved road on the other side. I longed to be able to walk along it; freedom seems so precious when you not longer have it. It was at this time that I made a firm resolution to escape, somewhere, sometime. I would get away.

On 4 August a large group of us were loaded into trucks and driven to a camp at Chartres. When we arrived, fifty or sixty of us, all aircrew personnel, were marched to a former convent and billeted in what had once been the chapel. With others already there, our group consisted of British, Canadian, Australian and American aircrew, and British and Free French paratroopers. I was there for only a few days.

I did get to meet (very briefly) one unusual prisoner who was to stand out in my memory. He was well tanned and wore the uniform of a French paratrooper. Of medium height, he was exceptionally muscular and well built, one of the strongest men had ever seen.

He kept to himself, speaking to no one. Other prisoners told me they had tried to speak to him in English and French but he never responded and they left him alone. A couple of days later, when there were few others around, this man approached me and in heavily accented English asked me where I came from. When I told him I was from Scotland, he appeared pleased and proceeded to talk in a quiet voice. It turned out he was Spanish and had been fighting the Germans since the days of the Spanish Civil War. When World War II started he had joined the French army and after the fall of France had got away to England where he was trained as a paratrooper with the Free French forces.

It seemed he had a need to talk to someone, but he was very wary. The Germans were known to plant their own men among prisoners to pick up information. He believed that if they found out who he was he could be shot. He had decided no German could speak English with an accent like mine! I felt really pleased about that and we talked some more, until some guards came in. Then he drifted off to be by himself again.

Early next morning, when I was being moved on, he smiled and waved to me. Somehow, I felt honoured to have made this brief acquaintance. I never saw him again.

On 8 August a number of us, all aircrew, were being moved again. This time we were told we were going by road to Paris and then by train to Frankfurt. We set off in darkness and as the sun rose, we could see we were in the outskirts of a city. It seemed rather strange to be in one of the world's most beautiful cities (relatively unscarred by war), not as a tourist but as a prisoner in the back of a German Army truck with armed guards as our "guides".

In due course we arrived at the Gare de L'Est, where we were shepherded into a large room on the second floor, overlooking the interior of the station. It was pretty crowded in this room, with just enough space to lie down on the floor at night to sleep. Two guards were posted at the door at all times.

This seemed a good time to have a stab at escaping–while we were still in Paris–so I began to look around. There were two windows that looked down on the interior of the station. Few trains moved in or out and the majority of people we saw were German military personnel. At the back of the room was a single window. As the weather was fairly hot, we were allowed to have it open. It appeared to have possibilities.

The window was located on the outer wall of the station and because of the slope of the ground, it was three floors above street level. The street itself was narrow and cobbled. Although not all that busy, it was never deserted; it seemed the only way to go.

The next day, after our morning meal, I positioned myself by this window. The wall below was constructed of large blocks of cut stone with a gap of about one to one and a half inches between the outer edges of the stone blocks. Reaching down I felt into one of these gaps. It seemed to me there was enough room to fit fingers and toes into the grooves to climb down. It was worth the chance, but it would be better to wait until early evening.

Around 1900 hours I stuffed my rope slippers and socks into my pockets and with the help of two of my fellow prisoners, I started down. I managed to fit my toes into one of the grooves, my fingers into another, then slowly and carefully I started my descent.

All went well for a short time. About three or four blocks down I heard from my left the sound of marching boots. I froze and slowly turned my head to have a look. From the side-road a squad of German soldiers appeared, marching up the street toward me. I had visions of being caught like a fly on a wall and the guys at the window above called to me to come up. Somehow I was able to climb back up more quickly than I had come down. My arms were grabbed and I was pulled back into the room. Thus ended my first attempt at escape.

At about ten the next night we were moved down into the station and marched to a platform where carriages were drawn up. We had thought we'd be put into cattle trucks, so these railway cars were a surprise. On the platform we were turned over to the men who were to form our guard for the rail journey to Frankfurt.

The guard was made up partly of older men in their fifties and sixties and partly of boys about sixteen or seventeen. They were heavily armed and under the command of an NCO who spoke very good English. He had the appearance of an experienced, disciplined soldier and proceeded to tell us his rank was the equivalent of a sergeant-major in the British Army, that he was being returned to Germany for officer training, and that he had no intention of allowing his record to be marred in any way. Any attempts at escape would be dealt with severely. He was an impressive figure and I had every reason to take him at his word.

We were put on board, eight men to a compartment. A guard with a machine gun was posted at each end of the carriage and others patrolled up and down the corridor. Soon the train started to move, but for the next hour and a half we were shunted back and forth as other cars were added to make up the full train. In the dim light we could see that other cars were filled with German troops, ours being more or less in the centre. At about 2330 the train started to move slowly out of Paris.

Over the next couple of days or so our train made its way through the countryside, often on single-track lines and with stops due to air-raid alarms. On one occasion it was attacked by USAAF Lightnings, a rather frightening experience feeling the impact of their ammo hitting the train somewhere up front. However, it was a brief attack and whatever damage was done was not enough to halt our progress.

During one of the longer halts–from mid-afternoon until nearly noon the following day–I formed an escape plan. The only way out was through the compartment window. The lower half of this window could be unlatched and moved upwards, but a horizontal metal bar limited the opening created. This bar was held in place by two metal brackets, one at each end, and fastened to the woodwork by two slotted screws. It was a way out. The train would have to be moving at a the right speed and the attempt would have to be made under cover of darkness.

Using the end of my nail file I had kept concealed, and with some effort, I was able to loosen one screw. I immediately tightened it again. The others in the compartment, all USAAF personnel, wanted to know what I was up to and I told them of my plan. They agreed to help me; three of them said they would follow me out the window if things went right. With their help, the other screws were loosened.

At 1700 hours the train pulled into Laon. We were allowed to get off to be given some food on the platform. I got close to the Senior British Officer (an Australian squadron leader) and told him of my plan to escape during the coming night. He gave it his approval and agreed I had the right to go first. The stage was set.

At 2200 we pulled into Rheims where the train remained until midnight before moving on. I felt we should be ready for the attempt, so with the help of others I loosened the screws holding the window bar in place. This had to be done between the periodic inspections by a guard coming along the corridor with a flashlight. Ii took quite a while, but at last we were able to remove the bar and stow it under the seats.

I decided I would wait until well into the night before jumping, and so we all feigned sleep. At about 0500 I decided to go; it was now or never. After a guard had passed we eased the window up as far as we could. Climbing up on the seat and staring out into the darkness with the train moving at a fair clip but not too fast, I gave the others a wave before heaving myself out into the black of the night.

The impact of hitting the ground was less than I'd anticipated. I landed on the side of my body rather than my legs and rolled a few times before stopping. I saw the other coaches passing and the glow of a cigarette. To avoid being shot at, I scuttled close to the rail and lay almost beside it for protection. I lay like that until the train disappeared from sight. I got up, dusted myself off, and checked for injuries. Apart from a few scrapes there were none. I felt elated and did a little dance of joy right there on the tracks. I was no longer a prisoner!

Now I had to meet up with the ones who were to come after me. The idea was that the first two out would walk up the tracks in the direction the train had taken and the last two would walk back and we'd meet in the middle. I walked on for about a mile before sitting down and waiting for about an hour. Nobody appeared. I was never to learn what happened to the others.

I was now on my own and had to decide what to do. The sun was coming up and I could see the countryside was wooded. I had to get away from the railway tracks. Setting off in a south-westerly direction through the trees I found myself in open uncultivated ground with bushes and small trees growing here and there.

All through that day I ate wild blackberries and drank from small streams. There were no roads, only narrow cart tracks with no movement on them. I spotted a faded signpost. It was in French. This was important to me as it meant the train had not crossed into Germany when I jumped.

It was a beautiful day as I continued my cross-country hike, enjoying my freedom. In the afternoon I spotted the wreckage of a crashed aircraft through some trees. I approached it slowly. On getting closer I recognised that it as a Lancaster. There was indication of fire although I couldn't tell how long it had been there. Tire tracks led up to the crash site and away from it, but these were not recent. I hoped the crew had escaped.

On I went with the idea of getting as far away from the railway as possible and avoiding towns or villages; but as the day wore on I began to realize that I should try to find help. My reasoning was that I didn't really know where I was or where I was heading and the wild fruit I found wasn't enough to sustain me. Moreover, my rope slippers were falling apart; they were not up to hiking over rough country. I decided the time had come to seek assistance from the local population if I could find somebody friendly.

Ahead of me was hilly ground toward which I headed so as to get a better view of the countryside. From the hilltop, there it was–a small village that seemed fairly quiet. About halfway down the hill, I squatted down on a ridge to study the lie of the land. The village was quite small and the part that could be seen had an unpaved road along which were situated houses and barns. Very few people were about and although I watched for an hour or so, there was no sign of German troops. This was it.

I got up, took off my battledress tunic, turned it inside out, and put it on again, not quite sure why. I think it was because it might make me look less military. I went down the ridge and started walking along the road, keeping to one side. Nobody was in sight. The road curved slightly into the village. Just where it curved was a house with a barn opposite.

A man came out of the barn. He was middle-aged and looked like a farmer. I walked slowly towards him. He hadn't yet seen me and started to close the barn door. Then, turning, he spotted me and froze, a puzzled look on his face. I must have presented a rather weird picture, a total stranger, scruffy looking, unshaven, coming out of nowhere. I went up to him and smiled.

"RAF...RAF...Ecossais." I didn't know what else to say.

He seemed startled and taking hold of my arm, he tore open the barn door and drew me inside. He put his finger to his lips to indicate I shouldn't talk. There were bales of hay in the rear half of the barn and he motioned me to conceal myself there. Then he left.

I didn't know what to make of all this. He might return with German troops, which made me think about getting off into the woods again, but I decided to wait it out and see what happened. It grew dark. Then I heard the door being opened again and I grew tense until I saw it was the same man, this time with a young girl. I began to relax. The girl was staring at me, a little scared. I smiled at her. Her father took me by the arm and all three of us crossed the road quickly into the house opposite.

This turned out to be an important meeting, not only for me but also for the family I was introduced into; we were to become part of each other's lives for the next three weeks or so. The family consisted of the farmer, his stout, middle-aged wife and their three daughters. As we sat down to a hot meal together, I felt very fortunate to be with them. I was extremely hungry and had to restrain myself from gulping the food down ravenously.

Afterwards we talked. None of them spoke English, but the little girl spoke good French and I struggled with my school French to converse through her. Their story gradually came out.

The family was Ukrainian. The parents, M. and Mme. Milasczurk, had left the Ukraine some years before the start of WW II and settled in Poland. Then, being concerned about what was happening in Germany, they had managed to leave Poland and get to France, where they had settled to farm.

The three daughters were named Katrina, about 22; Anna, about 19; and the youngest, Hélène who was ten. The parents spoke only Ukrainian but the two older girls knew a little French and Hélène translated my halting French for them. I learned that evening that the name of the place was Auberive and that a small German garrison was stationed at the other end of the village. It was lucky for me that I had entered where I did.

They asked me to stay hidden in the barn by day and only come over to the house at night when someone came to get me. Young Hélène would bring food for me in the morning and again at midday. She would sit outside and sometimes we would talk quietly through the open barn door. It was her idea that if she saw anyone approaching she would start to sing and this meant I had to go to the back of the barn to conceal myself in the hay. I think she enjoyed her role of lookout. Most nights I ate with the family and we would talk. One Sunday evening Katrina's fiancé was there. I cannot recall his name. He, too, was Ukrainian, a rather wild-eyed young man, with a mop of tousled hair. He proudly told me he was a member of the Maquis and had a rifle hidden at his home. He hoped he would have a chance to use it. He was the only other person to know of my presence in the village.

He was interested to learn I was a pilot and wanted to know about the aircraft I had flown and about flying training. When I said I'd trained in Canada, M. Milasczurk, the father, started to question me. It turned out that he and his wife had relatives and friends who had emigrated to western Canada in the thirties.

Later that night, back in the barn, I couldn't help reflecting on this unusual situation—that I, a Scot, should be talking with a Ukrainian family, in a small farmhouse in France, about Canada.

Days passed uneventfully and then one evening the family told me that on the following day a gendarme was due to visit the village on a monthly "inspection trip". He evidently came by bicycle from a nearby town. They wanted me to talk with him. I agreed, for I desperately wanted to know what was going on with the Allied Forces.

In training I had been told that gendarmes were reliable and could provide advice, even help.

The next day he turned up at the barn. How they got him to come there without arousing the suspicion of others, I haven't a clue, but they did. He was a pleasant, middle-aged man who spoke quite good English. He told me the Allies had broken out of the Normandy bridgeheads and were advancing through France while the Germans pulled back.

This was great news. He also told us that instructions had been issued for all escapers: if an escaper could remain safely hidden until the area he was in was liberated, he should do so.

His advice was that I should stay put and that if anything went wrong he would come back to put me in touch with the underground and I would be moved in stages to Switzerland. So that was it; I should stay where I was and continue to lie low.

A few days later things started to change More German troops arrived in the village. My evening meal was brought to the barn and it was obvious the family was worried. They felt it was too risky for me to stay where I was and decided that next morning, at first light, they would smuggle me out to the fields hidden in the farm cart.

Continued on page 362

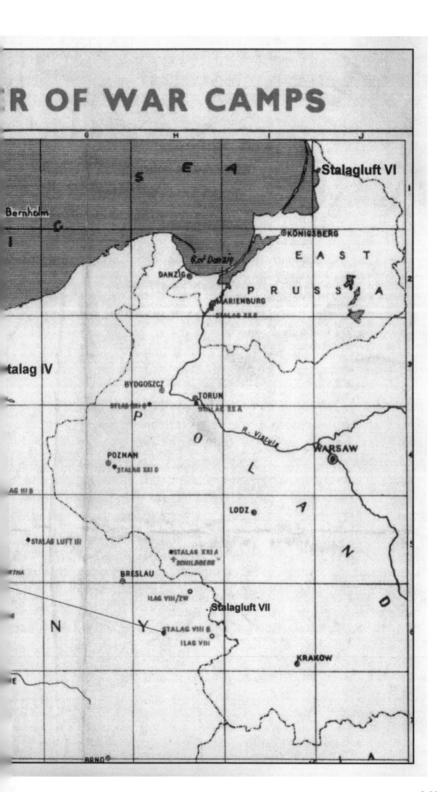

Stalagluft VI

Bornholm

S E A

KÖNIGSBERG

E A S T

Kof Danzig

DANZIG

P R U S S I A

MARIENBURG

STALAG XX B

talag IV

BYDGOSZCZ

TORUN

OFLAG XXI B

STALAG XX A

P

O

R. Vistula

WARSAW

POZNAN

STALAG XXI D

L

AG III B

LODZ

A

STALAB LUFT III

N

STALAG XXI A

SCHILDBERG

KTHA

BRESLAU

D

ILAG VIII/ZW

Stalagluft VII

N

Y

STALAG VIII B

ILAG VIII

KRAKOW

E

BRNO

A

Of course I agreed. In the morning, just as the sun was rising, I was whisked out of the barn and into the cart, where I was covered up with some sacks. With Katrina and Anna sitting at the rear edge of the cart and their father at the front guiding the horse, we set out for the fields.

After jolting over rough tracks for about an hour, we came to a stop. I got out. We were on the edge of cultivated land. Along this edge ran a depression where trees and bushes grew. One large bush had thick foliage reaching to the ground and this was the place they had picked for me to hide. They left me a package of food and drink to last for a day and a blanket to cover me at night. Then on they went to work elsewhere in the fields.

I was to remain out there for three days, an experience I thoroughly enjoyed. That first day I explored the adjacent area, careful to keep out of sight. I saw no one. It was exhilarating to be able to move around in relative freedom in the open air and that night I slept well under the stars.

In the morning I ate my remaining food and lay watching for my friends from the village. Pretty soon I saw the horse plodding along, following a track by the edge of the field. I noticed that this time the father had Anna and little Hélène with him. They told me there were still a lot of German troops in the village and that it was best to stay where I was. Leaving me more food, they went on to work. Once again I was on my own.

During that second day I ranged further over the countryside. Around noon I saw a ridge of high round ahead of me and decided to climb up to the crest. As I walked up I heard the roar of a powerful engine; startled, I dropped to the ground. And then I saw it! An Fw190 rose up into sight and climbed away at a fast clip. I was amazed at this happening out here in this quiet countryside and had to investigate. So I worked my way to the top, keeping under cover.

A grass airstrip ran parallel to the ridge. On the far side was a large stand of trees and dispersed among them were more 190s. The whole place was a hive of activity with refuelling trucks moving around and men working on aircraft. For a time I had some wild thoughts of getting over to where these aircraft were, attempting to get into one, taking off and heading for Normandy–but it was a crazy idea.

As I watched for nearly two hours, more 190s taxied out and took off. It seemed as though they were abandoning the airstrip.

Next morning when I met my friends from the village, they told me that the German troops who had recently come to the village had left and only the usual small garrison remained. They felt I should come back with them that evening. That night I was back in the barn.

It was about two days later that everything began to change completely. While I had breakfast everything was normal, quiet and peaceful. A few hours later I heard noises that seemed like shouting coming from the main part of the village. I opened the door slightly and saw Katrina and Anna running towards the village while their mother looked anxiously after them. About half an hour later they came rushing back with the news that the German soldiers had left in a great hurry, not even waiting to pack their supplies. The village was no longer occupied.

By mid-afternoon on 30 August the picture became completely clear. A group of heavily armed US Army jeeps swept into the village. Auberive had been liberated. Two of the jeeps pulled up outside the barn and I came out and joined the Milasczurk family, all laughing happily. The Americans looked at me curiously. I went up to a lieutenant in one jeep and told him who I was and how I came to be there. We shook hands. He informed me his group was an advance reconnaissance unit of General Patton's Third Army. Evidently the German forces were pulling back in a hurry along a broad front and units like his had to keep after them and keep them moving. He said the main force was not far behind and they should know what to do to help me. Soon after that he and his men moved off.

My adoptive family and I walked up the road to the centre of the village. All the people we met had to be told who I was and that I had been hidden there for about three weeks. I found myself rather a star attraction, with people shaking my hands and even hugging me. It seemed that the people of the village looked upon it as a great honour that I'd been hidden there, even though they'd known nothing about it. It was decided that on the following day there would be a victory parade.

That night I slept in the house, my first time in a bed for many weeks. It was absolute luxury.

The next day we assembled in the village square for the parade, which was to be led by the mayor, the Milasczurk family and me. We were followed by a small band who were a bit out of practise and out of tune but still added to the festive spirit. We marched round the square visiting many houses where we had to receive hospitality–food and a drink or two, invariably schnapps. It was powerful stuff and by late afternoon I was feeling no pain. That night I slept like a log.

Next day a US Army unit camped just outside the village. I contacted an Admin. Officer who promised that on the following day his unit would take me by jeep to Rheims, which was closer to the British sector.

That evening was to be my last in Auberive; I had a pleasant meal with the family, Katrina's fiancé and some of their friends. It was a joyous occasion. The following morning the family came with me to the US Army camp and we said our farewells. It was an emotional parting. They were a simple farm family who had taken in a stranger and provided so much and not without risk to themselves. As we sped off I waved to them until they were no longer in sight.

In due course we arrived at Rheims, where I was billeted at a small hotel in the city square, one of very few guests in a place formerly used by German officers. Two days later I was driven in an RAF vehicle into the British sector and on to an airfield on the outskirts of Douai, near the Franco-Belgian frontier. It was being used by RAF and RCAF squadrons, two of them Mustang units. I met some friends from OTU days and that night, over a few beers, we had a great talk together. Next day, 9 September, I was put on board a USAAF transport aircraft returning to SW. England.

My adventure in France was over.


On his return to UK, Jack was debriefed and gave details of the assistance the Milasczurk family had given him—very much at their own peril for hiding an Allied airman was punishable by death. He was told that the British government would make payment and award a medal to the family. When the war was over, Jack corresponded with the family and met Mme. Milasczurk in Oshawa in 1948. Ed.

# EARL TAYLOR

*Earl was born in Grandview, Manitoba on 26 May 1919. He joined the Canadian Army in July 1940 and transferred to the RCAF for aircrew training in June 1941. After receiving his Air Gunner brevet in May 1942, he was posted to the UK and completed his operational training there. He joined 207 Squadron in February 1943 and was shot down over Berlin six weeks later. He remained an unwilling guest of the Reich until liberated in April 1945. After discharge in September 1945, he rejoined the RCAF, this time .as a Pharmacist and Medical Supplies Officer. He resigned in 1953 to move to Victoria. He retired in 1984.*

## Spam, Sprouts, and Kohl-Rabi

In the spring of 1942 I completed the Air Gunner course at Mountain View, Ontario, and proceeded to the Aircrew Reception Centre in Bournemouth, England. Gunnery School at Storry Down, Wales, followed and then it was on to 1654 Heavy Conversion Unit at Wigsley, Lincolnshire, where I joined a crew captained by (RAF) Sgt Fransden. Here we converted on Manchesters and then Lancasters. On returning from leave in December 1942, I found that Sgt Fransden and the rest of the crew had been posted back to OTU, leaving me as a "spare bod". On the arrival of a new draft from OTU, I was fortunate to join a very good crew captained by F/0 Denys Street.

Sgt Gilbert Gray wrote of his time at Wisley: "This place seems to be miles from anywhere ... there are no canteens... there's no cinema... the mess isn't exactly attractive... the ablutions are crude... we are in Nissen huts... the airfield is a couple of miles away . . . goodness knows who invented this place . . . transport is very poor." He summed up conditions very aptly.

What followed is best summarised from the following entries in my logbook in 1943

**February 12**: posted to RAF 207 Squadron, Langar, Notts.

**February 13-26**: air firing, formation flying, cross country, high level bombing, fighter affiliation, lectures, emergency procedures, parachute and dinghy drills.

**February 26**: mine-laying off the West Frisian Islands. Three new crews on this op; two aircraft attacked by night fighters and one gunner killed, but the crew made it back even though the aircraft was badly damaged and on fire.

**February 28**: bombing attack on the U-boat pens and docks at St. Nazaire, France.

**March 1**: target Berlin. Returned to base with mid-upper and rear turrets unserviceable.

**March 2-7**: poor weather but we managed some training. On the night of the third of March we flew with a new engineer: Sgt Dudley. Our former engineer flew with another crew and went missing on a mine-laying trip in the Bay of Biscay. *According to an entry in Bomber Command Losses of the Second World War, his body was washed ashore in May 1943.*

**March 13-22**: on leave. On returning to the squadron we found our wireless operator was missing. Evidently he had been taken to hospital in Nottingham. To take his place RAF Sgt Blake joined the crew.

**March 26:** target Duisburg. Very bad weather. The Pathfinders were late and we had to stooge around in the heavy flak until they arrived to mark the target. We finally bombed on sky-markers through ten-tenths cloud.

**March 27**: target Berlin.

**March 29**: target again Berlin. Take-off was delayed because of the bad weather. Prior to setting course we were to orbit a searchlight at Skegness. While circling we narrowly avoided colliding with other aircraft and we were glad to finally set course for Germany.

*The Bomber Command War Diaries had this to say about the weather over the North Sea: "Very severe icing-electrical storm conditions". The book The Valley of the Shadow of Death described conditions thus: "It was doubtful whether the operation would take place, because of bad weather conditions en route, but at the last minute the go ahead was given. A total of 329 aircraft took off from their bases, but an exceptionally large number of aircraft (95 or 28.9%) returned after meeting very severe icing and electrical storm conditions over the North Sea . . . searchlights were operating in groups of 30 to 40 with predicted moderate to heavy flak over the capital city . . . The Command suffered heavy losses because of this ill-advised operation. Twenty-one aircraft failed to return."*

On our run-up the flak gave us a menacing welcome. As we approached our aiming point we found the marker concentration was poor, so we went round again and bombed a good concentration on this second run. The anti-aircraft welcomed us with heavy fire as we were on our camera run.

With three engines on fire, and following an attack by an Me110 that took out our port inner, we abandoned the aircraft. We all landed in the vicinity of the fighter station at Brandenburg and within a day or so were invited to be guests of the Third Reich. Since we had no choice we accepted the invitation. While waiting on the station platform for the train to take us to the Interrogation Centre at Frankfurt, a German officer came up and spoke to the skipper. He asserted that he was the fighter pilot who had delivered the *coup de grâce* to our aircraft. It is possible this was Hauptmann August Geiger, of NJG1, holder of the Oak Leaves to the Knights Cross, who had five victories that night. Hauptmann Geiger had a total of 53 victories before being killed in action in September 1943. *(Reference page 234 History of the German Night Fighter Force 1917-1945 by Gebhard Aders, 1979).*

At the Interrogation Centre we were put in small isolation cells and left alone for a day or so to ponder an uncertain future. Eventually an interrogation officer showed up. He was very friendly, spoke English fluently, offered cigarettes, and asked one of us to fill out a fake Red Cross form so that our parents could be informed of our safety. He was very plausible but the squadron escape lectures had warned us of this. He became quite annoyed when given only our name, rank, and number and nothing about our aircraft or squadron. He told us the names of other crews and personnel on the squadron, so we knew he was very well informed. Other tactics were to turn up the heat in the cell so that it would become uncomfortable and later to

Photograph courtesy of Bob Masters

turn all the heat off so that the room became very chilly. Later, a second intelligence officer showed up and offered the fake Red Cross form again.

The cell did not allow one to see out, so it was hard to tell the passage of time. After a number of days we were released to the main camp and put on a train to StalagLuft III at Sagan. Here we met some old friends who had been shot down before us.

On 18 June 1943 all the NCOs were sent to a new camp, StalagLuft VI, at Heydelkrug in East Prussia, near the Lithuanian border. With nothing to do time passed slowly, but on 7 January 1944 I was fortunate to obtain a job as a laboratory technician in the camp hospital. Our two British Army doctors, Dr. Pollock and Dr. Forrest-Hay, had both been captured at Dunkirk. I enjoyed the work in the hospital although it did not last very long. On 19 July the camp was evacuated because the Russian Army was approaching through Estonia and Latvia. The hospital personnel and POWs in K Lager, an American compound, were taken by train to the harbour at Memel and transferred to the hold of an old coal barge, the SS Insterburg. We spent the next three days in the hold as the ship slowly followed the coast to the German port of Swinemünde. Conditions were very crowded, and we had to sit up for the whole voyage. We were given no food and little water. During the voyage we had visions of the mines laid in the Baltic by the RAF. Any noise gave rise to apprehension as we pictured the ship's hull caressing the horns of an RAF mine just before it exploded. At one point, perhaps early in the third day, there was talk of overpowering the guards and sailing the ship to Sweden. Fortunately wiser heads prevailed and the idea was abandoned. It was just as well because when I was allowed on deck to relieve myself in the scuppers, I saw we had a wicked-looking E-Boat as escort. This effectively killed all talk of taking over the ship. The live-steam hoses held by the guards also acted as a deterrent.

When the ship docked at Swinemünde, we were hustled out and over to a train of cattle cars, the famous 40 and 8. Our shoes were taken away, and we were squeezed into the partitioned half of the car. Suddenly air raid sirens began to wail. The American Airforce carried out a small raid to add to the excitement.

Later the train pulled out and eventually, after a tiresome journey, we arrived at the small town of Kiefheide, to be greeted by a crowd of guards with Alsatian and Doberman dogs. They proceeded to run us up the road to our new camp, StalagLuft IV, a distance of some three kilometres. During this run the guards beat any laggards and stabbed them with bayonets. The run was made more difficult as we were burdened with our packs and many of the men were handcuffed together in pairs. We spent the next two days in an open field outside the camp perimeter with no food and very little water even though the days were terribly hot. Finally we entered the camp through the main gate where some naval personnel had formed a gauntlet and beat us as we passed in. A strip search and confiscation of all private possessions finally ended the welcome to our new home. Our accommodations consisted of tiny huts built like dog kennels that held ten men. We could not stand up in these huts and had to sleep jammed together on the floor. All in all it was not a happy place. On 20 August we were moved to another compound, where RAF and RCAF personnel were housed together. August, September and part of October were months of food shortages, no recreation facilities, and no Red Cross parcels. The latter half of October saw some improvement in conditions. A shortage of fuel made for miserably-cold barracks, but in December the fuel supply improved. Then on 25 December we were surprised and delighted to receive some Red Cross food parcels. The weather turned very cold until the end of January 1945.

On 6 February we left the camp and started marching west as the German Army was retreating before the Russian advance. Each day was miserable, marching through the snow. At night we stayed in barns or pigsties and if none were found we lay in open fields in temperatures well below zero. The food we had managed to take with us soon ran out and we subsisted on what we could steal from farms or dig out of the frozen ground. Soon everyone was suffering from severe diarrhoea. Dr. Forrest-Hay was with our column; each night he would set up a Medical Inspection Room staffed by our hospital personnel. We treated blistered feet and minor aches and pains but there was little we could do for the really sick. Cases of pneumonia were left with the Germans. On the march some people could not go on and dropped out of the column. Some of these simply disappeared and were never seen again.

On 6 March our column arrived at Neu Brandenburg some sixty-five kilometres north of Berlin. The camp was overcrowded but Dr. Forrest-Hay persuaded the Commandant to accept eight of our people. We were quartered in a so-called sick bay, an ordinary barrack block holding 180 people, all with severe diarrhoea, frost bite, gangrene, pneumonia and malnutrition. Conditions were very bad; filthy accommodation, little food, everyone crawling with lice, and once it began to warm up every bed a haven for countless bedbugs. Several men died from malnutrition and pneumonia. The one Allied doctor, an American, had no medication and could do little to help. The (British) Airborne captured at Arnhem were wonderful, coming each day to help where they could with the worst cases. Finally, sometime in April, The Royal Air Force made a paradrop of medical supplies. This drop was preceded by marker flares lighting up the camp and we thought bombs would follow. We were delighted to find that only medical supplies were dropped. These supplies helped to improve conditions for the worst cases.

At around midnight on 28 April, Russian troops of Marshal Rokossovski's Northern Front Army liberated the camp. They treated us well and allowed us some freedom. They moved us out of our filthy accommodations into a former Panzer Officers' Training School where conditions were much improved.

On 14 May an RAF Liaison Officer and driver arrived and negotiated our release. The Russians drove us to the American lines and passed us on to the British lines at Luneburg Heath. Here we were deloused and given new clothes and wonderful meals. On 19 May we were flown back to the UK. We returned to Canada on the SS Louis Pasteur. In England I learned that our skipper, F/0 Denys Street, had been murdered by the Gestapo following the mass escape from Stalaguft III in March of 1944.

Thinking back over my time in the service and as a POW, I realize my best memories of those days are of the fine people I was privileged to be with and I am happy to say some of them are here in Victoria as members of the Aircrew Association.

The following four letters were received by Mrs. R.J. Taylor, my mother, in the months following my capture and imprisonment. They were written by Sir Arthur Street, the Under Secretary of State, Air Ministry, and are therefore of considerable historical and human interest.

FIRST LETTER
31st March 1943. Dear Mrs. Taylor,
You will have heard the sad news that the Lancaster, of which your son was Air Gunner, is missing on the raid on Berlin on the night of 29/30 March. My son, Denys, was her captain and I would like, for my own part -

and I know that it would be in accordance with his wishes - to send you a word of sympathy in our common misfortune.

We must not, of course, abandon hope. The gallant crews on this raid had to fly through some of the worst weather they have had for weeks. Clouds, thick with ice, were banked up over the North Sea and our pilots had to climb almost the whole way to get over them. There were hail and rain and many aircraft ran into electric storms.

In such weather as this, it is quite possible that the crew of the aircraft in which you and I have a personal and anxious interest, had to bale out before reaching the target or on their way back. Let us hope, then, that we may have better news in course of time. We know that Air Force prisoners are well-treated.

My wife, who has a sure instinct in these things, is convinced that they are safe. And I would add this. Those who are competent to judge have always rated my son very high as a pilot. He was capable and efficient and just the sort of boy to get his crew down safely, if airmanship and coolness and courage count for anything. Moreover, he loved his crew and their welfare was always his first concern.

So I beg of you to hold fast to such hope as there is and I pray that God will keep you brave and strong to face the anxious time that lies ahead of us.

If they are safe, we must not expect news for two or three months. I will see that you are immediately informed if any news reaches us here and I should be glad if you would let me know if you hear anything at any time.

I am writing a similar letter to the next-of-kin of all the members of my son's crew.

Yours very sincerely,
(signed) A.W. Street.

SECOND LETTER
23rd. April, 1943. Dear Mrs. Taylor,

You will now have received the good news which reached us through the International Red Cross Committee this morning that your son, Sergeant Taylor, is a prisoner-of-war. All the crew of the aircraft are prisoners-of-war, my son included, and so far as we know they are all uninjured. It will be some time before we hear from the boys themselves what exactly happened to them, but I cannot but feel that my son, as Captain of the aircraft, must have done a good job at the critical moment in getting them all down safely. If I hear any further news, I will let you know and it would be good of you to keep me similarly informed. If there is any way in which I can be of assistance to you, please let me know.

When you write to your son, as you will now be able to do, please make no mention of me or of my position here. It is better that the Germans should not know that my son is in their hands. I am pretty sure that he will not tell them himself who he is and I do not think that his crew had any inkling of it.

Yours sincerely,

(signed)    A.W. Street

P.S. It follows from what I have said in the last paragraph of my letter above that it would be inadvisable to give any publicity, even in Canada, to the letters I have written to you. I am sure that I can rely on you to refrain from giving any information about them to the Press because of the risk of the information getting to the enemy. We have reason to know that the Germans watch the Canadian newspapers with great care from day to day. AWS.

## THIRD LETTER

28th April, 1943. Dear Mrs. Taylor,

I have to-day received a letter (undated) from my son in Germany. He says that all is well. He says that they had bad luck, that he held on to the last to make sure that all his crew could get out, and then only just managed to make it himself. He also says that they completed their mission, which means that they baled out on their return journey. We shall have to wait some time yet before we know what forced them down.

If you hear anything about their experiences, it would be good of you to let me know.

Yours sincerely,

(signed) A.W. Street.

## FOURTH LETTER

4th July, 1943. Dear Mrs. Taylor,

A day or two ago I received a further letter from my son who is a prisoner-of-war in Germany. It was dated May 20th. I thought you would like to have this extract from it:-

I cannot obviously tell you the story of how I became a POW till later, but we were shot up and despite all our efforts, I had to give the order to bale out. I saw all the crew out, then jumped myself, and you will be pleased to hear that they are all safe and well. They were all glorious and behaved with great fortitude. I wonder if Father would be so kind as to write a letter to their next-of-kin on my behalf saying they are all O.K. and were absolutely grand.....

Yours sincerely,

(signed) A.W. Street.

*Following years of detective work, the RAF Special Investigation Branch tracked down the Gestapo murderers and brought them before the court, where they were tried and found guilty. The full story of this investigation and its legal outcome are set out in Allan Andrew's book "Exemplary Justice". Ed.*

# AFTER THE BATTLE

With the onset of the Cold War, the initial reductions in RCAF manpower were reversed and the Service began to re-equip with modern aircraft and weapons. In 1949, NATO (North Atlantic Treaty Organisation) committed Canada and the US to supply land, sea, and air forces in support of a free Europe. Jets such as Vampires and Meteors replaced Spitfires and Mustangs, and these were soon replaced by F86 Sabres and Hunters in the early 1950s.

Soviet bombers could reach Canada and the US. To counter this threat and that of intercontinental missiles later on, the two countries signed the NORAD (North American Air Defence Command) agreement in 1958. Three lines of early warning radar were built across northern, central and southern Canada. RCAF squadrons were re-equipped with CF100 all-weather fighters, later replaced with supersonic CF101s, the Voodoo.

Soviet nuclear submarines could remain submerged and operative for months carrying missiles with nuclear warheads of far reaching capability. The RCAF countered with large, long-range anti-submarine aircraft with crews of fifteen to eighteen and modern electronic equipment to detect and destroy submarines.

Throughout the Cold War technology advanced rapidly. Jet engines became extremely powerful; planes climbed at incredible rates and flew at supersonic speeds. Aerial dogfights were replaced by air-to-air missiles of great accuracy and capability. In emergency, crews used ejection seats to shoot them up and out safely, even from ground levels on take-off or landing. The ever-increasing operational demands on aircrew were beyond human capability, and computers took over many of their duties.

Cockpit pressurization and weather radar coupled with jet power gave pilots a weapon against violent thunderstorms; they could avoid them or fly over. Avionics (aviation electronics) provided accurate navigation and approach systems; static free Ultra High Frequency radio; on board programming of direction, speed, altitude, and instrument approach landings and more.

In a few short years RCAF aircrew graduated from helmet and goggles, the restrictions of bad weather, and limitations of the internal combustion engine to highly trained, all-weather, jet-professionals. It was a fascinating transition.                    *Don Walker & Doug McLaughlin.*

# AFTER THE BATTLE
## CONTRIBUTORS

# HUGH YOUNG

*Hugh was born in Winnipeg in 1927 and in 1949 took a degree in mechanical engineering at the University of Manitoba. After graduation he went straight to Avro Canada at Malton, Ontario. After a two-year apprenticeship in the company's training programme for graduate engineers, he joined the experimental flight test department in 1951. His test-flying career as engineer, observer and surveyor was spent with both the Canadian and English Avro companies on military types and with the Air Registration Board in England on civil aircraft for military use.*

*He left aviation in 1959 and spent twenty-five years in vehicle safety, along the way writing the Canada Motor Vehicle Safety Regulations. He is retired and lives in Victoria.*

## Tales My Log Book Tells

A t the time I joined Avro Canada at Malton in 1949, the company (formerly the wartime Victory Aircraft Ltd. building Lancasters) was working on two designs. The first was a 30-passenger medium range four-jet airliner. The Jetliner, as it was christened, made its first flight in August 1949, a mere two weeks after the maiden flight of the de Havilland Comet in England (the world's first jet airliner) and *five full years ahead* of the American prototype Boeing 707.

In a macabre prevision of the ultimate fate of the Arrow (a much later supersonic fighter also from Avro) the only Jetliner built was cut up at the insistence of our wise leaders in Ottawa, lest future generations of young Canadians grasp what this country was, and is, capable of. Forty years would pass before the appearance of the next Canadian jetliner, the Canadair Regional Jet.

The other design, the first prototype of which was in final assembly at the time of my apprenticeship, was the CF-100 all-weather fighter with two Rolls-Royce Avon (later Avro-designed Orenda) jet engines. During the first retraction tests on the prototype CF-100 in the assembly bay with the aircraft, 18101, up on jacks, the nosewheel leg fairing in the retracted position did not lie flush with the skin ahead of it. The foreman, Bert Quinn, used a pencil to show me how to cut a piece of sheet alloy and use my imagination to fair it in. A draftsman produced a drawing of it and every CF-100 built had "my piece" under the nose; I have always been proud to shown it to my friends.

The first flight of the prototype CF-100 was on 19 January 1950; thus, I was on the scene at the very beginning of Avro's flight test programme. However, I made my early test flights with Avro in the comparative comfort of the Jetliner which, after all, had been designed to be comfortable. The Jetliner was a significant aeronautical improvement on the North Star and Avro paid me for flying in it while enjoying the quick and quiet of it all. The CF-100 was a whole new world.

Aspiring CF-100 flight-test engineers received all of fifteen minutes of hangar time in the back seat as a sufficient introduction to the ejection seat, the safety pin, the parachute, and the oxygen mask. Wild exaggeration? No, not really. As the Experimental Flight Test Department grew in size, all our neophyte engineers took their first flight "cold turkey". This, then, was the sum total of my basic training when my first flight in the CF-100 came round.

I happened to be the first flight test engineer to take the back seat of 18103, the first Mk 2, on its ninth flight. Don Ridler, one of the senior engineers, ushered me up the ladder, saw that I was facing forward and not sitting on my oxygen mask, and left me at the mercy of Peter Cope (one of the company test pilots). My first CF-100 flight, as was always the case with our greenhorns, required only perfunctory observations to be recorded by me, although Peter had a full briefing to work through.

After our "landing" back at Malton, Peter commented that although the airspeed indicator reading had been correct, he had thought at the time that the approach seemed slower than normal. It was. When Peter flared (pulled back on the stick) for the landing the right wing stalled and dropped, and we arrived on the starboard wheel, flap and wing tip, damaging the latter two. In the back seat, overwhelmed by the whole experience, I was aware only of an almighty crash and I remember asking myself if I would ever get used to this sort of life. The subsequent investigation located a misconnection to the airspeed indicator, which had caused 18103's speed on the approach to be significantly lower than it should have been. Well, so much for cool detachment and objectivity on the first flight.

Like me, all our new engineers would go haring off on their early assignments, innocent of any idea what to expect. This remains with me as one of two lasting memories of the experimental hangar. The other is the complete rapport that existed between pilots, flight test engineers, and the respective ground crews of each aircraft. One flight was delayed because I dropped a pencil in the rear cockpit and it rolled under the ejection seat out of reach. Although the engines were running and we were about to taxi out, I had no hesitation in informing Jan Zurakowski (ex-RAF, a renowned Polish test pilot known world-wide as "Zura") of the problem. Engines had to be shut down while crew chief Curly Ridley's men removed the seat and retrieved the offending pencil.

Not a word of reproach from anyone, but it didn't happen again. I spent 1952 at the parent Avro Company's flight test section at Woodford Aerodrome, Cheshire.

Back at Malton by the end of 1952, a lot of CF-100 flying ensued on Mk3 18120 with Zura, including climbs to a maximum of 42,000 feet. An indicated Mach number of 0.90 in level flight was attained, and 18120 was flown with long-range tip tanks for the first time on flight 31. This flying occupied March through May 1953.

The flight of 2 June 1953 was the most strenuous I had during my five years on the CF-100. To mark this day, Coronation Day, the Brampton Flying Club had organized an air show and the company had agreed to provide an aircraft. Coincidentally, I had some handling tests to do with Zura on 18120; these would be completed in time for Zura to get back and take the show in a production aircraft. We were no sooner airborne than Curly Ridley radioed that the production aircraft had a snag, and could Zura do the show in 18120? Zura insisted that he had too much fuel on board 120, making the aircraft too heavy for aerobatics.

There was Curly on the ground sweating bullets, Zura squeaking away into his mike apparently being awkward (anyone who ever heard Zura transmitting will agree he literally squeaked into the mike), and I in the back seat chuckling to myself because I knew what Curly didn't: Zura was burning off fuel just as fast as he could–full power at one hundred feet altitude. I was in for the ride of my life.

I remember the first low pass towards a grass field, and then Zura rolled inverted and I found myself hanging in my straps like a pendulum. Heaven knows how you fly an airplane like that. After that my world toppled. At one point, the Brampton Flying Club was revolving slowly in plan view but dead ahead, i.e. we were going vertically straight down. Zura did some tail slides (by closing both throttles in a vertical climb until the aircraft stopped and slid backwards). This later became a commonplace air show demonstration among the pilots, and would kill Glen Lynes (another company pilot). Zura then did the only falling leaf I ever was to experience in any aircraft, a sort of extreme alternating side-to-side sideslip. The airflow must have been mostly sideways across the canopy because there was a very loud swooshing noise I had never heard before, nor have heard since. In fact, we did everything but spins.

It was Don Rogers who later introduced me to spins on a production aircraft, checking spin recovery. A uniform rate of rotation was accompanied by pitching between nose on the horizon (or just above) to about 45° nose-down. The spin did not worsen as the number of turns increased, recovery was normal, and the general behaviour docile throughout. On at least one occasion Zura spun through some 20,000 feet as a convenient way of losing height between tests.

Glen Lynes also employed unconventional methods of getting through a briefing quickly. I had noticed that rate-of-roll tests always seemed to be done solo, and more from curiosity than necessity I took one such flight with Glen. The briefing called for 360° rolls in each direction at a specified series of speeds and altitudes. Well! Glen did the rolls, which were bad enough, but rather than give the Charlie in the back seat time to breathe between each test, he killed our speed with successive tight turns of several G, by this means arriving at the next lower test speed. This got through the briefing quite quickly and used up the flight test engineer even more quickly. I had no further curiosity about rate-of-roll testing after this.

Another CF-100 in which I spent a lot of time was 18187, one of the first Mk 4s. Our Chief Test Pilot, Don Rogers, and I carried out extensive icing trials during the first six months of 1954 to prove the electrically heated leading edge de-icing. This involved using the full endurance of the aircraft, and on the weekend of 8/9 May 1954 we flew a total of 11 hours 25 minutes in four flights; the longest of which was three hours.

One of our icing trips from Malton included a planned overnight stop at St. Hubert. During the outbound flight from Malton, busy gathering ice, the radio compass went unserviceable, leaving only the stand-by compass on the windscreen frame; this could best be described as only slightly accurate. Not to worry. Don raised a friendly tower somewhere that gave us impeccable courses to fly, until it became evident that the tower had been tracking a T-33, leaving us not quite lost but not at St. Hubert either. Don's voice betrayed no particular emotion, but he must have been having a baby because we landed straight in and the next morning Don was informed that dipping the tanks disclosed a final fuel state that would not have permitted even one circuit.

The squadron at St. Hubert put 18187 inside for the night. They were equipped with Mk 3s and had never seen a Mk 4 before, and their hospitality turned out to have a darker side. Don went off in search of friends while I hit the sack early, but all the while the squadron's pilots, hearing of the new arrival, drifted into the hangar for a look of anticipation. And then, during the evening, a Funny Thing happened.

There were some significant differences between the squadron's Mk 3s and the new Mk 4 in such matters as cockpit layout and various systems controls. Diligent application to these differences by some bright spark resulted in one of the engines running up to ground idle inside the hangar; not only that, they couldn't find out how to shut it down. A tractor towed the whole sensation out into the night air, where eventually peace was restored. Don and I were told about it the next morning at breakfast.

My own time on these icing trials totalled 81 hours 10 minutes in the course of forty-two flights. It was always a source of awe to me that the biggest Cunims (towering cumulo-nimbus clouds full of freezing moisture) were pitch black inside.

Despite the keenness of the flight test engineers, prudence sometimes dictated a solo test. Zura carried out such a series on the prototype Mk 4, exploring high Mach number dives. The trick was to get the aircraft into the dive as quickly as possible by half rolling and pulling back, starting from the absolute ceiling at which the half roll could be controlled. After a number of cautious dives there came the great moment when Zura rattled the office windows with a genuine sonic bang. To try and put a number to it, Don Whitteley, the senior flight test aerodynamicist, designed special instrumentation for the auto-observer (a camera recording a dozen or more instrument readings in flight) and a fellow engineer, Ralph Waechter and I stayed up past midnight doing the calculations, eventually arriving at a figure a mere whisker over Mach 1. With the bang to back us up, we had complete confidence in the calculated result--the first "made-in-Malton" supersonic bang.

Towards the end of my time on the CF-100, Peter Cope and I carried out target-towing trials on two specially modified Mk4s, using RCAF Trenton as our base. The winch with its drum of cable was installed in the gun bay in the belly, and all the winch controls were in the rear cockpit. The drogue target had to be jettisoned for each landing because the power of the winch was insufficient to pull it back in. A butterfly cutter was released to slide down the cable and cut the drogue free, and only the cable reeled back in. Peter and I persevered, enjoying a service Christmas and New Year at Trenton, and in due course proved the installation.

My last flight in the CF-100 was on 13 April 1955 with Zura in 18188. Later that year I left Avro and spent the next 4½ with the Air Registration Board in England, engaged on airworthiness test flying.

There was one flight I made that had no military connection, although it was in a very quick little jet and illustrates well the wilder shores of experimental test flying.

Hugh Kendall was a Canadian who went to England in the mid-30s and joined Miles Aircraft at Woodley Aerodrome, in the days when all that was required to build a light aeroplane was little more than a carpenter's level, a coping saw and a sharp plane. Pre-war, he had been approved for the design, construction and certification flying of aircraft. He was a one-man company. These approvals were grandfathered by ARB to continue after the war. The SK-1 was a joint venture with J.N. Somers, a businessman, to bring the jet age to British air racing as exemplified by the annual King's Cup race. It was a tiny single-seat aeroplane, span 22 feet length 20 feet powered by a Turbomeca Palas I, giving it a maximum speed of 332 mph. The turbojet engine was located on top of the fuselage, above the shoulder wing, and it had a vee tail and a retractable bicycle undercarriage.

It was built on the far side of Woodley Aerodrome, near Reading, in a dilapidated hangar, a feature of which was a roof that rested on top of the hangar door when closed. In order to move the aeroplane in and out with the door open, the roof had to be supported by a temporary inverted kingpost and guy wires that protruded downward into the door opening. This may have been why the SK-1 had a vee tail, to clear the king post!

The design surveyor at the Board was concerned about carbon monoxide contamination entering the cockpit from the engine, and I was assigned to organize a breathalyser sort of thing to take air samples in flight. I duly turned up and was met on the hard standing by Hugh Kendall, with parachute at the ready. I was not offered a 'chute, but being well brought up did not mention the matter; after all, it was a single-seater, or so I thought. When we reached the aeroplane I saw that there was a tiny space behind the pilot, just large enough to take anyone able to squeeze in, intended for carrying an engineer to races. This explained the absence of a 'chute for the surveyor. While I was settling myself in with the breathalyser, a pair of hands reached down and bolted into place a timber like a 2 x 4 with forgings at each end, hard down across my thighs. The fitter explained that this was the front spar. This made me feel better about the chute, but only for a moment, because I really wasn't much better off. I sought solace in the Observer's Creed: "In for a penny, in for a pound."

We taxied into wind, Hugh Kendall opened the tap, and the little aeroplane lunged forward across the greensward, quickly soaring into the air but only for several seconds, and then settling back onto the grass. With speed building up, we again took to the air and again returned to earth. I had a good view forward over Hugh Kendall's shoulder and noted with interest–quickening to concern–that the hedge appeared to be getting larger. Take-off number three was consistent with numbers one and two except at much higher speed–a brief flight of a few seconds duration and then a reassuring return to mother earth. By the time take-off number four was essayed–still in the original marathon but correspondingly faster–the little aeroplane had caught the hang of it and off we went.

As we passed through fifty feet I asked Hugh Kendall what that was all about. It transpired that the rearward movement of the stick was excessive, and the stop wanted moving forward a bit; full up elevator caused the tailplane to stall. Hugh Kendall continued, "It's nothing to worry about, though. It only happens on take-off."

The flight was a delight, a very smooth, slippery aeroplane. The carbon monoxide contamination was nil and my glass in the local pub after landing was unusually satisfying. Another type for my logbook.

My experimental test-flying career spanned 7 years 10 months, 358 flights in eighty-one different types or marks, totalling 502 hours 15 minutes. My choice of flight test after my apprenticeship had been deliberate: I was too young for the war, went ape at the thought of flying, and had a strong sense of a debt owed. In retrospect, two impressions remain indelible. The first is that although I had a private licence, I would never have made a professional pilot. Pilots are meant to have good reactions and test pilots the right reactions. I had no reactions at all; I was happy as a clam flying in anything with anyone.

And as I write this, I am caught by the second impression in the light of my reading of other stories in this volume coupled with all that I had learned about handling characteristics, namely the courage of wartime pilots and their confidence–typically having a minimum of relatively benign training–that their aircraft was "up to it" in terms of flying qualities. This was frequently not the case; witness the Halifax rudder over-balance. Geoff Howitt, one of the Board's pilots, had flown Mosquitos during the war and had an opportunity to fly one again for a special category C. of A. It didn't even begin to look at Civil Airworthiness requirements.

Inevitably, the moment came when the thought occurred to me for the very first time that there might be an element of risk in earning a living this way and, slowly going broke with inflation in England anyway, it seemed like a good idea to leave flying and return to Canada--but sometimes I wonder.

# JIM PARKER

*Jim was born in Calgary on 14 July 1946. He enlisted in the RCAF in 1964 (through Royal Roads Military College in Victoria) and graduated with a Chemical Engineering degree in 1968. Over the next twenty-seven years, Jim completed three tours on Trackers and Twin Hueys, served with the Personnel Group, was Zone Commander for Recruiting in Western Canada, and Registrar at RRMC until retirement in 1995.*

## Memories of A Peacetime Integration Pilot

My 32-year military career, which spanned the mid-sixties to the mid-nineties, began and ended in the same place: in Victoria, at Royal Roads Military College. In the middle ground was a grand circuit, living and flying over most of our fair land. I lived in all our provinces except PEI and Newfoundland. I received my wings (and my bride) wearing the distinctive blue Royal Canadian Air Force uniform, wore a "jolly green jumper" as one of Hellyer's hounds for the better part of twenty years, finished my active military service back in the blue uniform of the nineties Air Component-CF, and wore a dark blue suit with an Air Force lapel pin for the last few years of my career. I wore air force wings, but did all my operational flying for the navy and the army.

Somewhere in my readings about airplanes, pilots, and war, some author defined airline flying as roughly ninety-nine per cent boredom and one-percent stark raving terror. The same ratio worked about right for me. With 3500 hours of flying, that worked out to 35 hours of "really interesting stuff." Most of the following story is devoted to describing bits and pieces of those long 35 hours; the short-and-not-so-sweet bursts of adrenalin when my heart pounded in my throat or I challenged my version of immortality.

My flying training in Borden progressed smoothly and most of us graduated with the normal 25 to 30 hours of flight time. Then it was off to Moose Jaw for the next phase of our flying, which involved about 150 hours of flying on the basic Tutor jet aircraft. I received my first short dose of one-percent-terror, occasioned by an unpredicted entry into a full spin on my fourth solo trip.

Just before we started learning basic aerobatics, we went up with an instructor who demonstrated a few spin entries and recoveries, just in case we blundered into one on our early solos. Then it was off into lessons learning rolls, loops, cloverleafs, rolls-off-the-top, etc. After each dual trip we also had a solo trip to practice what we'd just learned.

So this intrepid student roars off on his solo flight after a great basic aerobatics lesson, does a few circuits, and heads out into the blue yonder. After basic loops and rolls he does a little slow flying and then notices that time is getting rather tight. So it's up gear and flaps, power up, and turn for base setting 30 degrees of bank on an attitude indicator (which of course is precessed out of its mind after loops and rolls.) Snap!

Suddenly the world is turning, turning, and the altimeter is unwinding, unwinding. OK, I know what this is. Power off, full opposite rudder, centralise control stick, and –judder, judder, snap! Now the world is spinning, spinning, whirling around in the opposite direction. OK, try it again. By now the altimeter is getting near ten grand and I'm getting rather concerned.

We'd been briefed that if we were down to 12,500 feet, in a spin and not in control, punching off the canopy could sometimes stabilise the aircraft. Well, I don't particularly like the thought of flying around with no canopy in –40° air, so I'll try it again. Full opposite rudder, centralise the stick, and the aircraft slowly stops spinning, almost starts to fly; then judders and snap! Now I'm right back where I started, spinning spinning, down, down, down. Only I'm now a lot closer to the ground; Old Wives Lake is about 2500 feet ASL (above sea-level).

The briefing had also decreed that if we went through 9500 feet and were still not in control of the aircraft, we should eject. I'm at that decision height now.

So as I'm dropping through 9000, I decide to make one more try. Now I'm talking to this chunk of metal that is stubbornly refusing to obey me. "One more time, beastie, and I leave via the nylon escalator!" Full opposite rudder, centralise the stick, and wait. This time the Tutor stops spinning, judders (my heart's up under my tongue), and then starts flying properly and quickly accelerates up to safe speeds. Oh heavenly bliss! Back to the base, call for a full stop landing, and get this crate back on the ground while still trying to act calm, cool and collected.

I guess I looked white as a sheet, because one of my fellow student pilots, also just walking into the blister, took one look at me, asked, "What in hell happened to you?" and towed me off to the instructor pilot who was monitoring all of us that day. I got a good blast for spinning through both canopy-fire and ejection altitudes, but it was a tempered blast, modified by the fact that I'd scared the bejabbers out of myself.

I was posted to twin-engined Expeditors in Portage la Prairie to become a multi-engine pilot. The training was fairly uneventful. Our only real excitement came in the late stages of the course, after we had mastered most flying techniques. My mutual partner and I were off on a navigation trip late one summer afternoon. Suddenly a line of thunderstorms rolled onto the base, and we were far enough away that we didn't get back before the first big black cloud was close enough to home to really stir up the winds and make the flying exciting.

By this time we'd already faced some pretty good crosswinds and knew what techniques were required. By mutual agreement it was to be my landing. However, just in the roundout, as the wings were jumping and the gusts were hammering us, my buddy decided that I needed some help and glommed onto the control stick. I was rather busy at the time, but not too busy to swipe him swiftly between the eyes with a backhand when he started to "help" me out. I obviously got his attention, and he let go of the stick. The remainder of the landing was rough, as we bounced down the runway until the speed bled off.

Taxiing was also a challenge, since the gusts made the plane want to "weathercock" into the wind.

Our 120 hours on "bug smashers" accumulated quickly and once again it was time to look forward to new pastures. This time we really didn't know what to expect, but we did know that the selection came from our favourite HQ again, and whatever the selection was would probably determine much of our future career. And sure enough, two weeks before grad, in came the posting message. On the fateful day we were all called into the Commandant's office and told that a new Tracker course had just been generated by our favourite HQ in Ottawa and we were all going to Dartmouth NS to fly Trackers. Dartmouth? Where's that? Trackers? We'd never even heard of Trackers. I was presented with my wings and I set off for Nova Scotia to find out what was up with this Tracker thing.

The Tracker was a twin-engined anti-submarine aircraft designed to be flown and operated off a carrier. It held a crew of four: pilot, co-pilot (really a navigator and tactician), and two back seat electronic operators. One of the back seats handled radar, electronic counter-measures gear, and radio duties. The other monitored the radio signals from sonobuoys and controlled the MAD gear (Magnetic Anomaly Detection–a device that detected a submarine). The Tracker came complete with folding wings, a hook for carrier landings and stops, crappy brakes, a radar dome under the belly which was lowered to do a radar scan, and a MAD boom which pushed out the tail of the aircraft. It had two huge nine cylinder, air-cooled, Wright single-speed supercharged 1820-horse radial engines; we could climb faster on one engine than some twins could with both straining. Of course the asymmetric thrust on single engine was awesome, and there was a big control system whereby nearly the whole tailplane became a rudder if one suddenly needed to fly on only one engine. The main thing in a emergency situation was to quickly engage the Single-Engine Rudder Assist, one of the things which was drilled into us on the conversion course until it became an automatic response.

After close to two years of co-piloting, it was finally our course's turn to get tested to be Crew Commanders and pick up our own crew. The last year and a half on VS880 went very quickly and I remember only two real frights. The first happened one dark and stormy night when I had to crew a mixed group (not my normal foursome) and we were paired up with the Commanding Officer (CO) of the squadron. We were to fly out 100 miles south of Shearwater to do some real submarine tracking with a target submarine. There was a cloud layer that extended from about 500 feet to 3000 feet above the ocean. Above this cloud deck it was clear to the moon, and below it was a 500-foot zone that had clear visibility but was dark indeed. To get our sub work done we had to get down near the surface of the water so that we could see our smoke floats and keep our bearings. We talked to the target sub, gave him the limits for the training exercise and then he dove. We were to do a simple 30-minute MAD tracking exercise with the two aircraft doing a racetrack pattern over top of the sub.

With two airplanes you could be back "on top" every 30 to 40 seconds, and we soon had a line of 6 to 8 smoke floats marking positions where we had sensed the submarine. The line of smoke floats had just started to jig to the right, indicating that the sub had made a turn, when my co-pilot looked up from his plot and said: "What the hell?"

As I rolled out of the turn at the back of the smoke floats, I too could see the wingtip and anti-collision lights of the other aircraft right in front of me. They should have been downwind and out of sight, but instead were getting bigger and coming down the smoke line from the other end. Obviously the CO or his co-pilot had lost track of what was happening, and they were now flying right at us, at our height. I didn't know what to do. Should I turn right and hope that he'd do likewise, or turn left, or what? Finally I decided that the only really safe manoeuvre was down, and we were already at 100 feet over the water. So I cut the distance to the water in half, and both the co-pilot and I watched as the green wingtip light of the other aircraft crossed directly above our heads. I pushed up the power, climbed into the goo, burst out the top of the deck into the moonlight, called the CO and said that I'd lost contact with the surface. My co-pilot wasn't very impressed with my go-to-50-feet decision but after I explained my reasoning, he agreed. It really was the only safe way to go with a disoriented crew coming right at you, and I knew exactly where the water was, thanks to the bobbing smoke floats.

Slowly our breath returned to normal and just then the sub called as she surfaced to finish the exercise. Our crew decided that one attempt to kill us was enough for that night, so we broke off the exercise and flew home. We met the CO and his crew later that night, and his co-pilot apologised for allowing the screwup. By the time he looked up from his plot, there we were coming directly at them and he was afraid to say anything to the CO, who just froze as the two airplanes closed on each other. Good thing I moved 'cause he sure didn't take any evasive action at all.

When it was time for our course to get posted out of VS880. I was sent right next door to the training squadron to teach other pilots how to fly the Tracker. My best scare while instructing came from my "best ever" student.

I was engaged in one of the most boring trips of the whole syllabus–Basic Instruments Technique, turns, climbs, descents, etc. My ace student was having no problems, so I told him to take a break from flying "under the bag", to drop down on the water, and to do a photo pattern around a Canadian Coast Guard cutter that was transiting Mahone Bay. Down we went to 100 feet. My student set up nicely and flew by the left side of the ship, then rolled on 60 degrees of bank and didn't apply any back pressure whatever. Of course the nose dropped instantly and we plummeted like a rock. I hollered "I have control", grabbed the stick, jammed up the power, and yanked the stick back as hard as I could. I rolled out level and felt the judder and buffeting as we nearly stalled. To this day I don't know how close to the water we were when we levelled off. After my heart stopped pounding, we did it all again. His technique was flawless the second time, and my hair was just a little greyer by the end of the trip.

I did have a few other excitements. Near the end of my tour, on a long-range navigation trainer, we had an engine explode and disconnect itself completely from the propeller. For the last ten miles to landing the only thing holding the prop on the front of the engine was the pressure of the air blowing past the prop as the plane flew through the sky. Since we had just completed a long, long patrol, which involved a search 250 miles off the coast of Nova Scotia, we considered ourselves very lucky indeed that the thing exploded just before we landed. If it had blown up an hour before it did, we'd likely have all gone for a swim.

Before I knew it the tour that I thought I'd hate was up. I did a tour as Assistant Registrar back at Royal Roads, then back to flying.

I was posted to fly the Twin-Huey Helicopter, designated as a UTTH-Utility Tactical and Transport Helicopter. It was a joy to fly for a jack-of-all-trades pilot. You could fly twenty days in a month and never fly the same type of trip twice.

It was one of those tactical trips that gave me another brief case of heartburn. Six Light Observation Helos (Kiowas) were acting as recce and path finders, leading three flights of eight Hueys loaded with army troops, hauling them all into a tactical area in a "surprise attack" scenario. It was to be a full live-fire exercise with artillery and tanks, so the briefings were long and elaborate. I was part of a four-plane section that was flying into the drop zone paired with another four-Huey section. We were led in into the landing zones by two of the six Kiowas.

After we loaded the troops, who had live ammo in their weapons, we edged up to the rendezvous to meet our pathfinders. Just after we picked them up, we noticed that the route we were taking into the live fire area wasn't the one that had been briefed. We thought that the pathfinders got updated info after the brief and the routing had been changed. It was a tactical exercise with radio transmissions allowed.

We approached the landing areas, warned the troops to get ready to leap out, and suddenly the other two groups of Huey eight-packs flew right into the same landing zones at the same time, coming at us from the opposite direction. Then the artillery opened up and shells started bursting in the treeline about a thousand yards from where we were. Even inside the aircraft we could feel the shockwaves of the shells raising hell nearby. Suddenly there were little brown helicopters going every which way just trying not to run into each other, desperately avoiding the artillery shell ones. There were 30 choppers in the same small clearing darting here and there, guessing where their chums were turning, 24 heavily loaded with live troops holding live ammo. The 155-mm shells were ripping up spruces, flinging up dirt and digging huge holes far too close for comfort.

Fortunately no one collided. The range safety officer stopped the artillery, and we all broke off back to the loading points. It turned out that our group's pathfinders had just plain screwed up.

I had only one other incident of notable excitement during my "fling wing" flying. I was co-piloting with one of the most experienced pilots in 1O Tactical Air Group. We were headed back to Edmonton after doing some work with the PPCLI Battalion in Victoria, when we hit a rapidly advancing cold front and spent ten long minutes twirling round and round in the midst of a mountain pass, totally out of directional control. The pilot just concentrated on keeping us right side up. Finally the winds calmed a bit and we were able to get down near the ground. We ended up landing in some farmer's corn patch near Lytton; we sat there for about half an hour before the winds fell off enough for us to shut down (the rotor can do some really weird things in super-strong winds). The other aircraft landed on a mountain opening about five miles away and also had to wait about half an hour before it was safe to shut down. I learned a lot about mountain winds on that trip and what they could do to unwary helicopter pilots.

That was the pretty well the end of my flying career. I retired in 1995 as Registrar of Royal Roads.

# DON WALKER

*Born in Ft. William, Ontario, in 1929, Don received a degree in mining engineering in 1951 and joined the RCAF. He completed pilot training and flew Sabres in the Air Division in Europe in the early fifties. Don was posted as a flying instructor on Harvards and then as an advanced instructor on the T33. Following a tour at AFHQ in Ottawa, Don flew the long-range anti-submarine Argus on the east coast. He left the RCAF in 1967, obtained a commission as a British Columbia land surveyor, and was appointed Manager of the Geodetic and Air Operations Section. Don retired in 1994.*

## Those Were the Days, My Friend

I was in my first year engineering at the University of Manitoba in Winnipeg in late 1947 or early 1948 when I heard a radio announcer telling us, in an excited voice, that there was a jet plane flying over the city. He was trying to keep us informed as to the movements of the plane, but it was obviously a hopeless task. People rushed out of their houses to get a look at the latest in aircraft technology–a plane without a propeller. This plane was one of the few jets in Canada at the time and was probably either a Vampire or a Meteor as a few had been undergoing evaluation at the Winter Experimental Establishment in Edmonton.

Two years later I was in residence at McGill University in Montreal. One of my friends in the residence was a pilot on 401 (F)

Squadron, a reserve squadron in Montreal. He flew Vampires on weekends and made a point of flying over the residence; sort of "showing off". This was more than I could bear and I made up my mind to join the RCAF after my graduation, rationalizing that there would probably be another war soon and I would be better off in the air than on the ground. The gods favoured me. I was selected for pilot training at Gimli and after getting my "wings", followed by advanced flying and pilot gunnery training on the Harvard, I was delighted to be posted to the Operational Training Unit (OTU) at Chatham, New Brunswick, for operational training on the F86 Sabre.

In August 1952, when I was en route to Chatham, I had a one-hour layover in Montreal before the train continued eastbound. It was during this hour that I saw a Sabre for the first time. It was flying about 3000 feet above the city and just streaked across the sky. I was very excited as I thought that in a month I would be flying one of those. These were the early days of jet flying in Canada. Flying jets was glamorous; the pilots were referred to as "jet pilots".

I arrived at Chatham on the 22nd of August and four days later I had my first flight in a jet aircraft, the T33. As there were no dual-seat Sabres, we received about a dozen flights in the T33 prior to taking a Sabre up for the first time. The T33s were borrowed from the USAF; some had ejection seats, some didn't. Bill Gould, my instructor, was short and stocky, so for better rear seat vision he always requested the ones without the ejection seats. Bill had flown fighters in WWII and had the distinction of flying the last RCAF flight of the war in May 1945. After the initial checkout on the Sabre and some familiarization flights we were handed over for operational training. F/O "Tiny" Thomson, one of our instructors, had an interesting habit. We flew in formations of four aircraft with Tiny as the leader and three trainees. Tiny would start his aircraft and after obtaining taxi clearance from the air traffic controller would move out without waiting for the others. He would then take off. If you were not able to catch up with him prior to take off you had to wait until he turned then you could "cut the corner". You certainly learned to do the pre-take-off checks quickly. In jet aircraft the power output of the engine was related to the pilot as "percent-power". Power for take-off was 100%. After take-off the power could be reduced to whatever figure the pilot wanted. Tiny would reduce it only to 97% for the remainder of the flight so the others flying formation on him did not have a lot of extra power to catch up. You concentrated hard on remaining in position at

392

all times. We called him 97% Thomson. Tiny died in a Sabre accident in January 1953, less than a month after I finished the course.

The Sabre was very sensitive; moving the control column a few inches would result in a fast roll. You could always tell the pilots doing their first few flights–their wings would wobble from side to side after take-off as they over-compensated on the controls. The Sabre was to become a classic fighter aircraft, the type that pilots would remember fondly for the rest of their lives. It was a beautiful aircraft to fly with a good cockpit layout and great visibility. It was designed by North American Aviation in the late 1940s and continually modified into the 1950s. Canadair of Montreal produced the aircraft under licence for the air forces of Canada, Great Britain, and Germany with some of those being subsequently turned over to Greece, Italy, Turkey and Pakistan. It is claimed that during the Korean War the Sabre dominated the skies with a kill ratio of 15 to 1 over the Russian Mig15. As the Sabre was a front-line fighter aircraft and the pilot training was not as intensive as it is now, the accident ratio was fairly high. Of the 1815 Sabres built by Canadair, approximately 540 were written off in accidents, resulting in about 200 deaths. The RCAF pilots flew over 925,000 hours in Sabres between 1950 and 1969. We never considered the Sabre a particularly dangerous aircraft to fly, but it did command respect.

After completing the OTU in December 1952, I was assigned to 427 (F) Squadron in St. Hubert, Quebec. The squadron had been re-activated after being disbanded at the end of the war. The squadron leader and the two flight commanders were wartime pilots; the rest of us were post-war and only recently graduated from OTU. The Cold War as at its peak at that time and Canada, as a member of NATO, had committed to establishing an air division in Europe.

The Air Division was to consist of four wings with three squadrons per wing. Two wings were already established, one at North Luffenham, England, and the second at Grostenquin, France. My squadron together with 413 (F) and 434 (F) Squadrons formed the third wing in Zweibrucken, Germany. We were to fly over in March of 1953. The fourth wing would be based at Baden-Sollingen, Germany.

This was a great time to be in the RCAF. Due to the cold war there was a recruiting drive to bring the strength of the air force up to about 50,000 personnel after a post war low of approximately 15,000. Morale was very good, money didn't seem to be too much of a problem, and we were all very optimistic that good times lay ahead. This was the beginning of the golden years for the RCAF.

We set a record for the crossing in March, not for the fastest crossing but for the slowest. It took thirty days; sailing ships did it in less time. We left St. Hubert on Saturday 7 March for Goose Bay, Labrador, left Goose on Saturday 13 March for BW-1 in Greenland, left BW-1 on Saturday 28 March for Keflavik, Iceland, left Kef on Saturday 4 April for Scotland and arrived in Zweibrucken on 7 April. I guess we should not have been surprised as the North Atlantic is not known for good weather at that time of the year, however we did not get any breaks. If I remember correctly, the forecast ceiling for both the departing airport and the destination airport had to be at least 10,000 feet before the Sabres could depart. There were no alternative airports on this route. As we had more pilots than aircraft, the first fifteen pilots reporting to the squadron flew the Sabres. The others made the crossing in a less pleasant but quicker way as passengers in the North (Noisy) Star. I lost out both ways. I was a spare pilot for the Sabres so I accompanied them on the thirty-day adventure as a passenger in a support aircraft. There were few memorable events during the journey; the walk to the glacier in Greenland, the all-day poker games that began right after morning briefing, and the long hours at the bar. On several occasions I was sure I would be called upon to fly a Sabre but all the pilots managed to recover enough by flight time to make the flight, although I am sure that some of them suffered greatly and were very happy to get on the ground again!

For me, the arrival at Zweibrucken marked the beginning of one of the best periods of my life. I was flying an aircraft that was probably the best fighter aircraft in the world and the other pilots on my squadron and in the other squadrons were the best bunch of friends I could have hoped for. It was an exciting time. Although we were at peace there was enough of a threat from behind the iron curtain to give a purpose to our flying. We had better be good–and we were. Beginning in 1958 the best fighter pilots in NATO competed for the coveted Guynemer trophy, named after Georges Guynemer, the great French ace of WWI. There were teams from the RAF, USAF, French, Dutch, and Belgian air forces, flying Mystères, Super Sabres, Hunters, Thunderbirds and of course our Sabres. The Canadians consistently won the competition.

The early days of flying in the Air Division were largely uncontrolled and we were pretty well free to do whatever we wished.

Dogfights were very common and on some days fights which began in the morning would continue till late afternoon. When a flight had to break off to return to base for refuelling it would be replaced with other flights. You could often tell where the fights were as the sky would be covered with contrails as the planes climbed through the contrail layer to reach operational altitude. At other times we would go sightseeing or low flying. As Germany was an occupied country at that time there were no complaints. It was this carefree attitude that got me into a bit of trouble one day. I was leading a flight of three. On the walk to the aircraft I asked the other pilots what they would like to do. One suggested that we visit the dams attacked by the famous Dam Busters of WWII fame. I hastily estimated the direction and flying time. At the appropriate time I descended through the cloud layer and there was a lake with a dam so I guess we had found it. I wasn't so lucky on the return trip. After flying an equal time on the reciprocal heading and letting down through the cloud (mistake!) I was over totally unfamiliar territory. We were getting low on fuel so I called for help and received a vector to the closest base, which happened to be a USAF base. The Americans had two bases close together; one served transports and the other was a fighter base. We arrived over the transport base first but I recognized it and turned away to the fighter base. My number three had lost radio contact and did not realise that there was the fighter base nearby. He was very low on fuel by this time and he told me later that he was very tempted to land at the first base, but as he couldn't contact the tower he decided to follow me although he thought he might have to eject shortly. I had hoped that news of this incident wouldn't get back to base, but that was a false hope—I think the news preceded us.

In February 1954 the Squadron flew to a French Air Force base in Rabat, Morocco, for air-to-air gunnery practice. The political situation was unstable, with the Moroccans struggling for independence and the French reluctant to grant it. We were told to do nothing that would aggravate the situation and in particular not to fly over the native quarters in Rabat. One Sunday morning one of our pilots had just completed a weather check over the range and on the way back did a few passes over those native quarters. Shortly after landing he was confronted by the Officer Commanding the detachment. The next day he was back in Germany and a few days later he was back in Canada and released shortly afterward. The wheels can turn quickly when necessary. There was another incident in Rabat that causes my heart to beat faster whenever I think about it. Two of us decided to walk the several miles from the base to the Atlantic coast. When we arrived at the coast we noticed signs in the field around us but as they were pointing away from us we didn't check them out until we left the field. The signs displayed large skull and crossbones with a message in French that we did not understand but assumed to state that the field had been mined during the war.

I flew the Mark 2 and the Mark 5 Sabre. The Mark 2 had a General Electric engine that produced 5200 pounds of thrust, giving it a maximum sea level speed of 679 mph, a cruise speed of 537 mph, and a service ceiling of 47,100 feet. The Mark 5 had a Canadian produced Orenda engine which resulted in 6500 pounds thrust, increasing the maximum sea level speed to 696 mph, cruise speed to 552 mph and the service ceiling to 50,700 feet. The last version produced was the Mark 6. This was even more impressive with a service ceiling was 54,100. The Sabre was capable of supersonic speed. To go supersonic in the Mark 2 required a very steep dive with full power; the dive in the Mark 5 didn't need to be quite as steep.

These good times came to an abrupt end in July 1954 when I was posted back to Canada to instruct basic flying on the Harvard. The shock of flying such a primitive aircraft after flying the Sabre was difficult to bear. Other pilots from the Air Division were suffering a similar fate; it was obvious that we were very unhappy. I'm sure that the Flying Instructors School was pleased when we finished the course! Fortunately, a year later I was back on jets, this time as an advanced flying instructor on the T33. I became very fond of the T33 but the Sabre remains in my memory as the best of the best.

The pilots who flew the Sabre in the Air Division in Europe in the 50s and 60s have such fond memories of that period that they have formed an organization that keeps them in touch with each other and they have a reunion every 2 years. The organisation is known as SPAADS–Sabre Pilots Association Air Division Squadrons. The last reunion, held at Calgary in 1996, was attended by approximately 750 pilots and their wives. Yes, those were the days.

# DOUG McLAUGHLIN

*After finishing High School Doug joined the RCAF in November 1942. He was sent home on deferred service until early 1943 and was then accepted for aircrew training under the BCATP. Doug received his pilot wings in early 1944 and was posted overseas. He was demobilised in March 1945 and spent four years in civil aviation before rejoining the RCAF in 1950. Following his discharge in 1972 Doug joined Transport Canada and worked with them until retirement in 1989.*

## From Military to Civil Aviation

As a BCATP graduate of 1944 it was too late for me to get into wartime operational flying, or "on ops" as the saying goes. There are neither wartime adventures nor misadventures in this story, only a few post-war reminiscences and reflections.

When I recall the wages paid in the 1930s and the scarcity of jobs, I find it interesting to speculate how life might have evolved for me had there not been a war. The armed forces together with a heated wartime economy altered significantly the way of life for many. No doubt many aircrew who joined up at eighteen or so will think of that period in their lives as being "prime time". The BCATP gave me a future; it trained me as a pilot permitting me to earn a living flying small aircraft post-war. For the unsophisticated young man wartime training was an interesting time; I wouldn't have missed it for anything.

My time in the RCAF certainly was a significant slice of my life. The discipline ("Wakey wakey, rise and shine; grab your socks; Hup-two-three-halt"), the camaraderie (we were a very closely knit bunch) and the joy of living, the interesting revelations of the Medical Officer concerning the physiological impact of certain diseases–all these had an influence on our outlook and possibly modified, and maybe even strengthened, our character.

The code of service discipline was properly leavened by another form of service "social" development. In essentially a male environment we socialized in the canteens and messes. Around the piano we sang "Nellie Dean" and "Down by the Old Mill Stream", favourite standards, though in a harmony not always perfectly executed. Other songs followed although their words have fortunately faded from my mind.

After induction at Manning Depot a course in English, mathematics and physics ensured that candidates were academically qualified for aircrew training. There were many of these War Emergency Training Plans (WETP) across Canada. Among other things we were quickly introduced to the acronym mode that characterizes much of the military and aviation lexicon. In this case the WETP course was followed by ITS, EFTS, SFTS and so on. In 1944 I had finished SFTS training and was overseas bound on the Empress of Scotland.

On disembarking at Greenock we went by rail to Innsworth, Gloucestershire. It was now July 1944 and overseas drafts of RCAF aircrew who previously would have been sent to Bournemouth were now sent to Innsworth. This was because, we surmised, of the Allied landings in Normandy that had begun a month earlier. AFU training continued. Then came good news and bad news. The good news was that pilot casualties to date were fewer than the number of graduates turned out by the BCATP. The bad news was that the surplus pilots would go to St. Athan to be trained as flight engineers on Lancasters and then posted to Bomber Command. As the course progressed we learned that if we did well on operations as flight engineers we could be allowed to do the second tour as pilots. Naive as I was I somehow figured there was condescension in that offer. Nevertheless this very interesting course finished in early 1945; but so did the war.

Returning home in 1945 I discovered that a friend of mine had bought a Piper Cub and a Cirrus Moth and set himself up in Civil Aviation. I straightaway acquired a Limited Commercial Pilot

Licence and began an interesting but low-paid career in civil aviation. In the next five years I flew a variety of light planes for a variety of owners. The pay varied but was consistent in that amounts were not great. In the non-scheduled airline business a fairly common pay scale was $140 a month plus three cents per mile–miles being measured in a straight line on a Transverse Mercator 1:500,000. Among other small types I flew the Seabee.

The Seabee was a most interesting aeroplane. A single-engine four-place amphibian early post-war design, it was an excellent one-person (pilot) plane; a good two-person plane; a fair three-person plane; and in certain circumstances an outright dangerous four-person plane. The problem was its performance on take-off at altitudes above sea level and/or temperatures above 59° F. For example a take-off at maximum all up weight on a cool summer morning would be safe, but when the temperature rose as the day progressed to 75°F the performance fell dramatically. A pilot unaware of the aerodynamic cause of this poor performance would face a dangerous situation. Once airborne it is essential to keep the nose down until the recommended climbing airspeed is reached. This standard procedure can take significant time and distance with a loaded Seabee taking off above sea level on a hot day. Small hills and trees could suddenly assume great significance. My Seabee employer liked to land on the various lakes around south-western New Brunswick. From time to time I was compelled to point out that while we could certainly land on a given lake, the Seabee would not fly us out

*Some years later I discovered in the RCAF trade journal "Flight Comment" that this interesting area of flight was defined as "the area of reverse command". Aircraft performance curves and ground effect were not identified in those days of wartime pilot training. Nor, as I recall, did we spend much time on the more esoteric areas of theory of flight such as increase in stall speeds with increased angle of bank. While sometimes one learned of these obscure elements of flight theory in manuals and occasionally through discussion with more experienced pilot, there were times when we learned the hard way–by bending an aeroplane.*

Seabee flying also extended to Grand Mannan and other Bay of Fundy points where some tough lessons were learned operating from Bay of Fundy swells. Such lessons as: innocent-looking ocean water sometimes ain't. Determine the swells and then take off along them. Better yet, use bodies of water where there are no swells.

Later on in the aviation business I learned about mind set. In 1947 I could not have spelled the term. A routine take-off from the airport turned out not to be routine when I allowed myself to become distracted. A short while later while setting up for a water landing on the Saint John River, it was the presence of a passenger in the rear seat who saved the day and possibly our skins. From the rear seat she suddenly spoke up. "Doug, I don't know if I should say anything but should those wheels be down like that?"

My aircraft maintenance engineer friend and I looked at each other. I said nothing, nor did he. I applied power, left the gear down and landed back on the ground surface at the airport. He and I knew that Seabees executing water landings with gear down simply flipped over. Few, if any, survived such mistakes. Post flight I expressed my gratitude to the lady but did not burden her with the possible outcome had she not spoken up.

In 1950 Canada's participation in NATO cranked up the RCAF aircrew training programme again. They began training navigators, radio officers, and pilots. The pilot training programme was offered to students from Belgium, Denmark, Italy, Norway, United Kingdom and Turkey. To meet the requirement for aircrew staff to handle this commitment the RCAF offered short service commissions to many wartime aircrew. These were interesting times because of Korea and the Cold War. In this post-war RCAF I had many interesting jobs: staff pilot on Dakotas, instructor on Harvards, the usual ground tour in administration, an all-too-short posting to 426 (Transport) Squadron, a tour in Maritime Command on 405 Sqn flying the Argus, and finally finishing up flying Dakotas out of Lahr, Germany, on transport missions. VIP flying was also involved at Lahr and I learned the Transport Command rule covering landings with VIPs: never early; never more than five minutes late.

Governments of two prime ministers interfered with my post-war military flying career. The government of 1963 (John Diefenbaker) cut short my 426 Squadron career by disbanding the squadron; the government of 1971 (Pierre Trudeau) cut short my posting in Germany and my RCAF career extension by changing Canada's participation in NATO. While I hold these PMs responsible I do not hold a grudge. Things did work out for the best and the cold cruel world turned out to be neither so cold nor cruel. After all, I joined Transport Canada and continued, as the saying goes, to live off the government teat.

The Department of Transport, or DOT as it was then called, had numerous areas of work for pilots. For my first three years I was a Civil Aviation Inspector (CAI for acronym addicts) working as a Regulator. This involved monitoring flight-training standards in the industry by flight testing candidates for various flying licences and licence endorsements. We tested each candidate's knowledge of the theories and principles involved in their work. In those pre-computer days we issued pilot licences, instructor and instrument rating endorsements, signing them on behalf of the Minister.

One excellent programme funded by DOT was the Civil Flying Instructors Refresher Course. Over the years this programme influenced considerably the quality of civil flying instruction. DOT inspectors flew with civil instructors to review the effectiveness of their teaching. Civil instructors then flew with each other to exchange and improve instructing techniques. Classroom instruction covered all the in-flight exercises and the flight theory behind them. Throughout this two week course there was much emphasis on how to teach. The atmosphere was non-challenging; it was a concentrated effort to improve teaching methods and to build the academic base an instructor needs to support those flying and teaching skills.

There were many ex–military pilots hired as Civil Aviation Inspectors and many with significant Transport Command experience. One result of this background was the introduction in DOT of instructor training modified from the old RCAF School of Instructional Technique. I think it's safe to say that the influx of the experience of ex-military pilots contributed a great deal to Canada's civil aviation body. But to keep things in perspective I can state that the best instructor and the best training pilot with whom I ever worked were products of the civil aviation system; i.e. they had no military background.

I cannot leave the subject of civil flying without noting the significant changes that have occurred in equipment and cockpit procedures. From the days when captains operated from memorized check lists and were expected to know all aeroplane systems thoroughly, we have moved to a "challenge & response" check list procedure. Today the First Officer calls the check list item and the Captain responds by executing or confirming. From the pre-start checks through in-flight procedures to shutdown–and in any emergency–the check list and company procedures must be followed.

The simplified instrumentation of the 1940s and 1950s has advanced to present day integrated flight systems with flat-screen colour presentation of flight and system data. Not surprisingly the Captain's job has evolved to include "Cockpit Resource Management". These days we read of the automation of space shuttle operations. Might automated airline travel be next?

The policy of equal opportunity for all Canadians was applied vigorously in Transport Canada. In the 1970s women began to appear in the Civil Aviation Inspector ranks. I had taught a couple of women to fly, flight tested many others and, while in Transport Canada, had done conversion-to-type training with five women who came to work as CAIs.

I recall one woman who particularly enjoyed the conversion training on the DC3 and flew it as if she owned it. When I queried her background I discovered she had begun commercial flying as a bush pilot in northern Manitoba. Prior to joining Transport Canada she had flown as captain on the Canso water bomber and also flown the Canadair water bomber. In the 1970s and 1980s more and more women selected commercial aviation as a career. As their numbers and experience increased they upgraded their Private Pilot Licences to Airline Transport Pilot Licence and ultimately flew with the airlines as well as with Transport Canada. A friend of mine is currently a First Officer on the Boeing 767. She has acquired seniority and will soon upgrade to Captain. One day, as the system moves on, a female Captain and her female First Officer will have their performance checked by a female check pilot.

# MICHAEL O'HAGAN

*Michael was born in London, England, in 1924. He joined the RAF in 1940 as an Aircraft Apprentice, training as a wireless operator mechanic. He passed out in 1942 and served on an OTU until posted to Bletchley Park, the centre responsible for decrypting enemy cipher traffic. He was commissioned in 1945 and served on the usual flying stations. Whilst engaged on radar design at the Telecommunications Research Establishment, Great Malvern, he was selected for language training in Mandarin, spent a happy three years at university, and then paid for it all with eight more years back on intelligence and radio warfare posts from which he did not escape until he attended Staff College in 1960. After Staff College, Michael worked at the Air Ministry on future communications for the RAF. He took early retirement in 1964.*

## Intelligence Gathering

It was during the Cold War, about 1954; the Royal Navy carrier HMS Bulwark was about to make a courtesy visit to Stockholm and undertake a bit of electronic reconnaissance on the way. Skyraider aircraft (I think that was the type) equipped with voice and radar receivers would simulate attacks on the Soviet mainland and record the Soviet reaction. The technique had been established in World War II. In the post-war years the RAF did the job from England, Germany, and Cyprus. These operations were the forerunner of the USAF's U-2 missions.

Using airborne receivers we could detect the enemy's radar

signals and determine the point at which we were "seen" and at which air-defence fighters were scrambled. And if we were really lucky, the enemy would switch on his specialized air-defence radars for us to record. There was just one snag: This was to be an operation from a carrier and the Royal Navy didn't have any officers knowledgeable about Soviet radars. So they borrowed me.

I flew on to the carrier from Lossiemouth, a naval air station in Scotland, and thoroughly enjoyed the cruise up through the Skagerrak, down the Kattegat, and into the Baltic. It was when the carrier was approaching the target area that I hit trouble.

The captain of the carrier wanted to sail close to and observe Oland, the long skinny island on the west side of the Baltic. But I wanted the maximum possible flying time on the Soviet side, the coasts of Lithuania and Latvia, then a part of the Soviet empire. It wasn't a fair fight; he was the captain of Her Majesty's aircraft carrier and I was a flight lieutenant.

Hat under arm in what I thought was true naval style, I marched in to see the great man. What followed wasn't so much an argument as a lecture on the privileges of rank and how that was something I should learn if I aspired to the dizzy heights of my lecturer. I would have lost and walked out with my tail between my legs except that this penetration mission had the backing of the Prime Minister. Suffice it to say we steamed up the Soviet side and my name was mud with the august captain.

Flying off a carrier was not the ideal way to gather intelligence. In later years, with the Comet and Canberra as the intercept aircraft, we had adequate navigation facilities and knew our position at the moment of each electronic intercept and we got tolerably good fixes. When flying from a carrier our knowledge of our position was less accurate.

It was all a game of cat and mouse. We were the mice and the Mig's were the cats. The idea was that because we were intercepting the ground control traffic, we would have the advantage of knowing when the Mig's would appear, but as neither the navy pilots nor I spoke Russian, the odds were slightly more even.

When the cats turned up, the Skyraider would drop down to sea level and high-tail it for neutral waters. Returning from one disappointing flight with no sign of Soviet opposition and nothing to record other than early warning radars, we were out of Soviet waters when the carrier suddenly gave the warning, "Bogies approaching from the north". The high-wing monoplanes came in sight and we dived almost to sea level. Three Swedish SAABs passed overhead with what I suppose was a friendly waggle of the wings.

On the homeward voyage the carrier's fighter aircraft conducted routine training flights and the Commander (Air) made it clear to the insignificant flight lieutenant that the Skyraider's task was complete and if O'Hagan wanted to attend the air briefings it would be as a silent observer learning how these things were done in the Senior Service. We duly steamed close to Oland as the captain wished.

The carrier was somewhere off Bornholm as I listened with horror to the day's briefing. The fighters were to fly south, dogleg west over land, and then turn north to rejoin the ship. Out of courtesy to the Commander (Air) I kept my mouth shut until the briefing was over; then I approached him in private:

"That is enemy territory."

"We've had enough of you bloody Air Force types" or words to that effect was the response I got for trying to help. I insisted this was Soviet-controlled territory and ended up being marched in to the captain again. The captain made it clear that he, too, had had enough of me, but he had the grace, or wisdom, to invite the Commander (Air) to display his charts. Good charts they were, probably produced by the Admiralty in time for Jellicoe to do his stuff at Jutland. The land over which the mission was to fly was part of East Germany and Soviet-controlled. I did my best to explain this. "A chart is a chart" is the essence of what I was told.

I was at an impasse. What was I to do? Sit back and wait for the inevitable international incident and perhaps the loss of naval aircrew or violate the strict rules of what Churchill called his ULTRA SECRET?

I asked to speak to the captain alone and produced my map of Soviet radar installations. There they were, right in the path of the proposed flight. I was shown out. Or was it thrown out? The air training exercise flight was cancelled, I was barred from all further air briefings, and as soon as we were within range of Lossiemouth I was flown off the carrier. The captain didn't come to say goodbye.

Back at base I was castigated for showing the captain material he was not entitled to see: "Surely you are aware, Flight Lieutenant, that rank has nothing to do with security clearance." An officer should show initiative, they tell you, but may the Good Lord help you if you do. That's when I realized I'd never become Chief of the Air Staff.

# PETER KEITH-MURRAY

*Born in Bath, Somerset, in 1935, Peter came to Canada and joined the RCAF in June 1954. He was commissioned in 1965 and ultimately rose to the rank of major. The wings he wears are those of an Air Weapons Controller. During his long career, Peter served in Canada, Germany, and the USA with NORAD and the NATO AWACS programme. Peter retired in 1991.*

## Outlasting the Cold War

My aircrew experience started with my selection for the NATO Airborne Warning and Control System (AWACS ) in October 1982 when it was decided Canada would participate and supply NATO with aircrew and ground personnel.

The main operating base was in Gelsenkirchen, in what was then the Federal Republic of Germany. When I arrived in early April 1983, our third aircraft had just been delivered and only one squadron was in existence. By the time I left in late August 1986, three operational squadrons had been formed plus the training squadron. All eighteen aircraft were assigned to the base, not to the individual squadrons, and were registered in Luxembourg; we thought this a bit odd as the country had no air force al though it was a member of NATO.

Gelsenkirchen is a great location. We could drive to the UK in one day; to Paris, Amsterdam or Lahr in six hours; Brussels in less than three hours; and to Köln or Bonn in just over an hour. We were in the British sector, watched Brit TV and used their NAAFIs, etc.

We were also most welcome at the US facilities. Baden-Baden, just north of Lahr, had a French commissary. What deals we got on red wines and canned snails!

Politics played a rather large role in every decision made in the NATO environment. The Americans and the Germans were usually at odds over something. We Canadians were there to help everyone compromise. To this day all NATO AWACS maintenance manuals and engineering orders are based on Canadian publications.

After about five months in the mission simulator and several training flights, usually of eight to nine hours' duration, I was evaluated as a *bona-fide* Tactical Director. Over 118 hours of actual flying time. I was duly awarded my air weapons controller wings *(AWC—read Fighter Controller for you old guys)* at the tender age of 48 and with 29 year's service. Who says you can't teach an old dog new tricks? By the time I finished flying with NATO on 31 July 1986 I had accumulated 1290 hours on 162 flights and was duly hosed down by the fire fighters on my final flight. I still don't quite understand why, but it was something we aircrew guys did.

The Boeing E-3 AWACS is a four-engined Boeing 707, designed many years ago; NATO E-3s were all built in the 1980s. The aircrew comprises four flight crew: two pilots, a navigator and a flight engineer. The mission crew consists of a Tactical Director, two or three weapons controllers, two or three surveillance controllers, two or three surveillance operators, plus a communications operator and technician, radar technician and the data technician (computer operator). The mission crew were referred to as back-end crew, never the rear-end crew. The E-3 is now in service with the USAF, RAF, RAAF and the French and Saudi air forces. The capability of this aircraft is mind-boggling.

The OTH (Over The Horizon) radar coverage was nearly 600 nautical miles; the downward looking Doppler radar over 250 nm. This is the area where most intercepts are conducted, within range of line-of-sight communications. While on station we generally flew a racetrack pattern with 60-nm legs at an optimum cruising altitude of 29,000 feet. The E-3 computer is so smart it pretends we are stationary when in fact we were flying at 360 knots. No wonder our mission call-sign was "Magic"

The Tactical Director can switch the radar to the maritime mode—there are thousands of fishing boats and other small craft in the North Sea and the Mediterranean. We could also set the radar picture to include a mix or combination of all three radars. We sometimes assisted the RAF maritime patrol Nimrod IIs by directing them to a target in their area of responsibility thereby saving them hours of unnecessary patrol time. The communications and data links on board were also very impressive. On one occasion on station over the Aegean Sea and linked up with the Greeks for the first time, I received a call from the Turks requesting our air picture be downlinked to them. I damn near blew it! The air picture they wanted included all of Greece. Luckily, a little voice said to me:

"Watch it, international incident brewing here."

I told him I'd have to check back with my Ops Centre. At that point the Turkish officer said, "It's OK; forget it".

Politics was something else in NATO. The general's position alternated between the Germans and the Americans; the Director of Operations was either a Canadian or a Dutchman. We referred to the individual squadrons by the nationality of their Commanding Officers. The American squadron was Squadron No. 1; Canadian squadron was Squadron No. 2; and the German squadron was Squadron No. 3. The Training squadron was commanded by an Italian, but we never called it the Italian Squadron. Some nations were very sensitive about to whom they reported. Greeks and Turks had little use for each other and the Belgian, Norwegian, Dutch and Danish contingents were seldom seen hanging around the German squadron. Before I left Europe, all the Forward Operating Bases (FOB) had been activated: Orland, Norway; Trapani, Italy; Preveza, Greece; and Konya, Turkey. SHAPE had decreed that the NATO airborne early warning force would not have all its eggs in one basket, so we usually had four to six aircraft away at the FOBs at any one time. From a personal point of view that meant our crews were deployed for eight days and seven nights every five weeks or so. That also meant three or four flying sorties during that temporary duty period. We also deployed to RAF Waddington (near Lincoln) for several years while the Brits were going through a very difficult period trying to get their Nimrod III (AWACS) airborne.

In August 1986 I was transferred on what was probably one of the longest postings (distance) in the peacetime Canadian Forces: from Gelsenkirchen to Anchorage, Alaska. That's from 7 degrees east to 150 degrees west longitude.

My four years of service in Alaska proved interesting. I was a staff officer with the Alaskan NORAD Region. My duties included flying on the USAF E-3 AMCS as NORAD Airborne Battle Staff (NABS). There are two positions on the NABS, a full colonel Airborne Battle Commander (NABC), and his NORAD Weapons Resources Officer, usually a senior captain or major. The NABC is airborne in case we lost not only our ground control facilities but also our "Brass" on the ground too. In Alaska most peacetime intercepts were conducted by our hunter-killer package against the Soviet TU-95 "Bear Hs" and infrequently the TU-22 supersonic "Backfire". These aircraft have the capability of launching multiple warhead cruise missiles against North American targets. The hunter-killer package consisted of two F-15C Eagles that were usually scrambled from one of the two FOBs, Galena or King Salmon, a KC-135 aerial refuelling tanker from Eilsen AFB (near Fairbanks) and an E-3 AWACS from Elmendorf AFB (near Anchorage). The two aircraft would act on intelligence warnings, scramble individually to meet at a predetermined point many miles off the coast. The Soviets were surprised on many occasions to be intercepted so far out. In fact, we were so successful that when Gorbachev and President Reagan met in Iceland in the summer of 1988, both agreed that intrusions into one another's airspace was counter-productive and unnecessary. And just like that, it was all over.

During my time in Elmendorf the USAF had one of their many administrative inspections and it was discovered that the Canadian aircrew hadn't completed Arctic Survival training, which was a USAF requirement if one flew in Alaska. In spite of our best efforts to scuttle it, we were posted to a Canadian Forces Arctic Survival course in Resolute Bay, North West Territory. After a week at CFB Namao for ground school, off we went. On that first night there were eight of us in an S&R tent. We were warm when we stood up but terribly cold when we lay down. Thirty or forty degrees below all the time, it really didn't matter which scale was used. It was cold! Daylight about two hours a day. Time to build an igloo. Our Inuit instructor demonstrated how to build one in less than an hour. Most of us were still trying to build one hours later. Finally, all the cracks filled in between the snow blocks, ready for something to eat and retire for the evening. Jeez, how come all those holes are developing in the wall? Our little "Bunsen burner" (camp stove) is melting the chinking in the cracks. Had to turn the heat down and re-chink the igloo all over again! Migawd, what time is it? We'd been working on that igloo for over eight hours! Miserable night: cold, cold and bloody cold.

*The key to the whole ordeal was to keep moving and keep busy.*
*Two nights in that igloo was enough; our last two nights were sheer*
*heaven, we built (excavated) a snow cave. After several hours of hard*
*work we move in, do a little cooking, light some candles (they formed*
*their own little alcoves, wherever you placed them on the wall of the*
*cave); it's actually quite pretty and warm. We are comfortable sitting*
*around in just our underwear.*

A great course. I really felt that had we gone down in the Arctic
and not been injured, I'd survive until rescued. I was fifty-two, the
oldest successful graduate of the CF Arctic Survival Course.

I mentioned earlier how things had changed. In the summer of
'89 the Soviets made history when they arrived in Elmendorf with
two MIG-29s and their AN-225 cargo aircraft, bigger than the USAF
C-5A. The Soviets had been invited to the Abbotsford International
Airshow and had brought Canadian dollars but no US currency. So
the Commander decreed that while the Soviets were on base the
Canadian buck would be accepted at par at the Base Exchange.
Suddenly we were all scrambling for Canadian dollars.

Another significant event the previous year was when I was
President of the Mess Committee at the annual RCAF Anniversary
Mess Dinner. As all participants appeared to be enjoying themselves,
I thought it was a good time to ask the Alaskan Air Command
Commander if he'd consider changing the command motto to "Top
Cover For North America" rather than "Top Cover for America". We
Canadians liked to think we were contributing to our country's
defence as well as to that of the United States. He stood up and
decreed on the spot that it would happen immediately. When I left
two years later a couple of his top advisers (senior colonels) still
hadn't spoken to me.

As my Canadian boss pointed out, while he thought it was a
terrific idea, some people in Ottawa didn't want to give the impression
that the US provided "Top Cover" for Canada, particularly in the
North. Once again I learned there are two sides to every story.

I left Alaska in August 1990 for Victoria and after some special
leave my final duty day was the 15 January 1991. I had helped to
keep the peace for thirty-six plus years. The very next day Canada
went to war in the Persian Gulf.

# HU FILLEUL

*Hu was born in Innisfail, Alberta. He joined the RCAF in 1950 and was awarded his Radio Officer brevet. He served with 426 Squadron during the Korean Airlift and subsequently as an instructor before moving to 412 Squadron on various aircraft, including the Comet Mk1, Hu did staff tours in Canada and Germany, retiring in 1974 to serve as civilian staff officer in Winnipeg and Victoria until retirement.*

## Special Flight to the North Pole

Canadians believe that they own the arctic lands and contiguous waters north of their mainland to the pole. As we know, this claim has been disputed at times by American nuclear submarines, supertankers and icebreakers.

It is also little known that between March of 1946 and September of 1947 three long-range reconnaissance B29s of 4149th AAF Base Unit of Air Materiel Command carried out a comprehensive aerial reconnaissance of arctic North America out of Edmonton, Alberta and Fairbanks, Alaska. These flights lasted for up to 22 hours and navigator F/Lt Keith Greenaway was one of the members of the RCAF who took part in that operation.

The Canadian government subsequently recognized that it had to establish its interest in the area and in March of 1954 laid on an operation for the first overflight of the North Pole by a member of the Canadian Cabinet. No. 426 Squadron at Lachine was given the job although we were a distinctly non-VIP outfit. However, one of 412 Squadron's passenger North Stars, two flight stewards and a VIP pilot, F/Lt Dean Broadfoot, were provided for the trip. The

Honourable Brooke Claxton, Minister of National Defence, led the official party and was accompanied by:

His Excellency R. Douglas Stuart; United States Ambassador to Canada

Leonard Brockington, Esq., an eminent advisor to the Liberal government of the time

General A.G.L. McNaughton

Gordon Robertson

Dr. John A. Hannah

And a number of aides and a four-piece band.

We carried a double crew captained by F/O Ron Kyle, with S/Ldr Greenaway from NDHQ along as passenger liaison and arctic navigation expert. The flight departed Ottawa on 27 March 1954 for Fort Churchill and it was there we found out why the band was on board. They were much appreciated as impromptu entertainment at the parties organized by the Minister of National Defence during each stop. The crew suffered a casualty at Churchill when F/Lt Broadfoot came down with the mumps and had to be left behind. That left us with two pilots as our double crew only had three to start with.

After spending an extra day at Churchill we flew six hours to Resolute Bay, a small RCAF outpost on the south side of Cornwallis Island. The weather being fine, we did a further 11-hour flight to the North Pole and back. The most memorable part of that flight was being served a steak dinner by the stewards while circling the north pole in brilliant sunshine. We knew we were at 90° north because F/Lt Mickey Majoca, the crew navigator, said so and S/Ldr Greenaway didn't argue the point. I always had my doubts; Santa's workshop was nowhere to be seen.

Invited by the United States Ambassador to visit the USAF base at Thule, Greenland, on 30 March, we were again royally entertained. While there we got a look at the revolutionary above-ground arctic sewer and water system that was being installed in insulated conduits called thermadors. From Thule the next stop was Goose Bay, Labrador, for another joint Canadian/American party and then back to Ottawa. The total distance travelled was 7476 nautical miles in 38 flying hours. Shortly after returning each member of the party received a beautiful framed-and-coloured lithograph scroll as a memento of Special Flight 73, an unsung bit of Canadian history.

S/Ldr Greenaway also presented each of us with an illustrated book covering the 1947 B29 reconnaissance missions. Published in

May of 1948 by the Joint Intelligence Board in Ottawa and originally classified Confidential, it had been downgraded to Restricted by the time we received it. Although the photography is all black-and-white, it was beautifully done and still provides a graphic portrait of Canada's wonderful northern lands.

In commemoration of the first flight over the North Pole by a member of the Cabinet of the Government of Canada,

The Honourable Brooke Claxton,

Minister of National Defence.

The S/Ldr Greenaway of this memoir
was the F/Lt Greenaway of the 1946/1947 B29 flights

# D.V. "BADGER" BERGER-NORTH

*Born, raised, and educated in Maidstone, Kent, England, Badger saw WWII through the eyes of a schoolboy. There were few dull moments as German bombers and RAF fighters met overhead. As the war ended he joined the Combined Cadet Force while at school, obtained a flying scholarship and awaited his compulsory service with anticipation. Badger joined the RAF in January 1955, was awarded his pilot wings in 1956, and served to January 1961. He and his wife emigrated to Canada, and in 1963 he joined the RCAF, serving to his retirement in 1985*

## There's No Life Like It

January 1955. My introduction to the lifestyle of the future, after receiving a personal invitation from the Queen to assist in defending the realm was, "Gentlemen, this is my parade square. When we're on this parade square you call me Sir and I call you Sir, the only difference being you mean it and I don't".

I was selected for pilot training in Canada under the NATO scheme. There were four Basic Flying Schools in Canada at this time: Penhold and Claresholm in Alberta; Moose Jaw, Saskatchewan; and Centralia, Ontario. After orientation we moved to 4FTS Penhold.

We flew the Harvard IIs for aerobatics and general handling (they're the ones that had the castering tail-wheel you couldn't lock and were prone to ground looping), and the heavier IVs for instrument and navigation trips. The Harvard was a great machine, but for the first few hours it was all you could do to hang on and go along for the ride. Of the original 38 who started on E Flight, 12 Norwegians, 5 Danes, 7 RAF, and 1 Canadian hung on to the end, despite the efforts of the instructors.

F/Lt Ritchie. "You can teach a dog to fly if you give it enough instruction."

F/O Boutin. "From the back seat they all look the same, anyway."

Those of us who survived the "Yellow Peril" were posted to 2AFS Portage la Prairie, Manitoba, for T-Bird training to wings standard, the other Advanced Flying School being 1AFS Gimli. The T-33 was so different: fast, quiet, fitted with ejector seats, and we were introduced to "bone domes" and oxygen masks. It was here that we joined up with the Turks and found that they had a very different attitude to life and death. This was 1956, and between Portage and Gimli there were quite a few fatal accidents. In spite of this we received our wings; it was the proudest day of my life. Back to UK to RAF Worksop to fly Vampire FB 5s and 9s, and T11 two seat trainers (before ejector seats). On to Meteor T7 and fighter F8s and then transferred to RAF Bassingbourn to Canberra 231 OCU to learn medium and high level visual and radar bombing. Upon completion posted to No. 12 (B) Squadron, RAF Binbrook, Lincolnshire.

No. 12(B) Squadron's origins go back to WWI, having been formed from C Flight of 1 Squadron. We were very proud of the squadron and considered ourselves far superior to the other two squadrons on the field; 9 and 139. No. 9 Squadron had the same rôle as 12, but 139 was the Pathfinder squadron. No. 9 Squadron's motto was "Per Noctem Volare" and their crest featured a bat with wings spread. They had a caged fruit bat named F/O Tom Dooley because he was always hanging around with his head down. No. 12 Squadron's motto is "Leads the Field", which just about tells it all. About half the aircrew were ex-WWII and I felt very fortunate to be able to learn from their vast experience. We spent deployments in Malta (Luqa) and Libya (Castel Benito) and flew around the Med. using bombing ranges at El Adem (south of Tobruk), Filfia (off Malta) and Tarhuna (south of Castel Benito).

Many incidents stand out, but one especially at El Adem when my bomb aimer (who was newly married and not quite with it) incorrectly identified the target on a first-run attack at 35,000 ft., let the beast go (a live thousand-pounder), and yelled "Strike! Good one!" upon seeing it explode. We received a simultaneous hysterical transmission from the Range Safety Officer to the effect that we had bombed the Domestic Site, just missing the Quadrant Hut. We returned to Malta to await the arrival of our CO. We were sipping our John Collins in the bar when W/Cdr Alex Blyth arrived in great haste and asked me what had happened. I explained with some trepidation, and when I finished he let out a sigh of relief:

"Christ, Badger, I thought you'd bent one of my aeroplanes!"

Fortunately the bomb was tail-fused, landed in soft sand, blew out a few windows and knocked some beer cans off the NAAFI shelf. W/Cdr Blyth was a Canadian in the RAF; the Service was very cosmopolitan, with members from all over the Commonwealth as well as from other countries. With 9 Squadron we were converted to nuclear capability which, because it gave us carte blanche in low flying, we thoroughly enjoyed. This we did on routes all over UK and Germany.

Lots of stories:

*throttling back and diving at yachts in Morecambe Bay, applying full throttle and pulling up in climbing turns to see if they were blown over; descending through cloud from about 45,000 ft. after a radar bombing exercise, cross-checking altitude every 5000 ft. while discussing the mission, calling altitude at 15,000 feet just as we pop out of cloud into a valley in Scotland, below 5000 feet in a dive; flying down autobahns the wrong way; zipping across abandoned Diepholz airfield past the control tower at about 50 feet and scattering little Piaggios, finding out on debrief that it had just opened as Germany's basic training school; did a simulated run on the Möhne Dam and found it hard enough without anyone shooting at me (my respect for those on the raid rocketed); crossing a road as a timing mark on a low level and getting the impression of hundreds of chickens disappearing in the back door of a farmhouse; why do sheep always run to the centre of a field and bang into each other when you fly over them? Coming up one side of a sand dune and surprising wild camels doing the same on the other side; flying across the desert as low as you dare towards a mobile oil rig, wondering why the crew "bale out" running like mad, and realising you have your bomb doors open; thinking you are low flying at about 50-100 feet and glimpsing a photo-recce Swift from Gütersloh on a crossing track below you; who's more terrified when your engine quits, you or the seagull that just got swallowed? Low level over Germany evading ducks when a generator fail light comes on and, on landing, find a large hole in the wing and the generator ripped off the engine by a kamikaze duck.*

We experienced being fired on only once. That was by the Maltese Artillery after we had taken off from Luqa, Malta, to return to UK. They *were doing AA practice and were supposed to be pointing their guns out to sea. We were over land and, seeing the flak bursting around us, wondered where the shrapnel was landing.*

The defences around Tobruk were still in evidence, as were the remains of dumps out in the desert. The Marble Arch (that Mussolini had built for his triumphant entry into Tripolitania, I believe) was still there on the coast road. Last away trip on Squadron was to Bahrain, via Malta, Cyprus, and Turkey. My next scheduled trip was to have been to Malaya. A wonderful time to be flying, with any fear being of one's own making.

1960. Posting to 1 Squadron, RAF Leeming, Yorkshire, a part of 228 OCU, the All Weather Fighter (AWF) Conversion Unit. The OCU consisted of No. 157 (?) Squadron equipped with Javelin T.3 trainers and FAW.5s (fighter all weather) and 1 Squadron with eight Canberra T.11 AWF Trainers with radar noses (only eleven were built: our eight, two sold to Sweden, and one kept by Boulton-Paul for trials) and a T.4; twelve Meteor night fighter NF.14s and a T.7 trainer, and a Chipmunk. Twelve pilots (6 fighter, 6 bomber backgrounds) and twenty-three aircraft: pilot heaven

In 1963 the Royal Canadian Air Force was advertising for ex-aircrew to be air traffic controllers, and I joined the RCAF on a Short Service Commission. After the course at Camp Borden, posted to RCAF Cold Lake. Busy! One-hundred-plus CF-104 Starfighters, CEPE (Central Experimental and Proving Establishment) with various aircraft, USAF SAC with KC97 tankers, Station Flight with four C47 Dakotas, a C45 Expeditor, and H-34s. Start of the 104 program, morale high, busy social life, hectic in the Tower. Scrounged flying time in the three Dak CF-1047 trainers with the 104 nose: "Woody Woodpecker", "Dolly's Folly", "Pinocchio"; the C45 "Bug Smasher," the Station C47, the H-34s, and some 104D and T-Bird time. When off duty, was often called to be second-dickie on the C-47 or C-45 for urgent medical evacuations or Search & Rescue missions. We lost quite a few 104s during this tour.

1967. SSC coming to an end and was offered a Permanent Commission if I would transfer to pilot branch. Ottawa had kicked out five hundred pilots just when the airlines were hiring, and about a thousand left the Service. They were obviously in a bind. Accepted and was sent to CFB Moose Jaw as an instructor. Didn't think I had the temperament or the ability but discovered it to be one of the most rewarding and satisfying positions in my life. Started as a line instructor, became an academics instructor, Deputy Flight

Commander, Flying Instructors School (FIS) instructor, the FIS Commander, "Trapper" (Quality Control & Evaluation), and achieved an A1 Category.

In 1975 posted to 407 Maritime Patrol Squadron, CFB Comox on the CP-107 Argus. Flew on various missions: hunting submarines, fisheries patrols, pollution patrols, search & rescue, assistance to other Departments, joint international exercises, and other tasking until St. Patrick's day 1977. CO called me in and said that the crew had apprised him of a problem. "Nothing wrong with your flying, Badger. It's just that the navigators and observers are bitching and complaining that you can't hear them bitch and complain."

After extensive testing in Victoria I was grounded due to "Aural discrimination loss". Destiny was to be on my side, for although I was now a "Penguin," I was given approximately thirty seconds to accept or reject a posting to Maritime Pacific Head Quarters (MARPAC), Esquimalt, as an operations officer (OPS). After completing five years in OPS to Compulsory Retirement Age, I was offered a two-year extension to serve as a supervisor controller in the Victoria Rescue Co-ordination Centre (RCC).

We covered everything west of the Mackenzie river and west of the Alberta-BC border right out to five hundred miles offshore. Although the smallest in area of all Canada's Rescue Co-ordination Centres, Victoria was the busiest and handled more than 50% of all Canadian incidents or accidents.

On a long weekend in the summer it was not unusual to have over a hundred Incident/Accident calls between a Friday evening and the following Monday morning. I became a qualified Canadian and American Search Master and finished a very rewarding and satisfying career in 1984, going the circle from possibly creating potential peril during the Cold War to saving those in peril at sea, on land and in the air.

# AUTHORS

# AUTHORS

# ACKNOWLEDGEMENTS

Members of the AirCrew Association, Vancouver Island Branch, acknowledge a deep debt of gratitude to the Book Committee who laboured long and hard to ensure that this book would be a lasting tribute to those who served their country in the Royal Canadian Air Force and Royal Air Force.

Aircrew used logbooks to record their every flight. Our veterans all retained their logbooks and this accounts for the ability to recall dates and times. Conversations given in direct speech necessarily represent an approximation.

| | |
|---|---|
| Jack Dixon | Chairman & Editor 1997 |
| Ken Pask | Chairman & Editor 1998 |
| Douglas McLaughlin | Secretary and Data Base |
| Chris Pike | Treasurer and Communications |
| Reg Lane | Historian |
| Bill Weighton | Proofing |
| Hugh Young | Proofing |
| Lefty Whitman | |

The Book Committee gratefully acknowledge the dedication that Michael O'Hagan brought to the task of steering our book through the editing, production, and publishing procedures. Without Michael's experience, erudition and enthusiasm this book would not have seen the light of day.

Our thanks also to Hu Filleul who brought to bear his consummate skills in scanning, cropping, and screening photographs and other documents.

And our special thanks to Rosalind, Alma, and Betty for their help, patience, and understanding without which we could not have completed our work

# LMF–Lack of Moral Fibre

One or two stories refer to LMF, a phrase developed by the RAF to describe "aircrew whose conduct may cause them to forfeit the confidence of their Commanding Officers in their determination and reliability in the face of danger." This quote is from an Air Ministry letter dated 10 September 1941. Today we would use the phrase "battle fatigue" to describe this complex psychological condition. Lord Moran, in his book "The Anatomy of Courage" warned "No man is immune from cracking if exposed to sufficient stress." He might have added "fear is cumulative".

Commanding Officers lacked any training in preventive action when battle fatigue was suspected. Medical Officers offered little help; they too faced a problem for which there was no immediate solution. Most importantly COs had to learn to recognise early signs of LMF. Quite often the solution was as simple as sending the man on leave; that was all that was needed for him to be in control again.

LMF was a delicate matter. To prove the need for drastic action was very difficult. Canadian books on the subject are mainly clinical in approach and in some instances offer graphic stories. When a problem was suspected the man or men were immediately removed from operations and the squadron since fear is contagious and spreads rapidly. It can undermine squadron morale in a matter of hours. Such rapid disappearances gave rise to apocryphal stories because nobody knew what events had transpired. Yet stories gained credibility through repetition and a degree of hyperbole, sometimes describing an outcome more suited to a French Foreign Legion movie of the times.

LMF was a very personal thing. It varied from case to case and manifested itself in different ways. One should not generalise when discussing this subject. Stories which sound extreme probably are and should not be taken at face value.

*Lt. General R J Lane DSO, DFC*, CD*

Copies of this book may be obtained from your bookseller or direct from the publisher

In Canada;    $27.95 post paid

In the U.S.:    US$19.95 surface mail
                US$19.95 plus $3 air mail

In the UK:     £11.95 plus £3 for surface mail
                £11.95 plus £5 for air mail

Cheque or money order to:
The Victoria Publishing Company Inc.
309-11 Cooperage Place
Victoria Publishing Company British Columbia
CANADA V9A 7J9

Fax     (250) 361 1574
Voice: (250) 361 1436

## Sir Christopher Foxley-Norris
Battle of Britain Fighter Association
*It may perhaps be thought that the fund of available stories about WWII has dried up and that nothing of value or novelty remains to be told. Not so, because the value of these stories lies in the fact that they are first hand, i.e. they are factual rather than fictional. They remain as vivid and fascinating as the events they portray. As such they must not be allowed to disappear because they are irreplaceable.*

## Air Chief Marshal Sir Andrew Wilson
President, The Aircrew Association
*This book is a glowing tribute to the skill and courage of aircrew in WWII; to those men who gave so much.*

## Robert E. Beamish MD, FRCP.
Editor in Chief, Canadian Journal of Cardiology
*A masterful gem—heroism and history vividly but modestly told—incredible stories with details never before revealed but never to be forgotten.*

## Lieutenant General A. Chester Hull
*This book serves to remind us that ordinary men achieved extraordinary feats of high endeavour and courage. They gave all to the cause of freedom.*

## Major General Wendy A. Clay
Surgeon General, Canadian Forces.
*It is memories such as these that help to put a human face on the horrors of war and to remind all those of us who wear a light blue uniform today of the immense debt of gratitude we owe to those who served before us.*

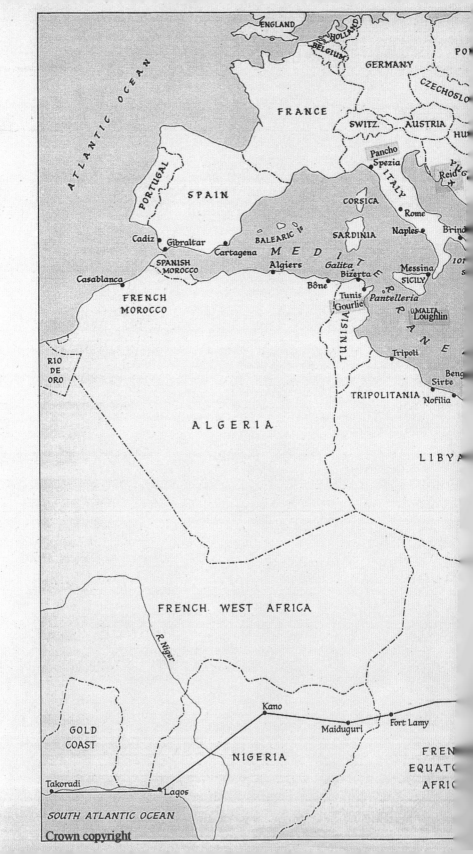

ENGLAND

HOLLAND

BELGIUM

GERMANY

PO

CZECHOSLO

ATLANTIC OCEAN

FRANCE

SWITZ.

AUSTRIA

HU

Pancho
Spezia

ITALY

Reid

PORTUGAL

SPAIN

CORSICA

Rome

Cadiz

Gibraltar

BALEARIC is

SARDINIA

Naples

Brind

Cartagena

MEDI

SPANISH
MOROCCO

Algiers

Galita

Messina

Casablanca

Bizerta

SICILY

FRENCH
MOROCCO

Bône

Tunis

Pantelleria

Gourlie

MALTA
Loughlin

RANE

R10
DE
ORO

TUNISIA

Tripoli

ALGERIA

Beng
Sirte

TRIPOLITANIA

Nofilia

LIBYA

FRENCH WEST AFRICA

R. Niger

Kano

GOLD
COAST

Maiduguri

Fort Lamy

NIGERIA

FREN
EQUATO
AFRIC

Takoradi

Lagos

SOUTH ATLANTIC OCEAN

15°    16°    2°W    17°    18°

Rauscha  Kotzenau  Steinau  Ostrzeszów  Wi
Kohlfurt  Prausnitz  Wohlau  Festenberg  Wieruszów
Haynau  Parchwitz  Oder  Kepno  Wieluń
Bunzlau  Oels
Görlitz  Liegnitz  Weide  Pitschen  Praszka
Goldberg  BRESLAU
Jauer  Canth  Namslau  Kreuzburg
Neustadt  Striegau  Ohlau  Klo
Hirschberg  Zobten  Wansen  Brieg  Rosenberg
Reisen  Gebirge  Jellowa
Gablonz  Waldenburg  Grottkan  Oppeln  Colonovska  Lubl
S  U  Münsterberg  Krappitz  Gr Strehlitz
Jelemnice  Trautenau  Braunau  Eulen  Neisse  Hinder
D  Gebirge  Krappitz
Dvur Králové  Náchod  Blatz  Potschkau  Zuckmantel  Holzen  Gleiwitz
Horice  Orlické Hory  Habelschwerdt  Ratibor
Nymburk  Tyniste  Rokitnitz  Würbenthal  JESENIK  Jägerndorf
Kolin  Pardubice  Kysperk  Grulich  Troppau
Kutna Hora  Chrudim  Vysoké Myto  Mährisch-Schönberg  Gratz
Golcuv Jenikov  Zwittau  Muglitz  Moravska
Zruč  Zdirec  Kornitz  Sternberg  Ostrava
Německý  Bystrice  OLOMOUC
Brod  Svitavka  Boskovice  Prerov  Valašské Mezíříčí
Pelhrimov  Jihlava  Prostějov  Vestin
Vel Mezíříčí  Tišnov  Hulin
Kamenice  Velká Bitteš  Vyskov  Kromenz  Visovice  Zilin
Telč  BRNO  Bucovice  Raje
Jindrichuv Hradec  Trebič  Jihlava  Uherske Hradiste  Vah
Neubistrita  Dacice  Moravsky Krumlov  O  S
Pohrlitz  Koby!  Wessely  L  O
Raabs  Drosendorf  Nikolsburg  Trenun  Ksinna
Waldhofen  Thayo  Zhaim  Hodonin  Svino
Horn  Laa  Poysdorf  Lundenburg  Myjava  Nove Mesto
Zwettel  Jablonica  Radošiná  Topolcany
Gerungs  Kamp  Ob Hollabrunn  Plavecky Svaty Mikulas  Topolcianky
Hadersdorf  Durnkrut  Trnava  Nitra
Krems  Stockerau
Martinsberg  Tulln  Zohor  Serad  Surany
Klosterneuburg  WIEN  Szenc  Nové Zámky
Weiselburg  St. Pölten  (Vienna)  Bratislava
Baden  Mödling  Bruck  Vagfarkasd  Somorja  Komárno
Hainfeld  Neusfeld  Bos
Gutestein  Magyarovar  DANUBE  Komárom
St Aegid  Neustadt  Hedervár  Györ
Mariazell  6763  Waller  Csorna  Kisber
Mürzsteg  Kirchbg  Sopron  Ndaa
Murzzuschlag  Lövö  Varsany
Aflenz  Ratten  Friedbg
Bruck  kt